# NUCLEAR ENDINGS

# NUCLEAR ENDINGS

## Stopping War on Time

## STEPHEN J. CIMBALA

PRAEGER

New York
Westport, Connecticut
London

Copyright Acknowledgment

The author gratefully acknowledges the permission of Lexington Books, Inc., for use of portions of *Extended Deterrence* (1987), Ch. 9.

**Library of Congress Cataloging-in-Publication Data**

Cimbala, Stephen J.
    Nuclear endings : stopping war on time / Stephen J. Cimbala.
       p.    cm.
    Bibliography: p.
    Includes index.
    ISBN 0–275–93165–X
    1. Nuclear warfare—Termination.    I. Title.
U263.C485   1989
355′.0217—dc19        88–27441

First published in 1989

Praeger Publishers, One Madison Avenue, New York, NY 10010
A division of Greenwood Press, Inc.

Printed in the United States of America

The paper used in this book complies with the Permanent Paper Standard issued by the National Information Standards Organization (Z39.48—1984).

10  9  8  7  6  5  4  3  2  1

To my father

# Contents

# Acknowledgments

I gratefully acknowledge the helpful suggestions of Leon Sloss and Richard Ned Lebow on various sections of the manuscript. I am grateful to Diane Wolf of Pennsylvania State University, Delaware County Campus, Media, for indispensable clerical support, and to Dr. Edward Tomezsko, Dr. Madlyn Hanes, and Ms. Jeanette Rieck of the same campus for their encouragement and assistance. I am also indebted to Susan Pazourek of Praeger Publishers for her interest in, and helpful suggestions with regard to, this and other works. Edward L. (Ted) Warner III and Notra Trulock III were kind enough to provide copies of unpublished conference papers and useful background information. Conversations with Bruce G. Blair, John G. Hines, Raymond L. Garthoff, Michael MccGwire, James McConnell, Phillip A. Petersen, and Notra Trulock III prevented other errors from creeping into the manuscript. None of these persons bears any responsibility for mistakes of form or substance. Finally, my wife and children are congratulated for having endured still another endless production with good grace.

# Preface

If a nuclear war between U.S. and Soviet forces or the forces of their allies were to start, how would it end? It is as difficult to envision how a nuclear war would end as it is to suggest how it might start. The issues of controlling and ending nuclear war break down into those of policy and those of strategy with the understanding that the two are linked. The issues of policy are the objectives for which the opponents are fighting, their expected gains and losses from various outcomes, and their willingness to seek war termination and on what terms. The issues of strategy are the derivation of military objectives from political ones, the translation of military objectives into force structures and war plans, and the capacity to adapt preset war plans to the demands of the situation. Thus war termination becomes a study not only of interstate relations during conflict and war, but also of intrastate organizational behavior that might contribute to, or detract from, efforts to bring war to a conclusion.

There are several reasons for studying war termination. The most important one is that no matter how low the probability of a nuclear war, it could occur; and if it does occur, we would like to terminate it with as little damage as possible.

A second reason for the study of war termination is to improve strategic war planning. Current and former U.S. war plans, and probably Soviet plans, are based on the infliction of damage. Damage expectancy is also the main criterion for force planning in many instances. The focus on damage infliction deemphasizes the importance of issues such as flexibility of force structure and options, and the durability of command, control, and communications under attack.

Third, the study of war termination may have some deterrent value. If potential opponents observe that the United States takes seriously the problem of nuclear war termination, they are less likely to attempt to box the president into an "all or nothing" situation. This view runs into two objections. Hawks contend that the study of war termination involves a prejudgment that core values might be surrendered instead of defended. Doves feel that improved understanding of war termination might make nuclear war more acceptable. The viewpoint here is that the study of how to end nuclear war purposefully suggests that we are serious about war, and also serious about thinking through its consequences.

Fourth, a focus on the problem of conflict termination in policy studies and government exercises should make leaders more familiar with the actual problems they might face if deterrence failed. On paper the United States for many years has had nuclear war plans that call for the refinement of options and the use of nuclear weapons only under the careful control of policymakers. However, much skepticism is implicit in the organizational ethos and standard operating procedures of the military services to which nuclear weapons have been assigned. Large bureaucratic organizations, of which the armed services are certainly one species, are resistant to tailor-made orders from civilian superiors if those orders conflict with what has been preplanned.

Chapter 1 provides a conceptual overview of pertinent issues in the literature of war termination. Three principal components of the concept are discussed with reference to historical examples. Those components are the notions of an "agreed battle," of escalation control and intrawar deterrence, and of coercive diplomacy. All are woven together in the complicated tapestry of nuclear war termination. Essentially they ask: How do theorists, and how would policymakers, understand the problem of war termination? Since there is no practice with nuclear war termination, some reliance upon the history of the prenuclear age is instructive.

An agreed battle is one fought deliberately within limits because both sides recognize that to exceed those limits would destroy their policy objectives. For an agreed battle to take place, both sides must remain willing to fight a constrained war despite the temptations to push against the boundaries of policy and strategy that limit war. One side may understand the war to be limited below certain thresholds, but the other may not reciprocate. An agreed battle at the conventional level may be prefatory to escalation that involves the superpowers in nuclear war, say in Europe.

Escalation control has been a prominent policy objective of U.S. war plans since the 1960s. After nuclear war has begun, this control will be tested severely. U.S. nuclear weapons employment policy has for several decades called for selective and discriminating uses of nuclear weapons even during strategic nuclear war. Whether the United States has the political and military attributes to carry out this policy guidance is controversial. Nevertheless, escalation control is central to the concept of war termination if the concept is to have any hope of convincing policymakers, and of finding its way into defense organizational repertoires.

Coercive diplomacy is the use of force as an agent of influence over the behavior of another state or other actor. This is distinct from the use of force to annihilate or destroy an opponent physically, without regard for that opponent's willingness to comply with one's demands. In the nuclear age, coercive diplomacy has assumed increased importance, and it has become the key to successful crisis management between superpowers. The Cuban missile crisis is an example of the successful use of coercive diplomacy as a crisis management tool. U.S. scholars have formulated the theory of coercive diplomacy and tested its hypotheses in cases of conventional wars and nuclear crises. Applying this logic to the more stressful case of nuclear war that has already begun, or even to superpower conventional war that threatens to go nuclear, is a task as compelling as it is intimidating.

The relationship between coercive diplomacy and escalation control is one of simultaneous tension and reciprocity. Indeed, each term individually connotes some tension or contradiction, as between "coercion" and "diplomacy" or between "escalation" and "control." Each term indicates some striving by leaders to obtain their objectives, but not at absolute cost. At some point on the hypothetical cost-benefit curve, the cost of continued fighting is no longer worth the investment of lives and expenditures. In nuclear war this point of diminishing returns would come very early for any objective other than national survival. The relationship between coercive diplomacy and escalation control is also kindred in another way. Both coercive diplomacy and escalation control represent perspectives on the relationship between force and policy that each side hopes, once the fighting has begun, the opponent has adopted. Otherwise there will be few, if any, limits to war's ferocity. The relationship between combatants then becomes a bargaining as well as a fighting one, and the bargaining can be as relentless and menacing as the fighting. Coercive diplomacy differs from escalation control in emphasis. The emphasis in coercive diplomacy is on the package of incentives and disincentives offered to the opponent to yield or keep fighting. Thus the perspective is essentially a rational model or black box.

Escalation control is more process oriented. The likelihood of escalation control is determined by the perceptions and expectations of policymakers as they are played through the decision-making process. That process acts very much like a pinball machine that causes those expectations and perceptions to carom from one flipper to another, and in different sequences. Policy outcomes are therefore congeries of outcomes that are not preplanned and do not occur in foreseeble sequences. What implications this process-oriented perspective will have for the control of nuclear war will be discussed in later chapters.

Chapter 2 considers the balance of terror and its implications for war termination. The superpower balance of nuclear forces is characterized by sensitivity and delicacy, but the debate is over the extent. Sensitivity implies that Soviet force building and crisis management are in part responsive to perceptions of U.S. behaviors, and Americans are responsive to their understandings of the Soviets. A delicate balance of terror is one in which each side fears imminent vulnerability to the first strike of the opponent, and so in time of crisis might be tempted to preempt.

The balance of terror is not evaluated as delicate here, although it is sensitive during crisis confrontations. This means that Soviet and U.S. leaders need not fear a "bolt from the blue" as much as a deepening crisis in which pessimistic expectations exceed optimistic ones. A first strike is not going to be attractive on the grounds of mathematical one-sidedness in counterforce capability. As long as neither U.S. nor Soviet leaders can expect to remove their cities from their hostage status to retaliatory strikes, the balance of terror should hold. Of course, it is possible that irrational action will cause a crisis to spill over into war. Here the superpowers' redundant strategic nuclear arsenals will pay ironic dividends. Even if hard pressed by totally unexpected events and making pessimistic assumptions about others' intentions, neither U.S. or Soviet leaders could consider a first strike that would allow their society to escape with impunity. This is reassuring, but no guarantee against deterrence failure. There are circumstances in which a first strike might appear to be "less worse" than waiting to be struck.

Chapter 3 considers U.S. strategic nuclear command vulnerability and its relationship to war termination. There are several important relationships here. First, the physical apparatus of command, control, and communications (C3) must survive all but direct attacks. Second, this surviving network of command centers, communications, and forces must provide policymakers as much flexibility in the selection among targeting options as is possible. Third, the opponent must not be given unnecessary incentives to escalate before the possibility of war termination has been precluded.

U.S. declaratory policy for the use of strategic nuclear forces, and employment policy (war plans) to a lesser extent, have evolved in the direction of demands for increasingly more survivable and "enduring" strategic command systems. On the other hand, the same policies have emphasized placing Soviet C3-plus-intelligence at risk, which seemingly creates disincentives for the Soviets to cooperate. Early U.S. nuclear strategies required only that forces and command systems provide for an early and comprehensive set of retaliatory strikes against a large Soviet target set. Beginning in the 1970s, U.S. planners sought to provide the president with options that could be tailored to very limited provocations. The concern was that the Soviet Union might use its strategic or other nuclear forces in an effective but less than total way, and that the United States would have no credible response. The Single Integrated Operational Plan for nuclear war has evolved into a highly refined set of targeting options for which the C3 may or may not be adequate, especially if these options are to be retained for use in the later stages of any nuclear war.

The canonical assumption about nuclear war, in contrast with the above, is that it will probably be short. One way to shorten it is to surprise the opponent with an attack that catches it off guard. Although nuclear strategists consider the "bolt from the blue" the least likely path to nuclear war, it is a more appealing path to desperate leaders who feel that war is probable and who assume that their intentions can be masked until very late in the game.

A true "bolt from the blue" would be struck against U.S. forces that were on day-to-day alert instead of being poised to retaliate. Such an attack would, by definition, come without a preceding crisis or conventional war that had alerted U.S. forces. A more plausible scenario is the dampening of a crisis followed by a surprise attack when the victim has let its guard down. The incentive for this would be the difference between the results of a first strike if the victim had adequate warning and the results of no or inadequate warning. This difference would have to be very significant for a preemptive strike to appeal to a desperate attacker as a best option.

However, if it did appeal, then the issue would be how the war might be stopped before it spun out of control. A "bolt from the blue," would catch the victim so unprepared that it might be more willing to acquiesce to adversary demands. On the other hand, if the victim retained significant survivable forces, these would likely be unleashed in one large spasm attack, precluding any sensible war termination. Strategic nuclear surprise might not be as implausible as some commentators assume, given a two-sided miscalculated escalation during a superpower crisis. Its implications for war termination are less straightforward. Strategic nuclear surprise might shorten the war by stunning the victim or deterring it from retaliation. It might make war termination more difficult by arousing the victim to an all-out retaliation. A true surprise would not allow to the attacker all the advantages, though; the attacker would have to strike with forces that were less than fully mobilized, for fear of giving away its intentions.

Chapter 4 deals more generally with nuclear surprise. Here we review nuclear surprise in the context of intelligence, warning, and related policy issues. Surprise attacks in conventional war have often succeeded despite an abundance of information on enemy preparations and intentions available to the victim. The reasons for the not infrequent success of surprise are as variable as the situations themselves. Some common- alities can be found in the expectations and perceptions of the victims relative to those of their attackers. If victims send signals of vulnerability that attackers can read correctly, the probability of surprise attack is thereby increased.

Surprise attackers are not always the most rational actors in deterrence theory terms. Rationality and credibility are not identical, although they are related. A rational attacker would never gamble in situations of great uncertainty where the odds of success were unknown. But historical attackers have so gambled, and their gambles have frequently paid off. From the victim's perspective, the preclusion of surprise attack requires something more than military preparedness. Preparedness must be translated into signals that reach the prospective attacker. Those signals must say loudly and clearly that retaliation beyond any acceptable price will follow any surprise attack, no matter how surprised the intended victim is.

For U.S. nuclear strategy, this means that the problem of avoiding surprise attack may be less a matter of "bean counting" than it is one of sending to the USSR clear signals of our capacity to retaliate. The United States must also limit the vulnerability of its forces and command systems, in order to make its retaliatory capabilities apparent. At the same time, the United States must signal that it is not intending a surprise attack of its own, even under the "worst case" conditions. It is reasonable for the Soviets to fear such in some circumstances, including a conventional war in Europe that is going badly for NATO. In this situation NATO sees its own nuclear first use as a limited one for demonstration purposes. The Soviet Union may see it as the first preplanned step in a larger process of escalation, in which the USSR had better not fall behind.

Chapter 5 considers Soviet strategy for nuclear war. Perhaps nothing has been so controversial since some U.S. analysts proclaimed that the Soviet Union was building a war-winning capability with its nuclear weap- ons. The Soviet view of deterrence is different from the U.S. one, not more sinister. Soviet military doctrine views the synergy of war and politics as important for victory. All wars, including nuclear wars, are political. This is very different from the Western view, which has it that nuclear war would be senseless madness.

However—and very important for Western understanding of the So- viet perspective—this does not repeal the laws of physics in the Soviet Academy of Sciences. The Soviet scientists can calculate as well as their U.S. counterparts. With current forces, they have no hope of surviving a U.S. retaliatory strike without unprecedented, and perhaps politically fatal, damage to their society. It can be debated whether the rulers in the Kremlin regard this situation of mutual deterrence as an inevitable misfortune imposed on them, or as a temporary expedient to be overcome in due time. Certainly the USSR has consistently shown its interest in deploying both active and passive defenses against enemy bombers and missiles, whereas the U.S. interest in missile defenses ebbs and flows with fiscal and political tides.

If war should appear necessary or unavoidable, the Soviets view the uses of preemption and active defenses as mutually supportive options. Their forces are prepared for any of three modalities in response to strategic warning of enemy intentions to attack: preemption, launch on warning/under attack, or second-strike retaliation. Soviet military writings of earlier decades stressed preemption because of the Soviets' comparatively fewer survivable retaliatory forces, but more recent sources allow for launch on warning/under attack or second-strike ride-out. There is also more emphasis in recent Soviet military writing on avoiding nuclear war entirely, and on preparedness for even extended global war without the use of nuclear weapons. How the Soviets might attack if they felt it necessary to do so is outlined in a number of alternative scenarios presented in this chapter.

Whether the USSR could execute any of its strategic options under wartime conditions would depend on the competence and flexibility of its command system. The Soviet approach to peacetime crisis management would also depend upon the performance of this system under unprecedented conditions. Compared with the U.S. one, we have too small a data base to make very confident statements about the Soviet command system for nuclear crisis management or war. This is doubly unfortunate: the Soviet system is worth knowing about in its own terms, and it interacts with the U.S. system during crises and wars.

What is known about Soviet military doctrine, force structure, and command systems for crisis management has some implications for the Soviet view of war termination. First, the Soviet command system must survive as a coherent system if it is to permit a negotiated war termination. Second, if the USSR follows a battle strategy not agreed upon and attempts to destroy the U.S. command system, it may well have forfeited any opportunity to achieve victory on other than Pyrrhic terms: mutual assured destruction. Some Soviet military writings seem to suggest that the Soviets expect to escape from this bind through a combination of active and passive defenses with counterforce preemption. But for the most part these Soviet writings are not expressing optimism about victory strategies; they are military-technical discussions of what the Soviets might do if they decided war were forced upon them. Third, the Soviet view of war is a holistic and longitudinal one: war is more than the exchange of weapons. It is an ongoing struggle between socialism and capitalism that should not be permitted to degenerate into wars that are losing propositions for the Soviet Union, which a general nuclear war surely would be.

War termination in Europe is taken up in Chapter 6, which considers the relationship between war termination and extended deterrence. "Extended deterrence" is itself a misnomer arousing some controversy. It implies that the United States must extend its nuclear umbrella over a prostrate Europe because of the weakness of the latter relative to the shadow cast by Soviet military power.

However, the USSR would contemplate war in Europe only under the gravest conditions. The alleged Soviet interest in a conventional-only option for war in Europe is no guarantee that the Soviets are optimistic that fighting can be controlled at that level. And they will be sensitive to the first NATO efforts to cross the nuclear threshold. Their doctrine and force structure permit very limited and proportionate responses to NATO nuclear first use. However, such a proportionate response cannot be guaranteed. It would depend upon the Soviets' theater-strategic political and military objectives, together with their optimism or pessimism about controlling war above the nuclear threshold.

For U.S. extended deterrence to work in Europe in a credible way, U.S. strategic nuclear forces have to be coupled in a credible manner to forces based in Europe. This implies that NATO conventional and theater nuclear forces are not ends in themselves, and that the Eurocentric balance of forces is not self-defining with regard to deterrence stability. It might turn out that deterrence would hold on the Central Front despite an imbalance of forces at the conventional level, provided the imbalance were not so one-sidedly in favor of the USSR as to lead to NATO intimidation.

NATO extended deterrence is also dependent upon its ability to control escalation. The control of escalation implies that NATO has both the capabilities and the doctrine that will allow for escalation control, and that the Soviets will have some incentive to reciprocate. NATO must also manipulate the threat to escalate to its own advantage, according to two somewhat different concepts of escalation.

The concepts of escalation inherent in NATO strategy are the deliberate and the inadvertent use of escalation. These are not necessarily contradictory in theory. Academic analysts can draw distinctions in theory that policymakers might find it hard to make in practice. The deliberate or "force dependent" model of escalation supposes that NATO can use superior forces, if it has them, to force the USSR to accept greater losses than it would accept if forces were essentially equivalent. On the other hand, the "risk provoking" model supposes that the USSR is sufficiently intimidated by the "threat that leaves something to chance" per se. The second assumption is that NATO, even with an unfavorable force balance, can credibly threaten to engage the USSR in an escalatory process over which both sides eventually lose control.

Both deliberate and inadvertent escalation can be threatened by NATO sequentially, if not simultaneously, provided the appropriate forces and command systems are in place, and provided the intended signals are understood by the USSR as NATO intends them. This is the indeterminate element in the U.S. maritime strategy, for example, which regards war termination as among its more important policy objectives. Maritime forces raise the possibility of applying horizontal and vertical escalation to turn the screws on the USSR during a war in Europe. Critics of the strategy regard its implications for the turning of the nuclear screw as too severe, since it threatens to degrade Soviet sea-based strategic retaliatory forces during a conventional war in Europe.

The potential collision between the deliberate and inadvertent models of escalation in NATO strategy is as serious a problem for NATO ground and tactical air forces as it is for its maritime forces. The Follow-on Forces Attack doctrine presupposes deep strikes with conventional high-technology weapons against Warsaw Pact second-echelon formations. Improved target acquisition and more accurate weapons delivery will allow some of these new conventional weapons to destroy targets formerly allocated to nuclear weapons. But the consequences for the cohesion of Soviet attack plans, if NATO doctrine is correct, are equally disruptive. Further, Soviet strategy for conventional war in Europe is understood by Western analysts to emphasize rapid and decisive thrusts into NATO's operational depth, in order to paralyze its command and control, destroy nuclear weapons and storage sites, and otherwise preempt a coherent defense before Soviet theater-strategic objectives are secured. It seems hard to imagine that either side's ambitious conventional war-fighting strategies could contain destruction, and expectations of further escalation, below the nuclear threshold for very long.

Chapter 7 focuses on U.S. maritime strategy and its role in the process of war termination. The U.S. Navy surprised not a few readers with its public exposition of the strategy by Chief of Naval Operations Admiral James D. Watkins in January 1986. War termination appeared as the central objective of the strategy, which was controversial even before its official public proclamation. The controversy had begun in the dissatisfaction expressed by U.S. Navy professionals in the late 1970s over the gap between their capabilities and the demands that U.S. strategy for conventional war would make upon U.S. maritime forces.

The Reagan administration declined to be specific about the numbers of conventional wars it would be prepared to fight simultaneously, but former Secretary of the Navy John Lehman, Jr., acknowledged that the United States would depend upon allied cooperation for war in Europe, apart from other distractions. The Navy offered the option of prolonging the war in Europe, perhaps to NATO's ultimate advantage, provided the ground and tactical air forces of the Western alliance could resist the initial Soviet attacks for several weeks. Critics charged that the Navy was following a unilateral strategy that was a rationale for force building. They also contended that the declaratory strategy for early attacks on Soviet ballistic-missile submarine (SSBN) bastions on the Kola Peninsula was impossible to implement or, if implemented, too risky of nuclear escalation.

The issues of simultaneous versus sequential conventional fighting strategies and of unilateral versus coalition warfare are perhaps over-blown by theorists. In the event of war, the tasking will be done by commanders in chief according to war plans that are much more detailed than the declaratory strategy that provides a generalized context for those plans. Nevertheless, declaratory maritime strategy was put forward by U.S. Navy officials as an answer to the problem of strategic, non-nuclear war termination. Here the issues of simultaneity and unilater-alism are directly pertinent to the choice of strategic concept. Horizontal escalation of conventional war into additional theaters of operation might bring about nuclear escalation. And a unilateralist approach could leave the United States disconnected from European members of NATO at the very time it was attempting to obtain closure on the conditions for ending a coalition war.

This last comment shows that critics of the U.S. maritime strategy feared that it would not work, and that it would. The same situation appears in Chapter 8, in which the potential implications of strategic defenses for American nuclear deterrence strategies are considered. Bal-listic missile defense (BMD) has for several decades been vulnerable to charges that it might work too well, and so destabilize deterrence based on offensive retaliation, or that it would not work, and waste money while creating an arms race spiral between the superpowers. Paradoxi-cally, both things could be true at different stages in the evolution of U.S. BMD capabilities: defenses could be technologically immature but useful as political bargaining chips. Later, they could be technically ma-ture but politically obnoxious.

Neither advocates of assured retaliation nor those of defense suprem-acy have made improved U.S. capabilities for war termination central to their arguments. Yet it would seem that if defenses improved U.S. capabilities for fighting and surviving nuclear wars, however those wars started, this consideration would be important to policy planners. To say that it might in principle appear important is not to say that the case for deploying defenses would ultimately prevail in the U.S. policymaking process. Thus far it has not, and for many reasons.

Among these reasons are some of the intellectual barriers to the study of nuclear war termination. The idea of engaging in nuclear war with any thought to acceptable outcomes strikes public and academic sensibilities as repulsive. And so it should, if it is the result of wishful thinking about capabilities that is disconnected from the realistic options that U.S. or Soviet capabilities for controlling war can provide. No nuclear war should be entered into with any optimism that it can be controlled. Nor should loss of control be guaranteed by failure to think about the problem before deterrence has failed.

Avoiding unwarranted optimism is not the same as accepting prevailing fatalism. If a nuclear war should begin, the appropriate objective of U.S. policy should be to terminate it as rapidly as possible on terms as favorable as possible. Despite Soviet declamations to the contrary, one suspects that, as their leaders stare into the abyss, the subject of war termination would not seem so implausible. It would remain difficult for both sides to achieve it once more than a few weapons had been detonated on their respective homelands.

U.S. and Soviet active defenses, including ballistic missile and air defenses, could contribute to war termination short of Armageddon. They could also create false hopes of prevailing in nuclear war. U.S. policymakers who favor deployment of missile or atmospheric defenses face the problem that they must overpromise in the public debate in order to obtain a system of limited, but perhaps significant, effectiveness. This limited but significant effectiveness would mean a system that protected U.S. retaliatory forces, command centers, and other targets defended preferentially, as opposed to a system tasked to provide comprehensive societal protection.

However, even limited BMD systems threaten the credibility of Soviet and U.S. limited nuclear options within and outside Europe. And a "limited" Soviet BMD system could render British and French strategic nuclear deterrents much less useful for coercive diplomacy, not to say retaliation, than they otherwise would be. In addition, limited Soviet and U.S. systems would pose the danger of the tapeworm that swallowed its host if they were based on more exotic technologies than their companion offensive forces. Budgetary pressures could then result in defense dominance by inadvertence, in which weak offensive forces faced competent defenses of uncertain effectiveness on both sides. Whether this condition would be more stable than the present condition is speculative.

The strongest argument against defenses, among audiences in Europe, is that U.S. and Soviet national, territorial defenses might make conventional war in Europe a more "thinkable" proposition in the future than it has been in the past. This argument is not unassailable. If the United States retains a survivable second-strike capability, then conventional war in Europe, with its attendant risk of nuclear escalation, should not be appealing to Moscow. The more serious concern would be if both superpowers deployed missile defenses with space-based components that were vulnerable to cheap defense suppression. If that occurred, then a crisis instability related to mutually vulnerable defenses might unravel an otherwise stable mutual deterrence on the ground. In a worse case, defenses would be vulnerable to one another and at least one side would fear that its second strike was doomed unless the opponent's defenses were first nullified. This is indelicacy with a vengeance. There is no reason that this condition, ipso facto, would make conventional war more probable, but it might make fear of escalation from conventional into nuclear war more unmanageable.

Chapter 9 reviews some of the major points stated throughout the text and draws together some threads previously separated. War termination, especially nuclear war termination, has received insufficient attention from theorists and policy planners. When it has been studied, it has not always been clear whether the investigators regard it as an outcome to be preferred or as a process to be manipulated or managed.

The first notion, of war termination as a preferred outcome, suggests that there is some less desirable outcome. Obviously there is in the case of nuclear war, even if the less desirable outcome is not as drastic as "nuclear winter." Outcomes are not always clearly connected to policymakers' preferences, and those preferences are infrequently organized into a coherent and systematic frame of reference. The outcome of war termination preferred by a policymaker in a specific context may not be predictable on the basis of generalized theories of deterrence. And deterrence theories are stronger on the issue of prewar decision-making behavior than they are on the subject of intrawar deterrence, which is virtually a void.

The process concept of war termination is as likely to draw upon a psychological view of decision making as it is to depend upon traditional categories of deterrence theory. A psychological perspective forces us to look inside the matrix of decision makers' choices, and not just at the "marginals" of a matrix or its outcomes. Analyses of decision making in crisis and wartime reveal that policymakers are motivated by biased reasoning and highly subjective preference orderings. Thus the "force dependent" logic of deterrence sketched for NATO strategy may be biased in favor of assuming too much abstract logical coherence on the part of policymakers. The "risk provoking" logic, on the other hand, may place excessive demands upon the willingness of opponents to "cooperate" by understanding U.S. signals to the effect that war may slip beyond unilateral or multilateral control.

Nuclear war termination demands much of scholars who will attempt to understand it and of policymakers who would have to implement it. No one would bet on the likely success of a managed nuclear war between superpowers or their allies. But the possibility must be provided for in war plans and in the training of policymakers who will order those war plans to be carried out. This implies preparedness for war termination at two levels: among politicians who will suddenly and unexpectedly find themselves confronted with the problem of crisis management and, if necessary, escalation control after deterrence has failed, and among military planners and operators who must execute the plans that have been adapted in order to provide for alternatives between deterrence and Armageddon. Should the preparedness fall short at either level, war termination is almost certainly excluded once a few nuclear detonations have occurred. The prophecy that there is no difference between some nuclear war and total war will then be a self-confirming one.

# 1

# The Theory of War Termination

This chapter broadly sketches the theory of war termination. War termination is bound up with other important concepts that will also be mentioned. It is related to, but distinct from, war objectives and war limits. There is no universally accepted theory of war termination in the very rigorous sense of the term "theory."[1] Instead there are conventions within scholarly and other professional discourse that will be followed here, although with adaptations for our purposes.

The theory of war termination posits two or more adversaries who are willing to fight for some objective that is less than total, within limitations imposed by themselves separately or jointly. Opponents, and especially nuclear-armed opponents, may not always be willing to do this. In this chapter we explore the conceptual issue of war termination as it might apply to superpower nuclear conflict, or to an outbreak of conventional war that might expand in that direction.

We will discuss three of the essential components of the concept of war termination: an agreed battle, escalation control, and coercive diplomacy. Each of these has its own implications for how wars in the nuclear age might be ended even after they have started. A preliminary caution is needed: that having an understanding of war termination is a necessary, but an insufficient, condition for bringing it about. This is especially the case in the nuclear age, for those weapons influence both the technological and the political expectations of leaders during crises and war.

## AN AGREED BATTLE

The first component of any concept of war termination is the idea of an "agreed battle."[2] An agreed battle is a conflict fought, by mutual agreement, for less than total objectives. Because it is fought for less than total objectives, or objectives smaller than each side might try to achieve without self-imposed restraint, it is conducted by rules that may be apparent only as the fighting unfolds. An illustration is provided by the conduct of the Korean war by the United States and the People's Republic of China (PRC). Each was determined to achieve certain policy objectives, but not at the cost of allowing the war to expand into total war. The Chinese limited their declaratory involvement to "volunteers"; the United States intervened in Korea, and later fought the Chinese who intervened, under the aegis of the United Nations. There were important restraints on how both sides conducted the fighting. The United States did not authorize bombing attacks on targets on the Chinese mainland, and China did not contest U.S. Pacific sanctuaries from which reinforcements and war-supporting matériel were provided. The war was thus frozen into a more or less tightly bounded geopolitical context, much to General MacArthur's displeasure and to the confusion and frustration of the American people.

What was most interesting about the Korean war as a limited war, however, was how the United States "discovered" the concept of limited war in the course of fighting it.[3] The United States did not plan to include South Korea within its strategic defense perimeter, as Secretary of State Dean Acheson had acknowledged in a speech in January 1950. Thus President Truman's reaction to the North Korean invasion surprised not only the North Koreans and the Soviets, but also many of the advisers in his own administration. At first the United States reacted by providing air support to the beleaguered South Koreans, but it soon became apparent that this support would be insufficient to stem the tide. Accordingly, Truman authorized intervention of U.S. ground forces, which at that moment were in a preparedness status far below that required for sustained combat in the Korean peninsula. As the North Koreans pushed U.S. and Korean forces into the Pusan perimeter in 1950, it soon became clear to Americans that they were in for a sustained commitment with apparently high costs.

But Truman was determined that those costs not be so high as to preclude the United States from assisting Europe in a defense against Soviet attack there, should it materialize. Nor was the United States so plentifully supplied with nuclear weapons that it could afford to use them in Korea without jeopardizing the stockpile that might be required for war in Europe. Moreover, nuclear weapons seemed disproportionate to the situation in Korea, since the North Koreans had attacked a U.S.

ally with conventional weapons, and the USSR had issued no nuclear threats to back up the North Koreans. There were few appropriate Korean targets for U.S. nuclear weapons, at least targets pertinent to the determination of battlefield outcomes. And after the Chinese intervened, the United States was determined not to expand the conflict into a war against the PRC mainland. Truman's military advisers noted that the United States lacked the wherewithal to fight the Soviet Union and the PRC simultaneously, and it was not clear that the United States, even with nuclear weapons, could accomplish any meaningful political objective in a war against China.

MacArthur was not alone among U.S. military commanders who failed to understand the evolving concept of limited war within the context of the larger "Cold War" now developing on several fronts.[4] Public confusion was also evident. Initially high levels of public support for U.S. intervention began to diminish as the war became protracted, costs mounted, and a clear and decisive outcome seemed nowhere in sight. This pattern was to be repeated in Vietnam, although other causes contributed as well. But one factor that made Korea different from Vietnam was that U.S. policymakers approached the second war after having lived through the first. The idea of self-imposed limitation in war with Soviet surrogates or allies was no longer in principle an apparent contradiction, although few of the critics of U.S. intervention in Vietnam would, by 1968, regard that commitment as limited in size or scope.

Yet surely it was. The United States did not officially declare war on North Vietnam or invade that country. It did not go to war against the Soviet Union or China, although both provided essential aid for the North Vietnamese military campaign against U.S. forces. And, most important, by 1968 the American policymaking process had made further increases in U.S. ground forces impossible, so President Johnson and his advisers were forced to limit their objectives even more. This had been foreshadowed in the conflict within the administration over prosecution of the air war against North Vietnam, when certain targets were kept off limits because of their political and symbolic impacts, despite military insistence that they be bombed because of their tactical or operational importance. Much to U.S. frustration, North Vietnam refused to acknowledge the concept of intra war bargaining and restraint.

The notion of an agreed battle might also apply to nuclear war, even war between superpowers, although there are no precedents as there are in conventional war. Although the superpowers have fought no agreed battles with either conventional or nuclear forces, they have conducted "agreed crises" with certain ground rules. During the Cuban missile crisis, for example, both U.S. and Soviet leaders refrained from actions that would certainly have provoked war, including a possible nuclear war. The United States sought to compel Khruschchev to with-draw the missiles by imposing a quarantine on Cuba. The quarantine was chosen because it was intended to send a message to the Soviets about U.S. resolve while allowing Khrushchev an opportunity to with-draw without humiliation.[5] Some of President Kennedy's advisers pre-ferred an immediate invasion of Cuba or a U.S. air strike against Soviet missile installations in Cuba. Although his "ExComm" group of hand-picked advisers appeared to favor the air strike during some of the tensest moments of the crisis, Kennedy held back from that option to allow Khrushchev more time to reconsider. Khrushchev neither directly challenged the blockade nor chose to confront the United States at some other Cold War pressure point, such as Berlin.

The Soviets, for their part, did not turn over to the Cubans either the offensive missiles or the decision to fire them once they were assembled, although they might have turned over defensive missiles. Thus, when Khrushchev finally acquiesced to Kennedy's demand for removal of the missiles, Castro was reportedly frustrated at his apparent irrelevance in Soviet decision making during the crisis. Yet the Kremlin could not turn over to Cuba a decision that might have resulted in World War III. The motives for Khrushchev's willingness to risk placing the medium-range and intermediate-range ballistic missiles (MRBM, IRBM) in Cuba were complicated to begin with.[6] More can be said about this under another heading, that of coercive diplomacy. But what is immediately pertinent is that the Soviet motives might not have been perceived correctly by the United States, with the loss of control over events to follow.

In similar fashion, U.S. actions during the crisis might have been misperceived by the Soviets. The United States apparently forced a num-ber of Soviet submarines in the Caribbean and Atlantic to surface during the crisis; some undoubtedly were nuclear armed.[7] A U.S. U–2 spy plane took a mistaken reading from a star and overflew Soviet territory, causing Soviet interceptors to scramble and Khrushchev to comment later, with some asperity, that the Russians might easily have interpreted that flight as a precursor of a U.S. first strike.[8] And the United States obviously drew the blockade line originally specified by Kennedy closer to Cuba at least once, in order to make a more unambiguous distinction between vessels that ought to be intercepted as suspect missile carriers and those that ought not.

That the crisis was conducted as an agreed battle is more evident from the U.S. side, because we have more testimony from U.S. participants than we do from Soviet participants. Khrushchev seems to have under-stood that once the missiles were discovered, although not yet in place, he had played his hand to the limit. Brinkmanship had now gone too far. Had he been able to emplace the missile complexes before their locations were verified by U.S. photographic intelligence, he might then have presented Kennedy with a fait accompli and offered to trade the missiles for a much higher stake than what he eventually got (Kennedy's pledge not to invade Cuba and, tacitly, the removal of U.S. missiles from Turkey). However, he was not prepared to gamble on provoking a U.S. invasion or air strike against Soviet installations on Cuba. The first of those two U.S. options, an invasion of Cuba, would have removed that country from the Soviet orbit and forced Khrushchev into some countermeasure to save face. U.S. officials eventually decided against the invasion on those very grounds, fearing a Soviet squeeze on U.S. and allied rights in West Berlin. The second of the two options, an air strike, would have destroyed Soviet property and killed Soviet soldiers. If the U.S. air strike were less than totally successful in taking out the Soviet MRBMs and IRBMs, then some of those missiles ready for launch might be fired at targets at the U.S. homeland, provoking U.S. nuclear strikes against the Soviet Union in retaliation.

The "agreed crisis" or nuclear analogue to the agreed battle in the Cuban missile crisis was conducted with the following tacit understandings by the participants. First, starting a nuclear war was not worth the stakes in Cuba, whatever they were perceived to be. Second, each side must have some face-saving story to present to political opponents and skeptics at home. For Kennedy, the discovery of the missiles was a great personal embarrassment in U.S. domestic politics, given his previous warnings to the Soviets and his promises to the public that "offensive" weapons would not be tolerated in Cuba. For Khrushchev, the discovery of the missiles before they were fully operational meant that he had to retreat in embarrassment or get from the Americans some face-saving promise about future U.S. intervention in Cuba.

Third, each side avoided, to the extent it was able to control them, side-of-the-board moves that would have suggested to the opponent that it was preparing to launch a nuclear first strike. The United States clearly threatened nuclear war against the Soviet Union in response to a Soviet nuclear strike anywhere in the Western Hemisphere; the implication is that any Soviet behavior less drastic would have met with a nonnuclear response, at least in the Caribbean. The Soviet Union did not, as it might have, pose a threat to Berlin immediately after the missiles were discovered and refuse to bow to the U.S. ultimatum. And even that ultimatum was not stated in terms that allowed the Soviet Union no options about how to carry it out; Kennedy did not set a time after which the United States would carry out any of its escalatory alternatives.

It is all very well to talk of crises as "surrogate agreed battles." The more difficult question is whether a nuclear war, especially one involving superpowers or their principal allies, could be so limited. We may consider whether such a battle could be limited by the ends for which the opponents fought, the means employed, or the conditions imposed by technology or other outside forces beyond their control.

The objectives attendant on such a conflict would have to be important; otherwise the use of nuclear weapons would not have been contemplated, let alone authorized. What objectives could be that important? A deliberate attack by one side against the homeland-based forces or society of the other would undoubtedly provoke retaliation. The objectives of that retaliation would be to reduce the arsenal of the opponent that remained following the first strike, in order to limit further damage, and to strike at other targets highly valued by it, to pose unacceptable costs. The expectation of unacceptable costs would in turn deter the opponent from a surprise attack in the first place. But if in a crisis the opponent appeared to fear the failure of deterrence and to contemplate preemption, then the expectation of losing its remaining forces would reinforce the deterring effects of paying unacceptable costs to its society. Thus, in standard deterrence theory both the expectation of societal costs and the anticipated loss of postattack military power are part of the calculus that deters the attacker. The expected loss of military power has two facets: the loss of forces and their supporting infrastructure, and the loss of command and control over those forces even if the forces themselves survive.

The reasons why an attacker might be motivated to strike—apart from these expectations of loss—are as unpredictable as the number of scenarios that strategists can conceive. In general, it is thought that a "bolt from the blue" by U.S. or Soviet leaders, in which one side strikes the other despite the absence of any apparent crisis or confrontation, is highly improbable.[9] A more probable path to war between superpowers is expansion of a conventional war, say in Europe, into a regional, and then a global, nuclear war.[10] War might also grow out of crisis misperceptions based upon prewar mobilization plans that were perceived to limit the choices of policymakers to striking while forces were prepared or relinquishing whatever objective was being contested to the adversary. Something like this characterized the July 1914 crisis in which the major powers of Europe, especially the Germans and the Russians, found themselves.[11]

However the Americans and the Soviets got into a nuclear war, and contrary to received wisdom, they might be strongly motivated to try to stop it. Unless the war has begun with an all-out "bolt from the blue" against one side's forces and urban industrial targets, there is no determinism about the escalation from limited to total war. This is certainly the case with regard to Soviet and U.S. behavior following exchanges of tactical nuclear weapons in Western or Eastern Europe. Assuming that these exchanges had been limited to targets within Europe outside the

Soviet Union, the USSR would, under certain conditions, have every incentive to stop the war at that point. Those conditions would include several variables. One would be the extent to which its prewar objectives had already been accomplished. The second would be the comparative weights in its calculus of what had been accomplished and what it feared NATO might destroy if the fighting continued in Europe. A third variable would be the Soviet expectation of whether the United States might launch a nuclear attack against the Soviet homeland, and under what conditions. This "worst case" assessment would prompt Soviet efforts to avert nuclear attacks against the USSR until they were perceived to be unavoidable; then it might motivate preemptive action against a comprehensive set of U.S. targets.[12]

The subject of escalation control is taken up more specifically in a later section. For the moment, we are reviewing the notion of an agreed battle after superpower nuclear war begins, and suggesting that it has several dimensions. First, there are certain obvious political and military thresholds. If they are crossed, the notion of an agreed battle withers away. The first of these thresholds is the actual shooting of Soviet forces by U.S. forces or vice versa: the outbreak of war. The second is the first nuclear detonation, with all its symbolism and suggestion. The third is the exchange of "tactical" nuclear weapons beyond the immediate battle area. The fourth is the exchange of nuclear weapons outside of Europe, perhaps at sea. A fifth is nuclear strikes against the U.S. or Soviet homeland.

This is not a single line of increment or decrement in devastation or escalation, because some of these thresholds could be crossed by more than one opponent or in more than one way. For example, the French might fire a nuclear weapon into Soviet territory before the Americans did (French doctrine is deliberately ambiguous on the timing of its initial nuclear strikes). Although France is a political but not military member of NATO, the USSR would probably take this as tantamount to a NATO-cum-France attack on its homeland. Strikes against U.S. or Soviet soil might occur from land or sea, and under auspices that somewhat disguised the source of the attack. Another possible threshold is attacks on the territory of one superpower by another with conventional weapons, which may become more feasible with new technologies. Some theorists of "catalytic" nuclear war have expressed concern that a third party might precipitate a U.S.-Soviet nuclear exchange in just this fashion.[13] It might be difficult to apply unambiguous national label to a submarine that fired a cruise or ballistic missile during an extended crisis in which all the major powers placed their forces on heightened alert and dispersed them widely.

The concept of an agreed battle seems at odds with Western understandings of Soviet military doctrine (of which more below). From some descriptions of Soviet geopolitical objectives, it would seem that the USSR is intent upon prosecuting any war with NATO or the United States to the fullest, including nuclear war if the Soviets are involved in it. Soviet doctrine is complicated on these points, but the notion of limitations in war, in order to further Soviet long-term political objectives, is certainly not. We can turn to no more unimpeachable source on this than Lenin himself. The czar and the Kerensky government sought to keep Russia in World War I at any cost, and the costs included (ultimately) the toppling of their respective regimes. Lenin recognized that the Bolsheviks could not consolidate their hold over the Soviet state and society, and at the same time continue to participate in the conflict on the Eastern front. Accordingly, in 1918 Lenin (amid much controversy among the leadership) instructed his delegates to sign at Brest-Litovsk a temporarily humiliating agreement to cede enormous amounts of the western USSR to the Germans. These concessions were later negated by the German defeat at the hands of the Western allies, but they bought Lenin precious time to consolidate his rule within the Soviet Union and to prevent his regime from suffering the fate of his immediate predecessors. As it was, the Bolsheviks would have to fight for several more years to establish their control over the larger territory of Russia in and outside of Europe.

Nothing in the Soviets' practice suggests that their leaders are unwilling to fight an agreed battle when it is to their advantage to do so or, in the negative, when other options appear worse. Events in Afghanistan in late 1987 and early 1988 seemed to bear this out. During his meeting with President Reagan in December 1987, Soviet General Secretary Gorbachev signaled Soviet interest in military disengagement from that conflict. This does not guarantee that an agreed battle can be conducted, only that it is not precluded by Soviet (or, for that matter, U.S.) ideology. U.S. history does not suggest that the idea of limited war is any easier for Americans than for Soviets to swallow, if we are speaking of politicians in general. There are differences in emphasis, as there are between Soviet military theoreticians and U.S. civil defense analysts. But the majority of U.S. military professionals are no more fond of fighting wars under restraint, other things being equal, than their Soviet counterparts. Wherever possible, professional military officers prefer to overcompensate, a judgment that is supported by the vagaries of combat and the history of war.

The concept of an agreed battle, described above, brings us to the related notion of escalation control. An agreed battle implies wide boundaries or constraints within which fighting, even ferocious fighting with heavy costs, may take place. The agreed battle has to do with those outer limits, set mainly by policy, beyond which the combatants choose not to go, regardless of what opportunities or perils are created by the instruments of war. Escalation control complements an agreed battle.

Loss of escalation control can erode the politically permissible boundaries established by the agreed battle. War aims can thus be subverted from smaller to larger and more ambitious or absolutist ones, despite policymakers' prewar preferences. Something of this sort took place when the U.S. forces in Korea were authorized to pursue the reunification of Korea instead of the status quo ante that had been the original mission. If an agreed battle establishes the outer limits of conflict, and does so mainly through policy, then escalation control has more to do with the inner limits of battle still bounded by policy but capable of slipping from one threshold to another.

## ESCALATION CONTROL

The second dimension of war termination as a concept is escalation control. The idea of escalation control suggests several things about war termination. First, wars have political objectives, and it sometimes contributes to accomplishment of those aims to limit war instead of expanding it. Presumably this also applies to limited nuclear war. Second, there are both voluntaristic and deterministic elements in limiting escalation. The process is partially controllable by the participants and partially beyond their control. Third, escalation is not always sequential or linear. It does not always proceed in small increments or in a direct line from one step to another. The idea of escalation is fuzzy at the edges, and it has become part of political argot apart from military studies, so some care must be taken with its usage.

In regard to the first point, it might seem self-evident that political objectives are important in determining the outcomes of wars. But those engaged in war or planning for war have not always understood this as clearly as scholars with 20/20 hindsight have alleged to do. Leaders have embarked upon wars with a series of carefully planned opening moves, which are sometimes brilliant tactical successes, without having considered "what next" or "how does it end?" Examples are the Japanese attack on Pearl Harbor, Hitler's invasion of the Soviet Union in 1941, and the continuation of fighting in World War I.[14]

The Japanese attack on Pearl Harbor surprised U.S. leaders, who had expected war but not an attack on the U.S. Pacific Fleet in Hawaii. The tactical success of this attack was spectacular. The U.S. fleet was severely crippled, and the simultaneous Japanese offensives against the Philippines also produced temporary victory. However, this attack did not succeed if success is measured by long-term political, as opposed to immediate tactical, accomplishments. The United States entered World War II and Japan had no hope of defeating the mobilized U.S. armed forces in a protracted war. By failing to consider how the war might end or by making unrealistic assumptions about war termination, Japan's leaders propelled the regime to its demise.

Hitler surprised his Soviet adversaries with his attack of June 22, 1941, and German victories in 1941 against a very underprepared adversary were stunning.[15] However, the Germans had underestimated the mobilization potential of the Soviet Union; and even if it had been correctly estimated, it had not been figured into any calculation of the political end game. This seems even more unfortunate for the Germans when it is recalled that Hitler gratuitously declared war against the United States immediately after Pearl Harbor. Thus the führer had assured himself of a multifront war against a coalition that was bound to defeat him. Given his psychology and ideology, this was perhaps understandable, but his military advisers might have had more misgivings about the gap between German aspirations and capabilities. The most critical advisers had been forced to resign or been deprived of power by the apparent success of German blitzkrieg tactics in France and the rapid defeat of Polish opposition even earlier. On the other hand, even Hitler should have been sobered by the unwillingness of the British to capitulate in 1940. To wage war on the Soviet Union in the hope that a defeated USSR would somehow inspire the British to give up was surely as wishful as wishful thinking can get.

World War I represents a case in which, on the issue of war termination, the twentieth-century democracies manage to look every bit as incompetent as their authoritarian counterparts. Both the Triple Alliance and the Triple Entente came about because their members could see war coming. But they expected any war in Europe to be on the periphery, say the Balkans, and to be contained there by a clever combination of military threats and diplomatic maneuverings. After all, in the preceding century Bismarck had enabled Germany to take on several opponents in succession, but for limited aims, and to arrange a postwar rebalancing of power that left Germany in an even better position. But Bismarck was no more, and the kaiser and von Moltke found themselves caught up in a crisis of competitive mobilization for what became a war of attrition. The rigid mobilization planning and the apparent irreversibility of the railroad-bound timetables have been alleged as contributory causes of World War I. No doubt they were, by July 1914, but much of the fat was in the fire earlier insofar as the political issues attendant to war were concerned.[16]

The political perceptions of leaders immediately prior to the outbreak of World War I were complicated by the commonality of their social lineage. They were an interlocking directorate of upper-class families, in a sense, who thought of war largely in personal terms. However, the technology of the day and the force of nationalism were moving against this self-contained system of policymaking by a closed circle of elites.

Some of the wretched military advice given to the principals in 1914 can be attributed to this sociological (in the worst sense) placement of people in top positions, both in governments and in their armed forces. Marx had anticipated that the workers of Europe would throw off nationalism and refuse to fight, and in this his heirs were disappointed. But his compelling metaphor about the existing order carrying within its womb the seeds of its own destruction was never more apropos.

Reactionary elites wanted to use nationalism for their own purposes, as Bismarck had done. But Bismarck had been willing to compromise his political objectives in order to have an improved war termination and postwar world; the successor generation of leaders was not. In 1871, Bismarck had grappled unsuccessfully with the problem of war termination. The French regime of Louis Napoleon collapsed, and no alternative coalesced immediately with the plenary power to make peace. Thus nationalism was wrongly construed to threaten the survival of the thrones of Europe by projecting itself across borders and divesting the ruling monarchs of their legitimacy, much as Napoleon had done a century earlier. This was not a correct perception of the problem. The danger was that nationalism could make a war, once it began, impossible to turn off, and that the absence of any script for war termination would destroy the monarchies and empires of Europe.

However, the democracies did no better, paying a heavy price for command systems that almost isolated the front from those responsible for devising theater war plans.[17] The British and French were as willing to continue the carnage on the Western Front despite the unprecedented losses and apparent military stalemate. When questioned in the British Parliament about war aims, the government responded with declarations that impugned the patriotism or morality of those posing the questions.[18] The French never considered negotiating for the return of Alsace or Lorraine and calling it quits, despite the centrality of those provinces in prewar explanations of why the Germans were likely to strike again.

Czarist Russia is perhaps the best example of a regime that self-destructed for want of considering the problem of war termination. Here again the highly stratified Russian society isolated the leadership from the tidal movements in nationalism and changes in technology that were rolling across Europe. Lenin, however, interpreted these tides with remarkable accuracy, having previously observed the Russian performance in the Russo-Japanese War. Although the regime saved itself after that debacle, it never fully restored the self-confidence of the leadership or the Russian military profession. And ordinary soldiers and sailors began to question the social dry rot that had infected their institutions, to the detriment of military effectiveness. Anti-regime terrorism was nothing new in Russia, of course, having flourished during the nineteenth century in various guises, most notably in People's Will (Narodnaya Volya).

Various anarcho-syndicalist parties of the left dotted the European land-
scape, and some of their theories found fertile ground among Russian
political activists. But for all of this preparatory work, the final push
could not be provided to the czarist regime until the pressure of war
going badly against it combined, during World War I, with the defections
of officers and their troops to the cause of revolution. Beginning in
Petrograd, these instruments of war and coercion were turned against
the regime by political activists who were able to pose the very question
that the czar would or could not face: How could Russia continue in the
war on acceptable terms? If it could not continue, for what would it
settle?

Political objectives can change during war. A government that has not
thought through its objectives prior to war may find that it is under
some pressure to invent them during it. And one that has thought them
through may be forced or otherwise motivated to change. In World War
II, important factions within the Japanese cabinet resisted surrender
even after the bombings of Hiroshima and Nagasaki, until Emperor
Hirohito personally intervened to settle the issue. Even then there was
rearguard, though futile, resistance to the decision. In the U.S. Civil
War, the prewar expectation on the part of the North's generals and
politicians was that military engagements between uniformed, combatant
forces would decide the issue of secession, and fairly quickly. A protracted war was not envisioned, and as the war became more costly, war
aims increased to include the destruction of the South's way of life and
the virtual incapacitation of its economy. The U.S. intervention in Vietnam during the Kennedy and Johnson administrations provided a kal-
eidoscopic review of rationales for involvement and its subsequent
escalation. U.S. aims were variously defined as keeping South Vietnam
free of Communism, making North Vietnam pay a price for its aggression, and, most tautologically, avoiding a humiliating U.S. defeat.[19] At
no time did the U.S. civilian or military leadership clearly define what
postwar policy objectives were most important, and thus worth paying
a higher price for, or, as an equivalent, what North Vietnamese objectives
were most important to them and what the cost of preventing them from
obtaining them might be.

Political objectives are especially difficult to define in low-intensity
conflicts, those falling into the border area between conventional wars
and terrorism or insurrection. Terrorist attacks are sometimes coupled
to a revolutionary war that has the aim of overthrowing the regime; at
other times they are attacks on officials with other objectives, including
the obtaining of publicity for the terrorist cause.[20] Low-intensity conflicts,
however they are defined, often have the character of ambiguous challenges to U.S. national interest instead of direct threats to obviously
salient objectives. Thus, those who use the techniques of revolution and

low-intensity conflict can take as much or as little of the struggle as they desire, while the authorities are kept off balance and uncertain as to the next point of confrontation. The war is more of a war of nerve and image, a competition to display for the population the competence or incompetence of the government in power. If the government cannot nip the revolution in its early stages, when trained cadres are organizing villages and preparing the infrastructure of later armed insurrection, then it will be handicapped at a later stage. At this later stage, military forces of the two sides are in combat but the fighting occurs in unorthodox styles, and the government forces are on the defensive. They must choose in many instances between overreacting to provocations or ignoring them. Armed forces trained for conflict with other national aggressors may resent "police" or counterintelligence duties that are required to root out the networks of cadres and sympathizers of the revolutionary cause.[21]

In the case of U.S. intervention in Vietnam, what began as provision of advisers to the government of South Vietnam became a U.S. war, although undeclared, against North Vietnam and its Viet Cong allies in South Vietnam. This transition was not sufficiently abrupt for policymakers to recognize that it had occurred. There was no dramatic moment when the war ceased to be "theirs" and became fundamentally a "U.S." conflict. Another uncertainty even after it was a clearly Americanized war was "against whom?" Was the United States fighting a revolutionary movement in South Vietnam, or the government of North Vietnam, or both? Was it also fighting indirectly against the Soviet Union and China, since both were providing aid to North Vietnam during the conflict? Sometimes it appeared that the United States was fighting with the government of South Vietnam, at least politically, and the divergence in war aims was very apparent during the negotiations that ended in the temporary peace accords of 1973.

The political debacle of the U.S. position in Vietnam that occurred two years after the peace settlement is one reminder that war termination may have a very different definition for two sides in a conflict. This difference may allow for a peace settlement that is a temporary fig leaf, behind which is a juggernaut to undo the arrangement. In 1975 the South Vietnamese found themselves on the receiving end of this juggernaut. Stalin had made a similar miscalculation in 1939 when he agreed to the pact with Hitler, assuming that this agreement would bind the German dictator at least until 1942. Of course, the Ribbentrop-Molotov agreement did not terminate a war, but it did terminate the immediate potential for the USSR to get into World War II on the side of the Allies against the Germans. This was no small benefit to Hitler, as he proceeded to show by invading Poland and dividing the booty with Stalin.

Another illustration of two sides' understandings of war termination is provided by the different expectations about their opponents' war aims held by Israelis and Egyptians prior to the October War of 1973. The Israelis judged that the Egyptians would not dare to attack them unless they had air superiority. Absent air superiority, the most the Egyptians could expect to do to the Israelis would be to knock them off balance temporarily, but not to achieve any permanent territorial gains. In particular, it seemed to Israeli officials and to some U.S. intelligence appreciations that the Egyptians would be foolish to start a war unless they could count on regaining the territories lost in 1967. And the Egyptians, in risking such a war, would have to reckon with the possibility of catastrophic losses should they fall short of their objectives. Here Sadat gambled that even if the concept of an agreed battle broke down, there were still possibilities for control of escalation short of total defeat for either side. This reverses the standard logic usually attributed to national leaders. As we have seen, defining an agreed battle would seem logically prefatory to establishing the thresholds and processes for control of escalation. As it turned out, escalation control was established during the 1973 war, but by exogenous forces in the form of superpower collusion, for fear they would be forced into direct confrontation.

However, Sadat's aims in the October War were not those judged logical by Israel. He apparently sought to dislodge the Israelis temporarily from their forward defense positions, including the Bar-Lev Line, and to demonstrate that Arab armies were not as feckless as they had appeared to be in 1967. Having regained some national honor and restored the appearance of a balance of power in the Middle East, the Egyptians could then negotiate for postwar political settlements with some bargaining power. However, Sadat's military strategy was less successful. The Egyptian Third Army was almost annihilated by the Israelis. Henry Kissinger's diplomacy saved Sadat further military embarrassment and prevented direct U.S.-Soviet confrontation. Kissinger's "shuttle diplomacy" prepared the way for the Camp David accords of the Carter administration, under which the state of war between Israel and Egypt was ended and diplomatic relations were restored.[22]

The character of the international system also influences the definition of war aims and the expectations as to which political and military objectives can be realized. Different kinds of international systems provide opportunities and disincentives for aggression according to different rules. In the classical balance-of-power system of the seventeenth century, limited wars were fought in order to sort out the basic distribution of territory and resources among the major European actors. This frequent use of limited war to restore the balance became less productive of system stability during the eighteenth and nineteenth centuries, when dynastic regimes felt the hot breath of nationalism mated to the sword of revolution. The Napoleonic Wars are well known for having marked turning points in military strategy (the "Nation in arms") but are less appreciated for their perturbation of the entire idea of systemic stability.[23] When systems are unstable, it is because powerful actors have antisystemic objectives, meaning that they would like to destroy the existing political order in addition to shooting up the battlefield. Napoleon, too, suffered the fate common to other military men who failed to consider a plausible script for war termination. His reach eventually outran his grasp, and so defeated itself.

Neither Napoleon nor Hitler could have withstood careful scrutiny of his strategic objectives on the grounds of war termination, for they had none. Their objectives were tactical or operational, although both entertained some vague notions that Russia would collapse after its capital had been invested. Napoleon learned firsthand that this was not the case, and Hitler repeated the plot with mechanized forces more than a century later, although he fell short of Moscow. It would be too cynical to ask whether either of these obsessive general/politicians had ever looked at a map of Russia, for their engrossment in conquering it was tied to absolutist political ambitions that knew no real limits. For leaders who are determined that history shall follow them, the distance in kilometers from one operational or tactical objective to another can easily be confused with victory in some politically meaningful sense.

Perhaps policymakers would be forced to think about their objectives for war termination if they had superior information about the costs and risks of involvement or escalation. However, military estimates are always subject to wishful thinking and distortion if hard questions about how war ends are not posed. Fred Charles Ikle discusses the illustrative example of Germany's unrestricted submarine warfare campaign in this regard. Chancellor Bethman-Hollweg was among those skeptical that the campaign could induce British capitulation, and feared that unrestricted submarine warfare would bring the United States into the war, perhaps decisively, against Germany. Careful military estimates were made, and they seemed to show a very convincing case for going ahead despite the risks. The estimates of British shipping losses during the months ahead in fact turned out to be very accurate. However, the assumption, based entirely on faith, that losses of that magnitude would cause Britain to capitulate was totally wrong. In addition, the article of faith that a certain level of shipping losses would result in the surrender of Britain was used to justify the risks of provoking U.S. intervention. It was assumed that Britain would capitulate before the United States could mobilize its power to intervene on Britain's behalf. Since the first assumption did not prove valid, the conclusion based on it had politically decisive, and disastrous, consequences for Germany.[24]

### Intentional and Unintentional Escalation

The second aspect of escalation control is whether the states in conflict can make escalation happen according to their designs. It is sometimes the case that crisis or war expands beyond the reach of those who seek to control it. This is the risk inherent in the tactic of brinkmanship, in which one nation is led to believe that another nation is more resolute about going to the brink of nuclear war than it is. Should one decide to be as resolute as the other, then deterrence will have failed and war will result. The relationship between the controllable and uncontrollable risks of war, or of nuclear war growing out of conventional war, cannot always be evaluated independently of the surrounding events.

President Kennedy is reported to have said, for example, that at the height of the Cuban missile crisis, he estimated that the risk of war breaking out was between one in three and even. Actually this was a metaphor as opposed to a statistical estimate, reflecting the president's weakening sense of control over events as the crisis progressed. Yet the incident is also suggestive of the difficulty that policymakers might have in deciding what the real risks of escalation are. There are some risks that either side might want to pose to the other that, once they have been posed take on a coloration transcending what was originally intended. An example is the problem of crisis management of nuclear alerts. During a level of alert above normal peacetime conditions, the United States or NATO might want to disperse theater nuclear weapons from storage sites to field destinations. This protective measure would be designed to assure that the weapons would not be destroyed in a surprise attack, should the USSR contemplate one. However, the very fact of dispersal of those weapons from their storage areas might send a message very different from that intended. It might suggest to the USSR that NATO was dispersing the weapons prior to launching a preemptive theater nuclear strike. The same risks of miscalculated escalation would apply to potential U.S. reactions to Soviet implementation of civil defense measures—for example, evacuation of major cities.

U.S. maritime strategy also raises the possibility of an unexpected collision between the deliberately imposed and the unexpected, but equally consequential, escalatory actions of naval combatants. The United States expects, during the early stages of a conventional war in Europe, to seed the Norwegian and Barents seas with attack submarines designed to destroy Soviet maritime forces, including their ballistic missile submarines (SSBNs).[25] The destruction of Soviet SSBNs by U.S. antisubmarine warfare might not be interpreted as a tactical event. Instead, the Soviet Union might perceive the destruction of SSBNs as a first step in an effort to destroy its nuclear retaliatory deterrent.[26] The Soviets might then react in one of several ways. They might accept destruction of their SSBNs if the rate of loss was thought not to be significant, and if the conventional war in Europe was otherwise going well. They might counterescalate by destroying U.S. and allied shipping with tactical nuclear weapons, leaving open the issue of escalation on land. They might launch a large nuclear strike against a comprehensive target set in Europe. Or, worse still for the United States they might strike preemptively, on the assumption that the United States was preparing a preemptive attack of its own.[27] Some experts contend that the USSR would be unlikely to use nuclear weapons first on land just because some of its strategic nuclear assets at sea had been lost. But NATO leaders would have no way of anticipating the Soviet calculus until conventional deterrence had failed, and then the USSR would be working actively to confound NATO estimates.

The problem of nuclear war at sea is complicated by issues apart from escalation control in Europe.[28] The traditions of the U.S. and other navies is that ship captains have a great deal of latitude with regard to self-defense and tactical improvisation. Modern surface and subsurface craft could not survive otherwise. Therefore, the intrusion of civilian controllers at long range is resented, and sometimes deliberately frustrated. The run-in between former Secretary of Defense Robert S. McNamara and the U.S. chief of naval operations George W. Anderson during the Cuban missile crisis, over procedures to be used in implementing the blockade, is so well known that it has become part of strategic folklore. In this instance, it appeared that McNamara had the better of the argument, at least from the perspective of controlling escalation along the lines preferred by the president. However, Anderson also had a point. If the president and the secretary of defense were to attempt to exercise control over the details of maritime operations throughout the duration of a protracted crisis or war, as opposed to the Cuban missile crisis of 13 days, the results would in all likelihood be counterproductive.[29]

The reason for this skepticism that policymakers can prevail over bureaucratic organizations, including military ones, for an extended period lies in historical experience. Large bureaucratic organizations are not very responsive to improvisation. They cope with their environments by adapting to certain repetitive and limited changes in familiar variables. If new conditions are assigned to familiar variables, or if totally unfamiliar variables are introduced, the system may respond inadequately or not at all. This tendency toward bureaucratic inertia is well established with regard to national military doctrine.

For example, between World War I and World War II, both France and Britain depended upon military doctrines that regarded attrition based on superior manpower, firepower, and material resources as the key to military victory. This doctrinal rigidity flew in the face of developments in technology and armored warfare tactics, which the Germans exploited in 1940. The results were twofold. From September 1939 to May 1940, the Western allies were deterred from attacking Germany in the west, although most of its forces were committed to the war against Poland. Because of their expectation that a war of attrition was unavoidable, France and Britain feared that it would take an industrial and military buildup of several years before they would be ready to strike at Germany. The second result was that the French were unprepared for the blitzkrieg launched by Germany in 1940 through the Ardennes Forest, which achieved what theorists would regard today as operational strategic results in the European theater of operations.[30]

Organizational rigidity is complicated by complexity and specialization. The existence of more specialized parts of an organization requires that more complicated systems of command, control, and communications be devised to coordinate their activities. Command systems consist of organizations, procedures, and technology.[31] As the organization becomes more specialized, the complexity of command and communications increases exponentially. Thus, the U.S. worldwide military command system has failed to send apparently simple messages to the correct destination because of compartmentation and incorrect distribution. This happened to the ill-fated intelligence ship *Liberty* in 1967 during the Arab-Israeli war, when messages from Washington to change its location were misdirected and the ship was attacked by Israeli combatants. The U.S.S. *Pueblo* was collecting naval intelligence off the coast of North Korea in January 1968 when it was attacked by North Koreans. It required a year to free the surviving members of the *Pueblo* crew. The entire fleet of AGER (auxiliary general-environmental research) surveillance craft was decommissioned shortly thereafter.[32] Compartmentation of messages contributed to the vulnerability of the *Pueblo*.

Nuclear command organizations are large and complex. Thus we can expect that they share some of the vulnerabilities to command and control complexity with other military organizations. False warnings of attack were recorded frequently during 1979 and 1980 at the headquarters of the North American Aerospace Defense Command (NORAD) at Cheyenne Mountain, Colorado. These warnings were almost all disproved immediately as misjudgments or artificially induced phenomena. However, one incident in 1979 and one in 1980 were more serious. In 1979 a training tape was played into the wrong console and simulated a Soviet attack much too realistically. In 1980 a faulty computer chip caused another simulation that resulted in the launching of alternative command post aircraft and other procedures that, during a real crisis, might have been provocative.[33] These incidents were contained because each could be isolated from any other incident and within an environment that was not conducive to exaggerated threat perception.

However, a more ominous possibility, during a superpower nuclear crisis or after conventional war has broken out, is the problem of malevolent redundancy in command systems.[34] This differs from the failure of a single part, such as the faulty rocket booster that caused the *Challenger* space shuttle disaster. Malevolent redundancy is the result of interaction effects between parts of a system that were not anticipated in the design of the system. A perturbation of one part of a complex system causes failure in another part, a relationship not planned for, and the related failure goes undetected until too late. Sometimes operators, not understanding the unexpected relationship between X and Y, make the situation worse in their (misguided) attempts to correct X in isolation.[35]

In U.S. and Soviet nuclear command organizations, malevolent redundancy may result from the unintended "wiring together" of these command systems in ways that are not fault tolerant. Each side's intelligence and warning systems are vertically integrated with their strategic retaliatory forces in order to preclude a surprise attack. Those intelligence and warning systems are constantly monitoring the opponent's forces and intelligence indicators. During a crisis confrontation or conventional war, the warning and intelligence systems of each side might reinforce the tendency of the opposite number to exaggerate threats, or misperceptions of threat.[36] The United States has not had experience with the managing of simultaneous Soviet and U.S. nuclear alerts. The USSR did place a number of airborne divisions on alert during the Arab-Israeli war of 1973. Some Americans regarded this as a substitute for actual willingness to intervene with force, and others took it as a more ominous signal. Accompanied by a Soviet threat of unilateral military intervention if Israel did not observe the cease-fire agreement sponsored by the superpowers through the United Nations, the Soviet military maneuvers did have reciprocal effects within the U.S. government. The United States raised its alert level to defense condition 3 worldwide to signify that the crisis had taken a new and dangerous turn, including the possible use of nuclear weapons if Soviet forces were actually used.

The relationship between deliberate and inadvertent escalation may also be that of a compound felony instead of mutually supporting misdemeanors. One side may wish to provoke a reaction from the opponent in order to force a showdown, in the expectation that the opponent will, in the end, back off. Something of this sort happened during the July crisis preceding the outbreak of World War I, in which various mobilizations were set in motion by the major powers. The mobilizations were not taken only as means of prudent preparedness. They were also regarded as signals to intimidate the potential adversary by warning its military establishment that its capacity to prepare for war was presumably inadequate, relative to that of probable opponents. Thus, when the Russian foreign minister sought to have his armed forces prepare a partial mobilization against Austria-Hungary but not Germany, he was rebuffed and informed that the choice was total mobilization or nothing. It is possible that the chiefs of staff were incompetent to provide such an assessment, but common sense would suggest that other political and military advisers to the czar should have pressed harder for alternatives. According to Richard Ned Lebow, who has studied this and other crisis events surrounding the outbreak of World War I extensively, Russia's inability to mobilize against Austria-Hungary was the result of a lack of consensus within the general staff, between officers favoring an offensive against Germany and those who preferred to attack Austria-Hungary. Since the general staff could not agree on either of these options, it chose to depend upon an unrealistic mobilization for both, simultaneously.[37]

This error of omission of alternatives was not committed only with regard to escalation control in the crisis management stage. It was also committed by the combatants after World War I began. It was certainly obvious by the end of 1914 that prewar expectations of rapid and decisive victory were not going to be realized. Political and military leaders failed to ascertain thereafter how the war might be ended on terms acceptable to either coalition. They made little or no attempt to define clear war aims. Each side, faced with the obvious defeat of its grand strategy, escalated the sacrifices and commitments required from its national treasuries and populations. A competition of escalation by endurance set in, in which the Triple Alliance and Triple Entente sought to outlast each other's capacity to suffer economic, military, and social privation.

This escalation of temporal and societal commitments is not always taken into account by military strategists and historians in writing about escalation. However, a war can be escalated by drawing it out in time, or by requiring larger social sacrifices, as well as by using more devastating levels of firepower. U.S. intervention in Vietnam illustrates this point. The United States assumed that its higher-technology base would allow it to escalate the conflict gradually. It did not actually try to win the war militarily by overwhelming the North Vietnamese and Viet Cong with crushing force. Instead, it attempted through ground and air operations within South Vietnam, and by air strikes against selected targets in the north, to intimidate North Vietnam into surrender. The analysis by North Vietnamese General Giap was that the competition in resolve was to be settled within the bodies politic of North Vietnam and the United States, as much as it was to be a contest of attrition within South Vietnam. The United States won the ground war of attrition, while North Vietnam won the competition in societal escalation.

It is, of course, much easier to see these things after many years have passed and hindsight has become prophecy. In the case of the Cuban missile crisis, some things are clearer as a result of recently declassified government documents pertinent to the "ExComm" deliberations of

October 27. They reveal that President Kennedy was not so willing to foreclose the option of trading U.S. Jupiter medium-range ballistic missiles in Turkey for Soviet SS–4s and SS–5s in Cuba as had been suggested in earlier accounts of the crisis.[38] This appears to suggest that Kennedy was more willing to make a politically obnoxious deal, from the standpoint of European NATO allies, in order to avoid a military confrontation with the Soviet Union over Cuba. As it happened, the United States was able to avoid having to make the decision openly and the episode passed from immediate public view. Still, this is a cautionary tale about the extraordinary level of control that modern presidents and national command authorities have over crisis events in the nuclear age. Given the consequences, Kennedy, and certainly any of his successors, would be reluctant to initiate nuclear war except under conditions in which they perceived no other option. The tricky case for controlling escalation, then, is less the crisis management before war begins than the threshold management of the barrier between conventional and nuclear war after conventional deterrence has failed.

This last statement might imply that where nuclear weapons are dispersed among U.S. conventional forces deployed far from the United States, the problem of peripheral threshold management is more serious than that of central control of escalation.[39] Land, tactical air, and naval forces engaged in combat against their Soviet counterparts may rapidly request contingent authority to use tactical nuclear weapons. Once that authority has been granted, albeit for the selective use of discrete packages of weapons and against specific targets, the problem of further restraint becomes enormous. The problem is not so much a technical as a political or organizational one. National command authorities in Washington, D.C., or the Headquarters, Supreme High Command in the Soviet Union may make the correct moves from the standpoint of crisis management logic, abstractly construed. The larger problem becomes that of implementation of that logic within organizations that have their own standard operating procedures, ethos, and institutional memories. Students of the U.S. nuclear command and control system have devoted a great deal of attention to the problem of command vulnerability due to the destruction of physical components or the disruption of important communications.[40] Perhaps equal attention ought to be given to the issue of implementation of policymakers' crisis or wartime expectations for force management and rules of engagement.[41]

## Incremental Versus Drastic Escalation

A third feature of escalation control has to do with whether escalation takes place in slow stages of relatively equal duration and severity, or whether it jumps spasmodically across many rungs of the escalation ladder at once. The danger is that theories or strategies predicated on a slow and linear escalation process may be confounded by the unwillingness of one of the parties to cooperate.[42] If one side has a doctrine of graduated escalation but its opponent does not, the side with the expectation of large jumps may interpret small escalations by its opponent as large changes in the status quo.

The problem of incremental escalation is inherent in NATO's "flexible response" doctrine. This doctrine calls for a graduated progression of conventional, theater nuclear and strategic nuclear responses to a Soviet attack on Western Europe. Of course, this progression might not be followed in actual fact; NATO has the capability to leapfrog levels of escalation if necessary. The NATO decision-making process requires approximately 24 hours from the time that corps commanders request release of specified tactical nuclear packages until release has been authorized and made its way back down the chain of command. It is expected that the initial uses by NATO of tactical nuclear weapons would be selective and controlled according to carefully drafted guidelines as to weapons, targets, and collateral damage.[43] Further decision to use nuclear weapons presumably would require additional consultation among high-level alliance political and military leaders. The objective of this selective and somewhat demonstrative use of nuclear weapons on the battlefield is primarily to signal the resolve of the alliance to continue its resistance, even at a higher cost. In effect NATO seeks to pose the risk of escalation in concrete terms. The tactical effects upon advancing Warsaw Pact divisions in Germany, while important, are a secondary consideration.

Soviet military doctrine expresses less apparent interest in employing nuclear weapons in a graduated way for signaling or coercive bargaining (see below). The Soviets do believe in selective uses of nuclear weapons, and for that matter of conventional weapons, according to the task assigned by army and front commanders. However, this does not bespeak any interest in Western theories of escalation control per se. A Rand Corporation publication that compared Soviet and U.S. doctrine on escalation stated:

There is little doubt that Soviet military thinkers *approach* the issue of escalation from a fundamentally different direction than do most of their Western counterparts. The roots of this asymmetry run deep and involve issues of culture, geography, and historical experience.[44]

This implies that the Soviet notion of intrawar deterrence might be very different, and involve fewer graduated escalatory steps, than the U.S. concept. The Soviets do not seem to accept the concept of signaling with nuclear weapons. It might be more difficult to get a decision from the

Soviet leadership, compared with the U.S. one, to release nuclear weapons to field commanders. But once release had been granted, Soviet commanders could be less inhibited than their U.S. and NATO counterparts as to timing and execution of retaliatory or initiatory strikes.[45] Much would depend upon the political objectives attendant to the Soviet attack or the Soviets' assumptions about NATO objectives after war began. But it seems apparent that Soviet worst case inferences about NATO objectives would result, should any nuclear weapons strike the Soviet homeland. It is also doubtful that Soviet leaders could distinguish between limited "surgical" counterforce attacks on Soviet territory and more comprehensive efforts to eliminate their deterrent—or that if they could distinguish, they would want to.

NATO's assumption that escalation must or will be graduated is in tension with its own requirement for credibly coupling the U.S. strategic nuclear deterrent to nuclear and conventional forces based in Europe. The U.S.-Soviet agreement on the elimination of intermediate nuclear forces (INF) worldwide caused some stir within NATO precisely over this issue. (More will be said about this in a later chapter.) NATO of course wants to have it both ways, with the USSR deterred by the difficulty of knowing exactly how tight the transatlantic coupling may be. Yet the possibility of keeping escalation under control if deterrence fails reassures the Americans (primarily) that a conventional war in Europe, or even limited exchanges of theater nuclear weapons, will not automatically engage U.S. and Soviet strategic nuclear forces. Here, too, divergent theories of deterrence, or at least conflicting emphases within a single theory, collide. Europeans emphasize the Soviet fear of a rapid engagement of U.S. strategic forces in any war in Europe as the basis of deterrence. Americans emphasize the credibility of graduated escalation as more persuasive to the USSR than a threatened "all or nothing" response.

The long-range theater nuclear forces, or INF, which the Americans and the Soviets have agreed to withdraw, were not necessary conditions for preserving deterrence in Europe. They were the result of modernizations whose controversiality went beyond the expectations of either Soviet or NATO leaders. Thus they became a political liability that greatly exceeded the putative military and political benefit they supposedly provided. The NATO rationale for the deployments of Pershing II and ground-launched cruise missiles (GLCMs) since they were first agreed to in 1979 was that the weapons would offset the Soviet SS–20 modernized IRBM, which the USSR began deploying in 1977. Europeans had raised the issue of offsetting Soviet theater modernization in view of the emergence of U.S.-Soviet strategic nuclear parity codified in the SALT treaties. A second rationale was that the Soviets might find it more plausible, and therefore deterring, that NATO would strike into their territory from Western Europe once Europe was attacked, as opposed to the lesser plausibility of U.S. strategic nuclear attacks on the Soviet homeland.

One controversial issue between Europe and the United States was whether enhanced nuclear forces increased the risks of escalation or reduced them. Part of the answer to that question depended on whether one could conceive of a theater nuclear war limited to Europe and not spreading into U.S. or Soviet territory. If the Euromissiles suggested to Europeans that they could get into a theater nuclear war faster by modernization than by deferring it, then the political premise of NATO strategy—that its theater and strategic nuclear deterrents contributed to stability and not to war —was called into question. NATO has escaped from this anomalous situation as a result of the U.S.-Soviet INF agreement, but only just, and by the ironic escape hatch of Gorbachev's acceptance of the "zero option" first proposed by Reagan (and extending it to "double-zero" with the inclusion of shorter-range INF).

## COERCIVE DIPLOMACY

The third component of the concept of war termination is coercive diplomacy. This has been alluded to in some of the discussions above, by example and by approximation, since there is considerable overlap between coercive diplomacy and escalation control. One might say that the objective of coercive diplomacy is escalation control while maximizing one's gains or minimizing one's losses in other respects.[46] Both escalation control and coercive diplomacy require some notion of an agreed battle, limitations upon ends and means for fighting war, and terminating war. Still, there are distinct issues associated with an appreciation of coercive diplomacy in its own right.

The first of these issues is suggested by the terminology itself, a seeming contradiction: "coercive diplomacy." This implies fighting and negotiating at the same time, which is precisely what is unique to it. The war is not fought, the opponent subdued, and terms imposed. One fights while negotiating, and desires to win at the lowest possible cost consistent with achievement of national objectives. However, this is easier said in theory than it is realized in practice. Those on the receiving end of coercive diplomacy may perceive the relative weights of force and diplomacy, or coercion and negotiation, differently from those who issue the warnings and threats.

Coercive diplomacy is not always successful. It requires that certain environmental conditions be present, and these cannot be guaranteed.[47] An erroneous appreciation of the environment is as likely as not to lead to misplaced signals or disregarded messages. The environment permitting coercive diplomacy must provide that, in general, (1) the party employing coercive diplomacy be able to threaten to do something to its opponent within a time frame that is meaningful to the latter; (2) the threatener have the capability to carry out the threat and be perceived as such by the opponent; (3) the threatener have the willingness to execute the threat and be so perceived; (4) the time between threat and its execution not be so long that environmental conditions change, making the threat irrelevant.

A classic example of a U.S. effort to apply coercive diplomacy that failed was the escalation of U.S. involvement in the Vietnam war. The idea was that North Vietnam would be made to pay an increasingly higher price for its aggression against South Vietnam. This was in all likelihood a very simplified misconception: a revolutionary war with some conventional features becoming confused with a conventional war per se. Accordingly, the United States assumed that the environmental conditions conducive to coercion of North Vietnam and its Viet Cong ally were present when, in fact, they were absent. The U.S. bombing of North Vietnam could not stop the flow of supplies into South Vietnam. The politico-military infrastructure of North Vietnam could not be subjected to blows that would disrupt effective management of its war effort. The morale of the North Vietnamese leadership could not be affected in a significant way. As for the war within South Vietnam, it was a collage of U.S. and South Vietnamese efforts to secure certain areas from further revolutionary activity while expanding the defense perimeter to include as much of the countryside as forces and strategy permitted. But reform of the government of South Vietnam, a prerequisite to mobilization of popular support for the government and against the insurgents, never materialized. The result was that the political environment within South Vietnam became more flabby as the United States increased its commitment of military personnel and equipment.

The U.S. command system in Vietnam was a cumbersome one for fighting the kind of war that revolutionary politico-military struggles are apt to be. The U.S. command system from Washington to Vietnam, and within Vietnam itself, was more like a sprawling corporate headquarters than a textbook military headquarters.[48] The volume of communications eventually cannibalized itself and precluded other than crude statistical assessment of wartime progress. Bureaucratic confusion in Washington abetted that in the field. This is perhaps well known, but the point here is that the United States was using an approach to war termination—coercive diplomacy—that called for a delicate blending of carrots and sticks, of incentives and threats; such blending requires a command system that is highly coherent and smooth in operation. This the Americans did not have, even supposing that their concept of the war had been correct—which, as we have just noted, it was far from being.

The coercive strategy has been tried in more recent U.S. foreign policy ventures, as in the U.S. flotilla assigned to patrol the Persian Gulf to protect reflagged Kuwaiti tankers against Iranian gunboats and missiles. President Reagan appeared in this instance to engage in coercive diplomacy without knowing it, and under conditions that were mostly unfavorable. The Iranian depredations having grown out of the Iran-Iraq war, any use of U.S. combat forces would appear to be taking sides in that conflict, which it was not official U.S. policy to do. The United States also had limited reach in terms of its ability to sustain a war in the Gulf and Southwest Asia, and countercommand attacks on Iran of the kind that were used against Qaddafi in Libya would be much harder to execute. Reagan in fact was rediscovering coercive diplomacy, for he had stumbled into it earlier in Lebanon, when the United States was forced to withdraw its peacekeeping mission under embarrassing circumstances. In Lebanon, the environmental conditions did not permit successful coercive diplomacy. The United States was unable to make meaningful threats or to offer useful incentives to halt the Lebanese conflict; in fact, U.S. intervention exacerbated it. Having arrived in Lebanon in the guise of peacekeeping forces, U.S. troops became highly visible targets for disgruntled factions in the Lebanese civil war. The United States could neither impose a settlement upon the disputants nor make its own role appear to be truly neutral, and thus escape collateral damage from terrorist wars.

Coercive diplomacy is of most interest to us in the context of a possible nuclear war or of a conventional war in Europe that has the potential to escalate into nuclear war. We saw earlier that the U.S. maritime strategy involves some ingredients of coercive diplomacy in order to induce Soviet interest in war termination prior to nuclear escalation. In this instance, the United States will use the threat to sink Soviet SSBNs as an inducement to the USSR to halt its aggression on the Central Front. In some variants of the U.S. maritime strategy, this coercive attrition of Soviet nuclear counterforce is accompanied by early attacks on the Soviet Northern Fleet in its home waters, perhaps including destruction of ports. Most of these latter and more uninhibited versions of the strategy are more rhetorical than operational expectations, and several flowed from the fertile pen of former Navy Secretary John Lehman.

Lehman's frequently cited desire to send the Soviet fleet to the bottom of the ocean at the early stages of any U.S.-Soviet global war is useful counterpoint to the theory of coercive diplomacy. The Lehman formulation is traditional military attrition without the niceties of bargaining while fighting. The opponent's targets are to be devastated as rapidly as possible. The operational U.S. maritime strategy, before and after Lehman, differed considerably from this ebullient and rhetorical one. The operational strategy, meaning the one that U.S. admirals were likely in fact to execute, called for a more gradual progression of fighting involving the use of U.S. attack submarines to protect sea-lanes and to establish pride of place in the North Atlantic and the Norwegian Sea.[49] U.S. carrier battle groups would be unlikely to storm the Kola Peninsula before these important waters were secured and the sea-lanes protected, no small tasks in themselves.

The risks of U.S. maritime strategy in crossing the threshold from conventional to nuclear war have been noted by critics of that strategy. However, this element is not necessarily inadvertent. The United States deliberately wishes to pose to the Soviet Union the "threat that leaves something to chance" when superpower maritime forces are engaged in direct conflict. As Thomas Schelling noted, there are two distinct issues here: the danger of escalation and the role that danger plays in a nation's strategy.[50] A strategy may deliberately pose the risk of inadvertent nuclear war because it is more persuasive to the adversary than threatening to start a general nuclear war. Forces at sea might stumble into the decision to escalate as a result of permissive interpretation of wartime rules of engagement unanticipated by the political leadership.

This, however, is a double-edged proposition, for the USSR in this instance must not anticipate that the United States will lose effective control of its own operations. U.S. forces might send this message without intending to. If the sinking of Soviet attack and ballistic missile submarines is accompanied by other indicators that Moscow interprets as preparations for a general preemptive strike, the benefits of U.S. nuclear coercion will become self-defeating, having overpersuaded the adversary of the risks involved. The United States had to walk this line between coercive persuasion and provocation during the Cuban missile crisis. An air strike against the Soviet surface-to-air (SAM) missile sites in Cuba (designed to protect their IRBM and MRBM installations) could have provoked Soviet retaliation against Berlin or other Western assets that were vulnerable to horizontal escalation.

The alternative of invading Cuba, deposing Castro, and removing the missiles also posed risks of widening the war and losing sight of the issue at stake. The line between deterrence and provocation of the USSR also had to be drawn when the implementation of the quarantine was discussed. A blockade that was too restrictive risked provoking the very war Kennedy was seeking to avoid. The U.S. objective was to get the missiles withdrawn without war, and even without local, conventional war. That the Americans could have smashed their way into Havana even without nuclear weapons is undisputed, but the costs even without Soviet escalation would have been considerable, and U.S. policymakers judged escalation as highly likely. Thus, the blockade seemed to be an incremental response to a very specific, although still dangerous, Soviet provocation, which left open the prospect of further escalation if the Soviets failed to comply. Of course, environmental conditions were extremely unfavorable to the USSR in this instance, and very favorable to the United States, once irrefutable evidence of missile installation in Cuba was made available to the Americans.

Another problematical issue in the application of coercive diplomacy for war termination is that it can be a two-sided affair. Each national actor or coalition may feel that it can up the ante without being vulnerable to a symmetrical escalation by the opponent. The opponent, in turn, may feel obligated to counterescalate for the sake of preserving its image of steadfastness or for the impact of steadfastness upon domestic political cohesion. During the war in Vietnam, the Johnson administration was marked by the fear that failure to stay the course in Vietnam would have domestic political repercussions, including a conservative backlash against a liberal Democratic president. Even the Nixon administration, a conservative-centrist coalition of domestic political actors, felt the perceived pressure of backlash in devising its strategy for gradual withdrawal, or deescalation. Thus the United States increased its commitment in the hope that the other side would give in, but the competition in tenacity ultimately exhausted the U.S. domestic political consensus.

A similar two-sided competition marked the war of attrition on the Western Front in World War I. Each coalition sought to exhaust the resources of its opponent. But coercion was used to complement the attrition strategy of exhaustion of resources. The German campaign of unrestricted submarine warfare was intended to disrupt the British economy, and thus destroy popular support for continuation of the war. Britain used its maritime resources in an attempt to strangle the German economy. During World War II, both sides attempted to bomb cities in the expectation that popular morale would suffer, and thus governments would be less willing to continue the fighting. In both twentieth-century global wars, then, coercion was exerted against national economies and popular attitudes, with mixed results, as a complement to the actual fighting.

In reference to Vietnam we noted the problem of deescalation as it related to coercive diplomacy. This relationship is very much in need of further study, as it would apply with particular force in a limited nuclear war between superpowers. The process of strategic deescalation is not well understood even in theory. We noted earlier that a linear progression up the rungs of the escalation ladder cannot be presumed in theory, let alone in practice. Neither can we anticipate that deescalation of an ongoing conventional or nuclear war between superpowers would occur automatically. It is sometimes supposed that after several limited exchanges of nuclear weapons, one side or both would come to their senses and attempt to stop the fighting. Even if this is so, it is not so clear that a cease-fire could be accomplished. Deescalation requires the cooperation of two sides, but escalation can be accomplished by one.[51] How difficult this would be in a nuclear war can be imagined from the checkered history of efforts to arrange the cease-fires and peace agreements attendant to conventional wars.

In Korea, deescalation of the war occurred only after the Chinese intervention had raised the risk of a conflict between the United States and the PRC that transcended the fate of Korea itself. However, deescalation did not occur immediately after the United States had rebounded from its initial losses at the hands of the PRC and reestablished something close to the status quo ante with respect to territory under allied control. Several years of protracted negotiations, marked by sporadic outbreaks of very intense fighting, continued. The Eisenhower administration may have sent signals that suggested an apparent willingness to escalate the war, including the possible use of nuclear weapons against Korean or Chinese forces.[52] This has been judged successful by some historians, although the primary sources do not provide a definitive verdict. However, the interesting thing for present purposes is that the Eisenhower strategy, if it did include tacit signals of willingness to escalate, also benefited from one deescalatory precedent. By the time Eisenhower was elected president, it was clear to the Chinese that the United States was not willing to expand the war into an invasion of their mainland territory, as they had feared in 1950 when MacArthur's forces neared the Yalu River. Several years of fighting within limits had established the precedent that if the conflict were to continue, it would do so as a limited war with limited objectives. The Eisenhower administration had somehow to offer the carrot of deescalation combined with the stick of a threat to disregard the "agreed battle" if negotiations did not bear fruit.

In Vietnam, the Americans used bombing attacks on Hanoi and Haiphong as coercive bargaining in 1972, in order to bring the North Vietnamese to the conference table and to obtain the peace accord of January 1973. It is not clear how much the bombing actually contributed to the contents of the immediate peace agreement, although it may have suggested to North Vietnam that Nixon was more unpredictable than his predecessor with regard to escalation. This raises the well-known and somewhat exaggerated issue of pretended irrationality as a coercive bargaining technique. In the Nixon administration this was referred to by policymaking principals as the "madman theory," which, if reinforced, would keep potential opponents on the defensive.[53] A statesman might strike a deliberate pose of irrationality, as Hitler did, in order to coerce his opponents and obtain his objectives with minimum, or no, bloodshed. Hitler certainly did this with regard to the capitulation of Czechoslovakia by intimidating its leaders and their supporters.

The "rationality of irrationality" stratagem has its limitations, however, apart from the risk that one irrational strategist may encounter another who equally discounts cost-benefit ratios. The rationality of irrationality deals with individual and collective governmental reputations. There is no assurance that the individual's reputation for irrationality will carry over to his or her successor, to the advantage of the state's objectives, as opposed to the individual's. Nixon's temptation to covet a reputation for being unpredictable apparently was not transferable to his successor, who presided while North Vietnam launched its final and successful offensive against South Vietnam. One might ask, in the context of a superpower nuclear crisis or ongoing war, whether a reputation for irrationality would destroy efforts to obtain war termination. Nuclear weapons having been used by either side, even against the allies of the other as opposed to its homeland, would change the symbolism of the conflict by breaking precedent dramatically. What would follow this precedent-shattering first crossing of the nuclear threshold by any member of NATO or the Warsaw Pact against any other? Undoubtedly consternation, and if either U.S. or Soviet leaders judged their counterparts in Moscow or Washington to be irrational (in the lay sense of reckless or in the precise sense of disregarding the calculus of expected gains and losses), the probability of winding down the conflict would almost certainly diminish.

Not only can there be irrational or crazy leaders, but there can be irrational command systems and states. This is true before war has begun and after conflict has broken out. Imagine a war in which some nuclear strikes have occurred against U.S. and Soviet homeland-based forces, leaving cities mostly intact. A rational command system would be able to assess how badly damaged surviving U.S. forces were, what further damage to Soviet forces or other objectives they could do, and what options were available to surviving leaders that could be executed by the forces and command system left. Whether such a postattack command system would exist after limited strategic nuclear war depends upon many unknowns. It may be very hard to communicate intentions clearly in the heat of battle, even if C3I is intact, a doubtful proposition. Targeting studies can distinguish on paper between targets that are destroyed in early salvos and those remaining unstruck, and computations can distinguish between probable prompt fatalities and those who survive the initial attacks.[54] It is more difficult to determine the postattack command system by extrapolating from the preattack one. A command system is a complicated and fragile gelatin mold of components. Organizational cohesion and standard operating procedures determine peacetime behaviors; wartime improvisations may differ unexpectedly from peacetime activities.

The physical apparatus of warning, intelligence, and assessment may be destroyed. But even if it is not, it may be disrupted in unpredictable ways, with information pathologies flooding decision makers with ghostly data bases and fictitious communications. It may be significant that the direct communications link (hot line) to enable prompt emergency communications between U.S. and Soviet heads of state is not hardened against direct attacks intended to destroy it. It would be useful only if it were not attacked; attacking it would violate the construct of an agreed battle by cutting off communications with the opponent's national command authority, and thus precluding war termination by agreement.[55] Other physical means of communication, apart from links between national command authorities, may of course exist, but authentication of persons using those links as authoritative is another matter.

Coercive diplomacy also depends for its success on the susceptibility of opposed coalitions or alliances to being divided. Certainly a hallmark of Soviet crisis management, if the USSR feels that war in Europe is about to break out, will be to create disagreements and division within the councils of NATO Europe. There are potentially many opportunities for doing so. Political parties, interest groups, and other organizations within NATO Europe will be poised to suspect the worst intentions on the part of their respective governments, especially if the genesis of the crisis is at all ambiguous. And, further to complicate alliance unity for the West, the causes for the outbreak of war might indeed be unclear. Revolts and insurrections in Eastern Europe could provoke Soviet military intervention to suppress them. Given the right environmental conditions, the conflict between revolutionaries and counterrevolutionaries could spread across the East-West border.

Nor are the Soviets immune from concerns about the solidarity of the Warsaw Pact. If conventional war broke out in Europe and the USSR won a quick and decisive victory while preventing NATO nuclear escalation, the non-Soviet members of the pact would probably hold fast under Moscow's lead. If, however, the war should spread into Eastern Europe, threatening its citadels of power, or threaten to go nuclear imminently, then centrifugal tendencies within the pact would surely assert themselves.[56] Rumania has already asserted its lack of deference with regard to pact maneuvers on its national soil (having observed, no doubt, the fate of Czechoslovakia in 1968 following such exercises), and the cooperation of East Germans in attacks against fellow nationals in the Federal Republic might be highly scenario dependent. The proposal by Professor Samuel P. Huntington of Harvard University to enable NATO to conduct a conventional retaliatory offensive into Eastern Europe, as soon as war begins on the Central Front, recognizes the vulnerability of the Warsaw Pact to divisive tendencies if prewar plans go at all awry.[57]

Potential divisions within NATO and the Warsaw Pact can be recognized, but whether they could be exploited in wartime is another matter. Here the issue of coercive diplomacy ties into that of escalation control.

Once war broke out on the Central Front or at the flanks of NATO Europe, the West would be attempting to coerce the USSR into stopping its offensive while continuing to fight in order to retain territory, population, and economic assets. All the while, the clock would be ticking against restraint in deciding upon nuclear first use. Within several days to a week, the NATO supreme allied commander would in all probability be asking for nuclear release. NATO and Soviet forces would be clashing in fast-moving engagements in West Germany and possibly elsewhere. In order to stop this conflict before it escalated into nuclear exchanges, the West would have to have in place some collective policy guidance about the instruments of coercion available and the conditions under which they might be used. These instruments might be diplomatic and economic as well as military.

We have certainly seen that peacetime economic factors, including the dependence of East and West on mutually supporting trade flow, investments, and loans, are important in preventing war in Europe. If war rapidly escalated into all-out nuclear exchanges, these factors would be irrelevant, but so would war termination. If a conventional war became protracted, and perhaps global, then economic and diplomatic instruments might move into the foreground as military forces fought to a stalemate.[58] It is not beyond the realm of possibility that the West could improvise exploitive uses of its collective economic power, including that of Japan, Western Europe, and the United States, in a protracted war. Certainly the Soviet Union can do its sums as well as NATO can, and can recognize the relative sizes of NATO and Warsaw Pact gross national products and economic potentials. In addition, even a short war that cuts off East-West economic intercourse raises disturbing problems for the imperial policing of Eastern Europe. The USSR can draw small comfort from the prospect of sacking NATO Europe only to find that it has unleashed an economic whirlwind behind the advancing Soviet forces, in the form of political and military revolts in Poland, East Germany, Czechoslovakia, and Hungary. This would be, from the Soviet standpoint, an ironic and posthumous triumph of Marx over Lenin. Workers' revolts would at last have destabilized governments dependent on capitalism in Europe, although they would be East European governments, cut off from access to capitalist goods, loans, and investments.

## CONCLUSION

The concept of war termination can be subdivided into components that include an agreed battle, escalation control, and coercive diplomacy. These are not independent concepts, for they overlap in theory as the behaviors they refer to overlap in practice. Having reviewed each component on its own terms to the extent necessary, it may be useful to summarize what they have in common.

First, war termination is not possible unless objectives are limited, and possibly restrained by self-imposed limitations as well as those forced upon the combatants by the situation or by each other. Self-limitation of objectives is contrary to some professional military traditions, and it very much cuts against the grain of U.S. historical experience. The Korean and Vietnam wars spawned deep resentment in the U.S. body politic, and the latter conflict still bears bitter fruit. Many Americans regard Vietnam as a war that the United States lost although its policy was to withdraw ground combat forces and turn the war over to the government of South Vietnam. Korea is regarded by those who remember it as a draw at best. In 1949, the Truman administration was pilloried by critics who felt that the United States had somehow lost China despite the U.S. inability and unwillingness to involve itself militarily.

Nor is there a great deal in Soviet historical experience to suggest that self-limitation of objectives in wartime is the norm. The Soviet experience with the two world wars, as well as the wars required to consolidate Bolshevik rule, was conflict for the highest policy stakes: control of the regime and survival of the state. The USSR has developed capabilities to fight limited wars, and has supported allies and proxies who have fought for territorial or other political objectives. It has used its conventional forces to enforce the Brezhnev doctrine (about the irreversibility of a successful Communist revolution) in Eastern Europe, and it has intervened militarily outside of the Warsaw Pact in Afghanistan, in order to replace one intransigent Soviet commander with a more compliant one. It was the assessment of the U.S. State Department and much of the academic community in the 1980s that the 1970s was a period of increasingly bold Soviet adventurism in the Third World, behind the shield of strategic nuclear parity. But others doubted that the reach of parity could extend to unconventional wars fought in developing societies by Soviet and U.S. allies and clients. Local conditions in these societies had seemingly more to do with the intractability of these situations, for U.S. and Soviet planners, than did the balance of nuclear power.

Although the experience might not be salutary, once major conventional or limited nuclear war has begun, the superpowers might find that cultural and historical differences mattered less than the stark facts of national survival. Solutions could be improvised and salient points of agreement would become self-evident through tacit bargaining and "dead reckoning."[59] History does not always repeat itself exactly, and the consequences of superpower nuclear conflict without any restraint are clear even to the most intrepid of national leaders. However, a salutary instinct against war *à l'outrance* is not equivalent to an established capability for imposing limitations upon oneself or upon the opponent.

Second, the present international system is no longer the tight bipolar Cold War confrontation in which any apparent gain for the Soviet Union was interpreted by U.S. leaders as an equally important loss for the United States. The system is now bipolar only at the level of strategic nuclear warfare, with other actors having major parts to play in finite nuclear deterrent and conventional forces. This multivariate system has multiple and conflicting goals with regard to stability. The apparent stability of the strategic nuclear balance has allowed an almost totally undisciplined rash of conflicts below the level of the nuclear threshold, save those which might bring the superpowers into immediate and direct confrontation. Cultural, ethnic, and religious pluralisms overlap with intrasocietal political fragmentation to create numerous small wars that the great powers, including the superpowers, appear powerless to stop.

The Iran-Iraq war of the 1980s provides a poignant illustration with all its attendant risks of expansion into a superpower conflict, like expansion of the conflict between Austria and Serbia in 1914. A further example would be another war in Lebanon in which Israel might strike directly at Syria, including Soviet forces acting in support of Damascus, and by expansion involve the Americans and Soviets as the two sides' principal suitors. If the U.S. policy of containment worked to limit the expansion of Soviet global reach for the first two decades following World War II, it has failed, once having stabilized the superpower relationship, to address the turmoil of the 20 years that followed. Thus far the superpowers have managed to keep their confrontations over Middle Eastern and other non-European wars at the level of coercive diplomacy short of violence. But there is no guarantee that this inhibition will endure forever or that the nonbloc actors who now predominate in the international system are prepared to play any significant balancing role.

Third, it is doubtful that either the United States or the Soviet Union can act out its part in any war termination drama if neither has rehearsed its lines. It is disconcerting that few U.S. presidents have expressed more than cursory interest in the contents of nuclear war plans, or in conducting the command post exercises that would familiarize leaders with the requirements of nuclear crisis management.[60] Whether Politburo members and general secretaries do any better is not available from the public record, but the compartmentation and secrecy evident in Soviet society suggest that nuclear crisis management procedures would be closely held within the Defense Council and other small groups of party and military principals.[61]

In this regard, the understandable urge of author-strategists of various persuasions to emphasize the costs of total war may impede efforts to obtain political support for the control of limited wars. The merchandising of Armageddon dulls U.S. public and congressional senses to the possibility that nuclear war, or conventional war against a nuclear back-drop, may occur unexpectedly. And if it does, policymakers who may never have thought seriously about what to do will be forced to place all of their trust in specialists who will be influenced by their own or-ganizational imperatives and professional biases. Largely unrehearsed defense communities and national command systems in Washington and Moscow are almost certain guarantees that the first nuclear detonation by either superpower will expand into self-destructive policide.

## NOTES

1. See Fred Charles Ikle, *Every War Must End* (New York: Columbia University Press, 1971); and Stephen J. Cimbala and Keith A. Dunn, eds., *Conflict Termination in Military Strategy* (Boulder, Colo: Westview Press, 1987).

2. The notion of an agreed battle is discussed with reference to nuclear war termination in Paul Bracken, "War Termination," ch. 6 in Ashton B. Carter, John D. Steinbruner, and Charles A. Zraket, eds., *Managing Nuclear Operations* (Washington, D.C.: Brookings Institution, 1987), p. 202.

3. On limitations in Korea, see Thomas C. Shelling, *Arms and Influence* (New Haven: Yale University Press, 1966), p. 130.

4. See Robert E. Osgood, "The Post-War Strategy of Limited War: Before, During and After Vietnam," ch. 4 in Laurence Martin, ed., *Strategic Thought in the Nuclear Age* (Baltimore: Johns Hopkins University Press, 1979), pp. 93–130.

5. There is a large literature on the Cuban missile crisis. For an authoritative political science account, see Graham T. Allison, *Essence of Decision: Explaining the Cuban Missile Crisis* (Boston: Little, Brown, 1971).

6. Khrushchev's reminiscences about Cuba appear in *Khrushchev Remembers*, Strobe Talbott, ed. and trans. (Boston: Little, Brown, 1970), pp. 488–505. It is sometimes argued that the balance of conventional and nuclear military forces in 1962 was so favorable to the U.S. side that the severity of the crisis was exaggerated by U.S. officials and by historians. Note, however, Khrushchev's remark: "The Americans knew that if Russian blood was shed in Cuba, American blood would surely be shed in Germany" (p. 500).

7. Allison, *Essence of Decision*, p. 138.

8. The U-2 pilot issued an open radio signal for help, and U.S. fighters racing to escort it home might well have confronted Soviet interceptors scrambled to observe it. See Allison, *Essence of Decision*, p. 141.

9. On the possibility of Soviet nuclear surprise, see William R. Van Cleave, "Surprise Nuclear Attack," ch. 21 in Brian D. Dailey and Patrick J. Parker, eds., *Soviet Strategic Deception* (Lexington, Mass.: D. C. Heath, 1987), pp. 449–466.

10. See Fen Osler Hampson, "Escalation in Europe," ch. 4 in Graham T. Allison, Albert Carnesale, and Joseph S. Nye, Jr., eds., *Hawks, Doves and Owls: An Agenda for Avoiding Nuclear War* (New York: W. W. Norton, 1985), pp. 80–114.

11. The crisis of July 1914 is treated exhaustively in Luigi Albertini, *The Origins of the War of 1914*, Isabella M. Massey, ed. and trans., vol. II (London: Oxford University Press, 1953).

12. See Stephen M. Meyer, "Soviet Perspectives on the Paths to Nuclear War," ch. 7 in Allison, Carnesale, and Nye, eds., *Hawks, Doves and Owls*, pp. 167–205; and Michael MccGwire, *Military Objectives in Soviet Foreign Policy* (Washington, D.C.: Brookings Institution, 1987).

13. For a discussion see Henry S. Rowen, "The Evolution of Strategic Nuclear Doctrine," ch. 5 in Martin, ed., *Strategic Thought*, pp. 131–156; Leon Sloss and Marc Dean Millot, "U.S. Nuclear Strategy in Evolution," *Strategic Review*, Winter 1984, pp. 19–28.

14. On this see Ikle, *Every War Must End*, passim.

15. John Erickson, *The Soviet High Command* (New York: St. Martin's Press, 1962), pp. 615–616.

16. A. J. P. Taylor, "Bismarck and Europe," ch. 11 in Taylor, *From Napoleon to Lenin* (New York: Harper Torchbooks, 1952), pp. 87–102.

17. Martin Van Creveld, *Command in War* (Cambridge, Mass.: Harvard University Press, 1985), pp. 148–188, discusses problems of command during World War II and technological and other contributory trends preceding that conflict.

18. Pertinent excerpts from British parliamentary debates during World War I are cited in Ikle, *Every War Must End*, pp. 76–78.

19. Leslie H. Gelb with Richard K. Betts, *The Irony of Vietnam: The System Worked* (Washington, D.C.: Brookings Institution, 1979), is an authoritative account of U.S. policymaking.

20. A useful compendium on this topic is Neil C. Livingston and Terrell E. Arnold, eds., *Fighting Back: Winning the War Against Terrorism* (Lexington, Mass.: D. C. Heath, 1986).

21. See Sam C. Sarkesian, "American Policy and Low Intensity Conflict: An Overview," ch. 4 in his *Beyond the Battlefield: The New Military Professionalism* (New York: Pergamon Press, 1981), pp. 59–74.

22. John J. Mearsheimer, *Conventional Deterrence* (Ithaca, N.Y.: Cornell University Press, 1983), pp. 134–164.

23. Michael Mandelbaum, *The Nuclear Revolution* (Cambridge: Cambridge University Press, 1981), pp. 57–58.

24. Decision making with regard to Germany's unrestricted submarine campaign in World War I is discussed in Ikle, *Every War Must End*, pp. 42–50.

25. An official statement of the U.S. maritime strategy is provided in Adm. James D. Watkins, USN, "The Maritime Strategy," *Proceedings of the U.S. Naval Institute*, January 1986, pp. 2–15.

26. Barry R. Posen, "Inadvertent Nuclear War? Escalation and NATO's Northern Flank," *International Security* 7, no. 2 (Fall 1982), repr. in Steven E. Miller, ed., *Strategy and Nuclear Deterrence* (Princeton: Princeton University Press, 1984), pp. 85–112.

27. For pertinent background, see Donald C. Daniel, *Anti-Submarine Warfare and Superpower Strategic Stability* (Urbana: University of Illinois Press, 1986).

28. See Desmond Ball, "Nuclear War at Sea," *International Security* 10, no. 3 (Winter 1985/1986): 3–31.

29. Lt. Michael N. Pocalyko, "25 Years After the Blink," *Proceedings of the U.S. Naval Institute*, September 1987, pp. 41–48.

30. Mearsheimer, *Conventional Deterrence*, pp. 67–98.

31. Van Creveld, *Command in War*, effectively demonstrates this point.

32. Jeffrey Richelson, *American Espionage and the Soviet Target* (New York: William Morrow, 1987), pp. 158–159.

33. Peter Pringle and William Arkin, *SIOP: The Secret U.S. Plan for Nuclear War* (New York: W. W. Norton, 1983), pp. 130–134.

34. Paul Bracken, "Accidental Nuclear War," ch. 2 in Allison, Carnesale, and Nye, eds., *Hawks, Doves, and Owls*, pp. 25–43, esp,. p. 36.

35. Charles Perrow, *Normal Accidents: Living with High Risk Technologies* (New York: Basic Books, 1984).

36. Richard Ned Lebow, *Nuclear Crisis Management* (Ithaca, N.Y.: Cornell University Press, 1987), ch. 3, pp. 75–103.

37. Lebow, personal correspondence with the author. See Albertini, *The Origins of the War of 1914*, pp. 539–549. Russian Foreign Minister Sazonov attempted to put pressure on Germany, in order to restrain Austria, by declaring a partial Russian mobilization. This partial mobilization supposedly was not directly threatening to Germany, but only to Austria. In contemporary jargon, Austria was being threatened with deliberate war and Germany with inadvertent war. However, leading Russian generals considered the proposal for partial mobilization dangerous; if activated, it would impede later efforts to implement general mobilization if the latter were necessary. Adding to the confusion, the czar apparently signed two ukases for mobilization—one for partial, and the other for total, mobilization of Russian forces—on July 29. One day later the czar ordered general mobilization, then canceled it at the last minute after receiving a telegram from the kaiser (ibid., pp. 555–558).

38. Recently declassified materials that shed new perspective on this appear in McGeorge Bundy, transcriber, and James G. Blight, editor, "October 27, 1962: Transcripts of the Meetings of the ExComm," *International Security* 12, no. 3 (Winter 1987/1988): 30–92.

39. Bracken, "War Termination," pp. 197–216.

40. Bruce G. Blair, *Strategic Command and Control: Redefining the Nuclear Threat* (Washington, D.C.: Brookings Institution, 1985), provides a very authoritative overview and an assertive argument about the extent of U.S. command vulnerability being insufficiently appreciated by policymakers.

41. See Norman Friedman, "The Rules of Engagement Issue," in E. F. Gueritz, Norman Friedman, Clarence A. Robinson, and William R. Van Cleave, *NATO's Maritime Strategy: Issues and Developments* (Cambridge, Mass.: Institute for Foreign Policy Analysis/Pergamon Brassey's Publishers, 1987), pp. 23–44.

42. The point is emphasized in Richard Smoke, *War: Controlling Escalation* (Cambridge, Mass.: Harvard University Press, 1977).

43. Catherine McArdle Kelleher, "NATO Nuclear Operations," ch. 14 in Carter, Steinbruner, and Zraket, eds., *Managing Nuclear Operations*, pp. 445–469.

44. Paul K. Davis and Peter J. E. Stan, *Concepts and Models of Escalation* (Santa Monica, Calif.: Rand Corporation, 1984), p. 15. Emphasis in original.

45. Until the mid–1960s, the Soviet KGB was responsible for custody and transport of nuclear charges, and the military was responsible for custody and transport of delivery vehicles. See Stephen M. Meyer, "Soviet Nuclear Operations," ch. 15 in Carter, Steinbruner, and Zraket, eds., *Managing Nuclear Operations*, esp. p. 487.

46. On the concept and applications of coercive diplomacy, see Alexander L.

George, David K. Hall, and William E. Simons, *The Limits of Coercive Diplomacy: Laos, Cuba, Vietnam* (Boston: Little, Brown, 1971); Phil Williams, *Crisis Management: Confrontation and Diplomacy in the Nuclear Age* (New York: John Wiley and Sons, 1976), ch. 7, pp. 135–191; and Schelling, *Arms and Influence*, ch. 1, pp. 1–34.

47. Alexander L. George, "The Development of Doctrine and Strategy," in George, Hall, and Simons, *Limits of Coercive Diplomacy*, ch. 1, pp. 1–35.

48. Inherently pathological tendencies of the U.S. command system for Vietnam are well documented in Van Creveld, *Command in War*, pp. 232–260.

49. Norman Friedman, "U.S. Maritime Strategy," *International Defense Review* 18, no. 7 (1985): 1071–1075.

50. Schelling, *Arms and Influence*, p. 109.

51. On deescalation, see Herman Kahn, *On Escalation: Metaphors and Scenarios* (New York: Frederick A. Praeger, 1965), ch. 12, pp. 230–243.

52. Although U.S. declaratory policy did not preclude the use of nuclear weapons in Korea if necessary, presidents Truman and Eisenhower differed in their expectations about the value of coercive nuclear diplomacy as opposed to battlefield applications. Eisenhower was apparently more willing to consider the potential value of actual use. See Richard K. Betts, *Nuclear Blackmail and Nuclear Balance* (Washington, D.C.: Brookings Institution, 1987), pp. 32–38.

53. Seymour M. Hersh contends that Nixon sought to emulate Eisenhower's success in ending the Korean war by applying the same approach to Vietnam, which, according to Nixon, meant the credible threat of overwhelming force, although not necessarily nuclear force. See Seymour Hersh, *The Price of Power: Kissinger in the Nixon White House* (New York: Summit Books, 1983), pp. 52–53. The "madman theory" applied in this context meant, according to Nixon: "I want the North Vietnamese to believe I've reached the point where I might do *anything* to stop the war" (ibid., p. 53).

54. See William C. Martel and Paul L. Savage, *Strategic Nuclear War: What the Superpowers Target and Why* (Westport, Conn.: Greenwood Press, 1986).

55. The point is made in Bracken, "War Termination," p. 198.

56. Peter H. Vigor, *Soviet Blitzkrieg Theory* (New York: St. Martin's Press, 1983), p. 7. According to the Soviet *Military Encyclopedic Dictionary*, edited by Marshal N. V. Ogarkov: "War puts to a stern test the strength and viability of a sociopolitical system" (vol. II, USSR Report, Military Affairs, JPRS, January 1985, p. 587).

57. Samuel P. Huntington, "The Renewal of Strategy," ch. 1 in Samuel P. Huntington, ed., *The Strategic Imperative* (Cambridge, Mass.: Ballinger, 1982), pp. 1–52.

58. See Gregory F. Treverton, "Ending Major Coalition Wars," ch. 6 in Cimbala and Dunn, eds., *Conflict Termination*, pp. 89–108.

59. Kahn, *On Escalation*, p. 211, notes: "One of the greatest misconceptions current in discussions of command and control is a failure to understand how well a central war might be run, at least initially, by 'dead reckoning'." This comment is made as part of a case against overemphasis upon the "fog of war" as an impediment to the conduct of nuclear operations.

60. Lebow, *Nuclear Crisis Management*, pp. 118–122, discusses U.S. leaders' ignorance of war plans and its implications.

61. On Soviet crisis decision making, see Meyer, "Soviet Nuclear Operations," pp. 497–512.

# 2

# The Balance of Terror

"The balance of terror" is such a familiar phrase that it no longer evokes the terror to which it refers. We have come to live comfortably with the balance of terror, so much so that the questions raised in the latter 1950s about how "delicate" the balance was now seem quaint.[1] Yet they are not. Although the most frightening scenarios for a Soviet "bolt from the blue" have been dismissed as improbable, this does not prove the indelicacy of the balance. There are several different and frequently confused facets of this issue, and they are discussed at greater length below.

We approach the balance of terror as a problem of perceived or actual vulnerability. This vulnerability may be one of forces, societal economic assets, or command systems; and of their vulnerability to a first or a retaliatory strike. It makes a great deal of difference what the intended targets are and, in a larger sense, what the two sides' war plans prove to be. It is conceivable or even likely that a poorly executed nuclear war plan could defeat one's opponent but not thereby guarantee victory for oneself.

Neither superpower has sought to imitate exactly the force structure of the other. Yet the action-reaction component of the arms race cannot be discounted. Each fears the potential vulnerability to a qualitative breakthrough or a quantitative breakout. So each deploys some insurance against worst cases while indicating willingness to negotiate at the margin. Arms control has not prevented either U.S. or Soviet planners from deploying systems that are considered vital to national security, but these have been included in arms limitation talks, and ultimately might appear in arms reduction agreements.

Consideration of the problem of the balance of terror, its basic stability, and the salient threats to that stability is basic to the understanding of nuclear war termination. If the balance of terror is basically stable, then the prospect for war termination on some basis is favorable compared with a situation of mutually perceived first-strike incentives. U.S. targeting policy has in the past rested upon a mixed strategy of counterforce and countervalue attacks, but U.S. declaratory and arms control policies have stressed assured retaliation against cities as the sine qua non of credible deterrence. Since 1974, U.S. targeting policy has evolved in the direction of flexible strategic options and escalation control, but the optimum limit of this process of refining strategic nuclear options may have been reached. It is impossible to prove that additional strategic options raise the probability of successfully terminating a central war between superpowers. However, it seems plausible that very restrictive war plans with fewer options tie policymakers' hands. One can go so far with flexibility, however, and it percolates into the repertoires of organizations much more slowly than it appears on the pages of scholarly writings.

## TECHNICAL VULNERABILITY

During the U.S. presidential campaign of 1980, Ronald Reagan spoke of a "window of vulnerability" for the U.S. strategic forces that an aggressive Soviet Union might exploit. Reagan's phraseology was based upon some very technical analyses that appeared in articles by Paul Nitze during the 1970s.[2] Nitze sought to illustrate the danger that the Soviet Union might exploit a temporary advantage in large, multiple-warhead, strategic land-based missiles (ICBMs) in order to eliminate the U.S. ICBM force in a surprise attack. Or, as a more likely possibility, the USSR would simply coerce and intimidate the United States into resignation in the face of Soviet adventurism, because of U.S. concerns about Soviet first-strike capabilities.

In fact, the scenarios were politically forced, for Soviet military planners could not have written a scenario for attacking the U.S. ICBM force in the 1970s—nor, for that matter, in the 1980s—without seeing their own society destroyed in retaliation. Thus technical vulnerability of the U.S. ICBM force to preemptive attack, even if it had been correctly calculated by pessimists, would not lead to effective strategic vulnerability. Strategic vulnerability imposed on the United States by the Soviet Union mandated that the USSR either find a way to disarm U.S. retaliatory forces across the board, or deploy a comprehensive ballistic missile defense system to deflect any U.S. retaliation.

The USSR was able to do neither of these during the 1970s or the 1980s, and the near-term prospect for its being able to do so in the 1990s was not promising. The calculations that had motivated Nitze and others to despair of the fate of the U.S. deterrent came down to the fate of the U.S. ICBM force. As the prestigious Scowcroft Commission rightly pointed out, the Soviet Union, in contemplating a first strike against U.S. forces or society, would have a substantial problem of attack orchestration.[3] It would have to launch its land-based and sea-based ballistic missiles (the latter SLBMs, for submarine-launched ballistic missiles) so that their warheads impacted upon targets either simultaneously or sequentially. Early-arriving SLBM warheads would alert U.S. warning systems and commanders to expect later-arriving ICBM attacks, and so allow for more ICBMs to be launched on warning or under attack.[4] If, on the other hand, the Soviets purposely delayed their SLBM detonations until their land-based missiles arrived at their assigned targets, then more of the U.S. bomber force thought to be targeted by SLBMs would escape.

Even this critique of the simplicity of stylized Soviet war plans (as developed by U.S. analysts) was itself very modest. It took for granted that Politburo leaders might decide upon an attack against the U.S. homeland on the basis of certain mathematical indicators that, if more unfavorable, would deter that attack. Yet it is almost certain that the mathematics of counterforce have little to do with the underlying strategic stability between the superpowers. This might seem reassuring to those who oppose improvements in U.S. and Soviet strategic counterforce capabilities, but it is not necessarily so. Counterforce superiority might have a talisman effect in a crisis, in which policymakers might be persuaded that their capability to make a disarming first strike was actual instead of notional. Therefore, the appearance of gross counterforce inferiority is to be avoided, and the effort to frighten the other side with it could prove to be counterproductive.

## CRISIS INSTABILITY

The concept of stability requires that we consider how the superpowers share vulnerabilty as a transactional attribute. Stability is that condition of the U.S.-Soviet nuclear balance such that neither side has anything conceivable to gain from the use of force or nuclear coercion. The second part of that sentence is frequently forgotten by enthusiasts of nuclear strategy. Nuclear weapons have been used primarily for coercion, or imposing one's will through fear of consequences, rather than as instruments of destruction. The problem for stability is the linkage between the two: they are credible as fear-inducing instruments only insofar as they are actual means of terrible destruction.

Stability of the balance of terror can be addressed at three levels. Basic stability is a condition in which neither side is deploying forces or building forces that over the long term threaten the other with loss of prelaunch survivability for its retaliatory forces. Crisis stability means that during periods of tension, neither side fears an imminent attack by the other. And arms race stability implies that neither seeks a technology break-through or a rapid numerical deployment of forces that would place the other side at a permanent disadvantage.[5] The condition of basic stability has obtained at least since the mid 1960s and, if some very cogent analyses of the Eisenhower years are to be believed, even earlier.[6]

If we factor out the matter of basic stability for the moment, we focus on the other two components, crisis and arms race stability. Crisis stability is the short-term component, so we will address it first, in the context of U.S-Soviet political relations and military preparedness.

The first thing to be said is that neither Soviet military planners nor their professional U.S. military counterparts expect that nuclear war will occur apart from other war. It is conceivable only by novelists that a "mad colonel" would somehow instigate an unauthorized detonation of a U.S. or Soviet nuclear weapon and thereby trigger World War III. Nor is it thought likely by U.S. experts that a war will begin with a Soviet nuclear attack "out of the blue" for which the United States has no prior political warning. Soviet experts apparently share this view relative to the Americans.[7]

The Cuban missile crisis stands as the nearest thing to a two-way confrontation of the superpowers that moved close to a nuclear ex-change. The crisis is often depicted as if the entire episode took place during a two-week period in October 1962. But of course it did not. The seeds of the Cuban missile crisis were sown in U.S. discovery of its own nuclear superiority following Kennedy's election and the public proclamation of same. There was also the impetuosity of Khrushchev, which made missile emplacements in Cuba a desirable way for him to accomplish several objectives, including a short-term adjustment of an unfavorable military balance. In addition, there were earlier reports of Soviet efforts to emplace the missiles well before October 1962, and President Kennedy had committed no small amount of his personal political prestige in reassuring Americans that installation of "offensive" Soviet missiles would not be permitted in the Western Hemisphere.[8] So to say that the missile crisis was a surprise to either side would be mis-leading in general, although the specific unfolding of events during October undoubtedly included some events that confounded the ex-pectations of both sides. And, further to emphasize the U.S. concern with technical, as opposed to strategic, vulnerability, accounts of the crisis note the hesitation in U.S. action until photographic evidence of the Soviet missile facilities under construction in Cuba was obtained.

The Cuban crisis did not grow out of a conventional war, although it did in part derive from political and diplomatic sparring between Ken-nedy and Khrushchev over Berlin, which might have resulted in con-ventional war. There is some theorizing that Khrushchev was emboldened to take the risk of putting missiles into Cuba on the assumption that, if challenged, he would put pressure on Allied rights in Berlin. In the event he did not choose to do that; but had he done so, he could have exploited the vulnerability of forward-deployed U.S. and other garrisons to East German and Soviet ground forces.

Given the strong likelihood that nuclear war will grow out of conventional war and not materialize totally unannounced, the problem of crisis stability (or instability) becomes greatly modified. Once conventional war has begun, the U.S. and Soviet nuclear forces will begin movement through a series of alert statuses, from peacetime slumber to near-to-wartime readiness. Although war itself might come as a surprise, its escalation to nuclear war would not. Forces poised and ready to retaliate against any surprise attack would pose a problem for any attacker, compared with forces that were on a lower level of alert or under normal peacetime conditions. Thus, the relationship between preemption and preventive war becomes a crucial one in understanding crisis stability. Preemption means a first attack by one side, in the expectation that the other side has already decided to attack it, in order to get in the first (and perhaps decisive) blow. Preventive war is launched at an opportune time to disarm the opponent, although there are no indications that it is preparing a first strike.[9]

The problem of crisis instability leading to nuclear war is a serious one. Some have compared the situation during July 1914 among the major powers in Europe with the possible configuration of superpower attitudes and behaviors at the edge of nuclear war. U.S. and Soviet leaders of the future might, as leaders apparently did in 1914, attempt to use brinkmanship, on the assumption that their opponents would back down before they did. Leaders of the future might stumble into war inadvertently, as did leaders of the past, excessively confident that they were maintaining control of events when in fact they were losing it.[10]

There is another side to the issue of crisis instability during superpower conflict, one that is perhaps more optimistic. This is the "crystal ball" effect that national leaders of the nuclear age would have as a result of their existing knowledge of nuclear weapons. They would not, as did their counterparts in 1914, enter war in the expectation that it would have limited consequences for their national and personal survival. If the Russian, Austrian, and German rulers of 1914 had had such a crystal ball, they would undoubtedly have settled for an early armistice or not begun the war at all.[11] The crystal ball does not require any murky divination about the alleged intentions of opponents with regard to the U.S.-Soviet relationship. The two sides' arsenals are so large and diverse that the foreseeable consequences of uncontrolled escalation are as obvious as they are terrible.

Of course, the war need not escalate out of control, and some have contended that this is the least likely outcome of a U.S.-Soviet nuclear exchange.[12] But this is not what will preoccupy national leaders during a crisis or after the first nuclear weapons have gone off. National leaders are going to be preoccupied with the absolute costs to their societies of continuing the crisis or fighting, if conventional war has already broken out. And if U.S. and Soviet conventional forces have begun exchanging fire, the likelihood is that the nuclear crystal ball will have imploded onto the desks of Politburo and National Security Council members alike.

Because national leaders with a nuclear crystal ball will be disinclined to optimism about the controllability of nuclear war, the problem of crisis instability is not as serious as some have made it out to be. The superpowers have decades of experience in nuclear crisis management, and have struggled through some cliff-hangers in the Cuban missile crisis, the Arab-Israeli war of 1973, and, according to former Secretary of Defense Robert S. McNamara, the Arab-Israeli conflict of 1967.[13] The cynic would say that these crises were too close for comfort, especially the Cuban one, and that future leaders would not be so fortunate. And, given the destructiveness of nuclear weapons deployed by U.S. and Soviet military establishments, one miss is sufficient. There will be no instant replays.

In this instance there is an ironical triumph of politics on behalf of common sense, and against the potential blinders of military specialization. The person who rises to the top of the U.S. or Soviet political pyramid is unlikely to have mastered the arcane details of nuclear war scenarios. He or she will be unfamiliar with many of the detailed procedures involved in nuclear force operations. This ignorance, contrary to popular supposition, acts as a barrier against a cavalier willingness to wage nuclear war. In the U.S. deterrence literature, for example, it is frequently lamented that presidents do not rehearse more often the protocols that would obtain under conditions of a Soviet surprise attack. Mostly they ignore the entire idea, including presidents of a hawkish reputation such as Nixon and Reagan. Only President Jimmy Carter could be persuaded to go through the command-and-control system rehearsal for nuclear doomsday in detail.[14] Carter, having been a nuclear engineering specialist in the U.S. Navy, perhaps had a more than usual fascination with the details of nuclear employment policy.

It seems to me that these presidential instincts against sober contemplation of the details of nuclear war, including the moment of their personal Armageddon, are far from counterproductive. It reflects the experience that any politician has of the unpredictable in human affairs, and of the tragicomic way in which things go wrong in political life. For a U.S. president or Soviet general secretary to be preoccupied with the postattack or postexchange world would be to divert his or her energies from more pressing and immediate matters. More important, it reflects U.S. and Soviet confidence that no leader would deliberately initiate a war that was suicidal. Although there are relative degrees of suicide, superpower nuclear war would be destruction without precedent, and this is not how most politicians want to go down in history. And if the past is prologue, they will do everything possible to avoid nuclear war, or even conventional war that has the potential to escalate into nuclear war.

## ARMS RACE INSTABILITY

If nuclear crises are more stable than some pessimists have supposed, there are those who argue that the balance of terror is unstable in the long run. There are various claims that the Soviet Union is moving into a position of military superiority compared with the United States and/or NATO. Harvard historian Richard Pipes argued in 1977 that the Soviet Union felt that it could "fight and win" a nuclear war with the United States because it had outbuilt the United States in strategic nuclear weaponry during the 1970s and because its military doctrine had a war-fighting, as opposed to a deterrent, cast.[15] Although controversial then and since, Pipes's argument raised the two most important issues relative to arms race instability. If either side could by virtue of superior force deployments or superior strategy for using equivalent forces, win a major nuclear exchange, then stability would be weaker.

Critics of the Pipes thesis misattributed to him and to others who shared his perspective the notion that crisis instability was weaker because of Soviet nuclear superiority. This was not Pipes's argument nor was it the argument of Nitze. Instead, they were suggesting that with superior forces or doctrine, the Soviet Union could intimidate the United States into surrendering vital interests and objectives without firing a shot. The NATO alliance would be forced to concede in a conventional war because the Soviet nuclear deterrent would deter NATO nuclear first use. And the USSR would make hay in the Third World because the United States would be deterred from major conventional escalations that it might otherwise undertake—for example, in Iran.

However, the Pipes-Nitze thesis of growing U.S. vulnerability posited a basically unstable balance of terror that, while not necessarily toppling now, could do so in the near future. The collapse of the balance was always a decade or so ahead; in the 1970s this meant that by the middle of the 1980s, if not before, U.S. leaders would be vulnerable to Soviet nuclear-induced coercion. The contrary assessment is offered here. As in the case of "doves" who argued that the problem of crisis instability was one of imminent danger, so for the "hawks" who argued that the USSR was winning the arms race, with fatal results for the West. Both underestimated the durability of the nuclear balance of terror and its overcompensating effects against nuclear adventurism. As suggested, there are two grounds on which Pipes and others rested their cases: improved Soviet forces and superior Soviet war-fighting doctrine. Let us take a closer look at each to see whether either, or both, could jeopardize the stability of the balance of terror.

### Superior Forces

Have the Soviets acquired strategic nuclear forces, or have they thought through a strategy, such that the balance of terror is more precarious than it was five or ten years ago? Those who answer "yes" give one of three reasons. The first is that the ability to retaliate against the cities of your opponent (countervalue strikes) is worth little or nothing by itself as a deterrent. The second is that asymmetries in counterforce capabilities, especially in the ability of each side to attack preemptively the strategic nuclear forces of the other, is vitally important to superpower deterrence. The third is that counterforce capabilities might not actually make a difference in wartime, but that the perception that one side is ahead will somehow weaken deterrence in the long run. (Thus this factor is categorized under arms race stability, although it also has serious implications for crisis stability).

The first issue with regard to superior forces is the charge that the ability to retaliate against cities following a surprise attack is insufficient by itself to deter an opponent under some conditions. It is argued that the Soviet Union, for example, might attack U.S. retaliatory forces with only a portion of its arsenal, holding the rest of its forces in reserve for retaliation against U.S. cities. By sparing cities in the initial attack, the Soviet Union would be creating every incentive for the United States to do likewise. Moreover, having done this equation in advance, U.S. planners would not respond to a threatened Soviet first strike, especially in a war in which the U.S. homeland had thus far been spared from attack.

The problem with this claim that retaliation against cities is not adequate to deter Soviet attack in all contingencies, is that it confuses a rational Soviet decision maker (by Western standards of rationality) with a believable Soviet leader. Retaliation against cities could happen whether the United States planned in advance for it to happen or not. It could grow out of a conventional war that escalated although no one expected escalation to occur. Retaliation against cities in response to anything less than a Soviet "bolt from the blue" against U.S. cities seems inappropriate because of the stylistic nature of war scenarios. The Soviet Union or the United States, once embarked upon a risky course of action, cannot be certain that the opponent is willing to make fine calculations of symmetry between attack and response. If the opponent is provoked enough, it may not calculate at all. Moreover, if it does calculate, it is likely to calculate the worst that can happen to itself, compared with the best outcome for the opponent. The United States or the USSR may then take the first option that seems to provide the opportunity to avoid the "worst-worst" case, in which the opponent maximizes its utilities and the United States or USSR minimizes its own.

The second claim that the stability of the balance of terror is at risk from force imbalances is that counterforce capabilities do matter. Faced with improved military outcomes made possible by counterforce capabilities, policymakers will be bolder in staking out their claims for vital interests. Thus the United States will be more inclined to come to the defense of Western Europe, and to invoke nuclear escalation there, if U.S. counterforce capabilities are superior to those of the Soviets. The United States would be in a position, in that instance, to dominate the escalation process as it moved closer to the top of the ladder: strategic nuclear forces. The USSR would eventually be forced to back down unless the dissolution of the Soviet empire was seen to be at stake.

Against this claim, it is doubtful that counterforce capabilities below a certain threshold matter very much as influences on basic deterrence stability. That threshold is the line that divides a credible first-strike capability from the capacity to do significant damage, short of a credible first strike, to an opponent's forces. Short of a credible first-strike capability, neither side has an incentive for preemption unless motivated by sheer desperation, which deterrence theorists have never laid claim to preventing. A credible first strike means that the opponent's retaliatory strike can be reduced to an "acceptable" level, whatever the first striker defines "acceptable" to mean. Given present superpower arsenals, it is inconceivable that either side could contemplate a successful first strike defined in this fashion. However, given greatly reduced arsenals that allowed for force asymmetries in certain categories, the redundancy and diversity of the present inventories of weapons would not be an available stabilizer. Some mechanism would have to be found to compensate for the stabilizing character of arsenals that are now, by dint of size and diversity, resistant to credible first strike even under worst case conditions.

The third claim of delicacy in the present balance of terror is one of perceptions. Although Soviet counterforce capabilities superior to U.S. ones might not make a real difference in war, in peacetime they provide coercive mileage to the superior side.[16] The United States might concede a vital interest that is being threatened by Soviet pressure, or it might refuse to escalate to nuclear first use in a conventional war because of superior Soviet counterforce capabilities. Soviet behavior in the Cuban missile crisis is frequently cited by U.S. policymakers as illustrative of this assertion. The willingness of Khrushchev and his Politburo associates to withdraw the missiles was a successful case of U.S. brinkmanship; and it worked, in this view, because of the inferiority of Soviet strategic nuclear forces compared with U.S. forces.

The Cuban missile crisis is more complicated than that. First, if counterforce superiority is so important, then Khrushchev should not have been willing to gamble on putting missiles into Cuba to begin with. The explanation that he did not expect to get caught does not comport with the Soviet military propensity for worst case analysis: they would insist upon a contingency for what to do if the USSR were caught. The plan had in fact been implemented by the Strategic Rocket Forces and Air Defense Forces in Cuba. They were to camouflage the missile emplacements, to surround them with air defense missiles (surface to air missiles), and to attempt to shoot down U.S. reconnaissance aircraft that might discover them prematurely. If discovered, the USSR was to announce that these missiles were Soviet possessions and that any attack on them would be considered a grave matter. Of course, Khrushchev gave way in the end, but not because of U.S. counterforce superiority alone. The United States also had substantial and probably decisive conventional superiority in the theater of operations (Caribbean and western Atlantic), including local maritime superiority.

Finally, the Soviets had attempted to build the missile installations without the political embarrassment of using a Third World country as a Soviet aircraft carrier. Khrushchev took a firm position on the role of the Soviet Union in supporting wars of national liberation in the developing countries. The diplomatic embarrassment that followed U.S. discovery of the missiles was equal to the military one. It showed that, on this issue at least, Castro was a puppet on which the USSR was pulling the strings, much to his embarrassment. He never again had the same credibility as a representative of nonaligned interests apart from the Soviet bloc.

Not only hawks argue the issue of perception, however. Doves worry that one side's counterforce superiority could provoke war. If one side were perceived to be superior to the other in counterforce capabilities, the other might, during a crisis, strike because of a "now or never" psychology. Thus the United States might, if its ICBMs were perceived to be vulnerable to preemption, launch on warning and on the possibly mistaken assumption that electronic indicators of Soviet launch were indeed valid. So might the USSR, in the face of U.S. systems such as MX/Peacekeeper, Trident II, and other prompt, hard-target counterforces. Here the issues of arms race stability and crisis stability come together. A race by the two sides to deploy counterforce capabilities, which are primarily designed to attack the forces of the other, will result in a self-defeating spiral of "trigger happy" forces that, during a crisis, invite attacks on themselves.

The concern that counterforce can be overdone is a valid one. There is a law of diminishing returns to accumulating warheads that can destroy the opponent's retaliatory forces *if they can do so in a first strike, and promptly.* If they cannot, things change, and so should perceptions. If U.S. and Soviet slow counterforce capabilities, such as those based at sea or airborne, are growing, then the balance is not necessarily less stable. Nor should it necessarily be perceived as such. If, for example, the United States and the Soviet Union were to deploy additional SLBMs, air- and sea-launched cruise missiles, and mobile land-based missiles while removing their silo-based ICBMs, then the net outcome could be favorable for crisis and arms race stability. Neither side would fear a prompt attack from an opponent whose forces were primarily deployed and designed to absorb a first strike and to retaliate.

However, this optimism must be qualified. Much would depend upon the accuracies of these less time-urgent, but still counterforce-capable, weapons. If they were sufficiently accurate to destroy an opponent's surviving forces in their entirety, then the slowness of their arrival might not mean much once war seemed imminent. Although it is more difficult to use slow counterforce systems like bombs and cruise missiles preemptively, it is not impossible. Given the correct strategy, an opponent's guard could be down with regard to attacks from slow as well as fast counterforce systems. The extents of U.S. and Soviet coastlines suggest some interesting vulnerabilities to mythical planners of attacks using cruise missiles launched from the sea or bombers outside air defense range.

Regardless of whether both sides' counterforce systems are primarily fast or slow, meaning whether they arrive at their targets within minutes or hours, they are likely to weigh less in the equation of any perception of a stable balance of terror. Perceptions are driven by ideology, motivation, and other subjective factors, of which missile and warhead inventories are only a small part.[17] If the Soviet Union perceives that the West has sufficiently hostile intent, its leaders will embark upon war as a matter of perceived self-defense. So, too, will the United States or NATO, vis-à-vis the USSR. The usefulness of military superiority or other relative measures of the military balance diminishes in proportion to the strength of two other variables. The first is the strength of commitment and motivation of either side to defend what is being threatened, or to take what is being refused. The second is the calculation on the part of each state of absolute versus relative losses. A state might be willing to fight a war in the expectation of serious absolute losses, in the expectation that its opponent would lose more. This was to some extent the expectation of the Union in the American Civil War. Wars of attrition have this character generally. To the extent that nuclear weapons have introduced anything new into warfare, they have altered this expected prenuclear relationship between absolute and relative losses. Now relative losses might not matter if the absolute ones were bad enough.

Nevertheless, the controlling point here is that the perceptual issue cuts both ways. Counterforce asymmetries might be meaningful if they were complemented by defenses that allowed either side to protect its homeland from retaliatory strikes. Without such protection for its homeland, either side must expect that counterforce attacks, even limited ones, open the door to a larger and more comprehensive devastation of its society. And even if the war is somehow stopped short of exchanges of attacks on cities, it is still likely to cause the loss of forces that make the United States or the Soviet Union a major power in the postwar world. When it comes to perceptions, a superpower computing the postattack balance following nuclear war would have to consider what other enemies remained. Thus the Soviet calculation would have to take into account China, and the possibility that war between NATO and the Warsaw Pact could allow the People's Republic to regain territories ceded to the czars in previous centuries.

What would a "return" to U.S. strategic nuclear superiority, by any reasonable definition of the term, imply? One definition has been proposed by Warner R. Schilling: Superiority is "a balance in which the death and destruction in the Soviet Union would be far greater than that in the United States" should war occur.[18] This definition has the advantage of deceptive simplicity, in that one can ask "damage for what political end, or to what targets?" But even so limited a definition of superiority, for the United States to aspire successfully to it, would require more than is now programmed:

...a return to American superiority would require the United States to do far more than add to the quantity and quality of its offensive forces (the MX, Trident II, cruise missiles, and a new strategic bomber). To reduce significantly the destruction the Soviet Union could cause in the United States would require a massive deployment of effective defensive systems: for ballistic missile defense; for air defense; for ASW; and for civil defense.[19]

In other words, a comprehensive defense would be needed to remove U.S. cities from their hostage condition. Otherwise they are vulnerable no matter how U.S. war plans are orchestrated. This bedevils Soviet planners, too, for they are unable to remove their cities from the same vulnerability. Thus their acknowledgment of a state of mutual deterrence, although not of mutual assured destruction as a preferred condition, was the basis for their willingness to sign the ABM Treaty of 1972, which limited missile defense systems to components incapable of providing national territorial defenses.[20] Of course, neither side had the technology in 1972 to provide such comprehensive defenses, but that is not the point. The point is that both forswore the objective of comprehensive defenses in favor of deterrence by threat of retaliation; the ABM Treaty is of unlimited duration, although subject to renegotiation and unilateral abrogation with six months' notice.

## Superior Strategy

The claim that either superpower can deploy forces that jeopardize the stability of the balance of terror is not sustained. What of the claim that one side, presumably the Soviet Union for Americans who doubt its intentions, can prevail in nuclear war with a superior strategy, despite forces that are not in themselves superior? Do the Soviets have any war-winning strategy if nuclear weapons are exchanged or if the risk of nuclear war is manipulated with sufficient credibility?

Two hypothetical war-winning strategies can be noted, and one has been mentioned already. The first, noted earlier, is the calibrated attack against U.S. strategic retaliatory forces that (mostly) spares U.S. cities from prompt destruction. Surviving cities are then held in reserve in order to force the president to capitulate. The second hypothetical war-winning strategy would be for Soviet offensive and/or defensive superiority to deter NATO nuclear first use, and so allow for a Warsaw Pact conventional war plan that would succeed without nuclear escalation.

Each of these war-winning strategies presents difficulties to war planners who must estimate conservatively. The first danger is escalation, that the conflict will expand beyond the boundaries within which nuclear first strikers or conventional war planners operated. Second, the side that instigates conventional war in Europe or nuclear war may find that its forces perform far below expectations. The friction attendant to war is a complicating factor: plans go awry, machines malfunction, people do unexpected things. Third, the absolute level of destruction in Europe, the United States, or the Soviet Union may be beyond whatever issue was being fought over in the first place. What issue over which the superpowers would fight a nuclear war would be worth the effects of that war, other than a retaliation in response to a nuclear attack? In this case the attack is the justification for a response, although not a self-evident one. Depending on the scale and character of the attack, the defender might not strike back right away, especially if the defender did not fear loss of control in the interim and expected to maintain survivable forces indefinitely.[21]

Therefore it is difficult, if not impossible, to identify a war-winning strategy for either superpower, given present offenses and nugatory defenses against them. The possibility of changing this condition fundamentally by deploying very competent defenses and drastically reducing U.S. and Soviet offenses presents a different challenge, which is taken up later. The present point is that there are neither war-winning forces nor war-winning strategies apparent on the horizon for either side. The balance of terror is not strained by the piling up of additional warheads and launchers, provided the numbers of these on either side do not approximate a credible first strike. Both U.S. and Soviet planners are very far from having that.

Crisis instability theorists link arms races to an inevitable denouement in which the sheer weight and mass of U.S. and Soviet inventories come crashing down. Even if U.S. policymakers were so committed to predestination, the Soviets are not. They believe that politics is the controlling faculty in war, and the political leadership would have exclusive right to decide to initiate the use of nuclear weapons at any level.[22] The careful study of the evolution of Soviet military objectives by Michael MccGwire suggests that present-day Soviet leaders are even less inclined than their predecessors to grant nuclear release. Or at least they have authorized geostrategic planning assumptions that treat the avoidance of nuclear devastation of the Soviet homeland as a primary global objective.[23]

## COMMAND VULNERABILITY

If the superpower strategic force balance is not conducive to instability, what else might be? Theorists have focused on the possibility that the U.S. or Soviet command, control, and communications systems might be vulnerable to disruption or destruction. Or, even if the systems functioned properly, political and military leaderships might be subject to "decapitation," and control over retaliatory forces thereby reduced to chaos.[24] Apparently U.S. policy planners during the Carter administration gave more explicit attention than previously to the possibility of targeting the Soviet political and military leadership, although options existed for withholding initial attacks against the highest level of leadership for bargaining purposes.[25] Both Bruce G. Blair and Paul Bracken have suggested that stylized attacks against principal U.S. command posts, communications networks, and other components of command systems could vitiate the strength and coherence of U.S. retaliation following a Soviet attack.[26] And some U.S. experts have noted apparent Soviet expressions of doctrinal interest in targeting the U.S. command system, along with other administrative and economic supports for post-attack retaliation and war recovery.[27]

There is some apparent indecision among U.S. experts about how the

USSR would go about this countercommand attack should Soviet planners conclude that it is possible.[28] Ashton B. Carter has outlined a notional series of targets that conservative Soviet planners might have to include in any comprehensive attack against the U.S. command system. He divides these targets into command centers, communication nodes, and warning and assessment sensors, and develops a plausible list of 650, 800, and 127 potential targets in each category, respectively.[29] The putative Soviet planner must intend to destroy more than a short list of targets in order to be certain that U.S. retaliation is paralyzed.

Of course, the Soviets need not paralyze the U.S. response entirely in all scenarios. If their objectives are more modest, then a partial disruption or destruction of the U.S. capacity to retaliate will suffice. However, this will not achieve the objective of reducing the destruction attendant to U.S. retaliation to acceptable levels. Only if the U.S. command system is virtually decapitated can the Soviets accomplish that. As Carter has noted, the performance standard required of the U.S. command system has much to do with the apparent attractiveness of Soviet attacks against it.[30] The system might be expected simply to respond with a gross and generalized coverage of as many Soviet aim points, in the shortest possible time. Or it might be expected to carry out a fine-tuned war plan through several stages of combat, including nuclear combat. But it cannot, in all likelihood, be designed for both contingencies: an extended or protracted nuclear war and an immediate spasm exchange of U.S. and Soviet arsenals.

Moreover, Soviet planners must assume that the United States has made some provision for delegation of presidential authority to release nuclear weapons under extreme conditions. In the event that the U.S. president were killed or incapacitated, the presidential Succession Act and the Twenty-fifth Amendment to the U.S. Constitution provide for an orderly transition of power to the vice-president and other designated successors.[31] The U.S. military chain of command runs from the president to the secretary of defense through the joint chiefs of staff to the unified and specified commanders of U.S. combat forces (commanders in chief for Europe, the Pacific, Strategic Air Command, and so on). These nuclear armed commanders have assigned weapons with which they could retaliate if their forces came under hostile tactical fire, once national command authority provided contingent authorization.[32] Electronic locks (permissive action links) are not required for nuclear weapons deployed at sea, including U.S. ballistic missiles launched from submarines. Soviet destruction of U.S. national command authority would simply ensure that eventually the submarine commanders would assume the responsibility for retaliation.

U.S. efforts to decapitate the Soviet national command authorities would be even more problematical. The USSR apparently has provided command bunkers around Moscow and in other locations for the highest party and state officials.[33] Military commanders have original and alternative command posts, including some that are mobile land based, airborne, or sea based.[34] Civil defense is given a great deal of declaratory emphasis in Soviet planning, although it appears more successful as a mobilization device than as a guarantor of nuclear immunity.[35] Soviet military planners acknowledge that a worst case scenario would require them to retaliate under conditions of no or very short warning (a true "bolt from the blue"), but they consider this a low-probability event. More plausible, in their estimation, is a nuclear war growing out of escalation from conventional war in or outside of Europe. Nevertheless, Soviet forces are expected to be prepared to preempt, to launch on warning/under attack, or to ride out a second strike, as the situation requires.[36]

Could a prolonged confrontation with the possibility of nuclear war looming as imminent create a leadership crisis in either U.S. or Soviet top circles. The selection process for U.S. and Soviet leaders is grueling (in different ways), and it seems unlikely that any individual president or general secretary will decide alone to launch nuclear war. Collective leadership is now the norm in the Soviet Union, at least since Brezhnev, whose regime sought to put behind it the image of Khrushchev's adventurism as manifested in Cuba in 1962.[37] Soviet military commanders would in all probability have to obtain approval from the very highest political levels in order to initiate the use of nuclear weapons. It is less clear whether in a crisis they would be given contingent authorization to respond when fired upon, or how massively they might respond to a selective NATO option. The imperative for topmost control of weapons of mass destruction derives from the categorically Marxist reading of the relationship between war and politics. According to the authors of *Marxism-Leninism on War and Army*:

Marxist-Leninist methodology makes it possible to solve the question of the interrelation between politics and armed force in the possible nuclear war in a consistently scientific way. As regards its essence, such a war would also be a continuation of the politics of classes and states by violent means. Politics will determine when the armed struggle is to be started and what means are to be employed.[38]

"Politics" in this context means the party leadership, which is especially sensitive to the risk of "Bonapartism," the emergence of men on horseback as political rulers. The continuation of the class struggle into wartime means that nuclear and other weapons of mass destruction will be used selectively as opposed to wantonly, to the extent that they contribute to the attainment of Soviet political objectives as set by the Supreme High Command. From the Western standpoint, the fundamental questions of command and control in wartime are technology or technique oriented, with major political issues taken for granted. In the Soviet case, there is a more complex interaction between political and technical factors, and with two objectives: defeat of the opponent's forces, and preservation of control by the party elite. The extent to which the preservation of top leadership and its control over forces and societal assets is important to the Soviet Union is indicated by its placement of the worlds' only deployed ballistic missile defense system to protect Moscow.

However, some Western inferences that the Soviet's interest in preserving top leadership can be used against them once nuclear war has begun may be misguided. Once at war, the USSR will have dispersed its primary and secondary command posts, and proliferated its communication and control nodes. The leadership is not a group of officials as much as it is an organization held together by standard operating procedures.[39] Those procedures in wartime will differ from those applicable in peacetime. Under wartime conditions the Soviet Union will almost certainly attempt to put into place a control structure derived from its experience in World War II. Martial law could be implemented in the various military districts of the USSR and in the theaters of military operations (TVDs) associated with the war effort. Under martial law, military commanders are given plenary authority to mobilize the entire resources of a territory according to state defense requirements. They are also empowered to deal with dissidence and resistance to such orders.[40]

Thus an attack on the Soviet control structure or command system would be an attack against the entire society, which would have to be virtually destroyed in atomic fire to prevent its reconstitution. But having done that, what would the West attempt to do then? Occupation of such a nuclear desert in order to install a Lockean regime in the Kremlin would be out of the question. To be sure, one could destroy members of the Politburo, leadership of the KGB, and other notables in the USSR; and if this were done selectively, it is conceivable that postattack negotiations could be carried on with some successors. But those successors would be as Marxist as their predecessors; and, being the perceived victims of nuclear aggression on their soil, they would be unlikely to be interested in war termination if they had forces with which to continue the fighting. By definition, such a war is a war between coalitions with decisive objectives for the triumph of socialism over capitalism or, Lenin forbid, vice versa. And Soviet military doctrine does not teach that the nuclear exchange is necessarily the end of a superpower conflict. Nuclear exchanges, especially if they are limited, could be preludes to an extended conflict in which the combined Soviet armies, air forces, and fleets proved to be decisive.

The key words above are "especially if they were limited," for the issue of limitations is central to the preservation of command and control into war itself. Here a paradoxical dilemma faces U.S. and Soviet leaders: destroying the opponent's command system promptly, in order to disable retaliation, versus sparing that command system to make later war termination possible. Some have argued that this idea of intrawar deterrence for war termination is a Western legend that would be rapidly disabused by Soviet behavior in the event. According to Bruce G. Blair:

But there is not a shred of evidence that the Soviet Union values nuclear diplomacy over brute force to achieve its objective of limiting damage to the Soviet homeland. By all indications, Soviet planners have long believed that exploiting C3I deficiencies is the only route to significant limitation. The high priority assigned to command suppression in Soviet military writings strongly suggests that Soviet strategy has been designed to fracture the command system and disorganize counterattacks rather than to deter U.S. commanders from ordering a counterattack.[41]

On the other hand, Soviet commanders are known to be loath to waste weapons on unnecessary targets, and they certainly will want to spare, to the extent possible, resources and assets that they might later want to exploit for their postwar recovery.[42] And the Soviet leadership might be less fatalistic about the outcome of war and the possible benefits of withholding if nuclear war is confined to Europe and has not yet expanded to the U.S. or Soviet homeland. Albert Wohlstetter and Richard Brody have suggested that the Soviet Union might take advantage of limited nuclear options of its own, including selective attacks on U.S. forces tasked for European reinforcement. These attacks would involve strikes at the U.S. homeland, but very selective ones against military installations, avoiding deliberate attacks against cities.[43] Regardless of the inherent plausibility of such scenarios—and they are arguable—the case can be made that during a crisis or conventional war, the Politburo would be more, instead of less, conscious of where its nuclear weapons were targeted and of the need for political control of unfolding military operations.

Here the difference between the Western and the Soviet view of "theater" versus "strategic" operations becomes critical. To U.S. planners, a war in Europe, even a nuclear one, is a theater campaign that has not yet become a strategic one. For Moscow, a war in Europe is a strategic war in the European theater of operations (Northwestern, Western, and Southwestern TVDs). This difference in perspective means that the U.S. and Soviet views of limited exchanges may differ considerably. The USSR can certainly conceive of a war in Europe that does not necessarily involve attacks on the Soviet homeland; if all goes well, from the Soviets' standpoint, a conventional war in Europe would have exactly that cast. However, they can also conceive of such a war getting very far out of control and expanding into nuclear attacks on Moscow itself. And the USSR, in viewing these scenarios, must take into account the plausible use of British and/or French nuclear forces against its major cities. The Soviet deterrent may be sufficient to prevent British or French first use of strategic retaliatory forces as a deliberate and calculated act. But those forces could be activated by a process in which Soviet conventional forces did some things that were required by their plan for attacking Germany and/or the Low Countries and ended up by triggering inadvertent nuclear war.[44]

In hushed tones, Western strategists on both sides of the Atlantic will acknowledge that part of the reason for the French and British desire to have nuclear forces of their own, apart from peacetime prestige, is to complicate the Soviet view of intrawar deterrence. The USSR might reason that the United States would indulge in skirmishing below the level of all-out exchanges against U.S. and Soviet cities, with Europe as the battleground. But Europeans want to create disincentives for this making sanctuaries of the U.S. and Soviet homelands, and to convince the Kremlin that it cannot separate theater from strategic nuclear conflict. De Gaulle's reasoning on this point has often been disputed, but never refuted convincingly: There is absolutely no reason why a U.S. president should choose deliberately to trade New York for Bonn, and deterrence is weaker to the extent that the choice of one can be decoupled from the other.

## CONCLUSIONS

Bruce Blair offers the following assessment of U.S. strategic nuclear vulnerability as of the early 1970s:

... the fact remains that U.S. command vulnerability and little else was responsible for creating a situation in which Soviet nuclear attack could have been a rational act, albeit an act of last resort. Command vulnerability was the main potential source of instability in a nuclear confrontation, and it represented a potential catalyst for intentional escalation on the part of both sides given the powerful incentive to strike first.[45]

Others have stressed force imbalances, the dynamics of crisis interactions, or the compound probability of simple bad luck as factors that make the U.S.-Soviet nuclear balance delicate. The view taken here is otherwise. The balance is not only not delicate, it is durable in proportion to the size and redundancy of the superpowers' arsenals. The larger and more diverse their strategic retaliatory forces are, the more improbable any first strike scenario becomes for either side.

This assessment has perverse implications for some canonical notions of arms control, including those which have influenced recent U.S. and Soviet proposals on nuclear arms reductions. It seems that, in principle, fewer weapons ought to be a better condition than more weapons, assuming equal reductions on both sides. However, the numerical balance has a tricky relationship to stability that is more complicated than common sense. Fewer weapons are not necessarily going to result in a more stable balance. Stability is the distance that both sides remain from a credible first-strike capability, and the security they feel against any contemplation of a first-strike possibility by the other. At greatly reduced and mutually agreed upon levels of strategic nuclear warheads, say 6,000, the superpowers may find that stability is reduced instead of enhanced. Much depends on how the reductions are implemented: which weapons, and in what phases. And U.S. and Soviet force modernization plans will become more significant, relative to the stability of the future balance, in an environment of significant force reductions of the kind discussed by Reagan and Gorbachev at Reykjavik in 1986.

Reductions in numbers of strategic weapons would contribute to stability, for example, if those reductions were taken in prompt counterforce systems such as silo-based ICBMs. Bombers and submarines with cruise and ballistic missiles are more survivable and versatile platforms than ICBMs, and therefore seem less threatening to stability. However, cruise missiles do raise the possibility of surprise attack in the absence of credible air defenses, which in the U.S. and NATO cases are deemed inadequate by many experts. And Trident II (D–5) SLBMs will be deployed by the United States beginning in 1989, with hard-target capabilities against Soviet silos and command centers presumably comparable with the MX/Peacekeeper ICBM. Both U.S. and Soviet planners seem intrigued by mobile ICBMs, with the U.S Midgetman intended for deployment in the 1990s, and the Soviet SS–25 and SS–24 (road and rail mobile, respectively) now deployed.

Based on past experience, it would seem that the shift from reliance upon prompt to slow counterforce systems would be stabilizing. This may not be the most important consequence of the shift, however. Slow counterforce systems lend themselves to use throughout an extended conflict. They would be harder to destroy in preemptive attacks, and might reasonably be expected to survive for weeks or months. Having diversified their arsenals with weapons whose survivability seemed so resistant to surprise, Soviet and U.S. planners might contemplate slow-motion nuclear wars for the future. Examination of slow-motion wars would show that, even in theory, the complexity of command and control increases enormously, and so does the potential for war termination. With systems dependent upon prompt launch, as ICBMs surely are, the superpowers cannot contemplate even limited salvos that cause less than massive collateral damage to populations and industry. Improvements in accuracy may allow cruise missiles and mobile sea- and land-based ballistic missiles to be used selectively against military targets while minimizing collateral damage. If accuracies improve sufficiently and can be mated to weapons that can survive almost indefinitely, as a sufficient number of cruise missiles could, then multiphase conflicts with selective nuclear strikes are no longer as inconceivable, even between superpowers.

Stability, then, is not only a function of first-strike invulnerability. It is also related to the expectation that if deterrence fails, one need not virtually exhaust one's arsenal against a comprehensive target set. Selective strikes can hurt the opponent, but not so badly that it has no incentive to negotiate. This kind of selectivity has not been available to U.S. and Soviet policymakers in the past. War plans can incorporate only so many options, and command post exercises can rehearse even fewer. Neither the superpowers' weapons nor their command systems have permitted them to contemplate seriously the possibility of a protracted, albeit limited, nuclear war.

We return to this matter later, but for now it is important to see that stability is not related only to time-urgent missile duels that take place in the first half hour of nuclear war, as is commonly supposed. Stability also includes the expectations that policymakers have about being able to continue to fight and to end the war on some terms that are acceptable to them and to their constituents. In the past stability has been supported by the sheer impossibility of doing this—thus the policymakers' basic horror of even launching a single nuclear salvo. Future force structures, more complicated and more survivable, may remove this deterrence by stark simplicity, and replace it with a more ambiguous complexity. Stability will then depend on expectations not only about how war begins but also about how it ends.

## NOTES

1. Albert Wohlstetter, "The Delicate Balance of Terror," *Foreign Affairs* 37, no. 2 (January 1959):209–234.

2. For example, Paul H. Nitze, "Assuring Strategic Stability in an Era of Detente," *Foreign Affairs* 54 (1976):207–233.

3. President's Commission on U.S. Strategic Forces (Scowcroft Commission), *Report* (Washington, D.C.: U.S. Government Printing Office, April 1983), pp. 7–8.

4. On the process of launch under attack for the U.S. ICBM force, see Ashton B. Carter, "Assessing Command System Vulnerability," ch. 17 in Ashton B. Carter, John D. Steinbruner, and Charles A. Zraket, eds., *Managing Nuclear Operations* (Washington, D.C.: Brookings Institution, 1987), pp. 578–582.

5. For useful clarification of the concept of stability, see Leon V. Sigal, *Nuclear*

*Forces in Europe: Enduring Dilemmas, Present Prospects* (Washington, D.C.: Brookings Institution, 1984), pp. 8–9.

6. According to Richard K. Betts: "In reality, the situation in the two decades after 1945 was never as rosy as those nostalgic for it seem to think, because there was never a time when leaders were *confident* that the United States could wage nuclear war successfully—that is, parry and repel a Soviet attack in Europe while restricting damage of the West to 'acceptable' levels." See Betts, *Nuclear Blackmail and Nuclear Balance* (Washington, D.C.: Brookings Institution, 1987), p. 144.

7. See Stephen M. Meyer, "Soviet Perspectives on the Paths to Nuclear War," ch. 7 in Graham T. Allison, Albert Carnesale, and Joseph S. Nye, Jr., eds., *Hawks, Doves and Owls: An Agenda for Avoiding Nuclear War* (New York: W. W. Norton, 1985).

8. Graham T. Allison, *Essence of Decision: Explaining the Cuban Missile Crisis* (Boston: Little, Brown, 1971), is a definitive account.

9. A lucid discussion of this is Richard K. Betts, "Surprise Attack and Preemption," ch. 3 in Allison, Carnesale, and Nye, eds., *Hawks, Doves and Owls*, pp. 54–80.

10. I am grateful to Richard Ned Lebow for helping to clarify some of these issues. See his *Nuclear Crisis Management* (Ithaca, N.Y.: Cornell University Press, 1987).

11. The "crystal ball" effect is noted in Albert Carnesale, et al., *Living with Nuclear Weapons* (New York: Bantam Books, 1983), p. 44.

12. For a discussion of pertinent concepts, see Herman Kahn, *On Escalation: Metaphors and Scenarios* (New York: Frederick A. Praeger, 1965).

13. Kosygin's threat during the 1967 Arab-Israeli war is noted in Robert S. McNamara, *Blundering into Disaster: Surviving the First Century of the Nuclear Age* (New York: Pantheon Books, 1986), p. 13.

14. Peter Pringle and William Arkin, *SIOP: The Secret U.S. Plan for Nuclear War* (New York: W. W. Norton, 1983), p. 216. Note Carter's atypical willingness among presidents to familiarize himself with the actual procedures to be followed in the event of nuclear attack.

15. See Richard Pipes, "Why the Soviet Union Thinks It Could Fight and Win a Nuclear War," *Commentary*, July 1977, pp. 21–34. See also Robert L. Arnett, "Soviet Attitudes Towards Nuclear War: Do They Really Think They Can Win?" *Journal of Strategic Studies* 2, no. 2 (September 1979):172–91.

16. For a useful analysis, see Richard K. Betts, "Elusive Equivalence: The Political and Military Meaning of the Nuclear Balance," ch. 3 in Samuel P. Huntington, ed., *The Strategic Imperative* (Cambridge, Mass.: Ballinger, 1982), pp. 101–140.

17. See Robert Jervis, "Deterrence and Perception," *International Security* 7, no. 3 (Winter 1982/1983), repr. in Steven E. Miller, ed., *Strategy and Nuclear Deterrence* (Princeton: Princeton University Press, 1984), pp. 57–84.

18. Warner R. Schilling, "U.S. Strategic Nuclear Concepts in the 1970s: The Search for Sufficiently Equivalent Countervailing Parity," *International Security* 6, no. 2 (Fall 1981), repr. in Miller, ed., *Strategy and Nuclear Deterrence*, p. 183–214.

19. Ibid., p. 212.

20. Raymond L. Garthoff, "Mutual Deterrence, Parity and Strategic Arms

Limitation in Soviet Policy," ch. 5 in Derek Leebaert, eds., *Soviet Military Thinking* (London: Allen and Unwin, 1981), pp. 92–124.

21. Stephen J. Cimbala, "How Should We Retaliate? Slow Down and Live," in Stephen J. Cimbala, ed., *Challenges to Deterrence: Resources, Technology and Policy* (New York: Praeger, 1987), pp. 268–288.

22. According to one authoritative Soviet reference: "The fact is that the decision to employ strategic nuclear arms must be made by the political leaders." See Col. M. P. Skirdo, *The People, the Army, the Commander* trans. by DGIS Multilingual Section, Translation Bureau, Secretary of State Department, Ottawa, Canada (Moscow: 1970), and published by the U.S. Air Force, p. 83.

23. On the evolution of Soviet military objectives from World War II to the present, see Michael MccGwire, *Military Objectives in Soviet Foreign Policy* (Washington, D.C.: Brookings Institution, 1987), esp. ch. 2.

24. John Steinbruner, "Nuclear Decapitation," *Foreign Policy* no. 45 (Winter 1981–1982):16–28.

25. Desmond Ball, "The Development of the SIOP, 1960–1983," ch. 3 in Desmond Ball and Jeffrey Richelson, eds., *Strategic Nuclear Targeting* (Ithaca, N.Y.: Cornell University Press, 1986), pp. 57–83.

26. For studies of the U.S. nuclear command system past and present, see Bruce G. Blair, *Strategic Command and Control: Redefining the Nuclear Threat* (Washington, D.C.: Brookings Institution, 1985); and Paul Bracken, *The Command and Control of Nuclear Forces* (New Haven: Yale University Press, 1983).

27. See Fritz W. Ermarth, "Contrasts in American and Soviet Strategic Thought," ch. 3 in Leebaert, ed., *Soviet Military Thinking*, p. 66; and Jeffrey Richelson, "The Dilemmas of Counterpower Targeting," ch. 7 in Ball and Richelson, eds., *Strategic Nuclear Targeting*.

28. This issue is explored in Stephen J. Cimbala, "Countercommand Attacks and War Termination," ch. 7 in Stephen J. Cimbala, ed., *Strategic War Termination* (New York: Praeger, 1986), pp. 134–156.

29. Carter, "Assessing Command System Vulnerability," pp. 561–562.

30. Ibid.

31. See Paul Bracken, "Delegation of Nuclear Command Authority," in Carter, Steinbruner, and Zraket, eds., *Managing Nuclear Operations*, pp. 352–372.

32. There are few good discussions of this very important topic. A useful contribution is Norman Friedman, "The Rules of Engagement Issue," in E. F. Gueritz, Norman Friedman, Clarence E. Robinson, and William R. Van Cleave, *NATO's Maritime Strategy: Issues and Developments* (New York: Pergamon Brassey's/Institute for Foreign Policy Analysis, 1987), pp. 23–44.

33. On the Soviet C3 or C3I system, see Desmond Ball, *The Soviet Strategic Command, Control and Communications and Intelligence (C3I) System*, (Canberra: Strategic and Defence Studies Centre, Australian National University, 1985); Stephen M. Meyer, "Soviet Nuclear Operations," ch. 15 in Carter, Steinbruner, and Zraket, eds., *Managing Nuclear Operations*, pp. 470–534; and Dr. John J. Yurechko, "Command and Control for Coalitional Warfare: The Soviet Approach," in Stephen J. Cimbala, ed., *Soviet C3* (Washington, D.C.: AFCEA International Press, 1987), pp. 17–34.

34. Soviet strategic nuclear forces must have the flexibility to respond to political leadership demands for preemption, launch on tactical warning/launch

under attack, and riding out a second strike. See Meyer, "Soviet Nuclear Operations"; and Robert P. Berman and John C. Baker, *Soviet Strategic Forces: Requirements and Responses* (Washington, D.C.: Brookings Institution, 1982), ch. 2.

35. See Harriet Fast Scott and William F. Scott, *The Soviet Control Structure: Capabilities for Wartime Survival* (New York: Crane, Russak/National Strategy Information Center, 1983); and P. T. Yegorov, I. A. Shlyakhov, and N. I. Alabin, *Civil Defense* (Moscow: 1970), translated and published under the auspices of the U.S. Air Force.

36. On this see Meyer, "Soviet Nuclear Operations."

37. Seweryn Bialer has suggested that the Western preoccupation with potential sources of internal conflict and instability in the Soviet Union has led to insufficient appreciation of its sources of stability. A more enhanced appreciation may result from analyzing the Soviet system as an authoritarian system instead of a totalitarian one. A modernizing authoritarian system would be prone to periods of instability and crises of legitimacy as part of a continuing effort to adjust authoritarian structures to new intrasystemic and environmental problems. See Bialer, *Stalin's Successors: Leadership, Stability and Change in the Soviet Union* (Cambridge: Cambridge University Press, 1980).

38. B. Byely et al., *Marxism-Leninism on War and Army* (Moscow: 1972), translated and published under the auspices of the U.S. Air Force, p. 28.

39. The difference between targeting organizations and groups is noted in Bracken, *The Command and Control of Nuclear Forces*, pp. 90–93.

40. The mobilization of Soviet societal resources under military command according to martial law is discussed in Scott and Scott, *The Soviet Control Structure*, pp. 12–18.

41. Blair, *Strategic Command and Control*, p. 216.

42. On Soviet targeting, see William T. Lee and Richard F. Staar, *Soviet Military Policy Since World War II* (Stanford, Calif.: Hoover Institution Press, 1986), pp. 138–167.

43. Views on the Soviets' willingness to engage in limited nuclear war differ. A case for their enhanced interest in limiting nuclear war even after it begins is presented by Albert Wohlstetter, "Between an Unfree World and None," *Foreign Affairs* 63, no. 5 (Summer 1985):962–994. On the other hand, according to Berman and Baker, "The USSR's operational philosophy reflects skepticism concerning the possibility (or desirability) of controlling escalation in a major conflict"(Berman and Baker, *Soviet Strategic Forces*, p. 34). For a Soviet view, see Maj. Gen. V. Zemskov, "Characteristics of Modern Wars and Possible Methods of Conducting Them," in Joseph D. Douglass, Jr., and Amoretta M. Hoeber, comps., *Selected Readings from MILITARY THOUGHT* (Washington, D.C.: U.S. Government Printing Office, 1971), vol. 5, part II, pp. 48–56. I am grateful to Notra Trulock for help in understanding this issue.

44. Barry R. Posen, "Inadvertent Nuclear War? Escalation and NATO's Northern Flank," *International Security* 7, no. 2 (Fall 1982), repr. in Miller, ed., *Strategy and Nuclear Deterrence*, pp. 85–111.

45. Blair, *Strategic Command and Control*, p. 178.

# 3

# Command Systems and Nuclear War Termination

This chapter explores the command system requirements for war termination. It reviews the missions and functions that strategic nuclear command systems are expected to perform. The problems attendant to the performance of these missions are also noted. Observations about the U.S. and Soviet nuclear command systems as they pertain to the problem of war termination will be made.

War termination is not a new theoretical expectation for the U.S. nuclear command system, as we saw in Chapter 1. However, the theory has not been followed up in practice to the extent that those interested in war termination might hope. The most serious deficiency is that of the U.S. nuclear command, control, and communications (C3) system. Whether this system could, after surprise attack, meet the requirements of general and gross retaliation is debated among experts. To expect it to do more than that—to provide for a controlled and selective response to provocations across the spectrum of conflict—is to expect what cannot be delivered in the near term, if ever.

With regard to war termination after the first exchange of nuclear weapons by superpowers that affect their own or allied territory, the C3 problems are not mainly those of hardware. Undoubtedly a sufficiently heavy Soviet attack would destroy principal and alternative command posts, sever communications links with forces, and cause other perturbations that might preclude the most preferred response to attack. However, an attack of this magnitude on either superpower's homeland, even against counterforce targets alone, could not be confused with a "limited" war in any sense by those on the receiving end of it. In terms of the discussion in Chapter 1, such an attack would violate the rules of an agreed battle and signal to the adversary that no limitations in ends or means were expected to hold.

The more difficult case to deal with is one in which the United States or NATO is reluctantly forced to consider a selective and constrained nuclear use, in response to either impending conventional war disaster or an opponent's first use. And this need not happen in Europe, which is the common setting for this type of scenario. Catalytic nuclear war between superpowers could result from a conventional war that began outside of Europe—for example, in the Persian Gulf. These cases, in which limited use might be followed by pauses for further threat and negotiation among the combatants and their superpower sponsors, would be the most stressful for the political leaderships and their command organizations. No textbook answers would be available. The command system would have to remain poised against the possibility of escalation while avoiding signals that seemed provocative.

Much attention has been devoted by scenario writers to the question of whether the United States or the Soviet Union could fight an extended nuclear war over many weeks or months. Since the Carter administration it has been U.S. declaratory policy that the United States should, for purposes of deterrence, appear to be able to do so. However, this question is based upon some misconstruction of feasible alternatives for forces, command systems, and national leaders. It is highly improbable that the U.S. or Soviet command system could survive as a cohesive entity for very long in the face of repeated, massive exchanges of nuclear weapons that struck each other's homelands. The U.S. nuclear command system does not need to meet this probably impossible standard. Instead, it should be designed to last into an extended phase of a war that is deliberately kept limited, an agreed battle. In such a war, however it takes place, each superpower would have to spare the most important components of its opponent's nuclear command systems from immediate attack. In fact, each might treat the homeland of the other as a sanctuary, a threshold above which all bets are off, but below which negotiation while fighting with limited nuclear and conventional weapons for war termination is acceptable. This is a more reasonable standard for the U.S., or the Soviet, system to meet.

There is further confusion about the issue of attacking the opponent's command system at the operational or strategic level. It is sometimes suggested that strategic countercommand attacks against the brain and nervous system of the adversary, including nuclear-armed attacks, can provide an economical recipe for victory that would otherwise be unattainable. If we are talking about one superpower winning an all-out nuclear exchange against another, the term is meaningless in form and substance. It takes on meaning, however, in the context of a global conventional war or a regional conventional or nuclear war. It might turn out that attacks against the military command systems of U.S. or Soviet allies—say, in NATO Europe—could appeal to desperate commanders who were unable to stop an opponent's onslaught. Were the U.S. Pershing II still scheduled for deployment in the Federal Republic of Germany, for example, it might occur to Soviet war planners that this weapon could be launched against command centers in the western military districts of the Soviet Union while the Soviet operational maneuver groups moved across the north German plain. This Soviet reckoning might be incorrect in the event, but a logical supposition to have drawn. The Pershing IIs are no longer a concern, assuming the INF agreement is followed through to their removal and destruction. However, the same problem applies to U.S. and NATO nuclear weapons of other ranges deployed in Europe. Even in a conventional war the USSR can hardly afford to leave them alone. If it attacks those weapons, and NATO moves to protect them, escalation could result from the appearance of preparation for NATO nuclear first use.

## BACKGROUND AND PROBLEM

A near consensus in the U.S. community of policy planners and strategic analysts has developed around the objective of improved strategic C3. Experts question whether U.S. strategic C3 can survive a Soviet attack.[1] The vulnerability of U.S. strategic "connectivity" among national command authorities, force commanders, warning and attack assessment sensors, and the forces themselves seemed apparent to national security advisers in the Carter administration.[2] After several studies, President Carter announced a number of directives calling for a robustly survivable and enduring (lasting into the first few weeks or months of a nuclear war) strategic C3 capability.[3] The Reagan strategic program includes large amounts of money for C3 improvements designed to implement the survivable and enduring connectivity recommended by military experts and policy analysts.[4]

The search for enduring C3 systems may divert attention from the search for forces and commanders that are "merely" survivable. The U.S.-Soviet arms race has been stimulated by the concerns of each side for the survivability of its forces and command structure against preemptive attack. Improved capabilities for protracted war do not necessarily lessen the danger of preemption, and may increase the danger. While the odds in favor of simple decapitation go down, the odds in favor of multiple dysfunction might increase. Social systems, including the command structures for retaliatory forces, cannot be programmed only to do what their designers expect, or hope.

## C3 AND U.S.-SOVIET STRATEGIC DETERRENCE

The issue of what deters the Soviet Union may never be resolved short of war.[5] Expectations are scenario dependent. Deterring a Soviet "bolt from the blue" attack against U.S. strategic forces seems less demanding than deterring a Soviet preemption in a crisis. U.S. strategic planners seem to agree that a Soviet preemptive attack would find U.S. forces on generated alert rather than day-to-day alert.[6]

U.S. experts regard the Soviet view of deterrence as differing from that of the United States in emphasis, if not in substance. Deterrence is not distinguished as sharply from defense in Soviet military writing; for Soviet writers, the best deterrent is that which also provides the most effective war-fighting and war survival capability.[7] Soviet leaders recognize the existence of mutual superpower deterrence but do not necessarily regard that situation as inevitable or desirable.[8] They have little apparent interest in the vulnerability of their homeland and forces to enemy retaliatory or preemptive attacks.[9]

Soviet military writers express no enthusiasm for the concepts developed by Western strategists to describe thresholds or crisis bargaining during strategic or theater nuclear warfare.[10] They are skeptical that nuclear war, once begun, can be contained. Their political expectations have as much to do with this pessimism about intrawar deterrence as do their technological assumptions. For Soviet military and political leaders, nuclear war with the United States and/or NATO would be a total, global confrontation involving nuclear, conventional, and other forces in diverse theaters of operations.[11] The war would not end until either the capitalist or the socialist camp was clearly defeated.[12]

Not surprisingly, given these doctrinal emphases, the USSR places highest importance upon preserving political control over the use of military force in wartime.[13] It would seem that this implies sensitivity to the potential vulnerability of adversaries if their command and control can be attacked and disrupted. But countercommand attacks at the tactical level (in our terminology) have different political implications and consequences than counterstrategic command attacks. Although the Soviets may be motivated to attempt counterstrategic C3 warfare once deterrence fails, they must estimate the potential costs and benefits with great care. More on this point appears below.

Whether the Soviets have ever endorsed any concept of strategic stability as discussed in the West is doubtful.[14] Nevertheless, they are aware of the conditions that superior or equal forces of opponents impose upon them. Soviet force modernization proceeds from domestic political imperatives that are not likely to fluctuate very widely in response to perceived threats.[15] U.S. strategic literature devotes much more attention to the perceived stability of the balance of terror, whereas Soviet writers refer to a more inclusive "correlation of forces." This latter term includes the military, political, economic, and psychological aspects of Soviet foreign and domestic policy.

Understood from the Soviet perspective as a correlation of forces, and from the Western as a more or less stable military balance, the superpower confrontation in doctrine yields a mix of apples and oranges. Doctrine provides only partial clues as to what decision makers would do in a crisis threatening nuclear war. A safe conclusion is that both Soviet and U.S. leaders would retaliate if they were attacked. U.S. policy is to absorb a first strike and then retaliate, although launch under attack has not been precluded as an option.[16] Soviet writers are more explicit about their willingness to preempt because they assume that the first blows with nuclear weapons may be decisive. Soviet military writers have been explicit on the purpose of nuclear or conventional fighting, which is victory.[17] Their concept of victory is contingent upon battlefield realities and conformity with Marxist-Leninist doctrine where possible.[18]

## WAR BY ACCIDENT OR MISCALCULATION

The superpowers have much to disagree about. One area of overlapping interests lies in the prevention of war by accident or miscalculation. These are related but not identical concerns. Accidental war implies the failure of negative control within the command and control structure of one party, with implications for the survivable forces or C3 of the other.[19] War by miscalculation implies erroneous estimates of the opponent's intentions, erroneous in the direction of making the outbreak of war more rather than less likely. It is also possible for wars to begin through both accident and miscalculation; World War I offers an example of both kinds of crisis behavior by national leaders.[20]

The prevention of nuclear war by accident rests primarily upon the command structure within each country. Nevertheless, even the most reliable of arrangements can fail during a crisis. Stressed personnel and faulty "wiring" can combine to produce accidental launch or warning of launch that is predicated upon computer error.[21] Accidental war might result not only from computer or human failures that release weapons without authorization but also from failure of the top-level "safety catch" holding back preemptive strikes by lower echelons.[22] For example if the U.S. president were unavailable during a crisis in which war seemed imminent, or were killed during the first few minutes of a nuclear attack, others in the military and civilian chain of command would by default assume control of retaliatory forces. Their views might or might not be consistent with the president's previously established policies for retaliatory strikes and war termination.

Some situations combine features of war by miscalculation with war by accident. Presidential disability during a superpower crisis is one of these situations. Although the Twenty-fifth Amendment to the U.S. Constitution has clarified the procedures for presidential succession in the event of presidential incapacity, it has its own problems in optimizing between positive and negative control. The president should not be removed from office as long as he is able to function, but he must lose effective control of the government if he is in fact incapable. The amendment attempts to resolve this dilemma by providing for cabinet and congressional involvement, and ultimate congressional resolution, in cases of apparent presidential disability.[23] The outbreak of war or the development of prewar crisis during a period of disputed presidential disability could create irresponsible pressures from other civilian or military leaders, either for preemption or for complacency.

War by miscalculation would be illustrated by the preemptive attack launched by either side in the expectation that the opponent had already committed itself to war. Most U.S. analysts consider this danger of war by preemptive attack more probable than a "bolt from the blue" or war by accidental launch. Scenario writers have been inclined to worst case estimates in the face of this danger.

Soviet preemptive attack on the United States could be aimed at the U.S. strategic nuclear retaliatory forces, strategic C3, or both, at least in theory. The possibility of countersilo preemption has occupied policy-makers and analysts in the Reagan administration, and was the source of considerable political debate during the presidential campaign of 1980. Studies making different assumptions about important variables such as U.S. silo hardness; Soviet warhead accuracy, yield, and reliability; and other factors reached opposite conclusions about U.S. ICBM vulnerability to Soviet preemptive strikes.[24] Other analysts, relying upon qualitative factors such as Soviet incentives and the intangibles of strategic nuclear war, seemed cautious but optimistic about the chances for avoiding Soviet preemptive attack on U.S. silos.[25]

The Scowcroft Commission resolved much of the political furor with a politically sensitive compromise. It recommended deployment of 100 MX missiles in Minuteman ICBM silos, and research and development toward the deployment in the 1990s of a small, single-warhead, potentially mobile intercontinental missile, dubbed Midgetman by the press.[26] The commission based this recommendation on the judgment that U.S. ICBM vulnerability was not significant to crisis stability as long as the rest of the strategic "triad" remained secure.[27] Mathematical models of countersilo attacks might show few U.S. ICBMs surviving such a first strike, provided the United States chose not to launch on warning or launch under attack, as proposed by some analysts.[28] Other experts questioned whether even the most robust launch-under-attack options could survive Soviet countersilo attacks.[29]

The Reagan administration has attempted to build upon the work of its predecessors in reaching agreements with the USSR to reduce the likelihood of accidental war. The superpowers, as is well known, established a direct communications link, or "hot line," in 1963 between Washington and Moscow. It has since been upgraded. Originally the system consisted of two teletype terminals, one wire telegraph circuit, and one backup radiotelegraph circuit.[30] Agreement was reached in 1971 to establish two satellite communication circuits for the hot line; these became operational in 1978.[31] The wire telegraph circuit remains as a backup for the satellite links.

In addition to these accords on improving the hot line, the superpowers have concurred on measures to reduce the risk of outbreak of nuclear war (Accidental Measures Agreement). Signed in 1971, that agreement requires the United States and the USSR to maintain and improve organizational arrangements to prevent the accidental or unauthorized use of nuclear weapons; to notify the other side of planned missile launches beyond the territory of the launching party, and in the direction of the other party; and to notify each other of incidents involving the accidental detonation of nuclear weapons that create a risk of war.[32] In 1973, the United States and the Soviet Union signed an agreement on the prevention of nuclear war that requires each side to refrain from acts that could lead to military confrontations, including nuclear war.[33]

The Reagan administration has offered the USSR several initiatives on the prevention of accidental war. President Reagan announced several confidence-building measures that he had proposed to the Soviet Union on November 22, 1982; American START and INF negotiators were instructed to discuss these proposals with Soviet representatives.[34] The Reagan proposals included advance notification of all ICBM, SLBM (submarine-launched ballistic missiles), and intermediate-range, land-based ballistic missile launches; advance notification of all major military exercises involving nuclear forces; and expanded exchanges of basic data on both sides' strategic forces.[35]

Also discussed within the Reagan administration were proposals to improve the fidelity of communications between the superpowers during crises and to clarify rapidly the technical issues bearing upon the possible initiation of nuclear war by either side. The Defense Department has proposed a high-speed facsimile capability for the hot line. This would allow rapid transmission of information as graphs, charts, and maps, precluding the necessary wait for translation in some time-urgent matters.[36] The Defense Department considered and rejected the idea of voice or video transmission for the hot line, a decision that deserves reconsideration.

Also considered was a proposal to create a joint military communications link (JMCL), parallel to the hot line, between the U.S. and Soviet national crisis control centers (for the United States this is the National Military Command Center in the Pentagon).[37] The purpose of JMCL would be rapid communication about a military incident that required urgent clarification but not direct contact between heads of state.

At the least, these measures for improved hot line capabilities, confidence-building measures, and a possible direct military communications link should contribute to crisis stability, if adopted by both sides. But they offer technical augmentation of existing capabilities more than anything else. They do not change the mathematics of the arms race or the political climate between the superpowers. They offer each side the opportunity to communicate rapidly and explicitly with the other during a crisis in which the sides have stronger incentives to avoid escalation or commitment than to resort to it. The United States and the USSR apparently used the hot line to communicate during the Arab-Israeli wars in 1967 and 1973.[38] Despite the agreements and initiatives, crisis stability remains precarious because it is scenario dependent. On the Soviets' side, it depends upon their assumptions about U.S. targeting (of USSR strategic forces and/or C3), U.S. C3 and force survivability, and U.S. propensities to launch on warning or under attack, as opposed to riding out the opponent's first strike. The signals that the United States sends about these matters are extremely important, and can be discussed at two levels: What should we want to say? What are we in fact saying?

## CRISIS STABILITY AND CURRENT OPTIONS

The extent to which U.S. arrangements for C3 contribute to crisis stability or crisis instability depends upon the "wiring" or connectivity among sensors, force commanders, national command authority (NCA), and retaliatory forces; the crisis-stable or crisis-unstable properties of the forces themselves; and the people, both civilian and military, who operate the systems and make decisions in time of crisis. Discussion of each of these three parts of the C3 story follows, with the admonition that some speculation is unavoidable. Some projecting of systems not yet in being and their probable impacts on Soviet intentions and behavior cannot be avoided, however tentative it must be.

### Wiring

As the United States becomes more dependent upon space-based communications for strategic warning, it gains something and loses something. It gains real-time transmission of information and faster interpretation of it. In a crisis involving possible U.S.-Soviet strategic confrontation, time is obviously crucial. It also gains better information. For example, deployment of the NAVSTAR/GPS system reportedly will inform users of their positions to within 26.2 feet horizontally and 32.8 feet vertically anywhere on earth; equally impressive readings on velocity and time are assumed.[39] The Air Force Satellite Communications System (AFSATCOM) became fully operational in 1983. Actually a set of radio relays on other satellites, AFSATCOM is designed to provide reliable one-way ultrahigh-frequency communications channels to transmit retaliatory orders from the NCA to U.S. strategic forces.[40]

The prospects are that NAVSTAR/GPS and AFSATCOM will improve the survivable communications that will ensure prompt transmission of orders to retaliate, assuming the systems themselves survive. If the systems are so easily destroyed as to invite preemptive attack, then they do not contribute to stability during crises. (The fragility of these important space-based assets can be compensated for by a variety of countermeasures, themselves inviting counter-countermeasures, and so forth.) But other aspects of the Reagan C3 modernization are less benign for crisis stability.

NAVSTAR/GPS will host the Integrated Operational Nuclear Detection System (IONDS), which will make possible the precise location and characterization of a nuclear explosion anywhere on the surface of the earth.[41] Scheduled to be fully operational in 1988, IONDS is an essential requirement for the conduct of controlled, protracted strategic war.[42] The same implications for protracted war fighting are apparent in the proposed MILSTAR (Military, Strategic, Tactical and Relay satellite communications program) system. MILSTAR will provide two-way, jam-resistant communications between commanders and their forces.[43] Hardened against nuclear weapons, MILSTAR satellites (probably four in geosynchronous orbit and three in elliptical orbits) should be fully operational in 1990.[44] MILSTAR and IONDS will allow battle management for protracted nuclear conflict; thus their capabilities are paradoxical. They are as necessary for protracted warfighting as they are encouraging to decision makers who believe such fighting is possible. Moreover, the improved accuracies of ICBM and SLBM made possible by NAVSTAR may move the United States toward a near-zero circular error probable (a measure of accuracy), a condition that can hardly be reassuring to the Soviets and increases their incentives to destroy the U.S. system in the early phases of an attack.[45] The USSR is preparing to deploy its own version of NAVSTAR, abbreviated GLONASS (for global navigation satellite system), but its capabilities should not be equal to those of a fully operational NAVSTAR.

Other improvements in strategic C3 proposed by the administration include the Ground Wave Emergency Network (GWEN) to connect the NCA to all major force commanders. GWEN would also provide communications connectivity among the North American Aerospace Defense Command (NORAD) headquarters, Strategic Air Command (SAC) headquarters, the strategic bomber forces, ICBM launch control centers, and important surveillance and warning centers.[46] At least 300 relay sites will be included in the fully operational system, expected in the late 1980s.[47] Airborne and ground communications with the strategic bomber force will be upgraded by the addition of low-frequency and extremely-high-frequency terminals.[48] Extremely-low-frequency communications with ballistic missile submarines (SSBNs) will be deployed in Wisconsin and Michigan, but the systems are not necessarily survivable. The only survivable C3 link to the ballistic missile submarine force is provided by TACAMO (Take Charge and Move Out) aircraft. The administration's TACAMO EC-X program will extend the range and speed of the aircraft, improve survivability through electro-magnetic pulse (EMP) hardening, and provide air refueling capability.[49]

Improved survivable communications to submarines contribute to strategic stability during crises. Submarines are the most survivable of U.S. strategic forces, but the survivability of their communications has been questioned.[50] The GWEN system contributes to crisis stability in that it provides alternatives to fixed ground stations that might be destroyed early in nuclear attacks. Still, like NAVSTAR/IONDS and MILSTAR, GWEN also has implications for protracted war fighting. When these improved C3 assets are deployed in space, they both contribute to U.S. C3 survivability and enhance the importance of their destruction in a Soviet preemptive attack. Moreover, if these superior U.S. communications are developed along with space-based offensive and defensive forces, there is an even higher premium for U.S. adversaries in attacking space-based assets. This scenario of increased U.S. dependency upon space for C3 and weapons platforms is imminent.

### Forces

Some of the Reagan strategic force modernization program would contribute to crisis stability, and other elements would raise the risk of war by accident or (more likely) miscalculation. On the positive side, the modernization of the SSBN fleet with Trident submarines and Trident II missiles adds increased capabilities to the most survivable part of the "triad."[51] The putative hard-target-killing potential of Trident II is a mixed blessing from the standpoint of crisis stability, however. Hard-target-killing, submarine-launched missiles that arrive promptly at their targets threaten the survivability of Soviet second-strike capability. Whether Trident II warheads would meet criteria of promptness is debatable.[52] Soviet worst case planners must assume that they would have the range, payload, and accuracy to destroy Soviet ICBM silos. Absent reconfiguration of the USSR retaliatory force, some 75 percent of its destructive power would be vulnerable to preemptive attack by a combination of U.S. MX ICBM and Trident II. By constructing a total of 29 Trident SSBNS and assuming the promptness of Trident II warheads, the United States could equal the prompt counterforce available for retaliatory strikes from 1,000 small ICBMs with single warheads, and the Reagan program for Trident SSBNs as it is now projected.[53]

Other elements of the Reagan strategic package are less encouraging from the standpoint of their probable effects on crisis stability. Deployment of 108 Pershing II ballistic missiles in West Germany, begun in December 1983 according to the NATO "two track" decision of 1979, was perceived by the Soviets as deployment of strategic, preemptive strike weapons. Although Soviet pronouncements on this point were to some extent designed to dissuade Europeans from supporting U.S. and NATO policy, the Soviet fear of preemption is genuine for reasons having more to do with C3 issues than with force characteristics. Launch of the Pershing II would provide little time for Soviet commanders to decide upon retaliatory options. If it has the range to attack important strategic or tactical command targets in the western USSR, the Soviets will be tempted (in their view) to preempt U.S. preemption in a crisis. Although in recent decades Soviet military writers have learned to use euphemisms for preemption, it is clear that the option is not foreclosed in Soviet policy for nuclear war.[54]

The administration's program to deploy thousands of nuclear-armed cruise missiles on surface ships and submarines as a secure reserve force is a mixed blessing. Cruise missiles are not fast enough to threaten most highly valued Soviet hard targets with preemption, provided USSR air defenses could limit the number of intruders reaching their targets. How secure the Soviets feel about their air defense capabilities to thin out U.S. cruise missiles launched from all azimuths at sea is not known. What is known is that U.S. analysts have already called for improvements in U.S. air defenses to deter attack upon the continental United States from Soviet submarine-launched cruise missiles. Closer deployment of Soviet cruise missile submarines to U.S. shores was threatened obliquely by President Andropov and Soviet military leaders when it became apparent that NATO deployments of Pershing II and ground-launched cruise missiles in Western Europe would go forward as scheduled.[55] If the scale of nuclear-armed cruise missile deployments by either side outruns too drastically the opponent's presumed defenses against those missiles, then preemptive attack at sea becomes a more attractive option. If, as some U.S. experts think, the oceans are becoming more opaque rather than more transparent, and detection of enemy craft will become more difficult for both sides, then the side with the larger numbers (the USSR) might prevail in some short-term scenarios.[56]

Most uncertain in their implications for crisis stability, when the complications of more robust C3 are taken into account, are the U.S. administration's programs for the military uses of space. Of principal and immediate concern are proposals following the president's "Star Wars" speech of March 23, 1983, for a comprehensive ballistic missile defense (BMD) system. Several advisory panels tasked to look into the technology for space-based and/or terrestrial BMD reported favorably on prospects for the near term (for somewhat crude systems) and for the long term (for more effective and more exotic systems).[57] The BMD in boost and postboost, midcourse, and terminal phases is designed to thin out a Soviet ICBM/SLBM attack so completely that the leakage would be tolerably small to nonexistent.[58] Designs range from the near-term proposal of the "High Frontier" group to the more futuristic X-ray lasers proposed by researchers affiliated with Lawrence Livermore Laboratory, including Dr. Edward Teller.[59]

Although the president called upon his military technocrats and bureaucrats to devise systems that could make strategic defense dominant over current and future offensive weapons, such an optimistic outcome is unlikely. One reason, of course, is that the Soviets are unlikely to concede U.S. dominance on the high ground of space without an arms race (if they feel competitive) or something more drastic (if they feel hopelessly outclassed). Their willingness to propose a treaty on antisatellite weapons to the United Nations, doubtless not without its self-serving elements, nonetheless reflects the Soviets' anxieties that they may be outgunned in antisatellite (ASAT) and other phases of space-based military technology.[60] The tested U.S. ASAT (now endangered by Congress) is by all accounts a more flexible and tactically superior design than the concept underlying the one ASAT tested so far by the USSR.[61]

When the deployment of ASAT and defensive satellite (DSAT) weapons and other weapons for ballistic missile defense seems imminent, both U.S. planners and their Soviet counterparts will face command dilemmas of serious proportions. The more dependent a nation becomes upon the early warning and battle management provided by satellites and their sensors, the more necessary it is to defend them against attack. Satellites can be attacked from a variety of earth- and space-based platforms, and future generations of ASAT should be more capable than current efforts.[62] The dependency of U.S. and/or Soviet strategic C3 on space-based assets is especially problematical. Some redundancy in ground-, sea-, and air-based systems can be created, but the time for national leaders on either side to react to an assumed provocation cannot be increased. For example, Soviet SLBMs fired from the Atlantic might reach Washington, D.C., in less than ten minutes. Firing those missiles on depressed trajectories would decrease the reaction time and might also be suggested if the USSR wanted to avoid U.S. space-based BMD, once it is deployed.

**People**

The persons who are involved in strategic C3 include civilian and military commanders, their successors in case of disability or death in peace or war, and the operators who must implement policies at the middle and lower levels of the bureaucracy. Some comments about each are appropriate now.

Commanders are those in the civilian and military hierarchies with the direct responsibility for ordering retaliatory strikes and/or for deciding which strikes to execute and which to withhold. They include the president and the civilian line of succession through the vice-president and cabinet members in order of the creation of their departments. It also includes the operational military chain of command from the secretary of defense through the joint chiefs of staff to the unified and specified commands in the field. In the absence of the president, the vice-president would preside over both hierarchies.[63]

The problem of presidential succession has already been alluded to. It is perhaps the least troublesome ambiguity. Whether the military chain of command would function to convey retaliatory orders to strategic forces that survived the initial attack is more problematical. An attack on U.S. strategic forces that included an attack on strategic C3 and the political and military leadership in Washington, D.C., would not allow the USSR to escape significant retaliatory damage to its economy and society.[64] But it might preclude the kinds of calibrated, controlled nuclear responses envisioned in the declaratory policies of NSDM 242 in 1974 and PD–59 in 1980.[65] John Steinbruner has suggested that even launch under attack would not be a feasible solution to the problem of U.S. ICBM vulnerability because of strategic command vulnerability.[66]

In addition to problematical scenarios, the people problems include individual and organizational variables. The relationship between organizational factors and C3 has been studied by Anthony Oettinger and his associates at Harvard University.[67] Their studies reveal that the U.S. strategic C3 systems are less the product of any coherent architecture than they are the results of technology pull, bureaucratic politics within the Department of Defense and the rest of the national security establishment, and demands of users for systems more responsive to their missions.[68] Moreover, organizational imperatives and bureaucratic politics outlast the tenure of office of even the most dedicated political and military chiefs. Follow-through on proposed improvements or changes must occur at the middle and lower levels of the bureaucracy, where people may be most resistant to change. In case of war, Paul Bracken has suggested, it might not be wise for Soviet attackers to decapitate the top of the U.S. command structure because middle- and lower-level commanders might fight an uncoordinated war to the bitter end, precluding war termination on terms favorable to the Soviets.[69]

People problems at the top are not limited to organizational and bureaucratic issues. There is also the question of physical or mental disability of top political leaders, or confusion during crises. During the last 4 centuries, at least 75 heads of state (real or symbolic) have led their countries while suffering from serious mental disturbances.[70] More typical in modern democratic societies is the problem of aging leaders whose grasp of the important issues may gradually diminish. Presidents Franklin D. Roosevelt and Woodrow Wilson were incapacitated or failing during critical periods of their terms in office: Roosevelt, during the Quebec and Yalta conferences; Wilson, during his last months in office.[71]

At the bottom of the pyramid are launch control officers who must fire missiles from silos or submarine launch tubes. Obviously these people are carefully selected, trained, and screened. But some investigators have found that there is pervasive uncertainty among ICBM launch control officers about whether they would actually fire their missiles if ordered to do so.[72] Numerous checks and balances built into the system to prevent accidental or unauthorized launch might interact unpredictably with procedures to preclude controlled retaliation, despite presidential orders.[73] Nor is it clear that commanders or launch control officers have been trained to recognize the "trap doors" that enemy espionage could build into software to divert systems from performing their assigned functions (and possibly cause them to perform destructive missions).[74]

## COUNTERCOMMAND ATTACKS

The trade-off between survivable and enduring C3 systems, if one exists, cannot be resolved only in the abstract. One must know what missions need to be performed and plan for C3 systems that can guarantee the connectivity to support those missions.[75] At present there is significant concern that U.S. strategic C3 is less survivable than the retaliatory forces it is designed to support.

How long C3 must endure once war begins is a matter that requires the consideration of policy and technology. Assuming that enduring strategic C3 technology becomes available, it may be provocative rather than deterring to the Soviet Union. If more enduring C3 infrastructure raises the stakes for preemptive attack against it, it might defeat itself in a crisis. Increased dependency upon space-based C3 makes more ambiguous the line between survivable and enduring C3; system survivability is dependent on the status of Soviet ASAT relative to U.S. DSAT capabilities or passive satellite defense techniques.[76]

Although it is counterintuitive to say so, neither the Soviet Union nor the United States has its best interests in mind (properly understood) if it contemplates destruction of the opponent's strategic C3 early in war. The plausibility of such countercommand attacks rests on the assumption that either side will fall apart if a significant proportion of its C3 is incapacitated. It is equally plausible that a disaggregated command structure would continue a disorganized war, in protracted salvos of nuclear strikes along with conventional and paramilitary conflict on a global scale.[77] The first priority of U.S.-Soviet arms control agreements in the 1990s should be mutual assured survivability of strategic C3. This cannot be done unilaterally, and the initiatives proposed by the Reagan administration in this regard (discussed above) are an appropriate beginning. Trends in technology for forces and U.S. strategic C3, unless deliberately controlled and modified to the contrary, will make preemptive attacks more attractive in the 1990s than they have been to date. This temptation to preemption for either side is the most basic disconnect in defense planning.

## PROTRACTED WAR

The expectation that the United States would fight a war over many weeks or months is charitable. Under present conditions, it would have to exert all capabilities to continue the war beyond several hours. Survivable rather than enduring control over U.S. strategic forces is the near-term problem for policy planners.[78] Several reasons for this are discussed below.

First, the logistical difficulties in preparing for protracted nuclear war are considerable. Command and control systems that endure through weeks of conflict are, even if feasible, useless if the strategic forces cannot be sustained.[79] Christopher Branch's monograph *Fighting a Long Nuclear War* is among the more recent expert testimonials to the problematical endurance of U.S. strategic forces.[80] One of his most interesting points is that the problems of providing bombers and missiles with the bases, supplies, and weapons they need for protracted war are far from solved. A particular weakness is the lack of reconstitution for airfields after they have been attacked and for missile silos following Soviet detonations.

Second, a protracted war implies sustained, methodical strategic exchanges during which bargaining on the conditions of war termination takes place. Evidence that the Soviets are attracted to this concept is sparse. They have the capabilities for protracted war at least equivalent to those of the United States, and the Politburo has always been sensitive to the preservation of top-level control over nuclear release. Once war actually began, conditions might differ. Soviet emphasis on the importance of the initial period of any war, and the decisiveness of any global conflict between the superpowers, provide little support for expectations about strategic nuclear war on the installment plan.[81] Of course, the deployment by either or both superpowers of more survivable forces and C3 (possibly protected by strategic defenses) could make extended war fighting seem more plausible in fact, although not necessarily more appealing to policymakers.

Third, the process of devising U.S. war plans seems more coherent for nuclear war plans per se than for the less bounded issue of protracted war in general. Any global war that became protracted would by definition be a limited one, relative to the total capabilities of the superpowers to destroy each other. Conventional and theater nuclear forces might have to be used together in operational campaigns that had never been tried before. Whether a global conflict between the United States and the Soviet Union is a rational choice is beside the point, for it clearly is not rational by peacetime standards. It is somewhat more to the point to ask how a global, extended, but still limited conflict could be contained without expanding into general nuclear war. Europeans in particular will want to know whether the containment of global war by superpower standards will include nuclear war in Europe, in which case it is catastrophic from their perspective.

## CONCLUSION

The nuclear command systems of the superpowers can be fine-tuned only so far before their tasking by policymakers outruns their capabilities. The problem is not amenable to additional dollars of research and development, although those dollars would contribute to some of the solutions to "micro" problems. But the "macro" problems are much harder. They have to do with the meshing and blending of people and bureaucracies, of expectations and fears, of contradictory imperatives for readiness to retaliate and for avoiding provocative moves.

The U.S. nuclear command system is not so vulnerable that it can easily be destroyed by the expenditure of small numbers of Soviet strategic nuclear weapons.[82] From the perspective of Soviet target planners, the U.S. strategic nuclear command system must look formidable indeed. An attack sufficiently large to guarantee destruction of the U.S. command system could not be disguised as a limited war, and no incentive would remain for the U.S. president or the presidential successor to withhold any remaining weapons. The U.S. system certainly has its deficiencies, but these are judged not so grievous that the system cannot guarantee, even under the worst conditions, some substantial retaliation against the society of any attacker.

However, the U.S. nuclear command system is wired to the NATO system, and here there is more room for mischief. The NATO nuclear command system based in Europe is encapsulated within a policy framework and general-purpose force structure not uniquely designed around the problems of using nuclear weapons, or for controlling nuclear war.[83] Even in conventional war under modern conditions, NATO might be swamped by a plethora of data and communications that made timely decisions impossible—or, if possible, erroneous. The time cycles associated with tactically and operationally driven decision loops in Europe would differ considerably from the time lines available to U.S. policymakers in Washington, assuming the U.S. homeland had not yet been attacked with nuclear weapons. Deterrence theorists have noted that NATO conventional forces are a fuse designed to detonate the theater and strategic nuclear deterrents that lie behind it.[84] They have less frequently remarked, with regard to the survivability and cohesion of the U.S. and NATO command systems in Europe, that the C3 fuses could blow out the fuse box in unexpected ways.

When problems attendant to nuclear command systems in Europe have been noted, they have generally concerned the management of alerts.[85] We have no experience with two-sided alerts of U.S. and Soviet nuclear forces, nor of fully alerted NATO forces.[86] The major problem of NATO preparedness for conventional war in Europe is not that of insufficient numbers of tanks, men under arms, or consumables, although the margins are precariously thin. The greater risk is that even limited Warsaw Pact mobilization would be followed by dilatory behavior in NATO capitals, which in turn would encourage the USSR to move. NATO would then face the operational problem of reconstituting its forward defense on the run while Soviet operational maneuver groups (OMGs) were painting on the canvas of the alliance's operational depth in West Germany. If the Soviets obtained their immediate tactical objectives and were on the verge of accomplishing their operational ones, the supreme allied commander, Europe, would almost certainly have requested nuclear release. His corps commanders might even receive it in time to influence the battle at the precise time and place deemed most critical. Repeated Soviet attacks on the NATO C3 system during conventional war will eventually reduce the efficiency of theater-based systems, especially their interoperability or transitivity from one member of the alliance to another.

If a short conventional war in Europe would place stresses on the NATO C3 system for conventional and nuclear conflict, a conflict that expanded beyond Europe would place even greater stresses on the U.S. and NATO European command systems. Such a war is even more improbable than a short war in Europe, and both are less probable than a continuation of deterrence. However, if deterrence should fail on the Central Front or elsewhere in Europe, NATO's force deployments and command systems might face an expanded war. The threat of early nuclear escalation is useful mainly as a deterrent to aggression per se. It becomes counterproductive to escalation control the moment the threshold of war and peace is crossed. To implement its declaratory strategy, NATO must use nuclear weapons within the first several days to a week of conventional war in Europe, assuming that current force ratios hold for the future. But in addition, NATO counts on using carefully circumscribed packages of nuclear response, which are designed not so much for their tactical effects as they are for communication of resolve to the opponent. The destruction is to be restricted; the message is to be stark.

The truth is that Americans and Europeans see this process unfolding in different ways, and have agreed to paper over their differences for the sake of harmony. The Americans since McNamara have genuinely hoped to keep nuclear escalation calibrated and selective (always preferring conventional war to nuclear war to begin with). The Europeans hope that escalation cannot be controlled, or that the Soviet Union will so conclude. Some Europeans would prefer not to give even a declaratory node to graduated escalation; others prefer to speak of it, sotto voce, within the alliance, but not within earshot of potential adversaries. These differences can be muted in peacetime, but during a significant crisis or after the onset of conventional war in Europe, they could be self-destructive. And without a consensus on how to control escalation, NATO has no strategy for war termination. There are two escapes from confronting this. The first is the Gaullist one: to rely upon the dread of strategic retaliation in order to cover the deficiencies in escalatory doctrine. The second is to rely on conventional defenses only, reserving NATO nuclear weapons as response to Soviet nuclear first use. It is doubtful that NATO can develop a cohesive military doctrine around either of these polar extremes. Flexible response has been too elaborately bargained over to be renegotiated. Therefore, NATO has to ask when a limited nuclear war would end, and how, and to assess the command systems with which it could bring about such an outcome. Otherwise, the European-based portion of the alliance command system is simply waiting to destroy itself, and its strategy along with it.

## NOTES

1. John Steinbruner, "Nuclear Decapitation," *Foreign Policy* no. 45 (Winter 1981–1982):16–28; Bruce G. Blair, *Strategic Command and Control: Redefining the Nuclear Threat* (Washington, D.C.: Brookings Institution, 1985).

2. Thomas Powers, "Choosing a Strategy for World War III," *Atlantic Monthly*, November 1982, pp. 82–110.

3. See Peter Pringle and William Arkin, *SIOP: The Secret U.S. Plan for Nuclear War* (New York: W. W. Norton, 1983), pp. 183–193, for a discussion of Carter administration planning and decisions in this regard.

4. The Reagan program for strategic and tactical C3I (command, control, communications, and intelligence) is outlined in Caspar W. Weinberger, *Annual*

*Report to the Congress: Fiscal Year 1984* (Washington, D.C.: U.S. Government Printing Office, February 1983), pp. 241–259. Our text refers to C3 rather than to C3I for the most part because the intelligence function is generic to decision-making problems beyond strategic connectivity.

5. Benjamin S. Lambeth, "What Deters? An Assessment of the Soviet View," in John F. Reichart and Steven R. Sturm, eds., *American Defense Policy* (Baltimore: Johns Hopkins University Press, 1982), pp. 188–198.

6. Congress of the United States, Congressional Budget Office, *Modernizing U.S. Strategic Offensive Forces: The Administration's Program and Alternatives* (Washington, D.C.: U.S. Government Printing Office, May 1983).

7. Fritz W. Ermarth, "Contrasts in American and Soviet Strategic Thought," in Derek Leebaert, ed., *Soviet Military Thinking* (London: Allen and Unwin, 1981), pp. 50–69; Benjamin S. Lambeth, "How to Think about Soviet Military Doctrine," in Douglas J. Murray and Paul R. Viotti, eds., *The Defense Policies of Nations* (Baltimore: John Hopkins University Press, 1982), pp. 146–153.

8. Raymond L. Garthoff, "Mutual Deterrence, Parity and Strategic Arms Limitation in Soviet Policy," in Leebaert, ed., *Soviet Military Thinking*, pp. 92–124.

9. The Soviet expectations for the conduct of global war are addressed in Maj. Gen. V. Zemskov, "Characteristic Features of Modern Wars and Possible Methods of Conducting Them," in *Selected Readings from MILITARY THOUGHT 1963–1973*, selected and compiled by Joseph D. Douglass, Jr., and Amoretta M. Hoeber (Washington, D.C.: U.S. Government Printing Office, 1974), pp. 48–56.

10. Benjamin S. Lambeth, "On Thresholds in Soviet Military Thought," in William J. Taylor, Jr., Steven A. Maaranen, and Gerrit W. Gong, eds., *Strategic Responses to Conflict in the 1980s* (Washington, D.C.: Center for Strategic and International Studies, Georgetown University/Los Alamos National Laboratory, 1983), pp. 347–365.

11. See B. Byely et al., *Marxism-Leninism on War and Army*, translated under the auspices of the U.S. Air Force (Washington, D.C.: U.S. Government Printing Office, 1972), esp. pp. 21–31; Harriet Fast Scott and William F. Scott, *The Armed Forces of the USSR* (Boulder, Colo.: Westview Press, 1982), pp. 37–67; John J. Dziak, *Soviet Perceptions of Military Power: The Interaction of Theory and Practice* (New York: Crane, Russak, 1981). The author is indebted to Edward L. Warner III for the opportunity to read his unpublished paper "Nuclear Operations in Soviet Military Strategy" (Santa Monica, Calif.: Rand Corporation, June 1983. An important discussion of Soviet doctrine on this point and its political implications appears in Maj. Gen. William E. Odom, "The Soviet Approach to Nuclear Weapons: A Historical Review," *Annals of the American Academy of Political and Social Science* 469 (September 1983):117–135, esp. 133.

12. Dziak, *Soviet Perceptions of Military Power*, p. 27.

13. On the Soviet high command in war and peacetime, see Scott and Scott, *The Armed Forces of the USSR*, pp. 97–129.

14. Soviet writers speak of the "correlation of forces," including military, political, social, and psychological (including morale factors) elements. On the implications of this concept for the controllability of nuclear war from the Soviet perspective, see Odom, "The Soviet Approach to Nuclear Weapons," p. 134.

15. Robert P. Berman and John C. Baker, *Soviet Strategic Forces* (Washington, D.C.: Brookings Institution, 1982).

16. Louis Rene Beres, *Mimicking Sisyphus: America's Countervailing Nuclear Strategy* (Lexington, Mass.: D. C. Heath, 1983), p. 25. See also John Steinbruner, "Launch Under Attack," *Scientific American*, January 1984, pp. 37–47; and Joseph D. Douglass, Jr., and Amoretta M. Hoeber, *Soviet Strategy for Nuclear War* (Stanford, Calif.: Hoover Institution Press, 1979), esp. chs. II and III.

17. Marshal N. V. Ogarkov, *Always in Readiness to Defend the Homeland*, Soviet Press: Selected Translations, 82, #11 and 12, p. 323; John Erickson, "The Soviet View of Deterrence: A General Survey," *Survival* 24, no. 6 (November/December 1982):242–251.

18. Too much can be made of the difference between Soviet and U.S. doctrine if nonparallel comparisons between U.S. civilian defense intellectuals and Soviet professional military writers are made. See Donald W. Hanson, "Is Soviet Strategic Doctrine Superior?" *International Security* 7, no. 3 (Winter 1982–1983):61–83. Some writers doubt that the United States has had *any* consistent strategic nuclear doctrine. See Aaron L. Friedberg, "The Evolution of U.S. Strategic 'Doctrine'—1945 to 1981," in Samuel P. Huntington, ed., *The Strategic Imperative: New Policies for National Security* (Cambridge, Mass.: Ballinger, 1982), pp. 53–99.

19. The concept of negative control is discussed in Steinbruner, "Nuclear Decapitation" and "Launch Under Attack." See also Paul Bracken, *The Command and Control of Nuclear Forces* (New Haven: Yale University Press, 1983).

20. See, for example, John G. Stoessinger, *Why Nations Go to War* (New York: St. Martin's Press, 1982), pp. 1–26.

21. "NORAD Computer Systems Are Dangerously Obsolete," *23rd Report of the Committee on Government Operations*, 97th Cong., 2nd sess., March 8, 1982 (Washington, D.C.: U.S. Government Printing Office, 1982); Pringle and Arkin, *SIOP*, pp. 126–152.

22. Bracken, *The Command and Control of Nuclear Forces*, passim.

23. United States Constitution, Amendment XXV.

24. Matthew Bunn and Kosta Tsipis, "The Uncertainties of Preemptive Nuclear Attack," *Scientific American* 249, no. 5 (November 1983):38–47.

25. Col. Thomas A. Fabyanic, "Strategic Analysis and MX Deployment," *Strategic Review* 10, no. 4 (Fall 1982):29–35.

26. Jonathan Medalia, "Small Single-Warhead Intercontinental Ballistic Missiles: Hardware, Issues and Policy Choices," Congressional Research Service, Library of Congress, Report no. 83–106 F (May 26, 1983).

27. President's Commission on U.S. Strategic Forces, *Report* (Washington, D.C.: April 1983).

28. Richard L. Garwin, "Launch Under Attack to Redress Minuteman Vulnerability," *International Security* 4, no. 3 (Winter 1979/1980):117–139. Steinbruner, "Launch Under Attack," contends that Garwin's proposal for launch under attack will not solve the problem of ICBM vulnerability because of command vulnerability or incapacity.

29. Steinbruner, "Launch Under Attack," and Congress of the United States, Congressional Budget Office, *Strategic Command, Control and Communications: Alternative Approaches for Modernization* (Washington, D.C.: U.S. Government Printing Office, October 1981), p. 19.

30. Secretary of Defense Caspar W. Weinberger, *Report to the Congress on Direct Communication Links and Other Measures to Enhance Stability* (Washington, D.C.: U.S. Department of Defense, April 11, 1983), p. 10.

31. Ibid., p. 10. See also Desmond Ball, *Can Nuclear War Be Controlled?* Adelphi Paper no. 169 (London: International Institute for Strategic Studies, 1981). Ball notes that the "hot line" would in all likelihood not survive the early stages of nuclear conflict—precisely when it might be most useful.

32. Weinberger, *Report to the Congress on Direct Communication Links*, p. 2.

33. Ibid., pp. 2–3.

34. Ibid., p. 3.

35. Ibid., pp. 8–9.

36. Ibid., p. 11.

37. Ibid., p. 12.

38. Ball, *Can Nuclear War Be Controlled?* p. 22.

39. Colin S. Gray, *American Military Space Policy* (Cambridge, Mass.: Abt Books, 1983), p. 32.

40. Weinberger, *Annual Report to the Congress*, p. 244.

41. Gray, *American Military Space Policy*, p. 28.

42. Ibid.

43. Weinberger, *Annual Report,... 1984*, p. 244.

44. Gray, *American Military Space Policy*, p. 31.

45. Ibid., p. 32.

46. Weinberger, *Annual Report... 1984*, p. 245.

47. Ibid.

48. Ibid.

49. Ibid., p. 246.

50. Ball, *Can Nuclear War Be Controlled?*, pp. 23–26, describes the C3 system for fleet ballistic submarines. He concludes that its survivability for controlled nuclear war fighting over a protracted period is dubious. Survivability of the submarines seems robust. See Richard L. Garwin, "Will Strategic Submarines Be Vulnerable" *International Security* 8, no. 2 (Fall 1983): 52–67. Garwin feels that the SSBN force can be controlled and communicated with "about as well" as a land-based force (p. 53).

51. Joel S. Wit, "American SLBM: Counterforce Options and Strategic Implications," *Survival* 24, no. 4 (July/August 1982):163–174; Desmond J. Ball, "The Counterforce Potential of American SLBM Systems," *Journal of Peace Research* 14, no. 1 (1977):23–40.

52. Congressional Budget Office, *Modernizing U.S. Strategic Offensive Forces*, pp. 56–57.

53. Ibid., p. 57.

54. Warner, "Nuclear Operations in Soviet Military Strategy," notes, p. 2.

55. See Donald C. Cotter, "Possible Soviet Responses to Pershings," *Wall Street Journal*, July 26, 1983, p. 32.

56. Lt. Com. Ralph E. Chatham, "A Quiet Revolution," *Proceedings of the U.S. Naval Institute*, January 1984, pp. 44–46.

57. "Star Wars Plan Gets a Green Light," *Science* 222, no. 4626 (November 25, 1983):901–902; Marcia S. Smith, " 'Star Wars': Antisatellites and Space-Based

Ballistic Missile Defense," Issue Brief no. IB81123 (Washington, D.C.: Library of Congress, Congressional Research Service, December 12, 1983), pp. 10–11.

58.  Gregory A. Fossedal, "The Pentagon Just Stays MAD," *Wall Street Journal*, December 1, 1983, p. 28.

59.  Gen. Daniel O. Graham, *The Non-Nuclear Defense of Cities: The High Frontier Space-Based Defense Against ICBM Attack* (Cambridge, Mass.: Abt Books, 1983); William J. Broad, "X-Ray Laser Weapon Gains Favor," *New York Times*, November 15, 1983, pp. C1, C2.

60.  An appraisal of Soviet military capabilities and intentions in space is provided by Stephen M. Meyer, "Soviet Military Programmes and the 'New High Ground,' " *Survival* 25, no. 5 (September/October 1983):204–215.

61.  Smith, " 'Star Wars,' " p. 6.

62.  Gray, *American Military Space Policy*, p. 10.

63.  Pringle and Arkin, *SIOP*, p. 209.

64.  See the remarks of Lt. Gen. Brent Scowcroft in Electronic Systems Division/MITRE Corporation, *Strategic Nuclear Policies, Weapons and the C3 Connection* (National Security Issues Symposium, October 1981), (Bedford, Mass.: Mitre Corporation, 1981), pp. 93–96. Scowcroft provides a balanced view of the president's preattack, transattack, and postattack C3 requirements and potential problems.

65.  On the "Schlesinger doctrine," see Secretary of Defense James R. Schlesinger, Press Conference, January 10, 1974, excerpts in *Survival* 16, no. 2 (March/April 1974): 86–90. On the implications of PD–59, see Desmond Ball, "Counterforce Targeting: How New? How Viable?" *Arms Control Today* 11, no. 2 (February, 1981), repr. with revisions in John F. Reichart and Steven R. Sturm, eds., *American Defense Policy* (Baltimore: Johns Hopkins University Press, 1982), pp. 227–234.

66.  Steinbruner, "Launch Under Attack."

67.  See, for example, *Seminar on Command, Control, Communications and Intelligence*, Incidental Paper, Program on Information Resources Policy, (Cambridge, Mass.: Center for Information Policy Research, Harvard University, December 1980).

68.  Ibid.

69.  Paul Bracken, *The Command and Control of Nuclear Forces*.

70.  Jerome Frank, *Sanity and Survival in the Nuclear Age* (New York: Random House, 1982), p. 59.

71.  Ibid., p. 60.

72.  "How Many Fingers on Trigger?" *New York News*, October 18, 1983, p. 12.

73.  Steinbruner, "Launch Under Attack," discusses this at length.

74.  "Pentagon Computers: How Vulnerable to Spies?" *U.S. News and World Report*, October 31, 1983, pp. 36–37.

75.  Harvard University, Program on Information Resources Policy, *Seminar on Command, Control, Communications and Intelligence*, esp. the discussion by Gen. Robert Rosenberg of the secretary of defense and the director of Central Intelligence colliding over the definition of priority mission for the RC–135 strategic reconnaisance aircraft, p. 63.

76.  Gray, *American Military Space Policy*, pp. 49–52.

77.  Bracken, *The Command and Control of Nuclear Forces*, p. 227.

78. Blair, *Strategic Command and Control,* passim.

79. For possible improvements in C3 survivability through mobility, see Alan J. Vick, "Post-Attack Strategic Command and Control Survival: Options for the Future," *Orbis* 29, no. 1 (Spring 1985):95–117.

80. Christopher I. Branch, *Fighting a Long Nuclear War: A Strategy, Force Policy Mismatch* (Washington, D.C.: National Defense University Press, 1984).

81. Soviet objectives and methods in general nuclear warfare are discussed in Col. M. P. Skirdo, *The People, the Army, the Commander* (Moscow: 1970), translated and published under the auspices of the U.S. Air Force pp. 16–23.

82. Ashton B. Carter, "Assessing Command System Vulnerability," ch. 17 in Ashton B. Carter, John D. Steinbruner, and Charles A. Zraket, eds., *Managing Nuclear Operations* (Washington, D.C.: Brookings Institution, 1987), pp. 555–610.

83. Bracken, *The Command and Control of Nuclear Forces,* pp. 129–178, discusses the problems attendant to command and control of nuclear forces in Europe. See also Catherine McArdle Kelleher, "NATO Nuclear Operations," ch. 14 in Carter, Steinbruner, and Zraket, eds., *Managing Nuclear Operations,* pp. 445–469.

84. I believe this analogy was first used by Michael Howard.

85. See Bruce G. Blair, "Alerting in Crisis and Conventional War," ch. 3 in Carter, Steinbruner, and Zraket, eds., *Managing Nuclear Operations,* pp. 75–120. NATO requires at least three days to deploy forces from peacetime to general defense positions. Mobilization of reinforcements must begin as soon as the Warsaw Pact begins to mobilize; any delays could prove costly, if not fatal, for NATO. U.S. and NATO officials assume strategic warning of enemy intentions would be available from a variety of political and military indicators filtered through U.S. and NATO intelligence collection and assessment. See Blair, "Alerting in Crisis and Conventional War," p. 81. The estimated 24 hours required for nuclear release to be obtained from the "bottom up" is notional; actual circumstances might dictate faster or slower speeds. The U.S. Army and Air Force in Europe have partially separate chains of command for nuclear release. Having obtained nuclear release from the United States and the United Kingdom, SACEUR [supreme allied commander, Europe] can bypass intermediate levels of command and issue "top down" orders directly to lower levels. See Kelleher, "NATO Nuclear Operation," p. 457.

86. Richard W. Betts, *Surprise Attack* (Washington, D.C.: Brookings Institution, 1982), p. 171.

# 4

# Conflict Termination and the Problem of Surprise

The problem of nuclear surprise attack is the benchmark case against which U.S. force planning has been developed for many years. This might seem unrealistic. The probability of nuclear war is judged to be low to nonexistent by most policymakers and expert analysts. Force planners are understandably cautious by temperament and training, however, and so overprepare for worst case scenarios. And the worst case of all could be a preemptive attack against the U.S. deterrent that left the U.S. president with the choice of suicidal retaliation against Soviet cities or acquiescence to Soviet demands.

The survivability of U.S. strategic forces cannot be taken for granted even if a technically survivable force structure is deployed. The distinction between technical survivability and actual survivability lies in the importance of strategic surprise. A surprised U.S. national command authority (NCA) could be much more vulnerable than an alerted one. U.S. strategic forces that were not fully alerted would be in very different condition compared with those which were, relative to their probable survivability against plausible Soviet attacks.

The political case for a Soviet or U.S. incentive to launch a "bolt from the blue" against the other has always seemed unconvincing to policy analysts. The risks would be enormous and the costs prohibitive. Why, then, have seemingly improbably scenarios been used as planning devices? Three reasons stand out: (1) traditional military conservatism; (2) simplicity in calculation, compared with messier scenarios; (3) policy pressures, in the form of efforts by the United States to incorporate more discriminating options into war plans. A real "bolt from the blue" might be a less than total one, calling for a less than total second-strike retaliation against a selective target set. Following a selective first strike and a constrained retaliation, real bargaining over war termination would begin. In some sense, it would have begun even before the first salvo was launched.

During the Reagan administration, policy officials and academic analysts have been forced to confront the issue of a potential "window of vulnerability" facing the U.S. ICBM force. But the issue is not a new one. It dates to the earliest days of the arms race. Individual components of U.S. (and Soviet) strategic retaliatory forces have always been vulnerable to some kind of surprise attack, *under normal peacetime conditions*. This is not news. U.S. and Soviet officials have obviously decided to invest in forces that are survivable overall *after* having been sufficiently alerted. This puts additional emphasis upon the intelligence and warning systems, and their fusion with the nuclear response mechanisms. Thus the strategic command system must, as we have seen, survive direct or indirect attack and provide for retaliatory strikes once it has been prepared to carry out this mission.[1]

Since the U.S. and Soviet nuclear command systems would probably be alerted if they were expected to respond at all, the probability of a truly unexpected attack might seem slight. As an abstract proposition this is undoubtedly so, but in the twilight of a particular crisis, policymakers will not want to depend upon general probabilities for consolation. And they will not have simple options, such as turning their nuclear command systems on or off in their entirety. The Soviet and U.S command systems will have to grind through procedures and organizational routines in order to move from a condition of lethargy to one in which they are poised for responsiveness. The actual unfolding of the alerting process may be more unpredictable than it was during rehearsals of the same event.[2] In turn, the Soviet and U.S. warning and intelligence systems will be watching each other for signs of preparedness—both preparedness for retaliation and, more ominously, preparedness for preemption. Each will read the other's tea leaves through the prism of its own procedures and strategic culture.

## STRATEGIC SURPRISE

Surprise, by definition, is whatever is not expected. Strategic surprise has a more specific meaning. (For more on definitional and conceptual problems associated with the issue of surprise, see Chapter 5). Applied to the failure of policymakers to anticipate events, including attacks, correctly, strategic surprise implies that the opponent's basic *intentions* or *capabilities* are misperceived. Strategic surprise is distinguished from tactical surprise. Tactical surprise is related to success in deceiving the opponent about single battles or campaigns. Strategic surprise misleads to a basic misunderstanding of overall methods and aims. Because of this more demanding condition relative to strategic surprise, one might expect to find that it is infrequent in the history of conflict among major powers. In fact, it is quite frequent. Not only are national leaders often surprised, they are not infrequently surprised catastrophically.[3]

Surprise is related to deception. Deception can be of two basic varieties, which Donald C. Daniel and Katherine L. Herbig have termed A and M type deceptions. In the A (for ambiguity)-type deception, deceivers attempt to confuse their targets by promoting at least two, or frequently more than two, possible interpretations for an event.[4] An example of this type of deception was the Bodyguard plan in support of the Normandy invasion during World War II. The anti-Nazi allies deceived the Germans by staging fictitious invasion threats against other targets throughout Europe. The second generic type of deception is the M (for mislead) type. In misleading deceptions, the deceiver attempts to focus the attention of the deceived on a false alternative. An example is provided by German planning for the invasion of the Soviet Union in June 1941. The Barbarossa plan attempted to exploit Stalin's preconception that Hitler would not attack without warning by making the German buildup near the Soviet border appear to be designed for another purpose (in this case, a putative invasion of Britain by the Nazis).[5]

As these examples illustrate, surprise is never total, a predatory aggressor falling upon an unsuspecting inert victim. At least, this has not happened in relations among major powers in this century. After all, attacks are usually preceded by some political disagreement or hostility; thus there is a general expectation that war might come about. In the above examples of deception, Hitler certainly knew that the Western allies were planning an invasion of his Fortress Europe. The trick was to estimate, correctly, exactly where and when. Stalin also knew that he could not fully trust Hitler, and prior to the Nazi invasion the Soviet leader received numerous warnings of Hitler's plans to attack. Although the "when" might be in some doubt, the "where" was clear enough. Stalin interpreted warnings of the Nazi invasion through the lenses of his own preconceptions. He did not want to believe that Hitler would attack in 1941 because he felt that the Soviet armed forces were not ready to repel such an invasion. The Soviets misestimated the German intentions and capabilities relative to Barbarossa. The Soviet high command expected that Hitler would repeat his performances prior to the invasions of Czechoslovakia and Poland, making political demands upon his victim and using military preparations to induce compliance.[6] The Japanese attack on Pearl Harbor in 1941 also illustrates the potential vulnerability of targets to deception, at least with regard to the time and place of attack. Although U.S. policymakers knew that they were drifting toward war in the Far East, and that a Japanese attack somewhere in the Pacific was imminent, they did not know exactly where, or how, the attack would be executed.

The consequences of a nuclear war between the United States and the Soviet Union would be devastating for both sides. Thus, no rational purpose seems to be served by launching such an attack. This condition of attack implausibility under normal peacetime conditions makes the probability of surprise higher under other conditions. Although U.S. forces can be alerted to various levels in response to perceived threats, the psychology of national decisionmakers is harder to change. So is the behavior of bureaucratic organizations that must respond to an unprecedented event that is a potential national calamity. Under pressures of time and circumstance, U.S. or Soviet leaders might want to believe that false warnings account for the blips on radar screens. And the belief would be reinforced in the U.S. case by an actual history of false warnings based on failures in microcircuitry or human error.[7]

In the event of rising tensions and a possible actual attack, U.S. leaders will have the uncomfortable choice of disbelieving plausible indicators of bad news or of believing those indicators with all the consequences they portend. And their counterparts in Moscow will be making their own estimates of U.S. responses to increases in the probability of a Soviet attack. U.S. analysts have emphasized that the U.S. or Soviet fear of surprise attack by the opponent could bring it about. That is one of the uncomfortable paradoxes of the nuclear age, and its resolution is one component of crisis stability. Less attention is devoted to the possibility that an attack (for whatever reason) could take place and not be believed. Desperate nuclear-armed opponents could at the same time fear the costs of war if they strike first, and so be inhibited, and fear being second in a nuclear exchange.

The discussion below considers the problem of strategic nuclear surprise in the context of survivability for U.S. forces and command, control, and communications (C3) and in the context of plausible Soviet deterrence and war-fighting strategies. No school solutions to the problem of surprise can be offered, but the recognition that favorable force balances in and of themselves are no protection against strategic surprise is important. Surprises are often surprises because they are not deemed efficient or affordable, as seen from the perspective of the state being attacked.[8] The more improbable a surprise is thought to be, the more it destroys the plans of the target state if it is carried out.

## SURVIVABILITY

The survivability of U.S. strategic forces means, in practice, that the United States can retaliate after absorbing an attack and inflict unacceptable losses on Soviet forces, military and political leaders, and society.

Whether U.S. forces have always attained that declaratory status, in operational capabilities, is debatable; forces have always been sized on the assumption of worst case threats.

The prelaunch vulnerability of U.S. land-based strategic missiles (ICBMs) to a Soviet first strike has been asserted by commentators since the mid–1970s.[9] ICBM vulnerability became a touchstone for the Reagan presidential campaign of 1980. Even U.S. analysts who disputed the imminent vulnerability of land-based missiles foresaw eventual vulnerability if the Soviet Union improved its ICBM accuracies as expected.[10] Whether the Soviets would attack U.S. ICBMs surgically or as part of a larger counterforce attack was scenario dependent. As has been noted, the authoritative Scowcroft Commission noted that the Soviet Union would have great difficulty attacking both U.S. bomber and ICBM forces without risking the self-destruction of its own war plans.[11]

Survivability of fleet ballistic missile submarines (SSBN) was taken for granted by many commentators until the question of the survivability of communications between submarines and higher-level commanders was studied extensively. Desmond Ball reported in 1981 that communications to the SSBN force might not survive the early stages of nuclear attack.[12] The Reagan strategic modernization program would reduce the force of U.S. SSBNs from its present size of more than 30 to about 20 at some time in the 1990s.[13] Breakthroughs in Soviet antisubmarine warfare could take advantage of a smaller number of U.S. platforms.

Bomber survivability depends on timely receipt of warning and bomber ability to be airborne before airfields are struck by Soviet submarine-launched ballistic missiles. Those missiles might reach inland bomber bases in the United States within 15 minutes if they were launched from favorable locations off the Atlantic coast.[14] Attacks on bomber bases could be timed to precede attacks on U.S. ICBMs from Soviet ICBMs on polar trajectories. Although such a strategy might allow more U.S. ICBMs to escape, it would more severely cripple the bomber force, which carries the largest share of hard-target warheads.[15] If the Soviets are concerned to limit the total megatonnage available in the U.S. retaliatory arsenal, regardless of whether it can be delivered promptly or slowly, then attacks against bombers pay higher dividends than those against ICBMs.

If the various components of the U.S. strategic "triad" are not necessarily survivable individually, they are by all indications survivable collectively. Vulnerabilities in one element of the "triad" are offset by different kinds of vulnerabilities in another. Thus, from the standpoint of managerial criteria, the redundancy in force structure may pay strategic dividends in creating cognitive complexity for Soviet attack planners. But this redundancy in forces contributes to cumulative force survivability only if U.S. strategic C3 is also survivable.

Such survivability cannot be guaranteed, according to expert analysts. John Steinbruner has suggested that the U.S. strategic C3 system may be disconnected by electromagnetic pulse and other residual effects of nuclear explosions.[16] Desmond Ball argues that commanders and their communications cannot be relied on to survive for very long after the first salvos of U.S. and Soviet strategic forces.[17] Paul Bracken notes the irony that Soviet attacks on the U.S. command structure (countercommand attacks) might succeed, although not necessarily to the ultimate advantage of the USSR. Success in disconnecting top U.S. political and military leaders from their force commanders might allow authority to cascade downward in the hierarchy, precluding war termination on favorable terms (or any terms).[18] A symposium at the Mitre Corporation cosponsored by the Electronic Systems Division of the U.S. Air Force reported testimony by experts that the C3 architecture was insufficiently enduring to conduct protracted nuclear war as apparently required in Carter and Reagan planning studies.[19]

The Reagan strategic modernization program will not alleviate all or even most of these force and command vulnerabilities. Deployment of 50 MX ICBMs in Minutemen silos does nothing to diminish their vulnerability to countersilo attacks, although the Reagan administration is now interested in basing the second allotment of 50 MX in rail mobile (and presumably more survivable) configurations.[20] Improved communications between strategic submarines and the NCA will be facilitated by the deployment of the extremely-low-frequency communications system in the Midwest, but the system will probably not survive the initial phases of war.[21] Deployment of the B–1 bomber to replace the B–52 as a penetrator of Soviet air defenses in the latter 1980s will not increase the warning time available to NCA or the Strategic Air Command (SAC) if the Soviets deploy their SSBN closer to their presumed targets or use depressed trajectories.[22] Proposed improvements in strategic C3 will provide more sophisticated attack assessment and real-time targeting information from satellites by the 1990s, but the survivability of the fixed national command posts (SAC, NORAD, the National Military Command Center in Washington, and the alternative NMCC in Raven Rock, Pennsylvania) remains doubtful.[23] At best, the president or successors could conduct the postattack war from airborne command posts for a few days if communications between the command posts and the strategic forces were still operating.[24]

## STRATEGIC WARNING AND CRISIS MANAGEMENT

The preceding illustrations are not worst case estimates. Almost all of these scenarios assume that the United States would be attacked after a significant period of strategic warning (after a crisis had developed).

This period of tension would result in alerted U.S. strategic forces (termed "generated") that are poised to retaliate, as opposed to those operating under day-to-day normal peacetime conditions.

Should the Soviets, for whatever reason, feel desperate enough to attack the United States with strategic nuclear weapons, attacking U.S. forces on generated alert would not be their best move. Studies show that U.S. forces on generated alert would inflict far more retaliatory destruction on remaining Soviet forces and society after a Soviet first strike, compared with U.S. forces on day-to-day alert.[25] A particular Soviet disadvantage in attacking alerted U.S. forces lies in the enhanced survivability of U.S. prompt counterforce, which poses a particular threat to Soviet forces withheld from the first strike. Alerted forces might resort to launch under attack or launch on warning—a possibility that could not be precluded by prudent Kremlin planners.[26]

Despite the comparative advantage for the Soviet Union in attacking unalerted U.S. forces, U.S. strategies tend to dismiss the "bolt from the blue" attack as a lesser possibility than attack following a prolonged crisis in which U.S. leaders and forces have advance warning about possible Soviet intentions.[27] The assumption that Soviet attack would not come as a "bolt from the blue" seems reasonable in situations that involve escalation to nuclear war from a conventional war in Europe. In those situations, it would come as no surprise to U.S. leaders to learn that Soviet preparations for possible theater and strategic nuclear attacks were in progress.[28]

In just those situations, however, expectations of possible Soviet attack could make the command system more difficult to manage. Sensitive balancing of positive and negative control would be necessary. Positive control ensures that forces perform their assigned missions in timely fashion. Negative control prevents unauthorized or accidental launch of forces.[29] For the purposes of this discussion, we will avoid quibbling over the terms "positive" and "negative" so long as the reader understands the intended meaning. During a protracted crisis, the emphasis would shift from the prevention of accidental or unauthorized launch to the responsiveness of the system to valid orders to retaliate.[30] The pressure to make certain that forces could not be disarmed would make it more difficult to maintain the layers or checks and balances against ill-considered use.

Throughout U.S. history, but particularly since World War II, U.S. presidents have had to exert strong personal control over crises to prevent standard operating procedures and organizational routines from propelling events beyond policy control. The Cuban missile crisis is one example. President Kennedy had to order the U.S. Navy to move its original blockade line closer to Cuba in order to provide decision time to Soviet leaders. Instructions about the interception of surface ships that approached the blockade line were important to the president and to Secretary of Defense Robert S. McNamara, who argued about the procedures with the chief of naval operations.[31] Political leaders failed to exercise equally strict control over U.S. naval antisubmarine warfare "hunter killer" exercises, in which six Soviet submarines were apparently forced to surface during the crisis before the president ordered the efforts curtailed.[32]

The mathematical probability that more U.S. forces would survive and destroy more Soviet forces if U.S. forces were alerted provides small consolation if decision makers cannot manage the alerts in a controlled fashion. The Soviets could exploit that inability to control the "alert bureaucracy" by first raising and then dampening the temperature of a crisis. These ups and downs of threats followed by appeals for peace have their precedents in Soviet crisis behavior: Khrushchev accompanied threats during the Cuban missile crisis with blandishments of his peaceful intentions. His two written communications to President Kennedy differed completely in tone and substance.[33] During the Yom Kippur war of 1973, Soviet leader Leonid Brezhnev offered to join forces with the United States in a joint expedition to restore peace. When this received no positive response, Brezhnev threatened unilateral Soviet intervention. Although in this instance the joint expedition was clearly an insincere proposal designed to buy time for beleaguered Egyptian forces, in a different crisis U.S. leaders might want to believe in the sincerity of a proposal that offered a way out.[34]

The Soviets could also exploit the "cry wolf" syndrome with repeated conventional exercises in Europe to which NATO became so accustomed that no single exercise would seem unusually threatening. Expectation of large Soviet maneuvers could become the norm rather than the exception, even during a crisis extending for weeks or months.[35] To some extent, a successful "cry wolf" attack is what the Egyptians accomplished against the Israelis in 1973. Israel had reacted to earlier mobilizations by the Egyptians that had not resulted in the actual outbreak of war. As a result, Israeli and U.S. leaders interpreted the events of September and October 1973 as more political posturing rather than as Egyptian military preparations for an actual attack.[36]

The fear that crises and alerts cannot be managed has prompted U.S. efforts to centralize command and control in order to attain more complete vertical integration among commanders, forces, and communications channels.[37] The concern about mismanaged alerts is frequently stated as a concern about failures of negative control, that is, accidental launch. But crises can be mismanaged in another way. The United States might need to respond to a crisis with heightened alerts maintained for long periods or, if deterrence fails, with retaliatory strikes. Whether it could do either successfully would depend not on a "game against nature" but on a competition with an opponent. The strategic doctrines and preferred war-fighting strategies of that opponent are thus relevant to our expectations about crisis management and war.

## SOVIET "DOCTRINE" AND WAR-FIGHTING STYLE: IMPLICATIONS FOR SURPRISE

The question of Soviet military doctrine is complicated by the plurality of references implied by the term "doctrine" in the works of many Western writers. The Soviets are more specific. Military doctrine is the policy of the Soviet state with regard to the kinds of wars it can expect to fight and the overall objectives in fighting them. Thus military doctrine is political guidance to the armed forces from the highest level.[38] Military art derives from military doctrine and military science, and applies at three levels: strategy, operational art, and tactics.[39] Also in contrast with the West, the Soviet definition of "strategic" is not based upon the kinds of technologies employed in warfare but on the objectives for which the war is fought.[40] Having committed themselves to battle, Soviet party leaders expect their generals to direct the combat to victory, at whatever level the combat is joined.[41] Victory is nothing less than the attainment of policy objectives; at a minimum, it includes the destruction of the opponent's military forces, command and control, and society to the extent necessary to retard the opponent's war effort.[42]

How these doctrinal precepts would play out in a strategic nuclear confrontation is particularly dependent upon circumstances. However war developed, the Soviets would have every incentive to attack the West on several fronts simultaneously. A war in which the U.S. and Soviet forces fought each other directly would have a high probability of spreading from one theater of operations to another; the Soviets set little store by intrawar deterrence, escalation control, and other refinements of Western deterrence logic.[43] The Soviet Union has historically shown great caution in committing its forces to war, but once in a war, has had little interest in reciprocal restraint in the face of political and military threats to the survival of the USSR itself. Although Soviet interest in the control of escalation and possible termination of nuclear war should be exploited to the extent that it exists, Western leaders should not build prewar policies on optimism about Soviet reciprocity.[44]

It is very unlikely that the Soviet Union expects to fight a nuclear war against the United States without absorbing significant and unprecedented damage to its society. Whether the balance of postattack megatonnage will favor East or West will matter less to the Kremlin than the comparative viability of Eastern and Western political systems and societies. An unsuccessful nuclear war threatens the Soviet's postwar political control if their society absorbs too much devastation and if their forces are too crippled to maintain internal security.[45] Even a best case scenario for the Soviet Union's postattack predicament allows for unprecedented death and destruction, as well as a possible return of the political anarchy that characterized Russia during World War I, or worse.[46] Although the Soviet control structure seems very pervasive by peacetime standards, Russian history is not reassuring to those who aspire to postnuclear totalitarian rule.[47]

What these doctrinal predilections and societal vulnerabilities imply is that the Soviets would emphasize surprise and the initiative in conventional or nuclear war against the West. Preemption is not foreclosed in Soviet strategy for nuclear war fighting, although some authors have been more willing than others to see preemption as central to Soviet planning.[48] The Soviet notion of preemption may differ from that of the United States, however. U.S. concepts of preemption emphasize almost certain detection of enemy intention to attack; Soviet preemption might be risked if the Politburo considered a U.S. first strike plausible, although not certain.[49]

From the Soviet standpoint, failure to preempt would be politically and militarily self-defeating and self-negating. Marxist-Leninist ideology and Soviet memory of historical experiences in this century would argue for avoiding another Barbarossa and getting in the first blow.[50] From the perspective of a detached scientific observer of arms races and wars, such a decision represents cosmic folly. Repeated scientific estimates concur on the possibility of mutually suicidal side effects from U.S.-Soviet nuclear wars in which large proportions of their arsenals are exchanged.[51] But in a crisis in which the Kremlin fears destruction of its imperium, scientific estimates may count for less than narrow military ones, even if the military ones are on the order of regressive fatalism.

Once convinced that war with the West was inevitable or highly probable, the Soviets might exploit substantial Western fears of war through combinations of carrots (peace programs and arms control proposals) and sticks (reminders of what can happen if Soviet proposals are not accepted). A certain minimum of Western psychological disarmament, in the form of disbelief that *anyone* could deliberately start a nuclear war, would be imperative to produce the necessary mind-set in the national capitals of Soviet opponents. That necessary mind-set need not be appeasement; a high state of ambiguity and uncertainty about real Soviet intentions would do, since the United States and its allies might not react to anything other than unambiguous warning of attack. And unambiguous warning is the last thing that Soviet leaders would want to give their victims. The West may be guilty of great misunderstanding of the Soviet perspective on this issue of warning sufficient for retaliation or preemption because of "mirror imaging" of Western and Soviet strategic perspectives. The Soviets might well assume that once U.S. satellites and computers have confirmed any attack, U.S. strategic retaliatory forces will be launched. U.S. policy does not preclude launch on warning, nor does it require it.[52]

If the Soviets have done their political preparations correctly prior to war, they may catch U.S. forces not fully ready because of disbelief by U.S. policymakers and/or clogged channels in the decision system. Catching U.S. forces less than fully alerted does not guarantee victory or even a prevailing outcome for the Soviet Union, but their recognition of this will not necessarily dissuade their attack in a crisis. Attacking from pessimistic desperation rather than opportunism, Soviet leaders might simply assume that striking first improves their postattack force survivability and societal recovery potential.[53] The greatest asymmetry between U.S. and Soviet strategic capabilities lies in the probability that U.S. policymakers may not believe an attack could happen. Therefore, they might continue searching for computer malfunctions, such as those of the past, while Soviet warheads rained on U.S. ICBM fields.[54]

## STRATEGIC DEFENSE AND SURPRISE

The possibility that by amending or abrogating the ABM Treaty, either the United States or the Soviet Union might deploy a ballistic missile defense (BMD) system to protect its retaliatory forces or many of its cities, or both, has technology and policy implications for the possibility of strategic surprise. Much of the debate about missile defenses and the Strategic Defense Initiative (SDI) of the Reagan administration, as discussed in another chapter, has focused on the mission of BMD: city defense versus protection of retaliatory forces. Although a distinction can be made in theory between these missions, in practice the distinction may not be so clear-cut. If technologies are developed and deployed for boost-phase defense, for example, they will contribute to the protection of retaliatory forces *and* cities because they will be attempting interception prior to the actual deployment of reentry vehicles on their separate trajectories (assuming MIRV, multiple warhead missiles).[55] For present purposes, BMD systems deployed in space or terrestrially might have more than one mission, or the mission might not be obvious to the putative attack planner.

One relationship between SDI and surprise attack has been noted in studies conducted for the Reagan administration, including the "Hoffman Report" on the policy implications of BMD.[56] A U.S. missile defense system adds to Soviet uncertainties in structuring their attack. This is important if their first strike is designed to destroy specific U.S. strategic force targets in order to blunt U.S. retaliation. Undoubtedly there are other ways to increase Soviet uncertainty in this regard; whether the most efficient way to do this is by deploying U.S. BMD systems to protect missile silos and other counterforce targets is debatable. But the relationship, once the defenses are deployed, is still as noted above: all other things being equal, even limited defenses complicate first-strike calculations by the opponent, requiring that it plan to expend additional warheads and decoys in order to assure the penetration of a sufficient number of warheads to achieve its objectives.

In the U.S.-Soviet case, the USSR may be willing to pay the price of deploying additional warheads to offset any U.S. BMD system until other elements of Soviet offensive forces (including bombers and cruise missiles) are modernized. The Soviets may also deploy their own defenses. If the Soviet defenses were approximately equal in capability (leverage against attacks) to U.S. defenses, then the superpowers' relative offensive capabilities, as now, would determine the stability of the balance. Although U.S. defenses would require the Soviets to use additional warheads to achieve objectives formerly attainable with fewer warheads, fewer of the surviving U.S. warheads would penetrate the Soviet defenses in retaliation, compared with the undefended Soviet case.

Much would depend on how and where BMD systems were deployed. If deployed in space, they would be vulnerable to attack from antisatellite weapons (ASATs) that the superpowers are now deploying or have deployed already.[57] Technologies suitable for ASATs are likely to be commingled with technologies required for the eventual deployment of space-based missile defenses. Thus the issue of defense in space may have to be confronted earlier for U.S. early warning and communications satellites that provide the eyes and ears for detection of Soviet launch. And Soviet fears for the survivability of their own warning and communications networks, also based partly in space, might contribute to a chain of events leading to their preemption of a feared U.S. attack in time of crisis.[58] The Soviet strategic command and control system is highly redundant, and is possibly less dependent upon space-based sensors and communications than is its U.S. counterpart. However, this does not preclude a pessimistic Soviet interpretation of U.S. ASAT activity during a crisis in which the United States has raised its level of strategic alert. Currently the United States has an ASAT that is thought to be more flexible and capable than the Soviet ASAT, but that latter has apparent capabilities to destroy U.S. satellites in low earth orbit.[59]

Some U.S. strategists might argue that the entire problem of crisis stability is overrated. The costs of superpower strategic nuclear war are so apparent, it is sometimes assumed, that neither side would launch an attack despite its crisis-induced fears, because the difference between striking first and striking second is (from the standpoint of societal destruction) meaningless. However, the more capable defenses are thought to be, the more they call into question this shared symmetry of societal vulnerability. Defenses for one side would obviously place the other at a disadvantage. Even defenses for both would complicate the simple doomsday calculus that now is thought by some advocates of assured destruction to keep the peace. Defenses do introduce complexity, but not necessarily crisis instability. Defenses deployed by one side that can eliminate the retaliatory strike of the other are certainly destabilizing. But a more likely outcome is the deployment of defenses by both sides with some capability to protect forces and command centers, and some more limited protection of cities and other socioeconomic assets. These partial defenses will be paired with offenses, perhaps with offenses limited by arms control agreements, but potent offenses nonetheless.

In this projection of two superpowers with partially effective defenses to which they are adding in modular fashion while maintaining some significant offenses, a mixed bag results for strategic surprise. It becomes more complicated to calculate how a surprise attack might be carried out. But the more implausible such calculations seem to be, the more politically vulnerable are the defender's expectations. A conservative attacker would overestimate the capability of the opponent's defenses; an audacious attack planner might underestimate them. Facing a mixed environment of offenses and defenses on both sides and seeing a crisis slide into war, or conventional war slide into nuclear war, Soviet leaders might decide to alert their defenses and opt for a "best of the worst" strategy. So might the United States. Neither side will have full confidence in the performance of its defenses or in the capabilities of its offenses against deployed defenses as opposed to simulated ones. If both sides make conservative estimates of their own capabilities (understating them) and conservative estimates of their opponents' capabilities (overrating them), then error on the side of prudence should serve to reduce incentives for surprise. But underestimating one's own capabilities and overestimating the opponent's contribute to crisis stability only if those prudent estimates do not become desperate ones, such that either side decides that it is "now or never," before the crisis escapes control.

## WORST CASES AND PROBABLE DILEMMAS

Concern about a "bolt from the blue" may be motivated by a form of worst case analysis that errs in two ways. It seems impractical to believe that either superpower would test the resolve of the other, given the consequences of guessing wrong for the society of the attacker. And theoretically, it is difficult for scenario writers to envision a surprise attack that succeeds in the same way that surprises seemed to work in the prenuclear era. However, and premonitory of the discussion in the next chapter, we have seen that surprises are not all of one piece. Surprise is a gradient, and so are the actual operations of strategic nuclear forces. They cannot suddenly be called from the "vasty deep" and ordered to carry out their missions in exactly the ways that policymakers and planners expect.

A war plan is a mechanism for coordinating warning, assessment, and response. Its purpose is to enable thinking about possibilities to be pinned down to concrete choices about radars, missiles, command centers, and other infrastructure of nuclear command system awareness and responsiveness. If one component fails unexpectedly, the entire system does not necessarily fail catastrophically. Nor can a nuclear cheap shot, even one that is unexpected, destroy the entire Soviet or U.S. nuclear command system. A massive attack would be required to destroy either side's nuclear command system; in the process, it would destroy much of its counterforce and countervalue target base as well. Moreover, if it succeeded, it would accidentally or deliberately preclude negotiations leading to war termination; the outcome would be determined by exhaustion of arsenals.

However, a less than totally destructive attack, against components of the U.S. or Soviet force structure and command system, could play havoc with any effort to retaliate against optimum mixes of target sets, as defined in prewar plans.[60] The irony is that this would make it more difficult to fight a limited war than a total one. A furious first strike by either side, involving thousands of warheads launched against the homeland of the other, would be devastating in its social consequences. But it would pose no serious decision dilemma for officials who had to decide upon a response; the response would be massive, and almost automatic. Such an attack could not be confused, and would not be, with an accidental launch or selective strike that left open the possibility of postexchange negotiation.

On the other hand, decision makers, if surprised by a sudden but limited attack on strategic nuclear forces not fully alerted, would have many things to sort out in a very short time. Assessment might be based upon partly degraded sensors, communications, and fusion centers. Space- and ground-based command systems components could be running at less than full strength. Commanders might assume delegation of authority according to standard operating procedures supplemented with plausible guesses about wartime improvisations. A partially degraded U.S. or Soviet command system could leave in place a central command apparatus operating at minimum efficiency, plus field commanders in possession of nuclear weapons who had differing assumptions about what they were now permitted to do with them. Central policymakers on either side might want to stop the war, while commanding forces in relevant theaters of operation would prefer to continue. The agony of decision in attempting to fight while negotiating does not present itself in the massive worst case "bolt from the blue" against which U.S. forces have traditionally been sized. A less than worst, but still terrible, case is more stressful.

## NOTES

1. Differences in the responsiveness of fully alerted and day-to-day alerted U.S. strategic nuclear forces are illustrated in Desmond Ball, "The Development of the SIOP, 1960–1983," ch. 3 in Desmond Ball and Jeffrey Richelson, eds., *Strategic Nuclear Targeting* (Ithaca, N.Y.: Cornell University Press, 1986), p. 81.

2. See Bruce G. Blair, "Alerting in Crisis and Conventional War," ch. 3 in Ashton B. Carter, John D. Steinbruner, and Charles A. Zraket, eds., *Managing Nuclear Operations* (Washington, D.C.: Brookings Institution, 1987), pp. 75–120.

3. Important case studies are presented in Klaus Knorr and Patrick Morgan, eds., *Strategic Military Surprise: Incentives and Opportunities* (New Brunswick, N.J.: Transaction Books, 1983).

4. Donald C. Daniel and Katherine L. Herbig, "Propositions on Military Deception," ch. 1 in Daniel and Herbig, eds., *Strategic Military Deception* (New York: Pergamon Press, 1981), pp. 5–7.

5. Ibid., p. 6. See also Barton Whaley, *Codeword Barbarossa* (Cambridge, Mass.: MIT Press, 1973).

6. Russell H. S. Stolfi, "Barbarossa: German Grand Deception and the Achievement of Strategic and Tactical Surprise Against the Soviet Union, 1940–41," in Daniel and Herbig, eds., *Strategic Military Deception*, pp. 195–223.

7. See Charles Perrow, *Normal Accidents: Living with High Risk Technologies* (New York: Basic Books, 1984), pp. 282–292, on the potentially error-inducing qualities of warning systems.

8. Michael I. Handel, "Strategic Surprise: The Politics of Intelligence and the Management of Uncertainty," in Alfred C. Maurer, Marion D. Tunstall, and James M. Keagle, eds., *Intelligence: Policy and Process* (Boulder, Colo.: Westview, 1985), pp. 251–252.

9. T. K. Jones and W. Scott Thompson, "Central War and Civil Defense," *Orbis* 22, no. 3 (Fall 1978): 681–713.

10. Matthew Bunn and Kosta Tsipis, "The Uncertainties of Preemptive Nuclear Attack," *Scientific American* 249, no. 5 (November 1983): 38–47.

11. Stephen J. Cimbala, "ICBM Vulnerability and Credibility Deterrence: Strategic and Theater Issues," ch. 10 in Cimbala, ed., *National Security Strategy: Choices and Limits* (New York: Praeger, 1984), pp. 267–279.

12. Desmond Ball, *Can Nuclear War Be Controlled?* Adelphi Papers no. 169 (London: International Institute for Strategic Studies, Autumn 1981).

13. U.S. Congress, Congressional Budget Office, *Modernizing U.S. Strategic Offensive Forces: The Administration's Program and Alternatives* (Washington, D.C.: U.S. Government Printing Office, May 1983), p. 57. See also D. Douglas Dalgleish and Larry Schweikart, *Trident* (Carbondale: Southern Illinois University Press, 1984).

14. President's Commission on U.S. Strategic Forces (Scowcroft Commission), *Report* (Washington, D.C.: U.S. Government Printing Office, April 1983).

15. Ibid., pp. 7–8.

16. John Steinbruner, "Nuclear Decapitation," *Foreign Policy* no. 45 (Winter 1981–1982): 16–28. See also Bruce G. Blair, *Strategic Command and Control: Redefining the Nuclear Threat* (Washington, D.C.: Brookings Institution, 1985).

17. Ball, *Can Nuclear War Be Controlled?* Soviet attack assessment systems may not provide a very complete or accurate picture of what is happening once war has begun. See Paul Bracken, *The Command and Control of Nuclear Forces* (New Haven: Yale University Press, 1983), pp. 120–128.

18. The Soviet command system may be resistant to attack, and it might not be desirable to destroy it even if it were possible. See Stephen J. Cimbala, "Countercommand Attacks and War Termination," ch. 7 in Cimbala, ed., *Strategic War Termination* (New York: Praeger, 1986), pp. 134–154.

19. Electronic Systems Division, USAF, and Mitre Corporation, *Strategic Nuclear Policies, Weapons and the C3 Connection*, National Security Issues Symposium, October 13–14, 1981 (Bedford, Mass.: Mitre Corporation, 1981).

20. Secretary of Defense Caspar W. Weinberger, *Annual Report to the Congress: Fiscal Year 1988* (Washington, D.C.: U.S. Government Printing Office, January 12, 1987), p. 205.

21. "Ex-Admiral Claims ELF Isn't Needed," *Milwaukee Journal*, February 22, 1984, p. 1; and Blair, *Strategic Command and Control*, pp. 183–184.

22. On bomber survivability, see Appendix E, "Bomber Launch Survivability," in Congressional Budget Office, *Modernizing U.S. Strategic Offensive Forces*, pp. 99–110.

23. Peter Pringle and William Arkin, *SIOP: The Secret U.S. Plan for Nuclear War* (New York: W. W. Norton, 1983).

24. See the comments by Brent Scowcroft in Electronic Systems Division/ Mitre, *Strategic Nuclear Policies, Weapons and the C3 Connection*, pp. 93–97.

25. Congressional Budget Office, *Modernizing U.S. Strategic Offensive Forces*, pp. xv, 21. See also Desmond Ball, "The Development of the SIOP, 1960–1983," in Ball and Richelson, eds., *Strategic Nuclear Targeting*, pp. 57–83, esp. p. 81. Ball cites a study positing that generated U.S. strategic nuclear forces could deliver 7,160 weapons on 8,757 targets, compared with day-to-day forces delivering 3,840 weapons against 5,400 targets.

26. Properly planned Soviet attacks on U.S. ICBM fields might not permit launch on warning. See John Steinbruner, "Launch Under Attack," *Scientific American*, January 1984, pp. 37–47.

27. Albert Carnesale et al., *Living with Nuclear Weapons* (New York: Bantam Books, 1983), pp. 49–50.

28. Richard K. Betts suggests that U.S. strategic forces have been planned for operations under conditions of surprise but argues that a "bolt from the blue" not preceded by crisis is improbable as long as the United States has survivable forces. See Betts, "Surprise Attack and Preemption," in Graham T. Allison et al., eds., *Hawks, Doves and Owls: An Agenda for Avoiding Nuclear War* (New York: W. W. Norton, 1985), pp. 54–79, and *Surprise Attack: Lessons for Defense Planning* (Washington, D.C.: Brookings Institution, 1982), pp. 229–238.

29. Strictly speaking, positive control implies that weapons will not be released until an affirmative order moves them beyond a status of readiness. Negative control means that commanders are understood to have authorization for dis-

cretionary launch unless higher authority interferes. Thus the U.S. strategic bomber force operates on positive control launch, while the ballistic missile submarines operate under negative control when communications are severed and war is considered imminent, or as having begun.

30. Paul Bracken suggests that under crisis conditions, information from warning and intelligence systems may overwhelm political authorities and their staffs. Some parts of the system will execute irrelevant standard operating procedures; others may hang in the air, awaiting orders that never come. *The Command and Control of Nuclear Forces*, pp. 58–59.

31. Elie Abel, *The Missile Crisis* (New York: Bantam Books, 1966). pp. 136–137.

32. Graham T. Allison, *Essence of Decision* (Boston: Little, Brown, 1971), p. 138.

33. Abel, *The Missile Crisis*, pp. 158–168.

34. See, for example, the description of the role played by Henry Kissinger in the 1973 October war in John G. Stoessinger, *Why Nations Go to War* (New York: St. Martin's Press, 1982), pp. 170–171.

35. Betts, *Surprise Attack*, p. 203.

36. Ibid., pp. 72–73.

37. A number of issues related to force management are addressed by various contributors in Carter, Steinbruner, and Zraket, eds., *Managing Nuclear Operations*.

38. See Col. M. P. Skirdo, *The People, the Army, the Commander* (Moscow: 1970), translated and published by the U.S. Air Force, pp. 98–99.

39. John J. Dziak, *Soviet Perceptions of Military Power: The Interaction of Theory and Practice* (New York: Crane, Russak, 1981), pp. 21–38.

40. Peter H. Vigor, *Soviet Blitzkrieg Theory* (New York: St. Martin's Press, 1983).

41. See John Erickson, "The Soviet Military System: Doctrine, Technology and Style," in John Erickson and E. J. Feuchtwanger, eds., *Soviet Military Power and Performance* (Hamden, Conn.: Archon Books, 1979), pp. 18–44.

42. William T. Lee, "Soviet Nuclear Targeting Strategy," ch. 4 in Ball and Richelson, eds., *Strategic Nuclear Targeting*, pp. 84–108.

43. Benjamin S. Lambeth, "On Thresholds in Soviet Military Thought," in William J. Taylor, Jr., et al., eds., *Strategic Responses to Conflict in the 1980s* (Washington, D.C.: Center for Strategic and International Studies, 1983), pp. 347–365.

44. Colin S. Gray, *Nuclear Strategy and National Style*, vol. I (Croton-on-Hudson, N.Y.: Hudson Institute, 1981); and *Nuclear Strategy and National Style* (Lanham, Md.: Hamilton Press/Abt Books, 1986).

45. Gary L. Guertner, "Strategic Vulnerability of a Multinational State: Deterring the Soviet Union," *Political Science Quarterly*, Summer 1981, pp. 209–223; John M. Weinstein, "All Features Grate and Stall: Soviet Strategic Vulnerabilities and the Future of Deterrence," ch. 2 in Robert Kennedy and John M. Weinstein, eds., *The Defense of the West* (Boulder, Colo.: Westview Press, 1984), pp. 39–76.

46. Normal Stone, "The Historical Background of the Red Army," in Erickson and Feuchtwanger, eds., *Soviet Military Power and Performance*, pp. 3–17.

47. Harriet Fast Scott and William F. Scott, *The Soviet Control Structure: Ca-*

*pabilities for Wartime Survival* (New York: Crane, Russak/National Strategy Information Center, 1983).

48. For differing views, see Robert P. Berman and John C. Baker, *Soviet Strategic Forces: Responses and Requirements* (Washington, D.C.: Brookings Institution, 1982), p. 36; Fritz W. Ermarth, "Contrasts in American Soviet Strategic Thought," ch. 3 in Derek Leebaert, ed., *Soviet Military Thinking* (London: Allen and Unwin, 1981), pp. 50–69, esp. p. 66; Bracken, *The Command and Control of Nuclear Forces*, pp. 41–48; and Stephen M. Meyer, "Soviet Perspectives on the Paths to Nuclear War," ch. 7 in Allison et al., eds., *Hawks, Doves and Owls*, esp. pp. 178–180. There is apparent consensus among U.S. experts that the Soviets expect to have strategic warning of U.S. plans for attack growing out of escalation from conventional war or directly from a superpower crisis.

49. Raymond L. Garthoff contends that the Soviet emphasis on preemption during the 1950s diminished by the latter 1960s, replaced by increased emphasis upon capabilities for launch on warning or under attack. See Garthoff, "BMD and East-West Relations," in Ashton B. Carter and David N. Schwartz, eds., *Ballistic Missile Defense* (Washington, D.C.: Brookings Institution, 1984), pp. 275–329, esp. pp. 309–310.

50. That this applies to nuclear wars as well as other wars is asserted in B. Byely et al., *Marxism-Leninism on War and Army* (Moscow: Progress Publishers, 1972), translated and published by the U.S. Air Force.

51. See, for example, U.S. Congress, Office of Technology Assessment, *The Effects of Nuclear War* (Washington, D.C.: U.S. Government Printing Office, 1979); and U.S. Arms Control and Disarmament Agency, *An Analysis of Civil Defense in Nuclear War* (Washington, D.C.: ACDA, December 1978).

52. Louis Rene Beres, *Mimicking Sisyphus: America's Countervailing Nuclear Strategy* (Lexington, Mass.: Lexington Books, 1983), p. 20.

53. U.S. Congress, Congressional Budget Office, *Retaliatory Issues for the U.S. Strategic Nuclear Forces* (Washington, D.C.: U.S. Government Printing Office, June 1978).

54. Postattack communications will be improved by several programs implemented during the 1980s, including the Ground Wave Emergency Network (GWEN), designed to survive the initial stages of nuclear conflict. Eventual full operational capability would include 300 nodes distributed throughout the United States. See Walter Pincus, "President's Command Jet Shifted Inland," *Washington Post*, September 23, 1983. The postattack reliability of this and other strategic communications systems is doubtful: see Blair, *Strategic Command and Control*, ch. 6, pp. 182–211. According to Blair, "A strategy designed to inflict as much damage as possible to U.S. C3I poses a much greater threat to U.S. second strike capabilities than does a strategy designed to inflict maximum damage to the U.S. force structure" (p. 208).

55. See U.S. Congress, Office of Technology Assessment, *Ballistic Missile Defense Technologies* (Washington, D.C.: U.S. Government Printing Office, September 1985).

56. For the Reagan administration view of BMD policy implications, see Department of Defense, *Defense Against Ballistic Missiles: An Assessment of Technologies and Policy Implications* (Washington, D.C.: Department of Defense, April 1984).

57. U.S. Congress, Office of Technology Assessment, *Anti-Satellite Weapons,*

*Countermeasures, and Arms Control* (Washington, D.C.: U.S. Government Printing Office, September 1985).

58. Soviet warning systems are described in Stephen M. Meyer, "Soviet Nuclear Operations," *Signal*, December 1986, pp. 41–56. The Soviet ASAT is depicted in U.S. Department of Defense, *Soviet Military Power: 1986* (Washington, D.C.: U.S. Government Printing Office, March 1986), p. 48.

59. According to the Office of Technology Assessment, the Soviet co-orbital ASAT interceptor may be capable of attacking satellites at altitudes of up to 5,000 kilometers (depending upon orbital inclination of the target). See OTA, *Anti-Satellite Weapons*, p. 5. For estimates of Soviet ASAT shots required to disable categories of U.S. target satellites, see Paul B. Stares, *Space and National Security* (Washington, D.C.: Brookings Institution, 1987), p. 94, and his comparable estimates for the U.S. ALMV (air-launched miniature vehicle) ASAT against plausible Soviet satellite target sets (p. 108).

60. For a discussion of this, see Ashton B. Carter, "Assessing Command System Vulnerability," ch. 17 in Carter, Steinbruner, and Zraket, eds., *Managing Nuclear Operations*, pp. 555–610, esp. pp. 561–573.

# 5

# The Soviet View of War Termination

The Soviets' view of war termination cannot be inferred from any single source or military exercise. Their historical behavior is perhaps more useful, although it occurred before the nuclear age and deductions must therefore be qualified. Nor is the Soviet view of war termination similar to the Western one, if the U.S. deterrence literature is taken to be representative of the Western view (on some issues this can be done without serious cost, but not on others). The Soviet perspective on war termination is as simple, and as complicated, as the Soviet view of war. Of paramount importance for understanding their perspective, the Soviets are aware that wars can result in military defeat and deposition of the regime in power, which happened to their immediate predecessors in World War I and almost happened to them in World War II.

The Soviets use "control" or "troop control" to include all those things that must be done to enable forces to accomplish their missions in wartime.[1] Generically this includes not only the technical apparatus for monitoring subordinates and for communicating orders to them. It also includes an understanding of the qualitative factors that influence leadership, the intangibles attendant to the motivation of combat forces, and the friction attendant to the unfolding of any war plans under battlefield conditions.[2] Thus the Western notion of control is a kind of systematic auditing or a systems analysis, whereas the Soviets' concept includes cultural and psychological components that are deeply rooted in their history and experiences. Above all else, the personal and professional memories of Soviet experience in the Great Patriotic War are ever present testimony to their commitment that war shall never again push the regime near the breaking point, nor the society near disintegration. Of secondary importance to World War II, but nonetheless memorable to students of Soviet history, the czarist regime crumbled during World War I after its war effort faltered and its armed forces rebelled.

Therefore, the issue of control in the Soviet Union begins with the control by the Communist Party of the Soviet Union over its armed forces in peacetime and in war. According to *The Officer's Handbook*:

The undivided leadership of the Armed Forces by the Party and its Central Committee is the objective law of their life and combat activities. This law is determined by the role which our Party plays in the life of Soviet society, as its leading and guiding force.[3]

The connection between the Communist Party and the armed forces affirms the theoretical connection between war and politics that is explained with the following emphasis:

War is inseparably linked with the political system out of which it grows. Politics engenders war. War is politics throughout, its continuation and implementation by violent means.[4]

Wars are evaluated by their political content, that is, in terms of the class interest on whose behalf they are being waged. Wars "in defense of the socialist Fatherland" are the most important and call for "a combination of the political, economic, military, moral, scientific and technical and other factors which determine the defense capacity and security of our own state and other socialist countries."[5]

Soviet military doctrine "determines the means, ways, and methods of ensuring the reliable defense of the Soviet Socialist State from imperialist aggression" by incorporating the nature of future warfare, methods of waging armed combat, and the preparedness of the armed forces and Soviet people to defeat any aggressor. Military doctrine has two aspects: political, concerned with the political evaluation of the military tasks of the state, and technical, which "determines the military-technical tasks of the armed forces, and the means, methods and forms of armed combat."[6]

These relationships between war and politics, on the one hand, and between the military-technical and the sociopolitical aspects of Soviet military doctrine, on the other, are not coincidental. They are formative even in the case of nuclear war. According to the authors of *Marxism-Leninism on War and Army*:

Marxist-Leninist methodology makes it possible to solve the question of the interrelation between politics and armed force in the possible nuclear war in a consistently scientific way. As regards its essence, such a war would also be a continuation of the politics of classes and states by violent means.[7]

Thus, apolitical wars are inconceivable, in the sense that all wars, and especially nuclear war, would have a political cause. This does not mean that any particular war would be politically sensible, that is, that it would advance Soviet aims as the leadership defined them. The Soviet leadership is very much aware that a U.S. or NATO nuclear attack on their homeland would create unprecedented societal destruction and jeopardize the stability of the regime. Thus Marxist-Leninist writers can at one and the same time aver that nuclear war is "the heaviest crime that could be committed against humanity" and task their armed forces to win such a war if it is imposed upon them.[8] The military-technical impact of nuclear weapons on combat operations and their control is acknowledged as revolutionary, even as the political character of imperialist wars is defined as immutable. According to Gen. Lt. I. G. Zav'yalov, writing in the Soviet military publication *Red Star (Krasnaya zvezda)*:

As a result of the influence of nuclear weapons, whole subdivisions, units and even formations can lose their combat capacity within a few minutes. Large territories will become useless for immediate continuation of the operation. Combat actions along many axes will become isolated and local in nature, *troop control will be interrupted*, and because of the break in the originally outlined plans for combat actions, *new decisions* will have to be made within *restricted time limits*.[9] (Emphasis added.)

Thus the devastation that nuclear weapons may do is not the primary concern of the Soviet commander, although collateral damage injurious to his own mission is unwelcome. More dissuading to him is the possible loss of control and the need to improvise decisions under stress, decisions that higher commanders might not approve and that the lower commander might not have practiced making. In addition, nuclear weapons have the potential to disrupt the entire linkage among the components of military art as perceived by the Soviets: strategy, operational art, and tactics. Nuclear weapons provide for the simultaneous accomplishment of strategic, operational, and tactical tasks.[10]

These military-technical implications of the risks for Soviet forces engaged in nuclear combat are not acknowledged at the cost of creating artificial barriers between conventional and nuclear weapons when properly employed. Many important principles of military art, in the Soviet view, apply to both conventional and nuclear war, including those principles of troop control. Admitting that new conventional and nuclear weapons make high demands on troop control, an authoritative Soviet writer explains as follows:

To control troops flexibly and effectively means to stay constantly informed about a sharply and rapidly changing situation, to foresee opportunities for switching from one mode of operation to another, to constantly maintain in readiness and bring into action at the proper moment those forces and equipment which can appropriately influence the course of events, and at the proper moment to make the necessary changes in established plans and relay these to the troops.[11]

Soviet commanders at the front (army group) and army levels may have the flexibility to improvise within the theater-strategic plan of the General Staff. But it is unlikely that this improvisation will be encouraged much lower on the ladder. Division commanders will have very specific orders about when and how they are to accomplish their missions. Deviation from the prescribed game plan poses a threat to a professional career, unless the deviation proves to have been successful after the fact. This may be a risk that Soviet unit and subunit commanders are willing to run in wartime, but they are almost certain not to take risks with their careers in military exercises.

There is also the problem for the USSR that its operational strategy for war in Europe is supposedly dependent upon marshaling numerous divisions from the western military districts of the Soviet Union. These are to join the battle near the forward line of troops that meanwhile has, according to Soviet expectations, been pushed somewhere into the midsection of the Federal Republic of Germany. However, those divisions from the Carpathian and Belorussian military districts of the USSR will be moving into aggressive air interdiction and other NATO onslaughts that are targeted against Warsaw Pact forces and command, control, and communications (C3) targets (or C3I with the additional component of intelligence). Unless the Soviet control system works very well and proves to be superior even to the German system that launched the blitzkrieg against France in 1940, it will have its work cut out to push its first-echelon forces into NATO's rear while giving sanctuary to its reinforcing divisions held farther back. In order to do this, the USSR must have a system that is reconnaissance pulled for its forward divisions and one that is command pushed for its rearward ones. The Soviet system will be more command pushed than reconnaissance pulled across the board, unlike the German panzers (although not all German divisions in World War II). A command-pushed system may have difficulty sustaining the flow of reserve divisions into the engagements that will take on the character of a helter-skelter battle throughout Germany. Of course, this problem of a rapidly changing template will also affect NATO C3, which has the added encumbrance of adjusting to a multinational corps structure with less than complete interoperability.

Much depends upon how much effective warning NATO gets and what NATO chooses to do with it. Effective warning means that NATO must respond within the decision cycle of the Warsaw Pact if the latter is weighing actual aggression in the balance. The most difficult case of the USSR would be one in which Soviet officials concluded (by whatever process) that there was a strong chance of NATO attack, although not a certainty of it. Soviet planners would be weighing the risk of preemption against the potential cost of not preempting. NATO would be deciding whether its intelligence and warning indicators had yet crossed the threshold of response, and if so, what kind of response would deter the Warsaw Pact from any premeditated aggression. Both sides would weigh the implications of protecting their C3, including commanders and communications. From the Soviet perspective, a faster and more decisive attack might allow them to maintain troop control, whereas a protracted conflict could dissolve it. Loss of control at the unit and subunit levels could then "trickle upward" into the truncation of the chain of political and military command theaterwide. The effects could range, in the Soviet view, from the simple loss of effectiveness to the worst case scenario, in which troop control breaks into a mobocracy of revolt.

## THRESHOLDS, ESCALATION CONTROL AND SOVIET C3

U.S. commentators misattribute to the Soviet Union perspectives that may not be transferable from one strategic culture to another.[12] Soviet awareness of Western theories of escalation control is not the same as endorsement of them. Hopeful proponents of controlled war fighting, conventional or nuclear, in Europe can draw upon a variety of Soviet and U.S. liturgical statements to support their views. Prominent Soviet writers can be cited as optimistic or pessimistic about the possibility of observing limitations on escalation once war has begun.

Despite their dissimilarities, NATO and Soviet concepts of escalation can be compared in order to derive insights about the expectations each might hold once war began. NATO strategy calls for direct defense with conventional forces; deliberate escalation to the use of theater nuclear weapons if conventional defenses cannot hold; and, ultimately, employment of U.S. strategic forces. Implicit in this strategy, adopted in 1967 as MC–14/3, is the assumption that NATO will field conventional forces adequate to avoid early first use of nuclear weapons. In fact, NATO has fallen short of this requirement. NATO's supreme allied commander, Gen. Bernard Rogers, has urged that NATO improve its conventional forces by having members increase their expenditures by an average of 4 percent in real terms (discounting for inflation) over the next decade.[13] This objective is unlikely to be met.

NATO's deficiencies in conventional forces create an expectation of early first use of nuclear weapons by the West. Concern that this expectation is self-defeating for NATO has been expressed by prominent former policymakers and strategists, including former U.S. Secretary of Defense Robert McNamara.[14] In his book *Blundering into Disaster*, McNamara endorses the recommendations of the prestigious European Security Study to improve NATO conventional defenses for four principal missions: blunting the initial Soviet/Warsaw Pact attack; eroding the attackers' air power; interdicting the follow-on forces and other reinforcements that the Pact would need to sustain an attack on Europe; and disrupting Soviet/Pact C3.[15] These deficiencies in NATO conventional forces relative to their plausible missions are all the more regrettable, according to U.S. analysis, because the USSR is now showing more apparent interest in a conventional phase during war in Europe, than formerly.[16]

Also implicit in NATO flexible response strategy is the assumption that U.S. strategic nuclear forces must be capable of dissuading the Soviet Union from initiating theater or strategic nuclear conflict if its conventional war plan is negated. This is not commonly understood, or acknowledged, by some writers whose understandable fears of strategic nuclear war have led to a diminution of the roles of strategic forces compared with other forces. The coupling of U.S. strategic nuclear forces to NATO theater nuclear and conventional forces is an intentional, and not coincidental, attribute of NATO strategy. It is not an unfortunate necessity that can be circumvented by improved conventional or theater nuclear forces. Quite the contrary; U.S. strategic nuclear forces must be highly competent relative to Soviet strategic forces, whatever the balance of forces in the European theater. Some advocates of the "572" deployments by NATO of Pershing II and ground-launched cruise missiles talked as if some balance of NATO and Soviet Eurostrategic forces, once attained, could substitute for any uncertainties about the employment of U.S. strategic forces. There is in fact no self-sufficient balance of theater forces that can be evaluated apart from the credibility of U.S. strategic nuclear forces. What will deter the Soviet Union from escalation to the level of operational-tactical (front level) or operational-strategic (theater of operations) is not only the expectation that it will be on the losing end of a regional firepower exchange, but also the expectation that the exchange will escalate to the use of U.S. strategic forces against targets in Europe and the Soviet homeland. Thus theater nuclear forces, however much they may be improved, are, like conventional forces, not a substitute for more credible U.S. strategic forces if Soviet first use, and subsequent nuclear escalation, is to be deterred.

The above argument has important implications, from the Soviet perspective. There is some evidence in Soviet writing and exercises that they might be willing to distinguish among tactical, operational-tactical, and operational-strategic nuclear employment.[17] The Soviets might recognize a threshold between operational-tactical and operational-strategic uses of nuclear weapons. In the former case, delivery means including SS–22 and SS–23 surface-to-surface missiles and frontal aviation that could deliver nuclear strikes against NATO surface-to-surface missiles, nuclear storage sites, and nuclear-capable aircraft, in addition to NATO air defenses, corps C31, and operational reserves. Operational-strategic employment of nuclear weapons would use intermediate-range and strategic ballistic missiles and long-range aviation against a variety of military and command targets, including NATO theater C31 headquarters.

On the other hand, Soviet ability or willingness to distinguish between theater-strategic nuclear war and intercontinental or global war would be very doubtful. So-called limited nuclear attacks by the Soviets, for example, against 34 U.S. bases that contained most U.S. combat tactical air and the military airlift to transport U.S. ground force divisions to Europe might be incorporated into their Eurostrategic war plan. The attacks, although directed against targets in the continental United States, could be accomplished with ten-kiloton airbursts at each base that minimized prompt fatalities. If the USSR also included 12 additional bases with U.S. ground force divisions, they would have targeted all U.S. general-purpose ground and tactical air forces that could affect the war in Europe for at least one month while keeping collateral damage well below the threshold of massive societal destruction.[18] It might seem obvious by peacetime standards that this was a strategic attack in the sense that it was comparable with a homeland-to-homeland exchange with ICBMs and SLBMs, but in the event, policymakers could decide otherwise, especially if they were Western policymakers with strategic nuclear forces at the best equivalent to those of the USSR.

Another illustration of the difficulty in preserving any distinction between European theater-strategic nuclear warfare and global war is provided by U.S. maritime strategy as promulgated by former Secretary of the Navy John Lehman and uniformed naval officers.[19] U.S. naval general-purpose forces would seek to establish primacy in the Norwegian Sea and to place at risk the survivability of Soviet ballistic missile submarines (SSBNs) in their protected bastions near the Kola Peninsula soon after conventional war had broken out in Europe. The Navy argues that progressive attrition of Soviet SSBNs during forward operations into Soviet-controlled waters will raise the perceived costs of escalation for the USSR and induce it to consider war termination on terms more favorable to NATO. According to Adm. James D. Watkins, then chief of naval operations:

The Soviets place great weight on the nuclear correlation of forces, even during the time before nuclear weapons have been used. Maritime forces can influence that correlation, both by destroying Soviet ballistic missile submarines and by

improving our own nuclear posture, through deployment of carriers and Tomahawk platforms around the periphery of the Soviet Union.[20]

The advisability of this strategy from an operational standpoint is not
at issue here, although others have judged it negatively.[21] The present
context is to note that these operations, if successfully carried out, would
create fewer incentives for a Soviet distinction, if NATO is counting on
one, between operational-strategic (theater-strategic) and intercontinental warfare, nuclear or otherwise.

The example of U.S. maritime strategy does raise another point, and
it has to do with the kinds of escalation that advocates of improved
conventional forces might substitute for the vertical escalation inherent
in nuclear weapons. The first alternative is horizontal escalation, the
extension of war in Europe to theaters of operation outside Europe.
The second is temporal escalation, the effort to prolong the war until
one side's resources have exhausted or stalemated the other. The third
is what we might call surprise escalation, in which unexpected operational and tactical maneuvers are converted into strategic and politically
decisive results. An example is the Nazi attack against France in 1940.

Horizontal escalation to theaters of operation outside of Europe is a
strategy that is not totally under the control of NATO for its successful
execution. Entry by the People's Republic of China into a NATO-Warsaw
Pact conflict would open a second front that might dissuade the USSR
from continuing the war in Europe; but, short of that, it is difficult to
construct a war-widening sequence that is unilaterally favorable to the
West (unless irrelevant to the outcome in Europe—for example, attacking Soviet client states in the Third World). The U.S. maritime strategy
offers a variant of horizontal escalation only if NATO can protect its
sea-lanes of communication between Europe and North America long
enough for strikes on the Soviet periphery to pay dividends, and provided that NATO ground and tactical air forces on the Central Front
are not summarily defeated.[22]

Temporal escalation is turning a conventional war in Europe into a
protracted war of attrition in order to stalemate Soviet advances and
then to terminate the conflict before NATO is required to use nuclear
weapons.[23] There are several problems with this alternative, which appears superficially attractive when static indexes comparing the economic
performances of the United States and its OECD allies, including Japan,
are compared with the Soviet Union and its allies. First, a protracted
conventional war under contemporary conditions, without the introduction by either side of nuclear weapons, is not likely to repeat the
experience of World War II by continuing for four years. Given reasonable projections about rates of personnel loss, rates of ammunition

consumption, and other expenditure rates in modern high-intensity combat, a period of three to four months would be a long war in Europe. Under those conditions, it is not at all obvious that the Soviet Union would be faced with sustainable inferiority.[24] Several years is of course a different matter, but a continuation of coalition warfare between the two alliances, under present conditions, for several years seems highly improbable, although protracted conventional war of uncertain duration is not excluded in Soviet discussions of wartime possibilities.[25] A second problem with the protracted war scenario, from the Western standpoint, is that it allows time for allied political consensus to disintegrate as the fear of nuclear escalation hangs over the battlefield and over efforts to negotiate an acceptable peace. A third difficulty is that an extended conventional war, if it successfully threatened the cohesion of the Soviet glacis in Eastern Europe, would almost certainly prompt Soviet use of theater nuclear weapons to break the stalemate in Western Europe.

A third option for either side that would, in theory, avoid vertical escalation is the option of surprise as to the kind of attack launched or the timing and character of the attack. The Soviet Union, for example, might attack from a standing start with its divisions in the Group of Soviet Forces Germany in a slash-and-grab thrust into NATO's operational depth, preparing the way for encirclement of NATO forward defenses.[26] As counterpoint, an unexpected and potentially decisive NATO use of conventional forces, according to Samuel Huntington, might be a conventional retaliatory offensive into Eastern Europe simultaneous with a Soviet conventional attack against Western Europe.[27] Each of these options, while appealing conceptually to expert analysts, has practical problems of implementation. In each instance, the Soviet blitzkrieg or the NATO conventional retaliation would be operating with a very thin margin of force structure relative to its probable success.[28] Intelligence misestimates or tactical contretemps could leave forward-moving forces isolated, and then destroyed. Moreover, each of these operationally daring approaches requires that real-time C3 operate with maximum effectiveness, while that of the opponent is seriously disrupted.

It seems fair to suppose, in view of the preceding discussion, that the problem of nuclear escalation cannot be avoided by NATO, and it is not obvious that it should be. NATO cannot go too far in the direction of making conventional warfare credible without lowering the threshold between no war and any war, which is far more meaningful than the thresholds separating kinds of war in Europe.[29] If the problem of nuclear escalation cannot be avoided by conventional deterrence and defense exclusive of probable nuclear use, then the other option is not nuclear avoidance but nuclear transcendence.

### Strategic Defense

If nuclear avoidance is not possible, nuclear transcendence is thought by some to be another plausible path to stable deterrence. A U.S. Strategic Defense Initiative (SDI) or Soviet research and development efforts might lead to nonnuclear defenses that could limit the damage from nuclear offenses and ultimately, make those offenses irrelevant. This vision was held out by President Reagan in his March 23, 1983, speech and is now institutionalized in the SDI Office in the Pentagon. We will not go into all the pros and cons of SDI here; a large literature has already accumulated. The present discussion will simply note some of the C3 issues attendant to moving from a world dominated by strategic offensive forces to one in which defenses are preeminent, if such an evolution can be brought about.

The first issue is that the problem of C3 for strategic defenses, U.S. and Soviet, cannot be disaggregated from the C3 requirements for strategic forces as a whole. In the foreseeable future, even if defensive technologies prove to be viable, they will be deployed alongside offenses, not in place of them. A mixed force of offenses and defenses will require subtle C3 arrangements for connecting national command authorities, force commanders, and command posts with the retaliatory forces.[30] Thus the problem of C3 software as discussed by software experts may make the task seem overly difficult technically, and insufficiently complicated from the perspective of group decision making. Providing the appropriate users with the information that they need, at the time they need it, and in a form useful to them will be more taxing to designers than writing millions of lines of computer code.

Second, the technologies that make possible credible U.S. or Soviet ballistic missiles defenses may be tasked to put those defenses at risk. The deployment of space-based kinetic kill vehicles as boost-phase defenses could work to the advantage of the attacker, instead of the defender, if the attacker used the same technology to suppress the defenses. And the prospect of defense suppression will be even more appealing if directed-energy weapons, such as lasers or particle beams, can be deployed in space and made invulnerable to attack from the ground. One can imagine two sides with space-based defenses that are also very competent antisatellite weapons, each capable of suppressing the other's defenses against ballistic missiles. Soviet doctrine, which has always held that offenses and defenses work together, will be less surprised than U.S. proponents of defenses, who find that defensive technologies have contributed to the possible success of an offensive strategy. This expectation by the USSR is evident in the statements of Soviet leaders in opposition to SDI as an alleged component of a U.S. credible first-strike capability.

Therefore, the primary importance of active and passive defenses, whatever they contribute to damage limitation, is what they contribute to deterrence. One issue pertinent to C3I in this regard, which requires more extended discussion, is whether U.S. SDI or NATO theater ballistic missile defenses could help to protect command centers and other potentially vulnerable targets, and thus reduce the temptation for early countercommand attacks at the theater or strategic (intercontinental) level. One of the unfortunate incentives for Soviet nuclear escalation in Europe is the possibility that theater-based C3 relevant to strategic deterrence would be destroyed much more easily by nuclear weapons than by conventional weapons, although both NATO and the Soviet Union are considering deep attack weapons of greater range and lethality.[31]

Third, U.S. strategic defenses could contribute to stability under some conditions by making retaliatory forces and supporting command systems less vulnerable to Soviet preemption. There is little doubt that U.S. ICBMs based in fixed silos will have to be launched under attack (if in fact they can be) in order to survive preemptive attack.[32] In addition, the perceived U.S. necessity for this operational capability, however far down it is thought to be on the preferred policy menu, raises the Soviet expectation that it will have to do likewise with its most capable and modern land-based missiles. Apparently the USSR is already prepared for preemption, launch under attack, or retaliation as a mode of operation for its ICBM forces, which constitute about two-thirds of its force loadings but approximately 80 percent of its ready inventory.[33]

The Soviet Union is already deploying mobile land-based strategic missiles, and the United States may follow suit with the Midgetman small ICBM in the 1990s or with 50 MX deployed in a rail mobile (rail garrison) configuration even sooner. Mobile land-based missiles would presumably add to ICBM survivability compared with fixed ICBMs, although there might be offsetting strategic and economic costs. The U.S. Midgetman was approved for full-scale development in December 1986 on the assumption that it will be a single-warhead missile with hard-target accuracy, although Congress allowed its weight to reach 37,000 pounds in order to accommodate penetration aids against future Soviet defenses, if needed.[34] Single-warhead missiles are not as attractive as targets compared with MIRV missiles, so the arithmetic of preemption looks less favorable to the prospective attacker and better to the defender. Soviet attackers would have to use megatonnage adequate to barrage likely Midgetman deployment areas, which could be quite substantial with even tactical warning; strategic warning would create an almost impossible problem of dispersal for prospective targeters. It is also not inconceivable that the small ICBMs could be defended with mobile or fixed terminal or terminal/midcourse defenses.[35] Midgetman will present new command and control problems, however, with enlargement of its dispersal area to include U.S. roads outside military reservations.

### Postattack Command and Control

In the worst case, outbreak of a U.S.-Soviet strategic nuclear war, the survival of commanders and the fidelity of the command structure will be as important as, or more important than, the survivability of forces themselves. "Fidelity" means that the command system must do more than survive incidental or deliberate physical attack on itself. Subsequent to attack it must perform with sufficient flexibility and continuity so that the United States is not forced to choose between gross retaliatory options or none. This point has been misunderstood by both "hawks" and "doves" in the strategic debate, so it merits expansion.

The first issue is crisis stability. If either side anticipates that its central political command will be destroyed early in war, then it has a strong incentive to preempt, and to preempt against the central political command of the opponent. However, that central command is not only a fixed physical entity. It is also a complex organism that may survive dedicated attack with unpredictable and pathological behavior. U.S. experts disagree as to whether the Soviet Union would deliberately attempt to suppress the U.S. national command authorities and highest military leadership if it felt war was unavoidable. It seems safe to assume that the U.S. leadership will not be deliberately spared from the collateral damage attendant to Soviet attacks against military and war-related economic targets. Soviet as well as U.S. planners could reason that U.S. leadership left intact with much of its country destroyed would have a significant incentive to settle for peace, compared with an uncertain or presumptuous leadership.[36]

However, the issue may not be drawn as neatly as this. The fear of command suppression will begin to be more realistic, on either side, after conventional war has begun and C3 based in the theater is attenuated. If the sharp operational end of theater C3 is gradually being disrupted deliberately or coincidentally, the expectation of more disruption to follow creates a serious pressure for escalation. For the Soviet Union, attempting to estimate the rate at which deterioration of C3 will become a strategic, as opposed to a tactical, problem, the concept of critical time for a mission related to control time for execution of authorized commands becomes very important. The USSR might, for example, react to survivability-enhancing deployments of Pershing II and ground-launched cruise missiles by nuclear preemption, especially if short-range nuclear forces had already been used and the "fog of war" made estimates very brittle.[37]

The second problem is delegation of authority. During a nuclear crisis, the United States wants to be certain that an authoritative Soviet leadership, in full control of its military forces and command system, correctly interprets U.S. signals and messages. If conventional war erupted in Europe, or elsewhere, involving direct conflict between U.S. and Soviet forces, the authenticity and cohesion of Soviet leadership would be an asset to NATO, not a liability. A succession crisis within the Politburo during a superpower confrontation might contribute to uncertain decision making in the USSR that the United States, under duress, interpreted as stonewalling while preparing to attack. Nikita Khrushchev's two very different messages to President Kennedy during the Cuban missile crisis offer indirect evidence that the Politburo was not of a consensual mind about how to handle the crisis once U.S. resolve to have the missiles removed became apparent. Although the U.S. president did present consistent positions in his communications to the USSR, the crisis management in the White House did not take into account important U.S. naval standard operating procedures, including those relevant to establishing the blockade line and to trailing Soviet submarines in Caribbean, Atlantic, and Pacific waters.[38] The U.S. situation illustrates something important about any large military command system, including the Soviet one. Delegation of authority is a misleading focus for understanding how the system may actually operate. Authority is a legal concept implying written delegation of plenary power downward from the top to the lower echelons of a hierarchy.

In command systems, as in other technologically complex and tightly coupled organizations, delegation of authority is less the issue than is effective assumption of the initiative by subordinates when the alternative is to suffer de facto loss of mission competence.[39] Command systems and commanders will not just drop dead, literally or figuratively. They will adapt to existing conditions to the best of their ability. Thus a proper understanding of the U.S. command system, and seemingly the Soviet system as well, is that delegation of competence will take place regardless of the arrangements that have been made for delegation of authority. Of course, one could argue, on the basis of Soviet World War II experience and the initial successes of the Nazi invasion of June 1941, that the Soviet Union might have more difficulty delegating authority and competence than would the United States or its NATO allies.

However, the Soviet World War III approaches cannot necessarily be projected from Soviet World War II experiences, since none of Stalin's successors has had a comparably tenacious grip on the system. The vulnerability of the USSR in June 1941 may attest to the weakness rather than the strength of centralized control, but despite his misestimates of Hitler's intentions, Stalin rapidly recovered his bearings and the command system adapted remarkably well over the long haul. Nuclear weapons might not give the Soviet command system the same latitude for mistakes in the future, however, which argues for U.S. sensitivity to the possibility of Soviet preemption in a crisis that appears to be escaping control. In the worst case for either superpower, theater commanders in chief who might be isolated from their national command authorities will strike back with an improvised and disaggregated war plan. Such a retaliation, however discombobulated it is, under present conditions would at least guarantee widespread societal destruction.

A third issue is the role of intelligence relative to ascertaining opponents' intentions and capabilities before and during war. The United States may now be correcting an unfortunate tendency of the past: to rely on the presumed infallibility of technical collection at the expense of intelligence derived from human sources.[40] According to Ernest R. May, prior to World War I the major powers made generally accurate estimates of one another's intentions ("proclivities") but failed to assess accurately their capabilities. Between World Wars I and II, the situation was reversed, with capabilities being more or less successfully estimated, but intentions not.[41] Of course, major intelligence services, given their scope and tasking, are bound to make both kinds of errors in the course of doing their jobs, and we are likely to know more about errors than successes on the basis of published literature.[42] Estimating is not a science but an art form that incorporates scientific inference and plain hunches, not to mention an element of luck.

On the edge of superpower confrontation, important information about the intentions of one side will be important to the other in the short term. Capabilities do not change rapidly relative to the gross size and flexibility of U.S. and Soviet arsenals. Therefore, erroneous estimates will be in predicting intent, not capacity. There is a subtle danger here of inferring intentions from capabilities. Although conventional wisdom might suggest that U.S. war plans and force acquisition ought to be based on worst case estimates, in the middle of an actual crisis a U.S. president would not want to exclude other than worst case assumptions. Kennedy's management of the Cuban missile crisis shows how this willingness to include hopeful alternatives in the decision maker's calculus can work to the benefit of war avoidance while still accomplishing policy objectives. Beginning with the blockade and leaving open the option of escalation, Kennedy allowed Khrushchev the option of not forcing the confrontation onto a more dangerous and crisis-unstable path. Moreover, the U.S. president also sought to provide the Soviet premier with a face-saving exit that would preclude the personal humiliation of Khrushchev as well as the national humiliation of the USSR.[43] This slow squeeze on the USSR while holding on to U.S. political demands allowed for Soviet misestimates of U.S. intentions that might have provoked war, had the United States in its initial response to the discovery of the missiles launched an invasion of Cuba or an air strike against the island.

Related to this concern is the problem of strategic deception, or *mas-kirovka*, as the Soviets call it. Soviet *maskirovka* is a multidimensional concept that includes both active deception and passive measures, such as camouflage and concealment.[44] The United States can expect that Soviet peacetime and wartime intelligence activities will include measures to deceive opponents about their intentions and capabilities, which are not as transparent as Western fetishists of technical collection might assume. Some very important things about the Soviet force structure, in terms of the ways in which it would operate following a Soviet decision that war was likely, are not known with high confidence by Western assessors. The USSR apparently has never placed its strategic nuclear forces on highest alert.[45]

The Soviet approach to deception is judged to be very different from the U.S. perspective, as the Soviet approach borrows from Pavlovian psychology, cybernetics, and Marxist philosophy. According to Roger Beaumont, "In any case, the Soviets have examined many aspects of command and control on much deeper and broader levels than has been the case in the West."[46] According to Donald C. Daniel and Katherine L. Herbig, the German effort to deceive the Soviet Union about the plans for Operation Barbarossa prior to the invasion of June 1941 il-lustrates the "M-type" deception, which focuses the attention of the tar-get on one wrong alternative. This is in distinction to the "A-type" deception, in which ambiguity is created to introduce confusion into the decision-making process of the target and thus preclude its focusing on the correct answer.[47]

Soviet military operations in World War II employed both types of deception noted by Daniel and Herbig. Operational planning for Soviet counterattacks at Stalingrad and the planning of the Belorussian cam-paign included considerable attention to *maskirovka*. Operation Uranus for the defense of Stalingrad was planned by marshals Zhukov and Vasilevskiy from September through November of 1942. This operation had to be prepared very carefully, in order to mask the counterattack that would follow successful defense of the inner city. Security was so tight that Soviet Army group commanders Rokossovskiy and Yeremenko were not informed of plans until the middle of October, when army groups were ordered to go on the defensive to deceive German intelli-gence. While visible efforts were directed toward the construction of defenses, the Soviets built up huge reserves 200 miles from Stalingrad and moved reinforcements only at night, under strict radio silence.[48] Another Soviet operational deception, Mars, was scheduled in case the Germans removed forces from their Army Group Center to support the attack on Stalingrad.[49]

The successful Soviet operational deceptions also hold lessons that are less obvious. They were made possible by a larger context in which the "victim" made self-defeating strategic and political errors of omission and commission. The Germans, for example, did not have to get several armies committed to the Stalingrad pocket; the capture of Stalingrad came to have more symbolic than operational or strategic significance. The inner city house-to-house (if not cellar-to-cellar) fighting was an art form in which the Russians excelled, and the costs paid by the Nazis were considerable. This is not the first occasion, nor undoubtedly the last, in which the capture of salient points on a map becomes an end in itself for commanders whose operational objectives are confounded by strategic confusion.

The larger issue in this regard, of course, was Hitler's willingness to engage in a two-front war with the USSR and its Western allies simultaneously, a high policy misjudgment that resulted in part from German underestimation of Soviet substainability for protracted conflict. The essential German misjudgment in this regard was not as is commonly supposed, an underestimation of Soviet reserve divisions and capabilities for industrial reconstitution, although that certainly occurred. The most important German misestimate was the assumption that Soviet strategic command and control would be unable to recover following early and spectacular operational victories by the Germans in the western USSR. This assumption was not so unreasonable, given the Nazis' experience with the French in 1940. The French were not militarily defeated so much as they were militarily disoriented and then politically discouraged. Nazi blitzkrieg operations fell not only upon defenders who were poorly prepared operationally but also upon French politicians whose repertoire included no alternative to conciliation. German operations created the potential for strategic political victory against the French, but French governmental fatalism and defeatism provided the coup de grace.

The collapse of the French command system in 1940, in contrast with the revival and eventual triumph of the Soviet system in 1945, carries significance beyond the illustrations of operational deception and Soviet interest in *maskirovka*. The greatest deceptions are self-deceptions. Deception is a component of surprise. Surprise includes deception and other measures to do the unexpected in implausible ways. The paradox of surprise is that the more improbable it is, the higher the payoff if it occurs.[50] Thus it may turn out that under some conditions of desperation or anticipation, a strategic nuclear surprise might take place despite the commonly held notion that nuclear war is irrational and self-defeating (this is discussed more fully in an earlier chapter). Paradoxically, the expectation that nuclear war is self-defeating may lead to vulnerability to strategic nuclear surprise. Strategic nuclear surprise would be most surprising if it were to remove key elements of the adversary's command system in the earliest stages of war. Undoubtedly, Soviet planners of strategic nuclear surprise would reckon against the obstacles to success, which are indeed formidable.[51] If we assume, however, that nuclear surprise might occur out of the "gray" instead of the "blue" after an alerted U.S. force was removed from alert, then it becomes somewhat less inconceivable, although not any less risky. Most analysts would agree that the risks under normal peacetime conditions are so awesome that only foolish leaders would risk nuclear suicide. During superpower crises, however, foolishness will appear to be wise to policymakers who fear preemption or loss of control.[52]

## STRATEGY, POLITICS, AND THE OFFENSIVE

The discussion of surprise leads naturally to the concern in the West about Soviet emphasis upon the offensive in operational and strategic writing. However, two different genres of Soviet discussion must be kept distinct. As Condelezza Rice explained it:

The tension between political activity and the military offensive has remained largely unresolved since Frunze. Modern-day Soviet strategy attempts to make a distinction between military-political doctrine, which is supreme and essentially defensive, and military-technical doctrine (similar to strategy), which upholds the primacy of the offensive and the need for surprise and initiative. This is a distinction that fails to remove the confusion, and the Soviets themselves elaborate no further.[53]

The distinction between military-political and military-technical doctrine might, in Western terminology, be better described as the difference between sociopolitical and operational modes of analysis, since both are so manifest in the work of Clausewitz and other noted Western strategists.[54] Western readers exposed to heavy doses of the "sociology of knowledge" literature will have some (limited) appreciation of the weltanschauung from which Marxism derives its categorical imperatives. The state must, as an essential matter, be prepared for war by anticipating the kinds of enemies it will have to fight and the character of the class nature of war causation. This last point is obscure to many Western readers, who assume that the distinction between bourgeoisie and proletariat is obsolete in the modern welfare state and/or that the Soviets no longer really believe in it. However, Soviet sociopolitical doctrine (military-political as above) is based upon the notion that wars are caused by the international class struggle. This class struggle has ontological significance in Marxist thought. In their view, its long-term implication is that no single conflict can eradicate the threat that imperialism and capitalism represent to the survival of Soviet socialism. This has serious implications for the Soviet distinction between military-political and military-technical thought as that distinction applies to nuclear war between the capitalist and socialist blocs. Raymond L. Garthoff noted, with regard to the development of Soviet military doctrine in the 1970s:

In its political, or war versus peace, policy dimension, military doctrine was thus moving *away* from the question of waging war to place greater stress on preventing war, although its military-technical or war-fighting component continued to emphasize preparedness to wage war decisively, and with a particular accent on offensive operations and on being prepared to wage all-out warfare if nuclear war should come.[55]

As reluctant cobelligerents in World War II, the Soviets are well aware of the costs of a major war, especially if they are forced to engage in it with underprepared command systems. Stalin's incapacity in the early days of Barbarossa is now legendary, but more important for Soviet field armies were the early and catastrophic operational losses sustained by their forces, which were poorly deployed and trained for the expected conflict. Soviet lack of preparation for the events of June 22, 1941, reflected in part the dramatic purges of the high command in 1937–1938 for reasons that are still not altogether clear.[56] If the "down" side of the Great Patriotic War for the USSR was its early defeats, the "up" side can be found in its adaptation under stress to the requirements for protracted war: sustainability and endurance. The major achievement of the USSR in World War II came not in the finesse demonstrated in military operations, although important and successful improvisation did take place, but in the capacity to mobilize the entire society and economy for war.[57]

For obvious reasons based upon the same experience, Soviet military leaders have decided that if they are charged with the responsibility to go to war by their political leadership, then surprise, boldness, and an offensive operational cast pay large dividends. This tenor in Soviet military scholarship has been apparent since the publication of an important work by A. A. Sidorenko.[58] Recent Western analysts make fewer references to Sidorenko because of his emphasis on the role of nuclear weapons in Soviet offensive theater operations. Contemporary U.S. analysis suggests that Soviet operational art now emphasizes a preferred model of theater-strategic conventional warfare with the escalation to nuclear use avoided if possible.[59] Part of the difficulty in estimating Soviet "operational" approaches from a Blue-views-Red perspective is that Blue is apt to define "operational" in at least three different senses. First, "operational" is a perspective on the conduct of actual campaigns, as opposed to the logistical or societal perspective.[60] Second, "operational" refers, in Western writing about "operational art," to campaigns from theater level down to division.[61] Third, "operational" represents a way of thinking about the conduct of theater-level campaigns, and in particular, about the command systems and its role in the success or failure of military operations.[62]

This third usage of the concept of "operational" can be applied to the

development of Soviet military thought by Triandifilov and Tukhach-
evsky, among others, about deep operations, based on their understandings of the World War I experience and on their contacts with Germans
during the postwar period.[63] It seems apparent that Soviet geography—
vast steppes, long borders, and the potential for encirclement by military
opponents—suggested an interest in operations of high speed and great
depth. Indeed, once they recovered their bearings and began to take
the offensive in World War II, the Soviets demonstrated, very much
against doctrinal expectations between 1938 and 1940, that they were
capable of conducting operations with unprecedented mass *and* mobility.
Study of the Russian Civil War had suggested to some Soviet analysts a
forecast of things to come. As Lt. Col. David M. Glantz indicated:

The concept of mobile operations on a broad front in great depth, the rapid
redeployment of forces over wide expanses of territory, the use of shock groups
for creating penetrations and the widespread use of cavalry forces as "mobile
groups" exploiting offensive success were all legacies of the civil war.[64]

Improvisation was made necessary by the requirement for the Workers' and Peasants' Red Army, created by decree in January 1918, to
adapt to the requirements of civil war and the expectation of continuing
external intervention in the revolution. Soviet military historians note
the conduct of fast-moving "meeting engagements."[65] Compulsory military service was introduced in 1918, against the earlier expectation that
the armed forces could be staffed by volunteers. Commanders, who were
from the "revolutionary strata of the proletariat and the soldier masses,"
however politically qualified, lacked "sufficient knowledge and experience and were not able to organize combat action and direct troops as
they should."[66] Former czarist military officers who were willing to serve
the new regime were called upon to provide professional leadership.

Superimposed upon this Soviet understanding of their unique historical experience has been the age of military automation and its attendant
high technology. For the Soviet Union, this influences expectations about
troop control in several ways. Future conventional military operations
that the Red Army may be required to carry out will take place at unprecedented speed and over great distances. Therefore, the Soviet emphasis on top-down command systems for the efficient carrying out of
a superior commander's operational-strategic concept must be combined
with allowance for tactical flexibility in maneuver battalions and divisions.
The United States has a difficult time doing this, and the requirement
for the Soviet Union to combine fixity and flexibility into one game plan
will be even more stressful.[67] However, according to U.S. Department
of Defense analysts John G. Hines and Phillip A. Petersen, the USSR is
now improving its operational-strategic command system by creating

high commands of forces for a theater-strategic military action (TSMA), of which the Western TSMA, commanded by Marshal N. V. Ogarkov, is an example.[68] These operational-strategic (or theater-strategic, in Western terminology) commands would direct many fronts simultaneously on behalf of the Soviet Headquarters, Supreme High Command.

This characteristically Soviet solution to the potential problem of expanding scope and speed of modern warfare may look better in peacetime than it performs in wartime. In contrast, the apparent Western disarray in NATO at the echelons above corps level may perform better than peacetime expectations would dictate. The Soviet creation of more inclusive command orbits with higher bureaucratic apogees does not necessarily yield a better fidelity in control of operations in the field. If the U.S. experience in smaller wars with regard to the operational reach of strategic command levels is any precedent, there is some substantial risk of overinvolvement by politico-military "sergeants" to the detriment of success in battle.[69] U.S. theater commanders in chief who might be tempted to disconnect their telephones would share grievances with Soviet commanders past and present who would prefer to see their political commissars disappear into a time warp. Here, too, one must make allowances for the fact that once war in Europe has broken out, the United States and its NATO allies would not be fearing a succession crisis, whereas it is not inconceivable that a leadership crisis could bedevil the USSR just at the time, especially if divisions existed within the Politburo and party leadership about the desirability of war.[70]

## WAR TERMINATION

We have reviewed Soviet doctrine and experience generally, with some emphasis upon its implications for individual components of war termination. But what of the overall picture? Does it make sense for us to conceive of the Soviet Union fighting a limited nuclear war in Europe or a limited global strategic war that it would then agree to terminate? We have seen that Soviet historical behavior has been adaptive to circumstances, and in some cases far more successfully adaptive than Western observers would have predicted. We have also noted that Soviet military doctrine is multifaceted with notable distinctions between its politico-military and military-technical aspects.

The above considerations, however, are arguably too technical for a complete grasp of the probable Soviet view of war termination. Consider first the political setting. The Soviet Union, from its perspective, is surrounded by class enemies. The two operative terms here are "class" and "enemy." Neither finds a comfortable niche in U.S. political discourse, and in Europe the references to a class are very bourgeois-ified (including those by self-described Marxians). By "class enemy" the USSR means that the international capitalist class acts more or less cohesively, and sometimes even conspiratorially, against the interests of the Soviet state. This might be considered a gloomy forecast, but it comes up against the self-confidence that the Kremlin exudes about the survival and growth of its own system. Western readers will gulp at this point and say that they have understood the Soviet system to be falling apart; that is why Mr. Gorbachev is insisting upon its "reform." This diagnosis of the Soviet system is misplaced Western conceit, and does no justice to Mr. Gorbachev.

Mr. Gorbachev is the personification of a collective leadership in a mature authoritarian state.[71] Cults of personality and adventurism of the kind demonstrated by the ebullient Mr. Khrushchev are passé as artifacts of another era. In that era, the socialist revolution in Europe was, from the Soviet perspective, still being consolidated against plausible threats from the West. The USSR has now surmounted these threats and has consolidated its basic political glacis in Eastern Europe; Polish up-risings in the early 1980s do not alter this. In various accords between East and West during the 1970s, the issue of legitimacy of Soviet rule over Eastern Europe and Western allied rights to permanent access to Berlin were settled permanently, from the Soviet standpoint. Mr. Gorbachev no longer has to defend the basic legitimation of his contiguous empire on the world stage. He is now defining the distance between the contiguous empire in Eastern Europe and its farther reaches, and this produces more disagreement within the Soviet elite (and therefore outside the USSR, among Soviet experts in other countries).

The misdiagnosis that the Soviet Union is on the verge of collapse politically or economically was articulated by various administration spokesmen during Reagan's first term. It was therefore judged appropriate to put pressure on the Soviet Union on all fronts, including military, diplomatic, and information policy. That Reagan's second term presided over a turnabout in these policies is testimony to the misplaced emphasis and aberrant judgments in the first instance. Presidential rhetoric aside, the administration behaved pragmatically toward the USSR in general, but its expectation that outside pressure might stress the Soviet system, because of that system's inherent weaknesses, to the point of collapse was folly in pursuit of myth. This was all part and parcel of the Reagan entourage's assault against the doctrine of containment as originally formulated by George F. Kennan, and with which U.S. neoconservatives have never been fully comfortable.[72] The Reagan approach to the Third World and the effort to support revolutionary movements against entrenchment leftist regimes there was derived in part from this anticontainment doctrine, which found its way into the higher echelons of Reagan's advisers.[73] These efforts were not necessarily misguided; they needed to be judged on a case-by-case basis. The point here is a different one: the assumption that ubiquitous U.S. sponsored insurgency would turn the tables on the Kremlin and not only contain it, but also roll it back to pre–1980, or perhaps pre–1970, dimensions.

However, one difficulty with any such assertive policy of anti-Soviet rollback, as the Kremlin leadership well knows, is that it is likely to go away with the next U.S. election. Certainly no continuity can be expected in any strand of U.S. policy beyond two presidential elections. This is the domestic political difficulty with it. Another difficulty is its assumption, as just noted, that the Soviet Union is besieged with internal economic and social weaknesses, near to toppling over with the help of aggressive U.S. prodding. If we reject that assumption in favor of one that recognizes the stability and continuity of the Soviet regime, instead of its imagined desperation, we are better prepared to recognize the implications for it of U.S. and other "class enemies."

One implication is that the status of Soviet class enemies is a categorical one. The very existence of capitalism as a social form is objectionable. Détente and cordial relations between individual leaders will not change this. This categorical status has both reassuring and discouraging implications for U.S. leaders, once the status is properly understood. The reassuring aspect is that a categorical enemy is not necessarily a provocative one. The Soviet Union does not need to fight a war against its class enemies in order to achieve its long-term objectives. Better that capitalism should sink through its own incompetence.

The second and less reassuring implication of the categorical nature of Western class enemies is that there is no such thing, from the Soviet standpoint, as a permanent plateau of political stability. After all, the Soviets are Marxists at least in name, and history was the midwife of social change for Marx, Lenin, and their philosophical progeny. Conflict and change are inevitable in human affairs, including the international politics of states. Wars on behalf of socially "progressive" revolutions are just wars, as opposed to the unjust wars that might be waged against socialism by capitalism, and especially those that might be waged against Soviet socialism.[74]

It follows from all this that the capitalists will attempt on occasion to trick the USSR into fighting wars that would turn out to be disadvantageous from its perspective. Therefore such wars should be avoided, and general nuclear wars are certainly at the head of this list. Otherwise, the capitalists may compensate for their domestic economic and political failures by their "imperialism" abroad, at the expense of the Soviet Union and its fraternal allies. It is difficult for Western analysts to take sincerely the Soviet framework of analysis just summarized, which posits that the Soviets are threatened by attack from without against the citadel of scientific socialism they have worked so hard to build. But this is just the image that their ideology presents of capitalist societies; and from the Soviet perspective, democratic capitalism is no different in this regard from more authoritarian regimes with the same economic base. Both threaten the Soviet Union by their very existence, and not only because they provide competition for the allegiance of people and for the ownership of factors of production. Either democratic or authoritarian capitalist regimes might stumble into war against the Soviet Union in the mistaken impression that the USSR lacked either the will or the capability for self-defense.

So the Soviet leadership will probably do everything possible to avoid a major war with the West, especially a war on disadvantageous conditions. If war cannot be avoided, this sociopolitical aspect of doctrine takes a back seat to the military-technical side. This latter emphasizes that if war cannot be avoided, it is the duty of the Soviet armed forces to prosecute that war, consistent with directives from national leadership, toward victory.[75] But the large nuclear arsenals of the superpowers complicate this simple equation. If those nuclear weapons are used on too large a scale, the will be self-defeating for either, or both, sides. If they are used on too small a scale, they may not be effective.

Once a war had started in Europe, would the Soviet Union recognize a threshold between few theater nuclear weapons and many? Or would the more meaningful dividing line lie between use of nuclear weapons outside Soviet borders and their use inside? Some U.S. officials have in the past expressed confidence that U.S. strategic nuclear forces could be launched against the USSR in selective strikes. This presumably would induce the Soviet Union to seek early war termination instead of responding by escalation of the conflict into all-out war. According to former Secretary of Defense James R. Schlesinger, control of escalation after strategic war began would be possible if the United States would

... maintain continued communications with the Soviet leadership during the war, and [would] describe precisely and meticulously the limited nature of our actions, including the desire to avoid attacking their urban industrial base.[76]

This "Schlesinger doctrine" was the first in a series of revisions in declaratory and operational strategy for U.S. strategic nuclear forces. And this approach of graduated escalation without precluding war termination has remained in the U.S. nuclear war plans to the present day. However, it is more convincing as a semantic exercise than as an operational reality. There are two basic problems in its execution. First, it requires a U.S. command system that is as fine-tuned as the list of options is elongated. Second, it requires Soviet cooperation, in the form of limiting nuclear war while fighting it.

Taking the first of these, the U.S. command system for nuclear war is a sprawling congeries of bureaucratic organizations, technologies, individual personalities, and institutional historical memories. There is no entity that can be drawn on a map to correspond to the "command system" in the same way that one can map ICBM silos or bomber bases. Thus, the results of attacks against the command system are not easily predicted on the basis of simple projections from its peacetime status. The command system might be eroded or destroyed in pieces, as we have seen, subject to the "fog of war" and disconnection of its disparate parts from the center. Consider the case of the U.S. nuclear command system, which might seem to be subject to early and prompt destruction by a small number of well-placed nuclear weapons in a surprise first strike against key command centers, communications links, and space- and ground-based warning and assessment infrastructure.[77] However, cautious Soviet planners could not count on inflicting maximum destruction with a minimum number of weapons. To be sure of destroying the most important parts of the U.S. command system in order to preclude effective U.S. retaliation against their forces and society, they would have to use thousands of reentry vehicles in order to compensate for uncertainties, including the problem that some elements of the U.S. (and Soviet) C3 system are virtually untargetable.[78]

As to the second issue, that of Soviet cooperation in targeting restraint and nuclear war termination, there are several dimensions. The first is Soviet willingness, and the second is Soviet capacity, to control escalation while fighting, and to do that over a short or extended period, for as long as necessary. A stronger case can be made for the second proposition than for the first. Willingness to negotiate during nuclear war would be prompted by the near certainty of bleaker alternatives: the USSR might fear that escalation to a higher level of exchanges would result in its defeat. So might the United States, in a nuclear war; and after the first exchanges of nuclear weapons, both sides might be probing for a way out. Skirmishing might go on among the superpowers' conventional forces and those of their allies even after a nuclear cease-fire had been reached. Or a nuclear cease-fire might be arranged for U.S. and Soviet homelands while conventional and nuclear war continued in Europe. It is easy to dismiss these possibilities in peacetime, when both superpowers can reassure their allies, without fear of challenge, that they will provide an all-or-nothing solidarity in the case of actual war. However, when war has begun and the superpowers have time to choose between regional and global devastation, it is not illogical for them to choose regional. Europeans are rightly concerned about this possibility, and so have prompted tight coupling of U.S. strategic nuclear forces with nuclear and conventional forces based in Europe (of which, more in a later chapter).

Could the Soviets' cooperation, even if it seemed preferable to them from a logical standpoint of minimizing their losses, be obtained? If superpower homelands had been struck, some means would have to be established for surviving national leaderships to communicate. The "hot line" between U.S. and Soviet leaders is not designed to withstand the rigors of nuclear war; it is a crisis management tool to prevent war. One important issue would be the cohesion or dissent within the Soviet leadership after nuclear war began. The Soviet Union has found the problem of political succession sufficiently difficult to handle in peacetime. The stress of nuclear war might well topple the political leadership that had failed to avoid it and to allow the armed forces sufficient time to prepare for it, at least in the judgment of the professional military.[79] During the Cuban missile crisis Khrushchev and/or Soviet leaders sent one message on October 26 that seemed to offer withdrawal of the Soviet missiles from Cuba, on the basis of a U.S. pledge not to invade Cuba. The next day, a second Kremlin message contradicted the implied contents of the first, stating that the USSR would require the withdrawal of U.S. Jupiter missiles from Turkey in order to obtain Soviet removal of MRBMs and IRBMs from Cuba.[80]

If the Soviet leadership remained cohesive under the stress of war and if nuclear attacks did not extend into the Soviet homeland, the scenario of limited nuclear war followed by war termination becomes slightly more believable, from their perspective. But only slightly, because even limited nuclear war would devastate parts of Eastern Europe, and the fallout would certainly appear in the western USSR. Nuclear exchanges between NATO and the Warsaw Pact might be confined to NATO territory, in which case the USSR might be more interested in dampening down the conflict but NATO still thirsting for escalation. NATO conventional strategy for war in Europe presupposes deep attacks against Soviet second echelons and other reinforcements very soon after war begins. This would mean air and missile attacks up to several hundred kilometers behind the forward line of troops. Based upon improved sensors, data fusion centers, and precision guided munitions, this conventional war subconcept intends to isolate Soviet reinforcements from their forward attacking echelons, and so stall the USSR war machine into a stalemate.[81]

Although NATO does not now field the technology to implement the deep attack concepts in their entirety, it will certainly have increased its considerable deep-strike capabilities by the mid–1990s, and even war remaining below the nuclear threshold will promise very heavy costs to Soviet invaders, if not outright defeat. If so, they may be the first to use nuclear weapons, if war is felt to be inevitable and if they are very concerned to attain their objectives quickly and decisively. The Soviets might conclude that their own strategic nuclear forces would deter U.S. escalation into homeland exchanges, and that the first decisive use of nuclear forces based in Europe would therefore provide them a position from which they could bargain with strength.

Soviet decision making has a certain opacity in the best of times, and under the stress of nuclear crisis or war, even more so, for Western observers. As Stephen Meyer has noted, the Soviet decision-making process is likely to vary considerably from peacetime, to crisis, to actual war.[82] A war that suddenly strikes the USSR as a "bolt from the blue" will not allow much time to improvise a response tailored to the nuances of the situation. The Soviets will be responding with prepared strike plans and a minimum of time for decision making. At the other extreme, once engaged in war, especially nuclear war, they will probably follow their World War II precedent, in which war-waging authority was concentrated in the State Defense Committee and Headquarters, Supreme High Command, at whose behest the general staff devised war plans.[83]

An extended crisis, say over Cuba or Berlin, could be more unpredictable in terms of Soviet decision making and response than a sudden disruption of peace that left little time for internal power struggles. However, Soviet planners apparently expect to have strategic warning of enemy intentions well in advance of any surprise attack; fewer of their retaliatory forces are in highly responsive states of readiness compared with U.S. strategic nuclear forces. No students of General Ivanov could forget the importance of the initial period of the war, and no Soviets who lived through June 1941 can do so. But the following observation by a noted student of Soviet military affairs is also pertinent here:

There is a dangerous asymmetry in East-West perceptions on this score. Many Western military analysts seem obsessed with the *politics* of the nuclear balance and focus on how the war might *begin*. Soviet military strategists formulate their plans with a steady eye on how the war might *end*.[84]

Withal, it would be optimistic for Western planners to assume that any particular scenario is more than speculative. A Soviet willingness to play by the rules of constrained nuclear war fighting presupposes their recognition of an agreed battle as discussed in Chapter 1. It also presupposes the presence of the other principal components of the concept of war termination: an interest in escalation control and in the use of coercive diplomacy toward some objective more limited than victory. Some Western planners have apparently assumed that in the event of actual war, the Soviet Union would quickly discover the logic of Western self-limitation or reciprocal targeting restraint. How the Soviets read Western intentions after nuclear war or conventional war in Europe has actually begun is almost entirely conjectural. Their military doctrine and experience do not suggest optimism about controlling any war, let alone nuclear war, that involves their forces in Europe and their East European allies, whose territories form a buffer between them and NATO Europe. Perhaps a reading of the Soviet preference hierarchy in the abstract, notwithstanding scenario dependency, would be first try to avoid war, especially nuclear war; if unavoidable, then try to win it, or not to lose it, as rapidly and decisively as possible; then, if it cannot be avoided, won, or stalemated, try to end it.

## NOTES

1. Soviet concepts of command and control are explained in John Hemsley, *Soviet Troop Control* (Oxford: Brassey's Publishers Ltd., 1982), ch. 1.

2. According to Clausewitz: "Everything in war is very simple, but the simplest thing is difficult. The difficulties accumulate and end by producing a kind of friction that is inconceivable unless one has experienced war." Carl von Clausewitz, *On War*, edited and translated by Michael Howard and Peter Paret with commentary by Bernard Brodie (Princeton: Princeton University Press, 1976), bk. I, ch. 7, p. 119.

3. Gen. Maj. S. N. Kozlov, *The Officer's Handbook*, translated by the DGIS Multilingual Section, Translation Bureau, Secretary of State Department, Ottawa, Canada (Moscow: 1971), p. 13. Published under the auspices of the U.S. Air Force.

4. Ibid., p. 41.

5. Ibid., p. 43.

6. Ibid., p. 62.

7. B. Byely et al., *Marxism-Leninism on War and Army* (Moscow: Progress Publishers, 1973), p. 28.

8. Ibid., p. 30.

9. Gen. Lt. I. G. Zav'yalov, "The New Weapon and Military Art," *Krasnaya zvezda*, October 30, 1970, repr. in *Selected Soviet Military Writings 1970–75* (Washington, U.S. Government Printing Office, n.d.), 206–213. See p. 209.

10. Ibid.

11. Ibid., p. 210. On Soviet military doctrine, see John J. Dziak, *Soviet Perceptions of Military Power: The Interaction of Theory and Practice* (New York: Crane, Russak, 1981), ch. III.

12. Colin S. Gray, *Nuclear Strategy and National Style* (Lanham, Md.: Hamilton Press, 1986), ch. 3, pp. 65–96.

13 Stanley R. Sloan, *NATO's Future: Toward a New Transatlantic Bargain* (Washington, D.C.: National Defense University Press, 1985), p. 141.

14. McGeorge Bundy, George F. Kennan, Robert S. McNamara, and Gerard Smith, "Nuclear Weapons and the Atlantic Alliance," *Foreign Affairs*, Spring 1982, pp. 753–768. See also Robert S. McNamara, *Blundering into Disaster* (New York: Pantheon Books, 1986).

15. McNamara, *Blundering into Disaster*, p. 120. See also *Strengthening Conventional Defenses in Europe: Proposals for the 1980s*, report of the European Security Study (New York: St. Martin's Press, 1983).

16. John G. Hines, Phillip A. Petersen, and Notra Trulock III, "Soviet Military Theory from 1945–2000: Implications for NATO," *Washington Quarterly* 9, no.

4 (Fall 1986): 117–137. Counterarguments to the argument that the Soviets are more interested in preserving conventional nuclear thresholds are noted in Joseph D. Douglass, Jr., and Amoretta M. Hoeber, *Conventional War and Escalation: The Soviet View* (New York: National Strategy Information Center/Crane, Russak, 1981).

17.  Paul K. Davis and Peter J. E. Stan, *Concepts and Models of Escalation* (Santa Monica, Calif.: Rand Corporation, 1984), pp. 26–27.

18.  Albert Wohlstetter and Richard Brody, "Continuing Control as a Requirement for Deterring," ch. 5 in Ashton B. Carter, John D. Steinbruner, and Charles A. Zraket, eds., *Managing Nuclear Operations*, (Washington, D.C.: Brookings Institution, 1987), p. 162.

19.  John F. Lehman, Jr., "The 600 Ship Navy," and Adm. James D. Watkins, USN, "The Maritime Strategy," *Proceedings of the U.S. Naval Institute*, January 1986, pp. 30–40 and 2–17, respectively.

20.  Watkins, "The Maritime Strategy," p. 14.

21.  On inadvertent war, see Barry R. Posen, "Inadvertent Nuclear War? Escalation and NATO's Northern Flank," in Steven E. Miller, ed., *Strategy and Nuclear Deterrence* (Princeton: Princeton University Press, 1984), pp. 85–112; and Paul Bracken, "Accidental Nuclear War," ch. 2 in Graham T. Allison, Albert Carnesale, and Joseph S. Nye, Jr., eds., *Hawks, Doves and Owls* (New York: W. W. Norton, 1985).

22.  John J. Mearsheimer, "A Strategic Misstep: The Maritime Strategy and Deterrence in Europe," *International Security* 11, no. 2 (Fall 1986): 3–57.

23.  John J. Mearsheimer, *Conventional Deterrence* (Ithaca, N.Y.: Cornell University Press, 1983), ch. 6, pp. 165–188.

24.  On the sustainability of NATO and the Warsaw Pact under standard mobilization scenarios, see William P. Mako, *U.S. Ground Forces and the Defense of Central Europe* (Washington, D.C.: Brookings Institution, 1983).

25.  See James M. McConnell, *The Soviet Shift in Emphasis from Nuclear to Conventional*, CRC 490, vol. II (Washington, D.C.: Center for Naval Analyses, June 1983).

26.  Peter H. Vigor, *Soviet Blitzkrieg Theory* (New York: St. Martin's Press, 1983), ch. 14, pp. 183–205.

27.  Samuel P. Huntington, "The Renewal of Strategy," ch. 1 in Samuel P. Huntington, ed., *The Strategic Imperative* (Cambridge, Mass.: Ballinger, 1982), pp. 1–52.

28.  Keith A. Dunn and William O. Staudenmaier, "A NATO Conventional Retaliatory Strategy: Its Strategic and Force Structure Implications," ch. 9 in Dunn and Staudenmaier, eds., *Military Strategy in Transition: Defense and Deterrence in the 1980s* (Boulder, Colo.: Westview Press, 1984), pp. 187–212.

29.  Benjamin S. Lambeth, "On Thresholds in Soviet Military Thought," in William J. Taylor, Jr., Steven A. Maaranen, and Gerrit W. Gong, eds., *Strategic Responses to Conflict in the 1980s* (Washington, D.C.: Center for Strategic and International Studies/Los Alamos National Laboratory, 1983), pp. 347–365.

30.  On C3 issues attendant to SDI, see Theodore Jarvis, "Nuclear Operations and Strategic Defense," ch. 20 in Carter, Steinbruner, and Zraket, eds., *Managing Nuclear Operations*, pp. 661–678; and Stephen J. Cimbala, "Artificial Intelligence

and SDI: Corollaries or Compatriots?" ch. 11 in Cimbala, ed., *Artificial Intelligence and National Security* (Lexington, Mass.: Lexington Books, 1987), pp. 203–214.

31. Wohlstetter and Brody, "Continuing Control as a Requirement for Deterring," p. 181.

32. Difficulties inherent in launching ICBMs under attack are discussed in Ashton B. Carter, "Assessing Command System Vulnerability," ch. 17 in Carter, Steinbruner, and Zraket, eds., *Managing Nuclear Operations*, pp. 578–582, esp. p. 580. See also Office of Technology Assessment, *MX Missile Basing* (Washington, D.C.: U.S. Government Printing Office, September 1981), ch. 4; and John Steinbruner, "Launch Under Attack," *Scientific American* 250 (January 1984): 37–47.

33. Stephen M. Meyer, "Soviet Nuclear Operations," *Signal*, December 1986, pp. 41–60.

34. See Blair Stewart, "Technology Impacts on ICBM Modernization: Hard Mobile Launchers and Deep Basing," in Barry Schneider, Colin S. Gray, and Keith B. Payne, eds., *Missiles for the Nineties* (Boulder, Colo.: Westview Press, 1984), pp. 29–41.

35. Near-term ballistic missile defense options are discussed in William A. Davis, Jr., *Asymmetries in U.S. and Soviet Strategic Defense Programs: Implications for Near-Term American Deployment Options* (Cambridge, Mass.: Institute for Foreign Policy Analysis, 1986).

36. On the problem of ambiguous command, see Paul Bracken, *The Command and Control of Nuclear Forces* (New Haven: Yale University Press, 1983), pp. 224–232.

37. Soviet writers have proposed three generic measures for assessment of control efficiency: critical time, control time, and performance time. Critical time is the time within which the mission must be completed to be successful. Control time is the time required by the decision cycle from intelligence gathering to the transmission of authenticated orders. Performance time is the time required to complete tasks once orders have been received. For an application to Soviet theater nuclear forces, see Stephen M. Meyer, *Soviet Theater Nuclear Forces, Part II: Capabilities and Implications*, Adelphi Papers no. 188 (London: International Institute for Strategic Studies, Winter 1983–1984) pp. 37–38.

38. Graham T. Allison, *Essence of Decision* (Boston: Little, Brown, 1971), p. 138.

39. On the concept of coupling in organizations, see Charles Perrow, *Normal Accidents* (New York: Basic Books, 1984), esp. ch. 3.

40. For illustrative evidence, see Adm. Stansfield Turner, *Secrecy and Democracy: The CIA in Transition* (Boston: Houghton Mifflin, 1985).

41. Ernest R. May, "Conclusions: Capabilities and Proclivities," in Ernest R. May, ed., *Knowing One's Enemies* (Princeton: Princeton University Press, 1984), pp. 503–542.

42. Christopher Andrew, *Her Majesty's Secret Service: The Making of the British Intelligence Community* (New York: Viking Books, 1986).

43. The importance of giving Khrushchev a way out in Cuba is stressed in Allison, *Essence of Decision*, pp. 223–228. The ExComm or special presidential

crisis management team had already decided that the U.S. response to a shooting down of a single U–2 intelligence aircraft by Soviet surface-to-air missiles (SAMs) based in Cuba would be to destroy the SAM site. If a second U–2 were downed, the United States would destroy all the sites; the Air Force had prepared plans for these contingencies. In the event, President Kennedy demurred, to allow more time for negotiations to succeed.

44. The *Dictionary of Basic Military Terms* defines *maskirovka* as a "form of support for combat operations, its purpose being to conceal the activities and disposition of friendly troops, and to mislead the enemy with regard to the grouping and intentions of such troops." *Dictionary of Basic Military Terms* (Moscow: Voyenizdat, 1975), translated and published under the auspices of the U.S. Air Force (Washington, D.C.: U.S. Government Printing Office, n.d.) p. 118.

45. Among the Soviet strategic nuclear forces, only ICBMs are thought to be maintained at day-to-day levels of readiness allowing prompt response to surprise attack. ICBMs that could be readied for launch on tactical warning or launch under attack within several minutes account for 80 percent of their ICBM launchers, and 95 percent of their ICBM warheads. About 20 percent of Soviet ballistic missile submarines are on station at any one time, and another 20 percent in port could contribute to launch under attack if they survived. Apparently no Soviet strategic bombers are maintained on air or ground alert. Hence Soviet prompt response is heavily dependent upon ICBMs, which include about 90 percent of the warheads available on day-to-day alert. See Meyer, "Soviet Nuclear Operations," in Carter, Steinbruner, and Zraket, eds., *Managing Nuclear Operations*, p. 494. The Soviet SS–18 Mod 4 force deployed in 1986 was estimated by the Pentagon to have the capability to destroy 65 to 80 percent of U.S. ICBM silos while retaining 1,000 unexpended SS–18 warheads for subsequent attacks. See U.S. Department of Defense, *Soviet Military Power: 1986* (Washington, D.C.: U.S. Government Printing Office, March 1986), p. 25.

46. Roger Beaumont, *The Nerves of War: Emerging Issues in and References to Command and Control* (Washington, D.C.: AFCEA International Press, 1986), p. 52.

47. Donald C. Daniel and Katherine L. Herbig, eds., *Strategic Military Deception* (New York: Pergamon Press, 1981), ch. 1, pp. 5–6.

48. For elaboration of these points, see Earl F. Ziemke, "Stalingrad and Belorussia: Soviet Deception in World War II," in Daniel and Herbig, eds. *Strategic Military Deception*, ch. 11, pp. 243–276, esp. pp. 247–254. Soviet operations in Manchuria also provide illustrative material: see Lt. Col. David M. Glantz, *August Storm: The Soviet 1945 Strategic Offensive in Manchuria* (Fort Leavenworth, Kan.: U.S. Army Command and General Staff College, February 1983), esp. p. 165.

49. Ziemke, "Stalingrad and Belorussia," pp. 250–251.

50. See Michael I. Handel, *Perception, Deception and Surprise: The Case of the Yom Kippur War* (Jerusalem: Hebrew University, 1976).

51. Benjamin S. Lambeth, "Uncertainties for the Soviet War Planner," *International Security* 7, no. 3 (Winter 1982–1983): 139–166.

52. On the limitations of deterrence as understood from the standpoint of rationality theories, see Patrick M. Morgan, *Deterrence: A Conceptual Analysis*, 2nd ed. (Beverly Hills, Calif.: Sage, 1983), esp. 4, pp. 79–102.

53. Condolezza Rice, "The Making of Soviet Strategy," ch. 22 in Peter Paret,

ed., *Makers of Modern Strategy* (Princeton: Princeton University Press, 1986), p. 675.

54. Clausewitz, *On War*.

55. Raymond L. Garthoff, *Detente and Confrontation* (Washington, D.C.: Brookings Institution, 1985), p. 780.

56. In 1941 the Soviet general staff planned for advance deployment of their forces in European Russia in five military districts from the Barents Sea to the Black Sea. Three of these were special districts, meaning they were operational groupings that could fight for a limited time period without mobilizing additional reserves. Actual frontier defense was assigned to the NKVD frontier commands, which were not under the operational command and control of the Red Army. Moreover, lack of preparation in signals and communications throughout the Soviet armed forces was notable. See John Erickson, *The Road To Stalingrad* (New York: Harper and Row, 1975), vol. I, pp. 68–73.

57. Rice, "The Making of Soviet Strategy," p. 671.

58. A. A. Sidorenko, *The Offensive* (Moscow: 1970), translated and published by the U.S. Air Force.

59. See Hines, Petersen, and Trulock, "Soviet Military Theory from 1945–2000."

60. My use of the term "perspective" is comparable with Michael Howard's "dimensions" of strategy. See his "The Forgotten Dimensions of Strategy," in *The Causes of Wars* (Cambridge, Mass.: Harvard University Press, 1984), pp. 101–115.

61. On Western usage of the term "operational," see Richard Simpkin, *Race to the Swift* (New York: Brassey's Defence Publishers, 1985), pp. 23–24.

62. John G. Hines and Phillip A. Petersen, "Changing the Soviet System of Control," *International Defense Review* no. 3 (1986): 281–289.

63. Rice, "The Making of Soviet Strategy," pp. 664–665; and Simpkin, *Race to the Swift*, pp. 37–39.

64. David M. Glantz, "Soviet Operational Formation for Battle: A Perspective," in *Selected Readings in Military History: Soviet Military History*, vol. I (Ft. Leavenworth, Kan.: U.S. Army Command and General Staff College, January 1984), pp. 2–12, esp. p. 3.

65. Col. A. Yekimovskiy and Col. A. Tonkikh, "Red Army Tactics in the Civil War," in *Selected Readings in Military History: Soviet Military History*, vol. I, pp. 48–57.

66. Ibid., p. 49.

67. See Hemsley, *Soviet Troop Control*, pp. 169–174, for an excellent discussion of pertinent problems and Soviet approaches. Additional perspective on Soviet approaches can be gleaned from V. V. Druzhinin and D. S. Kontorov, *Concept, Algorithm, Decision* (Moscow: 1972), translated and published under the auspices of the U.S. Air Force. Soviet command system weaknesses are discussed in F. W. von Mellenthin, R. H. S. Stolfi, and E. Sobik, *NATO Under Attack* (Durham, N.C.: Duke University Press, 1984), pp. 75–96, esp. pp. 83–93. According to these authors: "Given the long history of frictions and ambivalence in Soviet military command, it is clear that the Soviet military commander is constrained in his capacity for independent judgment and action to a degree that could be fatal in a high-intensity conventional war" (p. 91).

68. Hines and Petersen, "Changing the Soviet System of Control," passim.

69. Richard A. Gabriel, *Military Incompetence* (New York: Hill and Wang, 1985); and Edward N. Luttwak, *The Pentagon and the Art of War* (New York: Simon and Schuster, 1984), provide numerous illustrations of problematical reach in the U.S. command system.

70. Meyer, "Soviet Nuclear Operations," p. 485, indicates that the problem of succession might be most applicable to a surprise attack on the USSR in peacetime and less applicable to crisis or wartime operations.

71. For an assessment of the USSR as a developed authoritarian system, see Seweryn Bailer, *Stalin's Successors: Leadership, Stability and Change in the Soviet Union* (Cambridge: Cambridge University Press, 1980), esp. p. 145.

72. See the National Defense University symposium volumes edited by Terry L. Diebel and John Lewis Gaddis, *Containment: Concept and Policy* (Washington, D.C.: National Defense University Press, 1986), vols. I and II.

73. See Barry R. Posen and Stephen W. Van Evera, "Reagan Administration Defense Policy: Departure from Containment," ch. 3 in Kenneth A. Oye, Robert J. Lieber, and Donald Rothchild, eds., *Eagle Resurgent? The Reagan Era in American Foreign Policy* (Boston: Little, Brown, 1987), pp. 75–114.

74. Perspective on this is provided in Robert Bathurst, "Two Languages of War," ch. 2 in Derek Leebaert, ed., *Soviet Military Thinking* (London: Allen and Unwin, 1981), pp. 28–49.

75. Byely et al., *Marxism-Leninism on War and Army*, discourses as follows: "The types of wars in our time are determined by the main lines taken by the social struggle. These lines are: the struggle between the two world social systems—socialism and capitalism; the revolutionary struggle of the proletariat against the bourgeoisie; the general democratic struggle of the popular masses against monopoly associations; the national liberation struggle of the peoples against the colonialists; the struggle between capitalist countries for strengthening the positions of monopoly capital. *The main, decisive line of the social struggle is the struggle between socialism and imperialism* (p. 70, emphasis in original).

76. James R. Schlesinger, *U.S.-USSR Strategic Policies*, Senate hearing, p. 13, quoted in Bruce G. Blair, *Strategic Command and Control: Redefining the Nuclear Threat* (Washington, D.C.: Brookings Institution, 1985), p. 221.

77. This is one argument made in Daniel Ford, *The Button: The Pentagon's Strategic Command and Control System* (New York: Simon and Schuster, 1985).

78. Ashton B. Carter, "Assessing Command System Vulnerability," ch. 17 in Carter, Steinbruner, and Zraket, eds. *Managing Nuclear Operations*, pp. 560–573.

79. Meyer, "Soviet Nuclear Operations," p. 485.

80. Allison, *Essence of Decision*, pp. 220–223.

81. Gen. Bernard R. Rogers, "Follow-on Forces Attack (FOFA); Myths and Realities," *NATO Review* 32, no. 6 (December 1984): 1–9.

82. Meyer, "Soviet Nuclear Operations," passim.

83. Harriet Fast Scott and William F. Scott, *The Soviet Control Structure: Capabilities for Wartime Survival* (New York: Crane, Russak/National Strategy Information Center, 1983), ch. 4.

84. Steve F. Kime, "The Soviet View of War," in Graham D. Vernon, ed., *Soviet Perceptions of War and Peace* (Washington, D.C.: National Defense University Press, 1981), ch. 4, p. 58. Emphasis in original.

# 6

# War Termination and Extended Deterrence: U.S. and NATO Options in Europe

The matter of war termination applies to a U.S.-Soviet conflict in Europe at two levels or thresholds. The first of these involves the outbreak of conventional war between NATO and the Warsaw Pact before the first use of nuclear weapons; the second, afterward. One can imagine other thresholds, as some expert analysts have done.[1] However, the difference between war and no war in Europe, and that between no use and first use of nuclear weapons, are probably most significant from the standpoint of war termination. Time will still permit policymakers and military commanders to consider their options, surge their residual forces, and communicate their intentions to their adversaries. After the threshold of nuclear first use is crossed, the situation becomes more uncertain, although an expansion from first use to apocalypse is not guaranteed.[2]

We will take up the subject of war termination as it applies to conflict in Europe in the following order. First, we will discuss the question of military doctrine, of what U.S. and Soviet planners will expect to happen with regard to conflict expansion and war termination after deterrence has failed. Doctrines and expectations with regard to escalation will be of special importance here. Military doctrine deals with expectations. Therefore, a second issue will be the capacities of the two sides, insofar as they are known, to bargain for intrawar deterrence and war termination. Can either side fight a conventional war only, or a limited nuclear war, even if it wants to? Capabilities will be considered under several headings, including vertical command of forces, delegation of authority, and organizational responsiveness to the demands of policymakers.

A third issue, apart from doctrine or capabilities for escalation and war termination, is the possibility of attacks directed specifically at the highest political and military command centers of the superpowers. These kinds of attacks have at least been envisioned in the declaratory doctrines of both sides, and they raise grave issues. It would be naive to suppose that such attacks would not be tempting, and more tempting as the levels of destruction mounted on both sides. On the other hand, countercommand attacks designed to remove the opponent's leadership create fewer incentives, once they are done, to bargain for war termination.

Under these three general questions—of doctrine, capabilities, and countercommand attacks—we will consider the problem of ending war in Europe. The likelihood of war in Europe is judged to be small by experts. For that very reason, a war that began there would be unexpected, and even more unexpected would be the pathways for ending it. Peacetime preparedness for war termination might pay dividends that would be redeemed after deterrence failed for much more than their prematurity values.

## WAR TERMINATION AND MILITARY DOCTRINE

Neither the United States or the Soviet Union has stated a coherent politico-military doctrine of war termination. This applies to both nuclear and conventional wars. Indeed, the Soviet military doctrine hardly admits of the topic as such, as we have noted, whereas U.S. strategists who have written about war termination and its companion, escalation theory, are mostly civilians. The very term "military doctrine" does not have the same meanings for Soviet and U.S. leaders or military professionals.[3] Basically, Soviet military doctrine is the authoritative party-political expression on the nature of future wars, the probable enemies of the Soviet Union in those conflicts, and the responsibilities of the Soviet armed forces (in general) relative to the preservation and security of the state and its leadership.[4] Since the Soviet leadership is both the topmost layer of a bureaucracy and the embodiment of an international cause, its authoritative pronouncements on military doctrine are taken as starting points for debates on military art and science. Military art includes strategy, operational art, and tactics as they are known to Western audiences.[5]

U.S. and NATO military doctrine, on the other hand, reflects the democratic process of consensus building (intranational and international) and the relentless push of technological innovation in U.S. and European societies. Military doctrine as such is normally stated in manuals such as U.S. Army FM 100–5, *Operations*.[6] However, manuals such as this reflect individual service doctrines instead of national perspectives. The closest U.S. analogue to Soviet military doctrine is grand strategy, which combines the geopolitical outlook of the political leadership with some net assessment of the major threats to U.S. security. However, there are important differences between U.S. grand strategy and Soviet military doctrine, and these differences are worth pointing out.

One difference is that Soviet military doctrine is quite precise about who the principal opponents in a war are likely to be, as was noted in an earlier chapter. This is not a hortatory point; no one is claiming that the Kremlin will surge its forces west toward the English Channel within the next week or two. But it does mean that the Soviet Union is not at all in doubt about who represents the major threat to its security, in the judgment of its leadership. In theory, this is the capitalist class writ large. In practice, it is the United States as the leader of the capitalist and imperialist bloc.[7] The capitalist-imperialist bloc of course includes NATO, which performed the unforgivable (although convenient) task of absorbing West Germany into the Western alliance system while leaving the Soviet Union with the economically less desirable German Democratic Republic. This permanent division of Germany into NATO and Soviet halves also meant that the two superpowers would have a joint, tacit interest in keeping Germany divided.

For the West, it seems apparent that the principal challenge to its security lies in Soviet military power. But there is more optimism about changing Soviet intentions in the long run than there is realism on this issue. U.S. doctrine is often written as if the enemy is notional, a hypothetical opponent, although the real opponent is easily enough envisioned. Interest in détente and arms control on the part of U.S. and European publics further sparks resistance to the idea of permanent adversaries. States in conflict with the United States and its allies are thought to be misinformed or in the temporary grip of factions that will be superseded by moderates with whom the West can negotiate.

It is an article of faith in the Western and U.S. view especially that all conflicts are subject to negotiation and compromise. It is simply a matter of finding the specific terms. Therefore, Western negotiators are frequently surprised to find the Soviets more concerned about the political atmospherics and diplomatic fallout of arms control negotiations, for example, than the specific terms that are on the negotiating table at the moment. In the West, negotiation is undertaken after it is assumed that a conflict resolution is desirable in principle. In the Soviets' view of the world historical struggle, they are always fighting while negotiating, although not necessarily fighting with swords. "Peaceful coexistence" for the Soviet Union is not the cessation of conflict or the transformation of hostility into friendship. It is the continuation of conflict under other than military auspices.

Soviet and U.S. expectations about escalation and war termination, with regard to conflict in Europe, are likely to differ considerably. The Soviet Union at first saw little prospect that war between NATO and the

Warsaw Pact could be limited. Until the later 1960s, its authoritative policy pronouncements suggested that any war between the capitalist and socialist coalitions would be a total war and that nuclear weapons would be used early, and without limitation, by both sides in such a conflict. Beginning in the late 1960s and continuing to the present, Soviet policy statements have recognized the possibility that East-West conflicts, including those in Europe, might be less than total.[8] During the 1970s and early 1980s, the Soviet Union's political leaders, including General Secretary Leonid Brezhnev, began to state publicly that mutual deterrence between the superpowers was now operative as a fact of life.[9] This was an important recognition of the SALT I agreements and the ABM Treaty of 1972, which codified the existence of U.S.-Soviet strategic parity in strategic offensive forces. Soviet military leaders, including Marshal N. V. Ogarkov, former chief of the general staff, echoed the statements of political leaders to the effect that nuclear war could never be won by either side and must be avoided if at all possible. At the same time, Soviet spokesmen averred that should war be forced upon them (as they expressed it), they would not hesitate to respond with retaliatory strikes that would defeat the aggressor.[10]

Soviet and Western (U.S. and NATO) notions of escalation are not the same. The NATO doctrine of flexible response emphasizes a proportionate response to aggression by the Warsaw Pact. Faced with conventional attack across the inter-German border, NATO will respond in kind for as long as possible. If conventional defenses have failed or seem about to fail, then deliberate escalation through the controlled use of nuclear weapons is supposed to follow. NATO's conventional and theater nuclear forces are supported by U.S. strategic nuclear forces. These latter have been given flexible options at least since the 1970s, and probably before, for attacking targets of interest in Europe in order to forestall a Soviet invasion.

The NATO idea of limited and flexible uses of nuclear forces, especially U.S. strategic nuclear forces, is sometimes contrasted with the Soviet preference for grosser, and less discriminating, uses of force. It is true that the Soviet military literature does not emphasize intrawar bargaining and deterrence to the extent that the U.S. literature does.[11] However, this is very far from saying that in practice, as opposed to theory, Soviet commanders and political leaders would not be interested in establishing some thresholds rather quickly. Materials from the Voroshilov Military Academy in the 1970s became available to U.S. analysts of the Soviet armed forces during the 1980s. These materials suggested, along with other developments in Soviet policy, a greater pessimism about the impact of nuclear weapons on Soviet plans for conventional war in Europe. An important publication by Soviet military theoretician Col. Gen. M. A. Gareyev underscored the increased Soviet appreciation of the difficulty of conducting war with nuclear weapons. It also suggested a growing interest on the part of Soviet planners in keeping a war in Europe conventional, if it were possible to do so.[12]

Of course, both Soviet and NATO planners recognize that if the nuclear threshold is crossed in Europe, it will be difficult to limit the expansion of the war until it reaches the homeland-to-homeland exchanges so predominant in textbook scenarios. There is no automatic stopping point between small and large nuclear exchanges on European territory, a point of special concern to U.S. NATO allies. A tactical nuclear war in Europe would be a catastrophe for them, and a conventional war in Europe, fought for very long, would be almost equally daunting. This has led Europeans (speaking very generally) to emphasize the deterrence of war at all costs, and to regard nuclear weapons as a heavier makeweight than improved conventional forces. They are less inclined to view the importance of relative degrees of escalation, especially nuclear escalation. Conventional force improvements are seen by them as necessary expedients to placate insistent Americans, for political purposes, whatever the military rationale for those improvements.

Soviet planners, since the advent of NATO flexible response in 1967, have indicated greater interest in the possibility of a conventional phase, even a prolonged one, prior to the first use of nuclear weapons in Europe. It may be possible for them, under the best of conditions, to avoid the use of nuclear weapons altogether. The best of conditions for them, of course, would be to attain their objectives without nuclear escalation, by preventing NATO first use. This would mean seizing the initiative by driving through NATO's forward defenses on multiple axes of attack, encircling and bypassing defenders while disrupting the coherence of Western defenses.[13] NATO would be faced with the choice of escalation or acquiescence to Soviet demands. It is also assumed in this (Western) rendition of the Soviet conventional war plan that the USSR does not want to fight on more than one front at a time, especially on its European and Asian fronts simultaneously.

Students of this notional Soviet plan for war in Europe must note, however, that this is not a conventional war plan in the sense that it excludes nuclear escalation. The Soviet Union, despite its declaratory policy of no first use, will not hesitate to use nuclear weapons in order to preempt an anticipated NATO first use. And there is reason to believe that, faced with the alternative of the collapse of its control in Eastern Europe, Kremlin leaders would escalate a conventional war to the level of nuclear exchanges in Europe. They might do this because the alternative, loss of control over the glacis that protects them from Western invasion (as they see it), is too drastic to accept as a tolerable war outcome. They might also escalate to nuclear first use if the provocation were not so dramatic but simply politically inexpedient, if they felt optimistic about the ability of both sides to confine nuclear strikes to Europe, excluding the Soviet homeland.[14]

NATO flexible response strategy, in turn, invites Soviet exploitation of intra-alliance divisions and uncertainties with regard to the character of nuclear response and its timing. The Western notion of a gradual progression from one rung of a ladder of escalation to another is an optimistic one, assuming as it does that the rungs are clearly marked off. It is also assumed that they are carefully annotated with regard to the expectations at each level concerning appropriately deterrent, or compelling behavior expected of the opponent. For example, the U.S. quarantine or blockade of Cuba in October 1962 was designed not only to prevent additional nuclear-capable missiles from being shipped to that island, but also to compel the USSR to dismantle and withdraw the ones it had already sent there. Fortunately there is no superpower experience with nuclear war, but nuclear crisis and conventional war have not provided encouraging precedents with regard to keeping clear the distinctions among thresholds of escalation. Adversaries do not communicate well during crisis or war, even without the physical disruption of communications media.

For example, the U.S. attacks on North Vietnamese targets, in response to reported strikes against U.S. vessels in the Gulf of Tonkin in 1964, were described as controlled reprisals. They were designed to send a message to the North Vietnamese that the United States was capable of doing more damage and causing more coercive pain, if necessary, but that U.S. leaders would prefer that North Vietnam not repeat the behavior in question. How clearly this and other "slow squeeze" approaches were communicated to Ho Chi Minh is not clear, but in retrospect it is obvious that Ho interpreted many of these selective responses as indications of lack of U.S. resolve against superior North Vietnamese staying power. Military forces are blunt instruments with which to communicate, as the United States has learned even when its forces are committed to peacekeeping missions in Lebanon or the Persian Gulf. If by its naval deployments in the Persian Gulf in 1987, for example, the United States sought to distance itself from the Iran-Iraq war, at least in the sense of partiality, it did exactly the opposite. Riding shotgun for reflagged Kuwaiti tankers de facto, if not de jure, interposed U.S. forces as quasi combatants against Iran.

The last example makes a larger point about the constraints under which coercive diplomacy, as it is properly called, can be employed successfully. Coercive diplomacy implies the use of force or the threat of force in order to accomplish diplomatic purposes, a kind of persuasion short of war, and one not necessarily undertaken as a prelude to war. Coercive diplomacy can be a peacetime or a wartime activity, so to speak.[15] In peacetime it is often manifested in the show of force by maritime vessels sent for port visits or offshore visibility. During time of war, coercive diplomacy implies a limited use of force backed up by the threat of more, in order to induce the opponent to cooperate instead of pulverizing him into it.

Implicit in the notion of limited nuclear war, or even conventional war in Europe stopping short of nuclear escalation, is the idea of coercive diplomacy, of maintaining communications while the fighting continues, in order to arrest the process of escalation that might otherwise result. This would be especially important once nuclear exchanges had begun, but even the Western doctrine of how to apply coercive diplomacy in this situation is underdeveloped (to say nothing of Soviet doctrine). The difficulty with coercive diplomacy is that it works well only under certain very special conditions, which include (1) a clear understanding by the adversary of what is expected of it; (2) an adversary perception that the threatener is capable of carrying out the consequences of the threat; (3) an adversary perception that the threatener is willing to carry out the threat; (4) the lack of available alternatives for the party being threatened to avoid the decision calculus the threatener is attempting to impose.[16]

The last condition is especially severe, and it is one on which many an aspiring threatener has come a-cropper. Stalin's plan to put an economic squeeze on Berlin in 1948, in order to topple Western rights in that city, was an example of coercive diplomacy. Stalin thought he had succeeded, in that the onus was placed on the West to escalate the conflict to unacceptable levels (an actual shooting war, perhaps one with nuclear strikes). However, U.S. President Harry Truman conceived of an alternative that allowed the West to turn the situation around, or inside out (the airlift), and so to place upon Stalin the dilemma of escalation or denial of his objectives.

Cultural ethnocentrism may impede communication between adversaries, and mutual misunderstandings of what is desired by the opponent might precipitate war instead of avoiding it. Or, if contraction of the level of violence is sought instead of expansion, it might be difficult to establish this in proposals that are unambiguously clear to the intended target of the message. In revolutionary wars since 1945, there has been a combination of cultural ethnocentrism added to proposals not consensually understood between message sender and receiver. In the cases of France in Algeria and the United States in Vietnam, for example, the intended message was that the metropolitan/Western power would escalate in increments until the revolutionists yielded, assuming that some special magnitude of coercion would make resistance no longer cost effective. However, in neither case was the resistance based on perceptions of cost effectiveness, and the counterterrorist tactics of the French in Algeria and the United States in Vietnam (as in Operation Phoenix to neutralize Vietcong cadres) proved to be counterproductive to their objectives. Graduated escalation in both cases, but especially in the U.S. case, only provoked a more spirited resistance and an extended struggle.

The more dramatic case, of precipitating war instead of avoiding it, is illustrated by prewar maneuverings of the great powers in July 1914, on the eve of the eruption of World War I. The so-called July crisis proved to be beyond the capability of the Russian, German, and Austro-Hungarian leaders to manage, although "manage" may be the wrong word. There was certainly a shared misperception of perceived adversaries' intentions, inferred wrongly from mobilization timetables and inflexible military plans.[17] Having stumbled into war under misguided assumptions about the limits of their choices, the great powers compounded that mistake by persisting in fighting beyond the point of political and common sense. No notion of war termination was created in order to subordinate the fighting on the western front to the service of some meaningful postwar political objectives. In contrast, Lenin decided in 1918 that settling for half a loaf and saving the revolution in Russia was worth ceding large chunks of territory and enduring the humiliation at Brest-Litovsk. Unlike his Western counterparts, Lenin was attuned to the requirements of war termination even if he preceded by many years any explicit theory of such. Like Molière's bougeois gentleman who discovered quite accidentally that he was speaking prose, Lenin discovered the priority of war termination and cut his losses to do so, in order to give primacy to postwar political objectives (among them the survival of Soviet control).

Lenin was well ahead of his time, but until the 1960s, even the Western theory of war termination was almost absent from the literature. Fred Ikle's landmark *Every War Must End* did not appear until the 1970s, although the Hudson Institute and other U.S. government nonprofit agencies were doing termination studies in the 1960s.[18] Paul Bracken, one of the few persons doing systematic studies on war termination then and now, has rendered the somewhat surprising judgment that there exists today a fairly coherent and sophisticated body of literature on the subject.[19] This might be said of Bracken's writing and that of a few others, but generally even Western sources in the nuclear age do not provide much beyond hypothetical scenarios and conceptual structures that are mainly heuristic (Herman Kahn's metaphorical ladder of escalation, for example).

Even more problematical is the matter of escalation control, for this implies that in nuclear exchanges one can go down the ladder (deescalation) as well as up, or that one can freeze an escalatory process below a certain mutually recognized threshold. We will see in a moment what capabilities might be required to do so, but clearly, if the superpowers have done a great deal of planning for war termination after nuclear exchanges on their homelands or in Europe, it is a well-kept secret.

Western strategists have articulated concepts that are sometimes convincing and sometimes not, and the Soviet marshals have hardly exerted themselves to worry about the problem, especially in a nuclear context. However, the USSR has equipped its general-purpose forces with nuclear weapons, and conceivably has at least established planning contingencies for war in Europe in which nuclear weapons are exploded there, but not against the U.S. and Soviet homelands.[20]

The theory of war termination, such as it is, must also take account of the issues for which the two sides are fighting. In a nuclear war or a conventional war in which the possibility of nuclear escalation is seriously contemplated, the issues will undoubtedly be perceived as vital (unless the war has resulted from miscalculation and inadvertence, and even then some conflict over a vital interest might have motivated the inadvertent war). Certainly the first exchanges of nuclear weapons, even limited ones, will enliven the discussion in NATO headquarters and capitals, Politburo meetings, and National Security Council sessions. The difference between nuclear weapons and other weapons, among other things, is that once they are used, the character of the war, as well as its level of destruction, is at issue. The message being sent by the first side that engages in nuclear strikes in Europe, and how that strike is orchestrated, will matter more than which physical targets are destroyed and with what kilotonnage.

This transformation effect on political objectives after nuclear weapons have been fired has positive and negative implications. If a very destructive conventional war is suddenly stopped in its tracks by policymakers who are sobered by the first and few nuclear salvos, then some political point will have been made by those attacks, albeit with regrettable side effects. However, if the initial strikes are seen as preludes to more massive ones, then they invite a more massive response, and incentives to control escalation evaporate. Theorists debate whether the first nuclear strikes in Europe will lead to the imposition of control or the deterioration of control. In practice, military commanders will want to obtain preauthorization to disperse and protect possibly endangered weapons against first strikes, and those commanders may receive authority for preemption if need be. Once nuclear weapons become the issue instead of the instrument—and they will be after very few of them have been detonated—the containment of war in Europe becomes difficult if not impossible. In the case of oft-theorized limited strategic nuclear attacks against the U.S. or Soviet homeland, containment seems even more unlikely.

## CAPABILITIES FOR TERMINATION

Assuming that both sides want to terminate a war, which is assuming quite a lot, there remains the matter of capability to do it. Capabilities will be discussed here under several headings: vertical control of military forces; protection of national command authority or the delegation of command authority to others; organizational responsiveness and flexibility in implementing war plans or changing them; and communications between adversaries that make possible the sending of messages and their correct interpretation. Communications within each national command also are important, but they are discussed under organizational responsiveness.

## Vertical Control

Vertical control of military forces refers to the ability of policymakers at the top of the civil and military command structures to make those forces do what their top leaders intend. This is not as easy as it might sound. On paper, top leaders issue commands and subordinates carry them out. But in large modern bureaucracies this legalistic fiction is not really the case.

As orders cascade downward through a bureaucratic hierarchy, there is a selective filtering of them at the margin. It is not so much that the orders are explicitly disregarded. To do so is usually damaging to careers. What happens is more inadvertent. The orders are modified in subtle and unpredictable ways. The chairman of the U.S. joint chiefs of staff, for example, might issue a directive on behalf of the group that said security needed to be tightened at military bases. As this directive found its way to the Army, Navy, Air Force, and Marines, it would be interpreted by those at lower command levels in terms of their own prerogatives and perspectives. A general directive about base security cannot be implemented in the same way at every location. Base security means something different in Adak, Alaska, and Heidelberg, West Germany, for reasons having to do with geography, terrorist movements in Germany, and so forth. Moreover, our fictitious directive would be interpreted differently through the prism of Army, Navy-Marine, and Air Force established procedures. Army planners would worry more about helicopters than about fixed-wing aircraft, compared with Navy and Air Force planners.

Even within a single U.S. arm of service, there are significant differences in perspective and professional orientation. In the Navy, the aviators, submariners, and surface ship warriors form three distinct professional communities. So, too, do the tactical air and strategic bomber communities in the Air Force. The Army is no different. The special operations forces have for decades formed a distinct subculture, sometimes at odds with the mainstream promotional and reward structure. These subcultures of expertise and specialized training mean that the same orders will be implemented and interpreted differently as they (the orders) make their way through the bureaucratic maze.

An example of how orders might be filtered by habit and perspective, to the detriment of security, was provided at Pearl Harbor in 1941, resulting in the worst surprise attack suffered by the United States in its military history. The Army and Navy commanders at Pearl Harbor had been alerted by several messages from Washington that war was possible, although no one knew exactly where in the Pacific the Japanese would strike. However, the Navy commanders at the scene decided that an attack on Pearl Harbor was unlikely; the Japanese would be more likely to attack in Thailand or the Philippines. Therefore, the entire fleet was in harbor, vulnerable to attack. Army planners interpreted at least one war warning as a caution against sabotage of air bases, and grouped their planes wing to wing on runways, thus increasing their vulnerability to destruction from Japanese attacks from the air on December 7.[21]

Thus U.S. leaders, including the civilian cabinet officials in charge of the War and Navy departments as well as the army chief of staff and the chief of naval operations, felt confident that the fleet at Pearl Harbor was well protected. The warnings they received were not interpreted correctly as a result of filtration of information and differences in perspective. This filtration also occurred in the intelligence collection and estimation process that preceded the attack on December 7. U.S. intelligence at this time was poorly organized and underdeveloped compared with its wartime achievements. Important information about Japanese preparations for war in the Pacific was in the network, but it was synthesized within the intelligence arm of each service, Army or Navy. And not all the persons within each service who should have seen pertinent information actually had access to it. Thus, the estimation process was compartmentalized, excluding from the "need to know" some persons who actually did need to know. For example, the "Magic" intercepts of Japanese diplomatic communications were decoded by cryptographers but made available only to a select few officials in Washington. The commanders at Pearl Harbor did not have access to them because it was felt by higher authorities that their dispersal to the field would compromise security.

Illustration of stress and strain in the vertical control of forces is not limited to events preceding the nuclear age. Incidents have characterized the nuclear era as well. During the Eisenhower administration, Secretary of Defense Thomas Gates is said to have decided to order a worldwide military alert on the spur of the moment. Presumably this was done to test efficiency and responsiveness in emergencies. Gates envisioned that it would take place as a series of exercises known only to the military command structure. However, surprised lower echelons were not certain how to react to Gates's directive, and leaks to the press soon confronted the defense secretary with a major public relations problem.[22]

The problems of vertical control over U.S. forces during the Cuban missile crisis are well known as a result of Graham T. Allison's seminal study on the Cuban missile crisis of 1962.[23] Allison observed that rational policy models, in which objectives are clearly followed by the correctly chosen means to implement them, do not fully explain events that took place during the crisis. By introducing the "organizational process" and "bureaucratic politics" models, he enriches the analytical interpretation of the same anecdotal evidence. Perhaps the most frequently discussed of these insights derived by Allison, and alluded to by some firsthand accounts of the participants, is the gap between policymakers' and military leaders' expectations about military operations. President Kennedy and his advisers wanted to fine-tune the U.S. response to the crisis, in order to give Soviet Premier Khrushchev time to reconsider his threat to run the blockade and continue installation of the missiles. What was of paramount importance to Kennedy was not losing control of the crisis. However, military commanders also cared about not losing ships to the opponent, should war break out. Thus U.S. Navy antisubmarine warfare forced a number of Soviet submarines, which could have been carrying nuclear weapons, to the surface in the Caribbean and elsewhere.[24]

Nor was this example isolated. During the tensest period of the crisis, when U.S. officials were awaiting Khrushchev's final response to what was in effect the last U.S. ultimatum, a U.S. U–2 reconnaissance plane on a routine mission lost course and strayed into Soviet airspace. Soviet fighters scrambled to defend against what could have been a U.S. bomber attack or a reconnaissance prelude to such an attack.[25] Similarly, it is not clear whether the Soviets were fully able to control their own forces once the United States had announced discovery of the missiles and the crisis heated to boiling proportions. A U.S. U–2 overflying Cuba was shot down, and this loss almost caused Kennedy to order a U.S. air strike on the Soviet missile installations, with all the potential for escalation that this implied (since Soviet military personnel stationed in Cuba would almost certainly have been killed). It seems improvident for Khrushchev's efforts to control the Soviet options during the Cuban crisis that the U–2 would have been shot down at that time, although standard operating procedures under normal conditions would have called for it (as happened to Francis Gary Powers in 1960). Perhaps the Soviet air defense personnel who shot down the U–2 gave no thought to their action's implications for their leaders' subsequent freedom of choice, and they responded to an intrusion by carrying out standard operating procedures despite their consequences. Like U.S. Navy commanders, Soviet air defense officers may have concluded that their mission, narrowly defined, was the protection of valued assets, not the interpretation of political events.

It is this awareness, especially since Cuba, of the risks of control slipping away from leaders' grasp that has led to an increase in the attentiveness of policymakers and military leaders to the development of details and events in nearly real time. Leaders now want to know the details and to have control over them, especially during crises in which nuclear escalation or war seems possible. However, this increased attention from the top to events normally orchestrated at the middle and lower levels of the hierarchy is not without cost. At the very least, it rearranges previously established expectations about subordinates' discretion and freedom to take the initiative, which can introduce new complications into crisis and wartime decision making.

### Organizational Responsiveness

Related to the problem of vertical control of forces is the requirement for organizational responsiveness. However, though the two requirements might sound identical, they are different. Organizational responsiveness is the repertoire of organizational behaviors on which policymakers might conceivably call. In order to activate one or more than one of those behaviors from that repertoire, leaders must exercise vertical control. But they must do other things, too. In particular, they must understand the limits of organizational improvisation. The larger the organization and the more stressed it is, the less likely it is to be able to improvise, except in unwanted ways.

Bureaucratic organizations are characterized by large size, formal decision-making processes, and segmental assignments of jobs and responsibilities. No single person in the organization can know what all the rest are doing at any particular time. Accomplishing the organizational mission requires that each employee focus on his or her responsibilities to the nearly total exclusion of the concerns of others. This classical Weberian model of bureaucracy has been eroded at the edges as modern postindustrial U.S. and European management approaches have softened its rough edges. In professions and work places that deal in services or produce knowledge in some form, hierarchy is to some extent being displaced by a less stratified pattern of interaction among workers and bosses. Some call this matrix management, traditionalists are apt to call it confusion.

Notwithstanding these departures from the traditional bureaucratic model, the model still provides the basic framework for most decision-making in large organizations, especially military ones. The combination of hierarchy and specialization is necessary for very stressful missions to be accomplished with minimum disruption. However, hierarchy and specialization have their costs. The organizational focus and learning are subdivided, so that even those at the very top (or perhaps especially those at the top) are largely ignorant of what goes on at most other levels most of the time.

The consequences of hierarchy and specialization for nuclear command organizations have been studied by academic and other investigators. Nuclear command organizations, at least the U.S. variety, developed from the need to reconcile two apparently incompatible objectives. The first was the special treatment that nuclear weapons, on account of their destructiveness, were accorded by policymakers. U.S. President Harry Truman initially assigned control of U.S. nuclear weapons to the Atomic Energy Commission. Only later, and after much consideration of the possible implications, were they dispersed to the various unified and specified military commands that would use them.[26] Mechanical (and later electronic) safety devices were provided so that the weapons could not be detonated accidentally or illegally. Thus U.S. policymakers went to great lengths to insure against the possibility of accidental or unauthorized launch of nuclear weapons. And, although there have been several near misses, no accidental detonation of any U.S. nuclear device has been reported.

However, the objective of safety against accident or sabotage had to be reconciled with another, that of responsiveness. Once nuclear weapons had been dispersed to their assigned military commands, those commands would be expected to follow orders to retaliate once the orders were properly given. This required, in the case of U.S. strategic nuclear weapons such as land-based missiles (ICBMs), submarine-launched ballistic missiles (SLBNs), and bombers that organizations specially designed for the purpose of strategic nuclear bombardment (SAC) be created. The nuclear command system that grew up during the 1950s and 1960s in the United States was created with special properties in addition to the usual military and bureaucratic ones. These properties included safeguards against accident and responsiveness under fire. Once missiles replaced bombers as the primary weapons of choice for first strikes, the warning time for surprise attack was reduced from hours to minutes. This required changes in U.S. nuclear command organizations to ensure responsiveness even under the worst conditions of surprise attack.[27]

The question was responsiveness of what kind? Policymakers would want the best of both worlds, a response that was as rapid as it needed to be and as fine-tuned as it could be. They soon discovered that there were trade-offs here. Organizations can do only so many things at once successfully—or, to express it another way, the leaders of organizations can understand only a finite amount of what is going on. Initially the trade-offs between a rapid and a fine-tuned response were solved in favor of the former. The U.S. nuclear war plans of the 1950s emphasized early, and perhaps anticipatory, attacks against a wide variety of Soviet counterforce and countervalue targets. These targets were divided into Bravo (blunting mission against enemy retaliatory forces), Delta (destruction of the urban-industrial base and enemy control centers), and Romeo (retardation of Soviet troop advances into Europe).[28] Although the Eisenhower administration was marked by deliberations about preventative war against the USSR at the highest levels, the president never chose that option as preferred. But, as David Alan Rosenberg has recounted:

If preventative war was ruled out as a strategic option, preemption was not. In this era before ballistic missiles, preemption appeared to be both militarily and constitutionally feasible.[29]

Commander in Chief of SAC General Curtis LeMay is widely quoted as having stated, "if the U.S. is pushed in a corner far enough we would not hesitate to strike first."[30] This has been judged to be a highly provocative statement in retrospect, but in the context of its time it was taken by policy planners to be a realistic one. The statement is also less shocking than it appears if one realizes that today, taken all together, U.S. forces are much more capable of preemptive attack than they were at the time LeMay spoke. LeMay's insistence upon the need for preemption under some circumstances was in part derived from the limited options he would have in ordering his forces to war, since there were no U.S. ICBMs or SLBMs to call upon. And the blunting mission against Soviet nuclear forces was clearly given priority in planners' estimates, for the consequence of not striking first against the Soviet force was the possible vulnerability of the U.S. force, or a substantial proportion of it, to Soviet preemption.[31]

Neither the U.S. nor the Soviet bomber force could, in all likelihood, have completely surprised the other, and so allowed its society to escape unprecedented levels of destruction. U.S. retaliatory strikes from SAC in response to a Soviet invasion of Europe would certainly come as no surprise to the Soviets, and U.S. air defenses and attack warning systems of the 1950s would have prevented a totally successful (although it would still have been devastating) Soviet attack on the bomber force. Nonetheless, both sides feared nuclear preemption, and sought to provide command organizations that remained under policymakers' control while avoiding vulnerability to surprise attack.

As the Kennedy administration took office, the United States feared that it had fallen behind the USSR in developing its ICBM force, but the "missile gap" of the U.S. presidential campaign of 1960 turned out to be a myth, except that it was in the Americans', not the Russians', favor. However, the emergence of ICBMs paired with SLBMs allowed missiles to become the backbone of the U.S. retaliatory forces. This called for command organizations that could juggle a three-legged retaliatory stool and still retaliate while avoiding accidental or unauthorized launch. The twin demands placed upon a diversified "triad" of strategic weapons called for ingenious solutions, but those solutions, ingenious as they were, were imposed upon large mission-oriented military organizations.

Thus, SAC was not given the attack warning and assessment function, lest the arm of service designed for retaliation also hold the power to ascertain what kind of attack had been launched—or whether one had been launched. The development of U.S. warning and attack assessment systems has been described extensively elsewhere.[32] Warning and assessment was centralized in the North American Aerospace Defense Command (NORAD), which became an all-purpose fusion center with connections to the National Military Command Center in the Pentagon, the alternative NMCC at Ft. Richie, Maryland, SAC Headquarters at Omaha, and other key command posts.[33] As time went on, the inputs with which NORAD (a binational command with Canada) would have to cope expanded to include numerous space objectives as well as the monitoring of the peacetime and crisis conditions of U.S. and Soviet forces. For the latter task, NORAD receives information from sensors that include Defense Support Program satellites in geosynchronous orbit, land-based radars in the United States, Canada, England, and Greenland (called BMEWS and PAVE PAWS for detection of polar ICBM and SLBM launches respectively), and other land and sea-based sensors. Tracking information is also provided by the Enhanced Perimeter Acquisition Radar Characterization System about 20 minutes after Soviet ICBMs have been launched.[34]

NORAD would, under notional conditions of surprise attack, have very little time in which to ascertain that an attack had been launched, to contact the appropriate officials (including the president), and to provide a very accurate count of warheads and their intended targets. In all likelihood, the president would have to make a very rapid decision if, in the event, time permitted contact with him before Soviet SLBMs destroyed Washington, D.C. The pressure of time would be compounded by the probable lack of familiarity on the part of the president with the most recent version of the Single Integrated Operational Plan for nuclear war. Most presidents have shied away from the continuous briefings that would be needed to update their knowledge of the plan. A president so informed would have to choose among very general alternatives and leave the details of implementation to his military advisers. A very large response would undoubtedly be called for, and as rapidly as possible, under conditions in which the United States was struck by a truly "bolt from the blue" attack. However, this is not the most likely path to nuclear war between superpowers. A more likely path is escalation from a conventional war, and a war in Europe is probably going to push against the nuclear threshold rather quickly.[35] But would this mean that the U.S. president, given additional time to prepare the system for war, would be able to exercise increased control over it, and to fine-tune U.S. response to provocations?

Probably not, if the issue is war in Europe, although there is certainly the possibility of containing war within the European continent and not allowing it to spread beyond that theater to a general and global super-power conflict. Two kinds of containment would be important in limiting escalation and in making possible eventual war termination. The first would limit the war to one continent or theater of operations, horizontal containment. The second, vertical containment, would limit war below the nuclear threshold. The two kinds of containment interact. For hor-izontal, a war that spread outside Europe would be more difficult to keep below the nuclear threshold. For vertical containment, a war that went nuclear would have a greater chance of spreading beyond Europe, into the Soviet and U.S. homeland. Thus, horizontal and vertical esca-lation, which are sometimes seen as opposites, are actually linked. The choice of fighting a long conventional war or a short nuclear one may not be presented to policymakers as such. They may have to fight a war that begins as a conventional war in Europe, and ends as a global nuclear and conventional war.

### Delegation of Authority

Could a war of such scope and magnitude be terminated before it ended in nuclear holocaust? Perhaps it could. The first exchanges of nuclear weapons by superpowers and/or their allies may have a sobering effect, one that creates an open door through which policymakers may choose to walk. This door is not something that leaders can be forced to walk through. Before nuclear exchanges have gotten out of hand and after the war has spread beyond Europe, the superpowers may consider whether to impose some limitations on policy objectives and destruc-tiveness. Of course, it would have been better had they done so before, below the nuclear threshold and within Europe (although this is not the view of many Europeans, who would argue that a capability to limit war to Europe, or below the nuclear threshold, would weaken deterrence and invite war). However, it is easily agreed that conventional war is preferable to nuclear war, and war in Europe, however destructive, to war in Europe *and* outside of it. So the superpowers would still have some incentive to pursue war termination, provided some authority could be put into place to terminate it.

The discussion of arrangements for delegation of authority in the U.S. nuclear command and control system are closely guarded secrets; likewise for the Soviet system. Such knowledge is closely held because the opponent's knowledge of contingency plans for delegation of nuclear release authorization could be used against the effectiveness of those arrangements. In the U.S. case, release of nuclear weapons must be authorized by the president. However, the president may be among the first to be incapacitated or killed in a nuclear war. The heads of state in Western Europe might similarly fall early in war, even conventional war, to hostile actions. Therefore, prudent planners undoubtedly have worked out some arrangements for assumption of authority by lawful successors to chief executives, if those successors can be identified unambiguously (Alexander Haig's "I'm in command here" following the assassination attempt against President Reagan shows that this problem may not be trivial). The succession to the U.S. presidency is provided for by the Presidential Succession Act and the Twenty-fifth Amendment to the U.S. Constitution. In case of presidential death or incapacitation, the vice-president becomes president, followed by the speaker of the House of Representatives, the president pro-tem of the U.S. Senate, and the cabinet officers in order of the creation of their departments.

However, an attack that includes early nuclear strikes against Washington, D.C., might kill the president and many of his lawful civilian successors. Under those conditions, the last living successor might be difficult to identify quickly. The parallel military chain of command, running from the president to the secretary of defense and then through JCS to force commanders in charge of unified and specified commands, might take actual control of nuclear retaliation. A tendency for authority to cascade downward under the stress of actual attack, even if top leaders are not killed or incapacitated, is also likely.[36] Military commanders would have every incentive, and some contingent orders, to protect their forces from preemptive destruction. Standing rules of engagement might be implemented that allowed corps commanders in Europe or ship captains at sea to fire any necessary weapons, including available nuclear weapons, if enemy attack seemed imminent.

In fact, U.S. procedures undoubtedly do assign large amounts of discretion to force commanders even in peacetime. Rules of engagement may be spelled out in advance from Washington, but the commander in the field is to implement those rules with discretion, in order to minimize casualties and other losses. No one, for example, applauded the Marine commanders in Beirut in October 1983 when 241 Marines were blown up in their barracks, although those commanders were restrained by rules of engagement from taking more aggressive actions to protect themselves. In a crisis leading to superpower conflict, or after war had begun, the pressures against rules of engagement—to manipulate them permissively in order to provide for self-defense and advantageous initiatives—would be immense. This is a characteristic of nuclear crisis as well as of conventional wars: that engaged or endangered military commanders will take steps to assure that they are protected against worst case scenarios, even ones that are highly improbable from the standpoint of civilian policymakers.

Could a ship or submarine commander, or the commander of a U.S. division assigned to NATO Europe, initiate nuclear war on his own? The question is the wrong one. No one will do this insubordinately, for the risks are too great personally and professionally. What is risky is the indeterminate zone that is created by contingent delegation of authority: if you see this, then do that, and so forth. That is why contingent delegations of authority for the use of nuclear weapons will be given out sparingly by NATO and Soviet leaders, for fear that loss of control could turn crisis into war. But what incentive would they have to terminate war after nuclear exchanges or a large-scale conventional war in Europe had started, and on whom could they depend to do so?

Obviously delegation of authority is related to survivable leaderships who have some means of communicating with each other. Some peacetime preparations for this can of course be undertaken. Lists of persons can be established who, under such and such conditions, are authorized to exercise control over nuclear forces. This authority can be delegated all the way down the U.S. chain of command if necessary, and it is likely that de facto control over forces could devolve swiftly from higher to lower levels once nuclear exchanges began.

The slippage of control from the center to the periphery makes war termination more difficult to arrange. At the same time this slippage of central control is taking place, damage assessments and information about surviving enemy forces might be precarious. Paul Bracken has emphasized that the peacetime information regime will look very different from the wartime one, in the aftermath of nuclear attacks on NATO forces in Europe or North America.[37] Primary command posts might not have survived in Europe and in the superpowers' homelands if the war had expanded that far. Reconstruction of an information base necessary to turn the war off could prove to be a task beyond the competence of surviving commanders. One problem in a postattack environment would be the potential for wiping out much of the digitized data base on which correlation and interpretation are dependent. Some of the connectivity or communications pathways among surviving national leadership, force commanders, and fusion centers will be destroyed even in conventional war. In fact, this problem as it applies to Europe is insufficiently appreciated even by experts. Even conventional war in Europe in which no nuclear weapons have been exploded would destroy much of the infrastructure of communications and electronics needed for assessment of damage and estimation of the surviving forces on both sides.

In the Soviet case, the party leadership has made extensive preparations for its survival and control in the aftermath of war in Europe, or in the case of war involving the Soviet homeland. Making extensive preparations is not the same as guaranteeing that they will work, and the Soviets' diligence is unlikely to be rewarded unless they can terminate the war before most of the U.S. arsenal is expended. Preferably, they can terminate it before it expands beyond Western Europe or, if not, at least contain it outside the Soviet borders. The threshold of war engaging Soviet forces outside their borders is an important one; perhaps equally important for purposes of escalation control is the penetration of attacks, nuclear or conventional, into Soviet territory itself.[38] The Soviet command, control, and communications (C3) system includes underground command bunkers and protective facilities for numerous party, military, and government leaders in the Moscow area and beyond it. Provincial civilian and military officials also have protective shelters. Soviet force commanders have alternative command posts that are ground mobile, airborne, and sea based.

The Soviet C3 system also has substantial physical and electronic redundancy, with multiple communication paths connecting wartime military and political leaders with their general-purpose and other nuclear-capable forces.[39] However, there is some doubt whether the Soviet leadership would be able to cope with the wartime stresses that would drive effective control of forces downward into the hierarchy. Such an eventuality could spark paranoia about loss of control and might lead to intrawar efforts by political leaders to improvise additional controls over nuclear armed force commanders. NATO targeting strategy could, in turn, make this process of devolution of control more or less difficult for Soviet leaders to manage, and the possibility of decapitation attacks against regional or national headquarters has been an acknowledged component of U.S. declaratory policies.[40]

All of the above implies that, ceteris paribus, the U.S. problem of escalation control and war termination implies some notion of how much control the United States wants the USSR to be able to exercise over its own forces, as well as some sense of its own control. If the United States succeeds in destroying Soviet C3 competence early in war, it may find that the conflict cannot be ended despite the apparent intentions of both sides to do so. This would be ironic—the superpowers fighting to a stalemate by exhaustion (or extinction) on account of loss of control, whether deliberately intended or not. The irony is that the failure of escalation control would sever the connection between war and politics, turning the conflict into a mindless and savage ballet of destruction. To prevent this, as we have seen, issues of vertical command over forces, organizational responsiveness, and delegation of authority must be addressed before war actually begins.

## DEESCALATION AND WAR TERMINATION

Deescalation as a subject has received little attention compared with escalation. It is sometimes blithely assumed that if one can go up the ladder of escalation in increments, one can also go down in small steps. But historical practice does not bear this out. Often the fighting has to be stopped in its tracks, dramatically and suddenly, before negotiations toward a peaceful political settlement can take place. This stopping of actual fighting before the conclusion of final peace terms can come about from below or from above. The Bolshevik Revolution was given impetus by the desertions of soldiers from the front to join the discontented mobs in Petrograd. It was clear long before the Treaty of Brest-Litovsk that the Russians were beaten militarily. Actually, it had been clear since the battle of Tannenberg that Germany would prevail over Russia in a war of any duration. The irony was that prewar German planners assessed Russian capabilities as very formidable, and the Schlieffen Plan was designed to compensate for that by allowing for a quick, knockout blow against German enemies in the west so that Germany could turn its full attention to the Russian front later.

Sometimes deescalation does not led to war termination. During the "phony war" period of 1939–1940 on the Western Front in Europe, Germany was uncertain of its plans for following up the conquest of Poland. Several different campaign plans were drawn up for dealing with France and England. Hitler and his generals (he more impatiently than they) vacillated until the spring of 1940, when some of the ideas of panzer enthusiasts Erich von Manstein and Heinz Guderian found their way into the führer's favor (and into high-level briefings).[41] During this time Hitler also entertained some thoughts of peace overtures to Great Britain, in order to bring a stalemate on the Western Front. The French chose not to counterattack into Germany at this time, fearing that such an attack would not succeed militarily and that it might broaden the war beyond its present stalemate. The French hope was that Hitler could be induced to settle for the military status quo by the Maginot Line. Their refusal to invade Germany, apart from military pessimism, might also be seen as a tacit deescalation, the sending of a message that France would leave the German heartland alone if Germany would do likewise for France. Hitler chose not to understand any such signal, and in any case his war aims were implacable.

One of the interesting questions about World War I is why the fighting continued for so long after it was clear that none of the combatants were better off by prolonging it. Stubbornness is certainly one explanation, but the risk of losing throne and altar should have struck home to the rulers of Russia, Germany, and Austria-Hungary. The Austro-Hungarians chose an especially unfortunate course of action, from the standpoint of their imperial interests. They passed up opportunities to negotiate a separate peace with the Triple Entente and continued adhering to a pact with Germany that was destroying the cohesion of their state.[42] In the end, they lost their empire and the war as well. Italy, faced with the same choice, saw the handwriting on the wall and changed sides to its advantage, providing for itself a postwar position superior to what it would otherwise have obtained.

Deescalation would not be easily come by in a modern war in Europe, but it might make a great deal of difference to know how the war began, and what the disputants were fighting for. If the USSR, for whatever reason, had decided to embark upon the conquest of Western Europe pell-mell and could not be deterred from that misadventure, then the prospect for escalation control would be very slight. NATO doctrine and strategy are quite clear on this point; the West will not offer up Europe to Soviet control without using nuclear weapons, whatever that entails. However, this scenario, formidable as it is in the manuals of planners, is most unlikely to come about in reality. The prospect of a war beginning elsewhere and escalating to war in Europe is less remote, although not any easier to script.

A war that began, say, with a Soviet invasion of Iran, and then spread to superpower conflict in Europe, is one possibility. In fact, this is an interesting possibility because it suggests one of the roles that Western Europe and its vulnerability play in Soviet strategy. That role is hostage to Soviet escalation, in order to deter U.S. counterescalation. Consider, as an example of this phenomenon, the Cuban missile crisis. One might ask, apropos the resolution of that crisis, why the United States had to pussyfoot with naval blockades and diplomatic exchanges. Why not simply launch an air strike or invasion against Cuba, and sink Castro into the Caribbean once and for all? Had the superpowers' showdown over Cuba not involved any of their commitments elsewhere, this is what might have happened.

However, it must have occurred to U.S. policymakers, as it surely occurred to this writer, that an attack on Cuba might provoke a Soviet response against the vulnerable Western position in Berlin. U.S. and other allied garrisons are stationed there at Soviet sufferance, and could probably be extinguished by a sufficient number of well-armed East German security police. Thus the Soviets have West Berlin hostage to any reprisals they might care to execute in the event of a U.S. or allied response that is disproportionate to their aggression or coercion.

This is something different from a straightforward collision over U.S. and allied rights in Berlin proper, which took place in 1948, 1958, and 1961. Those crises were direct confrontations involving East and West, not conflicts that began outside of Europe and then spread to it. Theorists sometimes use the term "horizontal escalation" to refer to this spreading of conflict from one theater of operations to another, but this is somewhat misleading. The war can spread from the Persian Gulf or Sinai Peninsula, say either deliberately or inadvertently. If the latter, it is unclear whether horizontal escalation or a loss of control over vertical escalation has taken place. An expansion of war from Iran to Europe is as much the latter as it is the former, an eruption of a regionally limited (although serious) struggle outside Europe into Europe itself.

If such an eventuality transpired, the United States and its allies would be fighting on two fronts, Southwest Asia and Europe, while attempting to contain the war and reestablish the status quo ante before additional escalation, and possibly nuclear escalation, took hold. Another issue in deescalation of such a conflict beginning outside of Europe and then spreading into it, is what U.S. and Soviet maritime forces would be doing as the clash in Iran began to spill over into war elsewhere, including Europe. Would U.S. carrier task forces, for example, begin moving toward locations in the North Atlantic and Norwegian Sea within striking distance of Soviet shore targets? Would U.S. attack submarines move to establish a barrier at the Greenland-Iceland-United Kingdom gap in order to prevent surging Soviet wolf packs from threatening U.S. convoys in the sea-lanes connecting North America to Europe? Or, in the vision of former Navy Secretary John Lehman, would the U.S. carrier task forces actually sail into harm's way preemptively, moving as close to the Kola Peninsula bases of the Soviet Northern Fleet as they can get, as early as possible?

The U.S. "maritime strategy," as explained by Chief of Naval Operations Adm. James D. Watkins, was more cautious than some of Lehman's pronouncements.[43] But Admiral Watkins's official exposition of the strategy still called for assertive forward operations of U.S. maritime forces in the Barents and Norwegian seas, and those operations would quite obviously have to begin immediately after war broke out or even before, during the prewar phase that the Navy referred to as "violent peace." Certainly the outbreak of a direct engagement between Soviet and U.S. forces anywhere, including in the Persian Gulf, would alert both sides' naval forces to deploy to positions where they were less vulnerable. According to the U.S. maritime strategy as explained by Lehman and Watkins, aggressive forward operations or offensive sea control, including forays into Soviet home waters by U.S. attack submarines, would contribute to war termination on favorable terms for NATO while avoiding nuclear escalation.

However, one component of the U.S. maritime strategy had already become controversial as a result of selective briefings to the Washington community, and the public exposition of the strategy made it more controversial still. This controversial element was the surging of NATO submarines into Soviet home-water bastions where the Soviet strategic ballistic missile submarines (SSBNs) were protected by naval surface and subsurface vessels and land-based air power. The U.S. Naval rationale for this was that a steady attrition of Soviet submarines, which are part of the USSR's strategic nuclear reserve force, would dissuade the Kremlin from further prosecution of the war in Europe. Faced with a gradual diminution of its strategic nuclear reserve if its conventional war in Europe were not halted, the USSR would be compelled, in this vision, to desist and arrange acceptable terms for war termination. Indeed, war termination was described by Admiral Watkins as the predominant objective of U.S. maritime forces in conjunction with other U.S. forces and allies.[44]

Critics have suggested, however, that the use of U.S. forces in this "counterforce coercion" campaign against Soviet SSBNs could lead to vertical escalation by provoking a Soviet nuclear attack on NATO land- or sea-based targets in the western theater of operations.[45] The Soviets might also respond by attacking the U.S. homeland if they were sufficiently concerned that the destruction of their SSBNs was a prelude to a more comprehensive attack against Soviet strategic nuclear forces across the board. Some experts doubt that the USSR would so engage in comprehensive escalation in response to the gradual destruction of its SSBN force, since it would then be exposed to an equally comprehensive U.S. retaliation. If the Soviet Union is indeed deterred by U.S. retaliatory forces sufficient to accomplish the "assured destruction" mission of countersocietal retaliation, it does seem that this intrawar deterrence by the United States of Soviet nuclear escalation is readily accomplished. However, it also seems that the Soviet Union, by retaining a very small number of surviving forces relative to its prewar deployments, can do likewise. So the assumption that the Soviets can be induced to terminate a conventional war in Europe, especially if they are winning it, by progressive destruction of their SSBN force rests upon a weak foundation. If the Soviets saw their SSBN force undergoing attrition, and if they feared that this meant they would soon lose their strategic deterrent, they undoubtedly would be influenced to do something about it, although in what direction is far from obvious. The bulk of Soviet strategic nuclear force loadings are not on submarines, but on land-based missiles, and the United States lacks sufficient counterforce capability to destroy those Soviet ICBMs preemptively.

Another version of the "slow squeeze" that the U.S. Navy expects to put on the Kremlin lies in its ability to bottle up the Soviet fleets in their home waters, and so to prevent them from surging into the Atlantic and interrupting U.S. reinforcement of Europe. This is a more traditional, and less controversial, aspect of the maritime strategy, although why it is deemed necessary to fight this sea-based battle as far forward as the upper reaches of the Norwegian Sea is obscure to some naval analysts. It is certainly important to keep Norway out of Soviet hands and to prevent dominance of the Norwegian Sea and North Atlantic by Soviet land-based air forces. Perhaps the assumption is that the Central Front will collapse quickly and that the Navy has little time to turn the tables on the Soviets at sea before the game is up on land. Or perhaps maritime and continental strategies are dissociated because of their disparate service connections and their force building (or not building) implications.[46]

The question for present purposes is how those strategies might interact in the context of terminating a war in Europe, and probably a war that began outside of Europe. And, as indicated earlier, two prominent thresholds for war in Europe, however it began, would be whether Soviet territory had actually been attacked and whether nuclear escalation had taken place. In addition, if the war has spread to Europe from outside it, the global character of the conflict becomes important in its own right. Both sides would have to control their allies' or clients' propensities to escalate their local grievances into wider war. At the same time they would have to engage in mutual adjustment of their own conflicting interests. If, for example, war in the Middle East pitted Israel against Syrian, Egyptian, and other Arab forces, as in 1973, and this somehow spread to conflict between NATO and the Warsaw Pact, then containment of the Middle East crisis would be coupled to terminating war in Europe. In this instance the superpowers would have aims that were partly complementary and interdependent (containing regional war among allies and ending war in Europe) and partly conflictual (the terms on which either would be accomplished). Part of Henry Kissinger's success as a mediator of Middle Eastern conflicts as national security adviser and, later, U.S. secretary of state, was his ability to dissociate those two generic issues: joint interest in a settlement on some terms as preferable to continued war, and the specific terms on which a temporary settlement could be reached.

Of Europe itself, it might be supposed that even regional containment of the catalytic spark for war would still leave the superpowers with intimidating problems of war termination in Europe. So it would, but resolution of the "Balkan" problems that began the war would help to communicate a sincerity of intentions not to let the tail of force wag the dog of diplomacy, at least outside of Europe. If this could not be demonstrated on the periphery, so to speak, it is highly unlikely that the superpowers could impose a solution on themselves in the center. If the "balkans" could be resolved, a process of accommodation could be started toward adjustment of conflicting claims in Europe. This is not so improbable even after war has begun, provided the war has been confined to Germany, the Low Countries, and

Scandinavia; is below the nuclear threshold; and is without strategic conventional counteroffensives into Eastern Europe by NATO.[47] However, the onset of war in Europe would shatter expectations that had previously held both NATO and Soviet coalitions together, and these expectations would be subject to rapid change as the costs of war grew and the outcome remained uncertain.[48]

## CONVENTIONAL DETERRENCE AND CONVENTIONAL DEFENSE

The signing of the treaty on the elimination of global intermediate nuclear forces (INF) by President Reagan and Soviet General Secretary Brezhnev on December 8, 1987, called renewed attention to the importance of conventional deterrence in Europe. There are several trends pointing toward the increased importance of the NATO/Warsaw Pact conventional force balance, and toward decreased reliance by NATO on nuclear weapons for deterrence of any war in Europe. Several of the more important trends, and their implications for war termination, are discussed below. Chapter 7 provides an enlarged theoretical context for the problem of war in Europe as seen through the logics of U.S. nuclear strategy.

The first trend pointing toward an increased emphasis on the conventional force balance in Europe is the possible reconsideration of Soviet strategy for war in Europe. According to some expert U.S. analysts, the USSR has been reviewing its military doctrine and operational art as they apply to war in Europe.[49] It has seen a light side and a dark side as a result of these examinations. The light side is that it may be possible to fight a war in Europe, if all goes well from the Soviet standpoint, without using nuclear weapons. The dark side is that this would be a very large gamble against NATO, given the current numbers of weapons that NATO has deployed in Western Europe.

One has to be careful here. The Soviet Union might very well *prefer* to fight a war in Europe without nuclear weapons, on account of its putative superiority in numbers of conventional forces close to the inter-German and German-Czech borders. On the other hand, those larger numbers have to be qualified somewhat by recognition that the various NATO corps sectors in the central army group (CENTAG) and the Soviet forces in East Germany, Poland, and Czechoslovakia are organized differently. When we take into account those forward-deployed Soviet forces in Eastern Europe that would be the forces relied upon for hammering through NATO's forward defenses and penetrating into its operational depth, the estimates shown below result:

**Soviet Ground Forces (western theater)**

**East Germany (380,000)**

10 tank divisions

9 motor rifle divisions

other artillery, air assault, surface-to-surface missiles, and helicopter attack/assault and support

**Poland (40,000)**

1 tank division

1 motor rifle division

surface-to-surface missiles, helicopter attack and support

**Czechoslovakia (80,000)**

2 tank divisions

3 motor rifle divisions

other artillery, air assault, surface-to-surface missiles, and helicopter attack/assault and support

**Reinforcements**

3 groups of Soviet forces: Baltic, Belorussian, and Carpathian military districts

63 divisions (31 tank, 30 motor rifle, 2 airborne) plus 6 artillery divisions and 4 air assault brigades

*Source*: International Institute for Strategic Studies, *The Military Balance: 1987–88* (London: IISS, Autumn 1987)

In the NATO Guidelines Area (NGA) the Soviet and non-Soviet Warsaw Pact forces in East Germany, Poland, and Czechoslovakia match up against the NATO forces in West Germany, Belgium, the Netherlands, and Luxembourg as shown below.

**NATO and Warsaw Pact Forces**

|  | NATO | Warsaw Pact |
|---|---|---|
| *Manpower (thousands)* | | |
| Total active ground forces | 796 | 995 |
| Total ground force reserves | 922 | 1,030 |
| *Divisions* | | |
| Manned in peacetime | 32.33 | 48.66 |
| Manned on mobilization of reserves (only forces mobilized within NGA) | 12 | 8 |
| Total war mobilized | 44.33 | 56.66 |

*Source*: International Institute for Strategic Studies, *The Military Balance: 1987–88* (London: IISS, Autumn 1987), pp. 231–232.

These totals do not take into account other quantitative indexes of relevance to the battle on the Central Front, including comparative NATO and Warsaw Pact tactical aircraft and naval forces. Even with additional quantitative information, qualitative issues, including the opposed sides' wartime strategies and operational/tactical competencies, are more important.

These numbers, crude indicators as they are, do establish some things. They establish that there is no prima facie case for a Soviet walkover against the conventional forces of NATO properly deployed in response to timely warning. If, however, NATO fails to mobilize in a timely manner, and if its mobilization lags significantly behind that of the Warsaw Pact, then its forward defenses could be pierced and its strategy dissected rather quickly.[50] Peter H. Vigor, a noted scholar and close student of the Soviet military, has put together a hypothetical scenario for a Soviet blitzkrieg on the Central Front that is as plausible as any other. He acknowledges, nonetheless, that given present force balances, it will not be easy for the USSR to pull it off.[51] The USSR would have to be extremely daring and very lucky to mount an operational blitzkrieg against NATO that either prevented (by forcible means) or deterred NATO nuclear escalation.

The second factor contributing to a stronger emphasis upon conventional deterrence in Europe is the apparent Soviet and U.S. interest in making significant reductions in their strategic and European theater nuclear arsenals. It seemed a reasonable expectation that the INF agreement of December 1987 would be followed sometime after 1988 by a strategic arms reduction pact. The superpowers sought approximately 50 percent cuts in total strategic nuclear warheads during the START discussions, which would reduce each side to about 6,000, with an expected sublimit of 4,900 based on ICBMs or SLBMs.[52] Added to the INF reductions already agreed to, these cuts in strategic nuclear forces would lead to additional emphasis within NATO on the adequacy of conventional forces. Of course, 6,000 strategic nuclear warheads on missiles and bombers provide a substantial retaliatory capability, but in general, the fewer the strategic warheads, the more specific their tasking is likely to be. Pressures will mount to reserve nuclear weapons for response to nuclear first use by the opponent. Improved conventional forces will be expected to raise the nuclear threshold accordingly.

A third factor leading to additional NATO emphasis upon conventional deterrence is the U.S. interest in the strategic defense initiative (SDI) and the possible deployment, during the 1990s, of U.S. and/or NATO European strategic or theater ballistic missile defenses. Boost-phase defenses, which intercept missiles in their first few minutes of powered flight, before they disperse their warheads on assigned trajectories, would provide protection for both theater and strategic targets. The United States might opt to defend North America and leave Europe undefended, but this would lead to decoupling of the U.S. strategic deterrent from regional deterrence in Western Europe. Neither the United States nor the Soviet Union could deploy national territorial defenses without abrogating the ABM Treaty of 1972. Either might try to circumvent the ABM Treaty by deploying antisatellite weapons that were inchoate ballistic missile defense (BMD) weapons disguised for another mission.

The U.S. problem with regard to SDI deployment, as opposed to research and development, is that at the point of deployment, one must be explicit about who is protected and who is not. Leaving Europe out divides NATO, but including Europe in a U.S. strategic umbrella may be prohibitive in cost. Not all Europeans are equally enthusiastic about SDI, and some want no part of it. The United States might begin mini-SDI deployments in Europe under the ABM Treaty-permitted rubric of theater BMD. However, to be truly effective against Soviet nuclear intimidation or attack, Euro-strategic BMD would have to be linked with U.S. homeland defenses. One can imagine that some of the SDI-related technologies could be used to develop theater BMDs that have some utility in deterring conventional war in Europe or in reducing NATO losses if conventional deterrence fails.[53]

A ticklish issue connects superpower arms control to the credibility of U.S. extended deterrence in Europe. Would strategic defenses for the U.S. homeland make a U.S. threat to retaliate with its strategic forces against Soviet theater nuclear or conventional forces about to prevail in Western Europe more, or less, credible? Experts disagree. In theory, a defended United States might have more resolve than a United States whose cities were exposed to Soviet nuclear retaliation. If the United States could remove its cities from their hostage condition, so the argument goes, it could then threaten the USSR with impunity.

However, a complication of this argument is that it omits mention of what the Soviet Union has done in response to the U.S. SDI (or, for that matter, for the Soviets' own motives). If the USSR also has a defense, and that defense is as competent as the U.S. one, then the gain in extended deterrence provided by the U.S. system is presumably canceled out. Moreover, if the Soviet system reaches a certain absolute threshold of competence, apart from its competence relative to the U.S. system, it will restrict U.S. limited nuclear options on behalf of European defense. And, again, the Soviet system might be good enough to threaten the capacity of the British and French strategic nuclear forces to retaliate after their homelands were attacked by the Soviet Union.

Regarding the superpower relationship itself, there is also the question of defenses reducing, instead of increasing, crisis stability and arms race stability. Defenses could contribute to crisis instability if they were based in space and vulnerable to space-based antisatellite weapons that were cheaper. They could contribute to arms race instability if they encouraged the other side to improve its offenses to the point at which the original defenses were negated at cheaper cost. Of course, it is not necessary that defenses, any more than offenses, have these characteristics. The superpowers will be reluctant to abandon the threat of retaliation totally, although with defenses deployed, offensive retaliation will have to cover a smaller number of attack scenarios. Deterrence by denial (to the opponent, of its objectives) would now supplement deterrence by threat of punishment.

It will be many years before defenses of such competence are deployed that the U.S. or Soviet leaders could place high confidence in them. Meanwhile, both have problems of alliance management with regard to BMD, although those of the USSR are arguably less. The Warsaw Pact is not the kind of voluntary alliance that NATO is, and the USSR has already deployed a treaty-permitted limited BMD system around Moscow. One can imagine the Rumanians opting out of a Soviet regional BMD system, and one can also imagine that the Kremlin might not care less. But, overall, the competition of both East and West to develop and field theater ballistic missile and improved air defenses, against near-term threats from improved conventional forces, seems more imminent, and more operationally pertinent, than the longer-range competition to deploy national U.S. or Soviet systems.

What if conventional deterrence becomes more important in Europe, and nuclear first use less plausible? This does not by any means remove nuclear weapons from the NATO deterrence picture. Nor does it imply that Soviet doctrine will assume a NATO unwillingness to use nuclear weapons. The USSR will fight from a posture in which it anticipates that NATO might go nuclear at any time, and especially when NATO seems about to lose the conventional war.[54] Even after the INF reductions, NATO will have some 4,000 tactical nuclear weapons deployed in Europe (roughly those with ranges of less than 300 miles). These forward-deployed nuclear weapons could easily become embroiled in a conventional war in Europe once desperate NATO corps commanders sought, and were authorized, nuclear release.[55] No Soviet war planner would recommend a lunge across the north German plain in the expectation that NATO, facing imminent defeat on part or all of its territory, might not use nuclear weapons.

On the other hand, if the Soviet Union is losing a conventional war in Europe and appears to be falling short of its prewar objectives, what then? Would it introduce nuclear weapons into such a conflict if the West had not? The Soviet Union has publicly pledged not to be the first country to use nuclear weapons in war, but the Soviets do not consider that preemption, in anticipation of first use by the opponent, is equivalent to first use as defined by NATO. Thus, if fought to a stalemate on the Central Front and devoid of conventional options, the USSR might escalate, if that escalation could accomplish quickly and decisively what it could not otherwise accomplish with Soviet and other Warsaw Pact conventional forces. This would be one of the principal challenges for war termination: to create a disengagement of conventional forces after stalemate was obvious but before nuclear escalation occurred. The difficulty is compounded by the two conflicting motives for escalation by either side in a stalemated situation: desperation, for want of any perceived alternative, or opportunity, as a way to leap over the stalemate, to one's advantage. Or, perversely, both factors, seeming opposites in theory, could reinforce each other in practice, as desperate policymakers and commanders attributed false hopes to alternatives simply because they were available.[56]

There are two dangers for Western analysts and planners in placing more emphasis upon conventional deterrence, to the exclusion of a prominent role for nuclear weapons, if the above arguments hold. The first danger is that of underestimating the present conventional strength of NATO, which is considerable. It would not be an easy pill for the USSR to swallow, under the most favorable assumptions (for the USSR) about relative alliance force balances, mobilization rates, and coalition cohesion. It seems that a conservative Soviet planner must calculate that the odds are too long in Europe.[57] A too pessimistic self-diagnosis by NATO can exaggerate the real threat to unreal proportions, leading to nostrums that are misplaced. Whether, for example, NATO can defeat the Soviet second-echelon armies will matter less than whether it can prevent those of the first echelon from achieving a decisive breakthrough and disruption of its forward-deployed forces.

The second danger is that of NATO complacency, of assuming that force balances, mobilization rates, and alliance cohesion really do not matter very much because of the low probability of war in Europe under any conditions. This second danger is a very seductive one because it is largely true. The probability of war in Europe is certainly low, and the probability of a deliberate and unprovoked Soviet attack westward is even lower. However, it is just this improbable character of war in Europe that, if it happens, will make it unbelievable to policymakers.[58] And not only to NATO leaders, but also to Soviet ones, for the likelihood of war growing out of a failure within their system of control over Eastern Europe should not be underestimated. The social mobilization of the peoples of Eastern Europe has long been delayed by the rigidities of the Cold War. As those restraints are loosened—for example, in East-West arms control agreements—political quiescence will be more difficult to maintain in Eastern Europe on any basis other than adjustment to new public expectations about political rights and social entitlements.

## CONCLUSION

Theorists can posit a conventional war in Europe that is terminated at that stage. Or they can construct equally plausible scenarios in which conventional war slips across the threshold of limited nuclear use. Thereafter it becomes difficult to know where or when such a conflict would end. But it would have to end somehow, and the question for planners and policymakers is whether they have thought through the problem in advance, however difficult it is to engage the attention of the pertinent officials.

The notion of an agreed battle as it applies to war in Europe is a very problematical one. The restraints would have to be imposed by both sides very quickly, before the fog of war and the sunken costs of commitment overwhelmed policymakers and commanders. However, the notion of restraint is not irrelevant to fighting war in Europe. One important issue is where else the superpower coalitions are engaged in combat, with what weapons, and with what objectives. A global conventional war is larger and potentially less subject to control than a regional war, given the inherent undesirability of both. An important issue with no obvious answer is how the USSR would react to a NATO conventional retaliatory offensive into Eastern Europe (as opposed to limited tactical incursions by ground forces and deep air interdiction, which are now programmed).[59]

The second component of war termination, escalation control, is also a matter of some uncertainty once war begins in Europe. A smart analyst would not place very much reliance on containing war in Europe below the nuclear threshold. However, once war began, both sides would have incentives to limit war to the region, to keep it below the nuclear threshold, and to terminate it before it escalated into attacks on the U.S. and Soviet homelands. This issue has divisive potential within NATO more than it does within the Warsaw Pact. There is a fundamental and irrevocable difference between U.S. and European stakes in limiting escalation, as opposed to preventing war altogether.

Effective use of coercive diplomacy to terminate a war in Europe is bounded by the lack of environmental conditions permitting it to work well. Clear communication of intentions to limit war would become more difficult as the conflict expanded across Europe and the stakes rose proportionately. U.S. and Soviet strategic nuclear forces would be alerted and poised to retaliate, although how long effective alerts could be sustained is unknown. The U.S. maritime strategy includes some notions about the coercive use of naval forces to bring about war termination on favorable terms before nuclear escalation occurs (this will be taken up more specifically in a later chapter). It is important to remember that there is a diplomatic or bargaining factor as well as a coercive one in the term "coercive diplomacy," as stressed in Chapter 1. Thus, either East or West would have to offer some carrots as well as sticks.

## NOTES

1. Herman Kahn, *On Escalation: Metaphors and Scenarios* (New York: Frederick A. Praeger, 1965).

2. On this topic see Stephen J. Cimbala and Keith A. Dunn, eds., *Conflict Termination in Military Strategy: Coercion, Persuasion and War* (Boulder, Colo.: Westview Press, 1987); and George H. Quester, "The Difficult Logic of Terminating a Nuclear War," in Stephen J. Cimbala, ed., *Strategic War Termination* (New York: Praeger, 1986), pp. 53–74.

3. Fritz W. Ermarth, "Contrasts in American and Soviet Strategic Thought," ch. 3 in Derek Leebaert, ed., *Soviet Military Thinking* (London: Allen and Unwin, 1981), pp. 50–72.

4. See B. Byely et al., *Marxism-Leninism on War and Army* (Moscow: Progress Publishers, 1972); and Michael MccGwire, *Military Objectives in Soviet Foreign Policy* (Washington, D.C.: Brookings Institution, 1987). MccGwire is especially useful on the evolution of Soviet geopolitical objectives and their relationship to military strategy.

5. See John J. Dziak, *Soviet Perceptions of Military Power: The Interaction of Theory and Practice* (New York: National Strategy Information Center, 1981).

6. *Operations*, U.S. Army FM 100–5 (Washington, D.C.: Department of the Army, 1982).

7. For an informative essay on this, see Robert Bathurst, "Two Languages of War," in Leebaert, ed., *Soviet Military Thinking*, pp. 3–27.

8. Raymond L. Garthoff, "Conflict Termination in Soviet Military Thought and Strategy," ch. 3 in Cimbala and Dunn, eds., *Conflict Termination in Military Strategy*, pp. 33–58.

9. Raymond L. Garthoff, "Mutual Deterrence, Parity and Strategic Arms Limitation in Soviet Policy," ch. 5 in Leebaert, ed., *Soviet Military Thinking*, pp. 92–124.

10. Mary FitzGerald, "Marshall Ogarkov on Modern War, 1971–1985," Center for Naval Analyses, Working Paper, September 1985. See also Marshal N. V. Ogarkov, *History Teaches Vigilance* (Moscow: Voyenizdat, 1985).

11. For pertinent background, see Stephen M. Meyer, "Soviet Perspectives on the Paths to Nuclear War," in Graham T. Allison, Albert Carnesale, and Joseph S. Nye, Jr., eds. *Hawks, Doves and Owls: An Agenda for Avoiding Nuclear War* (New York: W. W. Norton, 1985), pp. 167–205.

12. Col. Gen. M. A. Gareyev, *M. V. Frunze—Military Theoretician: The Views of M. V. Frunze and Contemporary Military Theory* (Moscow: Voyenizdat, 1985), is being cited with increased frequency by Western military analysts of Soviet strategy. See John G. Hines, Philip A. Petersen, and Notra Trulock III, "Soviet Military Theory from 1945–2000: Implications for NATO," *Washington Quarterly* 9, no. 4 (Fall 1986): 117–137.

13. See Christopher Donnelly, "Soviet Operational Concepts in the 1980s," in *Strengthening Conventional Deterrence in Europe: Proposals for the 1980s*, report of the European Security Study (New York: St. Martin's Press, 1983), pp. 105–136; and John G. Hines and Phillip A. Petersen, "The Warsaw Pact Strategic Offensive: The OMG in Context," *International Defense Review*, October 1983, pp. 1391–1395.

14. The possibility that U.S.-Soviet nuclear exchanges might be confined to Europe was apparently suggested to U.S. officials by Soviet representatives during the Nixon administration. See Meyer, "Soviet Perspectives on the Paths to Nuclear War," p. 185.

15. On the theory of coercive diplomacy, see Alexander L. George, "The Development of Doctrine and Strategy," ch. 1 in Alexander L. George, David K. Hall, and William R. Simons, *The Limits of Coercive Diplomacy: Laos, Cuba, Vietnam* (Boston: Little, Brown, 1971), pp. 1–35.

16. This discussion adapts the framework developed in ibid.

17. See Barbara W. Tuchman, *The Guns of August* (New York: Macmillan, 1962).

18. A definitive study is Fred Charles Ikle, *Every War Must End* (New York: Columbia University Press, 1971).

19. Paul Bracken, "War Termination," ch. 6 in Ashton B. Carter, John D. Steinbruner, and Charles A. Zraket, eds., *Managing Nuclear Operations* (Washington, D.C.: Brookings Institution, 1987), p. 198.

20. See Meyer, "Soviet Perspectives on the Paths to Nuclear War," p. 185. Western and Soviet approaches to escalation in Europe are compared in Paul K. Davis and Peter J. E. Stan, *Concepts and Models of Escalation*, (Santa Monica, Calif.: Rand Corporation, 1984).

21. The definitive study in political science is Roberta Wohlstetter, *Pearl Harbor: Warning and Decision* (Stanford, Calif.: Stanford University Press, 1962).

22. See Scott D. Sagan, "Nuclear Alerts and Crisis Management," *International Security* 9 (Spring 1985): 99–139.

23. Graham T. Allison, *Essence of Decision: Explaining the Cuban Missile Crisis* (Boston: Little, Brown, 1971).

24. Ibid., p. 138. An application of these models in another context is provided in Leon V. Sigal, *Fighting to a Finish: The Politics of War Termination in the United States and Japan, 1945* (Ithaca, N.Y.: Cornell University Press, 1988).

25. Allison, *Essence of Decision*, p. 140.

26. On U.S. nuclear weapons safeguards, see Donald R. Cotter, "Peacetime Operations: Safety and Security," in Carter, Steinbruner, and Zraket, eds., *Managing Nuclear Operations*, pp. 17–74.

27. See Paul Bracken, *The Command and Control of Nuclear Forces* (New Haven: Yale University Press, 1983), pp. 11–18, on the development of U.S. nuclear command systems and vertical integration of warning and intelligence with nuclear forces.

28. David Alan Rosenberg, "The Origins of Overkill: Nuclear Weapons and American Strategy, 1945–1960," *International Security* 7, no. 4 (Spring 1983), repr. in Steven E. Miller, ed., *Strategy and Nuclear Deterrence* (Princeton: Princeton University Press, 1984), p. 113–182. See p. 144.

29. Ibid.

30. Ibid., p. 145.

31. Authoritative U.S. government estimates during the Eisenhower administration revealed that the United States might inflict more damage on the USSR than vice versa by striking first (preemptively), but the Soviet Union could still inflict unprecedented destruction on the United States in response. Thus the administration shifted, between 1955 and 1956, from a policy of superiority to one of sufficiency in strategic nuclear forces. See Richard K. Betts, *Nuclear Blackmail and Nuclear Balance* (Washington, D.C.: Brookings Institution, 1987), pp. 150–155.

32. Bruce G. Blair, *Strategic Command and Control: Redefining the Nuclear Threat* (Washington, D.C. Brookings Institution, 1985).

33. Daniel Ford, *The Button: The Pentagon's Strategic Command and Control System* (New York: Simon and Schuster, 1985), p. 125.

34. Ibid., p. 84. See also Desmond Ball, *Can Nuclear War Be Controlled?* Adelphi Papers no. 169 (London: International Institute for Strategic Studies, 1981).

35. For development of this topic, see Fen Osler Hampsen, "Escalation in Europe," ch. 4 in Allison, Carnesale, and Nye, eds., *Hawks, Doves and Owls*, pp. 80–114.

36. Bracken, *The Command and Control of Nuclear Forces*, pp. 196–197.

37. Ibid., ch. 4, pp. 98–128.

38. See Meyer, "Soviet Perspectives on the Paths to Nuclear War," passim.; and Meyer, "Soviet Nuclear Operations," *Signal*, December 1986, pp. 41–56.

39. See Desmond Ball, *The Soviet Strategic Command, Control and Communications and Intelligence (C3I) System* (Canberra: Strategic and Defence Studies Centre, Australian National University, 1985), for background and perspective.

40. For discussions of this issue, see Jeffrey Richelson, "The Dilemmas of Counterpower Targeting," ch. 7 in Desmond Ball and Jeffrey Richelson, eds., *Strategic Nuclear Targeting* (Ithaca, N.Y.: Cornell University Press, 1986), pp. 159–

170; and Stephen J. Cimbala, "Countercommand Attacks and War Termination," ch. 7 in Cimbala, ed., *Strategic War Termination*, pp. 134–156.

41. On the development of the plans for Germany's attack against France in 1940, see John J. Mearsheimer, *Conventional Deterrence* (Ithaca, N.Y.: Cornell University Press, 1983), pp. 125–131.

42. Ikle, *Every War Must End*, pp. 62–64.

43. Adm. James D. Watkins, USN, "The Maritime Strategy," *Proceedings of the U.S. Naval Institute*, January, 1986, pp. 2–17.

44. Ibid., p. 2.

45. John J. Mearsheimer, "A Strategic Misstep: The Maritime Strategy and Deterrence in Europe," *International Security* 11, no. 2 (Fall 1986): 3–57.

46. Robert W. Komer, *Maritime Strategy or Coalition Defense?* (Cambridge, Mass.: Abt Books, 1984).

47. The case for a NATO conventional retaliatory offensive is made in Samuel P. Huntington, "The Renewal of Strategy," ch. 1 in Samuel P. Huntington, ed., *The Strategic Imperative* (Cambridge, Mass.: Ballinger, 1982), pp. 1–52.

48. Gregory F. Treverton, "Ending Major Coalition Wars," ch. 6 in Cimbala and Dunn, eds. *Conflict Termination and Military Strategy*, pp. 89–108.

49. See Hines, Peterson, and Trulock, "Soviet Military Theory from 1945–2000."

50. Compare Mearsheimer, *Conventional Deterrence*, pp. 165–186; John J. Mearsheimer, "Maneuver, Mobile Defense and the Central Front," *International Security* 6, no. 3 (Winter 1981/1982): 104–122; and Barry R. Posen, "Measuring the European Conventional Balance," *International Security* 9, no. 3 (Winter 1984/1985): 47–88.

51. Peter H. Vigor, *Soviet Blitzkrieg Theory* (New York: St. Martin's Press, 1983), ch. 14.

52. *Aviation Week and Space Technology*, December 14, 1987, p. 18.

53. See Richard D. DeLauer, "Emerging Technologies and Their Impact on the Conventional Deterrent," in Andrew J. Pierre, ed., *The Conventional Defense of Europe: New Technologies and New Strategies* (New York: Council on Foreign Relations, 1986), pp. 40–70.

54. John Erickson, Lynn Hansen, and William Schneider, *Soviet Ground Forces: An Operational Assessment* (Boulder, Colo.: Westview Press, 1986), p. 55.

55. Catherine McArdle Kelleher, "NATO Nuclear Operations," ch. 14 in Carter, Steinbruner, and Zraket, eds., *Managing Nuclear Operations*, pp. 445–469, provides an overview of pertinent issues.

56. Robert Jervis notes that limits to rational decision making include the possibilities that decision makers may fall prey to overconfidence, to misperceived value trade-offs, to mistaken interpretations of new information in terms of preexisting beliefs, and to defensive avoidance. See Jervis, "Deterrence and Perception," in Miller, ed., *Strategy and Nuclear Deterrence*, pp. 57–84, esp. pp. 73–84.

57. Benjamin S. Lambeth, "Uncertainties for the Soviet War Planner," *International Security* 7, no. 3 (Winter 1982/1983): 139–166.

58. A point made in Richard K. Betts, *Surprise Attack: Lessons for Defense Planning* (Washington, D.C.: Brookings Institution, 1982), p.154.

59. See Huntington, "The Renewal of Strategy."

# 7

# Conflict Termination and U.S. Maritime Strategy

The U.S. maritime strategy has been advanced by Navy professionals and policy analysts as the U.S. answer to the otherwise unsolvable problem of global war termination without nuclear escalation.[1] The term is perhaps logically distinct from the phrase "Maritime Strategy" that marked the rhetoric of the Reagan administration and the office of the secretary of the navy. This second "Maritime Strategy" fulfilled various functions, not the least of which was to garner major shares of the general-purpose forces budget for the U.S. Navy compared with its Air Force and Army competitors. And in this regard John Lehman must be judged to have succeeded, since the 600-ship navy was well on its way to construction by the time he left office during Reagan's second term.[2]

But the battle of the Potomac over force structure is not identical to the preparation of wartime operations that U.S. Navy professionals must expect to fight. The U.S. maritime stategy in lower case was the generic strategy that carrier admirals, submarine commanders, and other combatants would have to execute with the forces available, and according to prewar plans offering limited, although still formidable, options. From the standpoint of these operational planners and potential war fighters, the Navy's task in a regional European or global conventional war against the Soviet Union was clear enough. It was to control the seas in order to make them safe for U.S. and allied shipping, and for those combat missions with which maritime forces would be tasked by national command authorities.

This tasking, however, was expected to be very demanding on a force structure that, however much of the Reagan pie it had received, was still dispersed over several oceanic theaters of operations in peacetime.

And during crises, such as the attacks on tankers in the Perisan Gulf in 1987, the United States would frequently turn to its forces afloat when the alternatives did not allow for coercive diplomacy as an option between war and peace (see Chapter 1). The ambitious wartime tasking for a NATO-Warsaw Pact conflict that might spread beyond Europe could strain U.S. capabilities to the breaking point, forcing a painful choice between nuclear escalation and conventional defeat. Looking for a way to maximize U.S. advantages and Soviet disadvantages, U.S. planners sought to put U.S. maritime forces at the forefront of war termination.

In so doing, as explained below, planners entered into considerable controversy. Some of this controversy was due to the confusion between naval political rhetoric and maritime operational realities, and some of the confusion was the result of strategic misexplanation by the Navy itself. Enthusiastic force builders have been known to slide over into operational hubris. Particularly controversial was the expectation by advocates of the U.S. maritime strategy that war at sea could somehow be conducted so that war on land was terminated according to U.S., and not Soviet, wishes. This was controversial as a strategic statement of preferred relationships between means and ends. It was also contentious as a question of operational feasibility: whether the U.S. and allied navies could make any significant difference in war outcomes before nuclear escalation in Europe deprived them of the opportunity.[3]

Critics of the U.S. maritime strategy are therefore correct when they note, as we shall see, that the U.S./NATO maritime strategy is irrelevant if the Central Front collapses of its own incompetence. Such a collapse is not the most probable outcome, unless NATO is truly sleepwalking into a Soviet "bolt from the blue." In other than this highly unlikely scenario, U.S. maritime forces may make the difference in whether NATO can extend the war in time and/or space as an alternative to vertical escalation. The discussion that follows first reviews the components of U.S. maritime strategy as that strategy has been publicly proclaimed by officials. It then looks at other questions of escalation and risk, comparing those risks inherent in U.S. and allied NATO strategy for land warfare with those thought to be inherent in war at sea. We also consider the likelihood that NATO has even a theoretical escape, let alone a practical one, from running the risks of nuclear escalation even apart from the decisions made about U.S. maritime strategy.

## THE U.S. MARITIME STRATEGY

The principal objective of U.S. maritime strategy, in support of national military strategy, is deterrence. A secondary objective, should deterrence fail, is to end the war on terms as favorable as possible to the Western alliance, short of defeat.[4]

This general statement applies to conflicts of all kinds in which the U.S. Navy might be engaged, including visible presence in the Third World, low-intensity conflict, conventional war in Europe, and nuclear war. No other arm of service is required or expected to be as versatile. None can provide the flexibility of demonstrative warning without political commitment. Policymakers' options are maximized by having at their disposal naval forces that can rapidly enter, or withdraw from, a zone of conflict without tying the hands of a U.S. president who commits them.

This flexibility has its own dangers, however. Policy planners can come to rely on maritime forces to show the flag on occasions when it might not be appropriate, or to bail out inadequate diplomacy. In the last analysis, maritime forces are combat forces. They are not to be squandered on missions that politicians should handle through diplomatic channels. Nevertheless, maritime forces can support diplomacy by sending a subtle reminder to diverse foreign audiences that U.S. diplomacy is ultimately supported by deployable power. Another potential danger of the flexibility built into maritime forces is the temptation to act without allies. Obviously U.S. national strategy does not envision fighting a global war with the Soviet Union without the armies and navies of the NATO allies. But one might ask whether unilateralism is any more appropriate in Third World conflicts, even when the United States has maritime superiority compared with potential opponents. Were the United States to take military action in the Persian Gulf against Iranian or other regional forces, for example, it might be preferable to be assisted by the allies even through the U.S. Navy would not require that assistance.

General guidance always leaves much that is scenario dependent. The U.S. Navy cannot foresee all the contingencies that might lead a president to call upon its services. Wars involve turns of events that are not forecast even when policymakers think that their objectives are clearly defined. And maritime forces will be called upon to fight or to establish a visible presence when objectives are not clearly defined, as in the commitment of U.S. forces to the multinational peacekeeping force in Lebanon in 1983, which resulted in the blowing up of a barracks and the deaths of 243 U.S. Marines.[5] A clearer definition of objectives does not necessarily imply that naval commanders will have more control over events in the combat theater of operations. In operation Urgent Fury in Grenada, most of the important combat action was on the ground even after naval surface and air forces had established a secure periphery within which that ground combat could take place.

Nor, it must be acknowledged, is the U.S. maritime strategy able to transcend the bureaucratic politics of defense organization. As has been well documented, the Pentagon is organized not to fight wars but to fight budget battles.[6] Service competition for missions and resources is part of the background against which strategic choices are made. Although Congress had made reorganization of the Pentagon a priority in passing the Goldwater-Nichols bill of 1986, not much is likely to change in the basic character of a pluralistic U.S. defense policy-making system.[7] The U.S. maritime strategy will be built upon the limitations imposed by budget battles, mission malaise, and interservice rivalry that have taken place since the National Security Act of 1947 was passed.

Finally, there is among those things that need to be pointed out about the matter of general guidance for maritime strategy, the requirement for a certain amount of deliberate ambiguity. Particularly with reference to what the United States might choose to do in a crisis confrontation or actual war with the U.S.S.R., it is imprudent for the Navy to engage in total candor about operations. This has led some critics of U.S. maritime strategy to discern malice aforethought in the strategy, including a casual disregard for the possibility of escalation from conventional to nuclear war. More will be said about this below.

## WAR IN EUROPE

In the case of war between NATO and the Warsaw Pact, the U.S. maritime strategy provides that the Navy must accomplish several missions. The most basic among these is protection of the sea-lanes of communication that connect the United States to NATO Europe. Disruption of those sea-lanes by Soviet surface or submarine forces, or land-based maritime aircraft (Backfire bombers based on the Kola Peninsula) would disconnect European NATO from its supply lifeline and prevent timely reinforcements from reaching their destinations.[8]

Much depends upon how long the United States and allied NATO ground and tactical air forces can hold out. Estimates vary, and are somewhat contentious. Apparent estimates by the supreme allied commander, Europe, (SACEUR) suggest that NATO conventional forces without significant improvements will be defeated within several days and will have to resort to the introduction of nuclear weapons.[9] John J. Mearsheimer states that the Warsaw Pact may be made to seem more imposing than it really is by worst case estimates and that NATO, given appropriate time for reaction in prompt response to warning, can withstand plausible Pact attacks.[10] C. J. Dick has noted that much depends upon the surprise attained by Soviet/Pact attackers and the momentum or tempo that is maintained by them against NATO resistance.[11] William W. Kaufmann developed a variety of estimates about the viability of NATO conventional defense postures and argued that incremental improvements in current conditions, including barrier defenses, could provide credible conventional defenses at affordable costs.[12] Jeffrey Record recommends that NATO reconsider the declaratory doctrine of follow-on forces attack promulgated by Gen. Bernard Rogers and concentrate on fixes in its current deployment posture, including permanent fortification at the inter-German border and more operational reserves.[13]

The U.S. maritime strategy and U.S. Navy can contribute to denial of Soviet objectives on land in Europe, but they cannot substitute for conventional forces or doctrinal deficiencies relative to the land battle. As Adm. Isaac Kidd is reported to have said, someone must take the land and say "This belongs to me": navies cannot do that, whatever else they may do. It would be wrong and misguided in the extreme for U.S. maritime strategists to offer their forces as substitutes for increased supplies of ammunition or additional operational reserves in Europe.

The reverse is equally the case, however, for NATO forces in Europe. U.S. and European ground forces cannot by themselves bring about war termination without escalating to nuclear first use. NATO flexible response doctrine promises to deter the Soviet Union from conventional war in Europe by direct defense with conventional forces coupled to nuclear escalation if direct defense proves to be inadequate. Ultimately nuclear escalation might proceed to the use of U.S. strategic forces against targets in the Soviet Union or elsewhere, although it seems probable that the first Western uses of nuclear forces would involve short-range theater nuclear forces.[14] The problem with flexible response strategy is that what makes it a successful deterrent—the likelihood of nuclear escalation if NATO faces conventional defeat—makes it more difficult to limit the consequences of war after deterrence fails. It is an all-or-nothing strategy, despite some optimistic expectations that nuclear use in Europe could be selective and controlled, including the selective use of U.S. strategic forces on European targets. The fact is that no one has written a credible scenario for limited nuclear war in Europe that does not sooner or later involve intolerable risks of escalation to strategic nuclear war.[15]

We return to this point about escalation as it applies to maritime strategy in the next section. But it must first be appreciated that however implausible the story for escalation control might seem with regard to global U.S.-Soviet maritime conflict, it is no less implausible with regard to limited nuclear war in Europe even without the use of any maritime forces.[16] At issue is not whether more discriminating weapons of greater accuracy and smaller yield can be built and deployed among NATO forces based in Europe; they can, and are. The issue is the collision of U.S. and Soviet political expectations during conventional war in Europe. For the Soviet Union, if not for the Western alliance, as Benjamin S. Lambeth has noted, the important threshold in such a war will not be the step from conventional war to nuclear war but the onset of war itself.[17] This does not mean that the USSR will be insensitive to U.S. crossing of that threshold, however. Should the Soviets detect preparations for NATO nuclear first use or events that they interpret to be those preparations, they might choose to preempt.[18]

The deficiencies in flexible response strategy are well known. First, the strategy means something different to Europeans and to Americans. Whereas U.S. strategists see flexible response as a way to preserve options even after deterrence fails, Europeans emphasize the coupling between conventional and theater or strategic nuclear forces.[19] In the U.S. formulations of flexible response, conventional forces in Europe are frequently discussed as denial forces, while Europeans envision those forces as creating a trip wire that triggers nuclear release that deters Soviet aggression.

Second, flexible response allows the initiative to the Soviet Union. NATO is by definition a defensive alliance, and even prudent military measures cannot be taken if they are deemed unduly provocative or politically ambiguous by alliance members. An illustration is the need for fortifications at the inter-German border, which have been precluded because they symbolize for some Germans the permanent division of their country into two parts. Another cost of conceding the initiative to the Soviet Union and the Warsaw Pact is that they can pick the time and place of launching an attack. This acts as a force multiplier that offsets some of the assets of the NATO side and makes it more likely that the Warsaw Pact can eventually break through in one or more sectors.[20]

Third, flexible response cannot compensate for deficiencies in conventional forces as denial forces by substituting tactical nuclear weapons, as is commonly thought. NATO theater nuclear weapons are useful as complements to adequate conventional ground forces, provided those forces are adequate to deny Soviet objectives. If they are not, tactical nuclear weapons do not necessarily favor the defense.[21] Soviet doctrine emphasizes a rapid and decisive breakthrough into the rear of the opponent in order to disrupt and confuse its defensive battle plan.[22] To accomplish this, specially tasked forces, including operational maneuver groups, will strike deep into NATO's vitals in order to isolate frontal defenders from their logistic and command, control, and communications (C3) support.[23] Successful preemption may preclude NATO nuclear release. Since the Warsaw Pact has the initiative, it can orient and concentrate its forces in advance; any delay in NATO reaction time could prove fatal.[24]

NATO, in partial recognition of these potential problems, has developed the declaratory doctrine of follow-on forces attack for deep interdiction of Warsaw Pact second-echelon forces long before they reach the forward line of troops.[25] Follow-on forces attack and other "deep attack" operations will be relevant if the Soviet/Pact first-echelon forces can be contained, but, as explained above, conceding the initiative to the attacker diminishes NATO's chances of preventing some potentially decisive breakthroughs against its forward defenses. The Soviets can concentrate forces for deep penetration behind NATO front lines and then encircle isolated defenders, while fighting rapid meeting engagements on the ground. This would be accompanied by a strategic-theater air offensive that neutralized NATO's conventional air defenses and equalized NATO and Pact tactical offensive air assets.[26] Destruction of Soviet second-echelon forces would not compensate for isolation and confusion among NATO's critical corps sectors at the Central Front.

## ESCALATION

Like war on land, war at sea between U.S./NATO and Soviet/Pact forces involves significant risk of escalation. No one can guarantee that this escalation can be contained short of strategic nuclear war. While this fact may be daunting for U.S. strategists, it should apply with equal force to U.S. estimates of Soviet calculations. The prospect of strategic nuclear war involving superpower homeland exchanges can be no more attractive to the Soviet Union than it can be to the United States, despite the expectation by some analysts that Soviet societal preparedness for post-attack recovery is superior to that of the United States.[27]

The question of escalation, however, involves more than the movement from conventional to nuclear weapons. Weapons employment is only one dimension of the problem of escalation and, thus, of escalation control.

Of greater importance once war begins will be Soviet and U.S. assumptions about wartime and postwar objectives. If the Soviet Union perceives that it is the U.S. or NATO objective to invade the Soviet Union or Eastern Europe with ground forces, for the purpose of reversing the "Brezhnev doctrine" (by which the Soviets declare that a regime communized within their contiguous empire cannot be dissolved), its incentives for escalation control are very few. This is the cautionary note that must be applied to the otherwise intriguing proposal by Samuel P. Huntington for a "conventional retaliatory offensive" into Eastern Europe by NATO forces immediately following the onset of a USSR/Pact attack into Western Europe.[28]

Although Huntington's proposal is problematical to implement without raising the risk of uncontrolled escalation, it is based upon a sounder deterrence logic than the objective of retaliation per se might suggest. Huntington has grasped the important point that nuclear deterrence and conventional deterrence are moving in ironic directions in Western Europe. What the United States will need in the future is a strategy of diversified deterrence in which conventional forces can contribute to deterrence not only because of their denial capabilities but also because of their potential retaliatory capabilities.[29] Huntington applies this insight to land forces, but it is also applicable to war at sea.

U.S. maritime forces can accomplish some of the retaliatory missions now assigned by NATO to strategic and theater nuclear forces, or by Huntington in his proposal to conventional ground forces. They can increase the costs of continuing the war for the Soviet Union and its allies, and create incentives for war termination. To do this, U.S. and allied maritime forces can exercise both denial and retaliatory options.

Denial options would ensure control of the sea-lanes and protection of U.S. and allied coasts and coastal waters against domination by the Soviet fleet. They would also encompass denial of Soviet maritime air superiority over the northern flank. U.S. maritime denial capabilities would force the USSR immediately to contemplate the prospect of a protracted war at sea, whatever the conditions on land.

The Politburo's contemplation of a long rather than a short war should also be stimulated by the use of maritime forces for retaliatory as well as denial actions. Retaliation in this instance would have two objectives: first, the destruction of Soviet naval forces that posed any threat to the survivability of U.S. and allied maritime forces; second, the attrition of Soviet ballistic missile submarines (SSBN) to the extent that those submarines cannot be distinguished from attack submarines (SSN) threatening the U.S. fleet.[30] These retaliatory options complement the denial options and pose short-term and long-term costs to the Soviets for continuing the war. In the short term, U.S./NATO domination of the battle for the Norwegian Sea will allow the protection of sea-lanes that are decisive for NATO reinforcement. This might not preclude Soviet occupation of parts of West German territory, but it should preclude the conquest of all of Western Europe with conventional forces alone. Another short-term implication of sea control is that the Soviet surface navy will be in a war of attrition that is a logical prelude to its total destruction, a long-term matter of concern to the successors of Admiral Gorshkov.

The retaliatory option of most long-term importance to the USSR might be the gradual attrition of its SSBN fleet, an important component of its strategic reserve. Much of the Soviet surface fleet is already devoted to protection of the waters within which this naval strategic reserve fleet conducts its patrols. Attrition of the Soviet surface fleet thus increases the improbability of protecting their bastions even before any SSBN are actually engaged. Once U.S. and Soviet submarines are engaged in "the battle of the Atlantic" if it comes to that, Soviet leaders will certainly anticipate that their SSBN will be fair game along with SSN. One can judge this from the absence of any Soviet statements promising that U.S. SSBN will be given sanctuary status in the event of global war, and from the conservative planning assumptions that cautious Soviet leaders are always presumed to make.[31]

Nonetheless, the risks should not be minimized. Barry R. Posen has cautioned that the attrition of Soviet SSBN could lead to the Soviet conclusion that strategic nuclear war was under way, regardless of U.S. intent.[32] Desmond Ball has noted that a substantial proportion of U.S. nuclear weapons are deployed on submarines and surface ships that would certainly be involved in any major war in Europe.[33] But there is another side to these observations about the dangers of escalation. Those dangers, apparent to Kremlin leaders as well as to NATO's, should dissuade them from further escalation if NATO has not muddled the issue of its political objectives, as opposed to its military operations. In other words, the clear and consistent communication of its political objectives, before and during war, will be as important to NATO as the conduct of its military operations. The maritime strategy in this sense is deliberately escalatory, designed to impose progressively greater costs upon the USSR and its allies should they choose to continue the battle for Europe. It is important to be clear about what is at stake in such a conflict. For the USSR to persevere in any theater war in Europe beyond the first few weeks, its objectives can be nothing less that the subjugation of that continent. For the West to acquiesce in this is nothing less than defeat, not only for NATO as an alliance but also for the United States as a putative superpower.

Participants in U.S. policy debates imagine that there would be various graduated stages of escalation during war in Europe and that the thresholds separating one stage from another would be clear and obvious. Entering war on this assumption could prove fatal. Essentially there are two kinds of wars that can happen between the NATO and Warsaw Pact coalitions: wars of very limited objective (probably developing out of crisis misperception) and strategic wars. In the second case, the objective is the conquest of continental Europe, whether by conventional or nuclear weapons. NATO strategy implies that the choice of weapons by the USSR, rather than the political objectives for which the USSR is fighting, will determine the degree of responsive escalation by the West. These objectives may be indistinct at the outset, but the distinction between a limited and a strategic war in Europe will be obvious before very long. A strategic war for Europe (or a strategic/theater war in Soviet parlance) is not necessarily a global war if horizontal escalation can be controlled, but it should be remembered that a strategic war in Europe is (ultimately) about the postwar balance of power in global terms. Thus, the Reagan administration's initial declaratory emphasis upon horizontal escalation, much maligned by critics, may have little value as declaratory policy but may in fact come to represent the actual state of affairs that is imposed on the West after war begins.

At the same time, NATO needs some options other than conventional retaliation into Eastern Europe or nuclear attacks into Eastern Europe or the Soviet Union in order to induce Soviet moves toward war termination along the lines of the status quo ante. It has no appropriate options that are not risky in this context. The choice is among several very risky options *by peacetime standards.* But none of these options would even be contemplated under other than wartime conditions, and under wartime conditions involving the entire European theater of operations or its most important territories and waters.

Peacetime comparisons make the maritime strategy seem riskier than it really is. So do comparisons with idealized versions of current NATO strategy for the defense of Europe. The multitude of nuclear weapons deployed in Western Europe and commingled with conventional forces do not constitute a precision instrument. Even apart from the uncertainty about the role of British and French strategic deterrents, nuclear weapons based on the European continent and in quick reaction aircraft create command and control uncertainties for NATO itself. As Paul Bracken has noted, the Soviets are as likely to fear NATO's loss of control over its short- and medium-range nuclear weapons as they are to fear the controlled and deliberate employment of them.[34] Once war in Europe began, NATO and Warsaw Pact forces would be nuclear-armed hydras stinging each other in the midst of a large conurbation of unprecedented congestion and chaos. Unlike deliberate or inadvertent nuclear war at sea, collateral damage is immediate and the attendant emotional reactions, predictable.

Nor should it be assumed that NATO will exercise the prerogative to cross the nuclear threshold, at sea or on land. NATO's conventional declaratory strategies do not seem as innocuous to the USSR as they do to their architects. An example is the recent set of U.S. Army tactical doctrinal refinements known as AirLand Battle.[35] AirLand Battle doctrine is based upon "securing or retaining the initiative and exercising it aggressively to defeat the enemy." The best results are obtained when "initial blows are struck against critical units and areas whose loss will degrade the coherence of enemy operations, rather than merely against the enemy's leading formation."[36] In case anyone wonders what this might mean in Western Europe, U.S. Army field manual FM 100–5, *Operations,* notes that opposing forces "will rarely fight along orderly, distinct lines," that "distinctions between rear and forward areas will be blurred," and

... air and ground maneuver forces; conventional, nuclear and chemical fires: unconventional warfare; active reconnaissance, surveillance and target-acquisition efforts; and electronic warfare will be directed against the forward and rear areas of both combatants.[37]

Army doctrine is not cited to be critical. On the contrary, it is remarkably realistic and straightforward. The point is that allegations that the U.S. maritime strategy creates unnecessary risks of escalation should raise the question "Compared to what?" Soviet planners offering reasonable interpretations of AirLand Battle to their superiors would conclude that NATO counteroffensives across the inter-German border, perhaps including early resort to nuclear use, are in the offing. This may be the reason that Gen. Bernard Rogers, SACEUR, has refused to endorse AirLand Battle, citing the obvious allied sensitivities to reference to nuclear or chemical weapons use initiated by the West, however hypothetical the discussion.

Nor should Soviet reactions to NATO escalation be misrepresented. The nuclear threshold should not be crossed lightly. But two superpowers at war in Europe would be hard pressed to avoid it. One Soviet sensitivity, to which this author wishes all U.S. strategists were more attuned, is sensitivity to attacks on their homeland by conventional or nuclear weapons. Soviet leaders might be persuaded that attrition of their SSBN force was occurring as part of a process of combat that was not fully controllable by either side. Attacks on Soviet ports, airfields, or other homeland territorial targets would have an entirely different symbolism, and the step should be taken by the West only after Warsaw Pact provocations have left no practical alternative.[38] It will be difficult for maritime forces involved in Arctic engagements to avoid creating the appearance of threat to Soviet homeland targets; nevertheless, gratuitous destruction of those targets would invite escalation to nuclear attacks on the continental United States if the Soviets feared they had nothing else to lose.

Another issue raised by possible attacks on the Soviet homeland, with conventional or nuclear weapons, is the widespread belief in the possibility of substituting horizontal escalation for crossing the nuclear threshold. Horizontal escalation is the expansion of a conflict to geographical theaters of operation outside of, and in addition to, those in which it began.[39] This notion was made popular by officials in the Reagan administration who have since departed, but its essence has survived changes in personnel. The idea of horizontal escalation was that the United States, perhaps on the defensive in Europe, might counterattack the Soviet Union or its allies and clients somewhere else in the world. As Robert Komer has suggested, attacking Soviet Third World clients such as Cuba would be small compensation for the loss of Western Europe; the United States is not committed by virtue of its maritime strategy to such a trade-off.[40] What is more problematical for U.S. strategy is the lack of adequate airlift, sealift, and prepositioning to sustain simultaneous conflict in Europe and another major theater of operations, such as the Persian Gulf. Horizontal escalation, whatever its conceptual appeal, does not provide an alternative to nuclear escalation or to conventional war that threatens to change the nuclear correlation of forces from the Soviet perspective.[41]

## THE MARITIME STRATEGY AND ITS CRITICS: UNDERFORMULATED ISSUES

One of the most significant criticisms of the Maritime Strategy is the contention that it might lead to inadvertent nuclear war instead of war termination favorable to the Western alliance. John J. Mearsheimer, in an article in *International Security,* provides an extensive critique of the Maritime Strategy alleging that the strategy is vulnerable on precisely this point.[42] According to Mearsheimer, the principal components of the Maritime Strategy include offensive sea control and counterforce coercion against the Soviet SSBN force. Although previous explanations of the strategy seemed to emphasize offensive sea control, according to Mearsheimer the January 1986 presentation by Admiral Watkins highlighted counterforce coercion. This, in Mearsheimer's judgment, involved unnecessary risks that nuclear escalation, rather than war termination, would result from any implementation of U.S. naval strategy.

Capt. Linton Brooks, one of the principal architects of the Maritime Strategy, expressed a more sympathetic view of the relationship between the strategy and escalation. Writing in the same issue of *International Security* as Mearsheimer, Brooks contends that by adjusting the nuclear correlation of forces in favor of the United States and its Western allies, anti-SSBN operations can provide leverage for war termination without carrying undue risks of escalation.[43] It is obvious that this argument is not going to be resolved soon, absent deterrence failure.

The answer to the question of escalation control is a compromise between deliberate and inadvertent escalation. The United States would want to be raising Soviet incentives to comply with its demands for war termination while avoiding the expectation in the Kremlin that compliance would imply something more drastic, such as the demise of the regime. Part of what is threatening about escalation, in horizontal and vertical dimensions, is that it cannot be fully controlled. If your opponent knows that you can turn escalation on or off at will, without regard to any countermeasures, then there is no uncertainty with which to couple threats to compliance. Whether NATO can create this uncertainty between threats and Soviet responses depends upon fulfillment of other conditions once war begins. And these other issues are far from having been fully resolved.

What is interesting about the exchanges of the Maritime Strategy advocates and critics, then, is that they have left some unanswered questions about several issues that need further discussion and analysis. Indeed, there is some surprising consensus between critics and advocates on issues about which both may be wrong. A few of these issues are discussed below, although they cannot be fully resolved here.

## Blitzkrieg

One of the first underformulated issues is the assumption shared by maritime critics and advocates that the Soviets are capable of mounting a successful blitzkrieg attack in Western Europe. In his very influential study *Conventional Deterrence,* John Mearsheimer argues that the key to deterrence on the Central Front is the ability of NATO to thwart a Soviet blitzkrieg.[44] According to Mearsheimer, should the Soviet Union expect to succeed in a rapid and decisive conventional war against NATO, deterrence will fail. However, he thinks deterrence in Europe is fairly secure because NATO has adequate regular forces, in his judgment, to thwart a Warsaw Pact blitzkrieg. Nevertheless, Mearsheimer shares the judgment of other experts that the preferred Soviet style for war in Europe would be a rapid and decisive thrust at NATO's vitals designed to win a rapid conquest of Europe in a style comparable with the German campaign against France in 1940.[45] Maritime Strategy advocates have conceded the point, for the most part, that the USSR may in this fashion rapidly and decisively achieve its aims, and thus make allied naval forces almost irrelevant to the outcome.

There are two problems with these assessments of Soviet operational style and its relationship to the probability of war and escalation. The first is that the Soviet capability to fight in the style of warfare employed by the Nazis in France (or, for that matter, by the Israelis in 1967) is very debatable. The Soviet command structure differs from the German World War II tradition of *auftragstaktik* and from that of the Israeli Defense Force. Command and control in the USSR ground and tactical air forces, which would be the decisive components of a blitzkrieg, are very hierarchical compared with the German and Israeli forces. Little discretion is allowed subordinate commanders, and the Soviet use of the term "initiative" bears little resemblance to its Western counterpart.[46]

That the Soviet Union would prefer a rapid conventional victory to a prolonged stalemate in Europe is not disputed. But Soviet capabilities for rapid and decisive victory in Europe may not depend upon a classical blitzkrieg, which has only some similarities to their preferred operational style. As Barry R. Posen has noted, some aspects of the Nazi blitzkrieg were fortuitous; the German army initially resisted the idea of mobile armored warfare.[47] What finally resulted in the field was an amalgamation of Guderian's thinking, Hitler's intuitions, and the army's adaptation of a nontraditional subcomponent into its organizational structure.[48]

The last thing that Soviet front and theater commanders will want is armored spearheads charging along improvised routes without concomitant fire preparation by artillery and preceding theater-strategic air offensives.[49] The Soviet recipe for rapid victory in Europe will not employ airpower in the same fashion the Nazis did. Although Posen contends with some justification that the Nazis did use the *Luftwaffe* against the command/control and logistics infrastructure of the opponent's rear, its most dynamic impact came in close air support.[50] The Soviet theater-strategic air offensive would be designed to open the way for a comprehensive grasp of Western Europe. Targets very deep in the theater of operations would be struck with the objective of collapsing NATO's rear and opening the way for decisive and complementary ground offensives based upon the rapid insertion of operational maneuver groups behind the forward line of troops within the first day of the war.[51]

The very style of NATO forward defense maximizes Soviet incentives not to rely upon the improvisation so characteristic of the Nazi blitzkrieg. The USSR will probably preplan several primary attack axes and reinforce the one that seems to be showing the most promise during the first hours of combat. It will then be a question of how rapidly and decisively additional forces can be rushed though the breach in NATO's forward divisions in order to complete the encirclement and isolation (and ultimate destruction) of those divisions. Rapid meeting engagements will undoubtedly characterize the tactical and operational style of this conflict, and uncertainties that obtain at those levels will undoubtedly be exploited by attacker and defender. Still, the point is that were Hitler to rule in Moscow today, and were he to propose something akin to the blitzkrieg against Western Europe, the marshals in the Kremlin would be reluctant to rely upon the high degree of serendipity implicit in the führer's estimate. The Soviet style of war is characterized by operational and tactical flexibility, but not on a theater-strategic scale.

There is also a taxonomic similarity between the Nazi version of combined arms for ground warfare and the contemporary Soviet version. Both share a preoccupation with the disruption of the opponent's command and control and the preservation of one's own amid fluid combat operations.[52] As Charles J. Dick has noted, the Soviets are extremely conscious of their ability to maintain a rapid tempo of operations against the enemy in order to collapse its ability to coordinate any coherent response.[53] However, although there is an abstract similarity in the objective of disruption of the opponent's command and control, Nazi German and contemporary Soviet forces do not accomplish this in the same way. Soviet disruption of the opponent's command and control in a theater of operations such as Western Europe will involve extensive reliance upon *spetsnaz* forces, (forces of special designation), airborne landings, and other unexpected behind-the-lines demarches in order to collapse enemy resistance, including assaults against political and military leadership.[54] More on this will be said below, for it would be most un-Marxist for the USSR to expect that its field armies alone will accomplish *strategically decisive* objectives in a war involving the scope and destructiveness of war in Europe.

## Flexible Response

If maritime strategists and their critics are too willing to concede that the USSR is capable of employing a Nazi-style blitzkrieg against NATO, their second shared deficiency is the incomplete understanding of flexible response. It seems that Maritime Strategy advocates and critics alike share the judgment that if NATO can delay a Soviet blitzkrieg to the point at which the ground/air war in Europe becomes a war of attrition, then the advantage shifts to the West.

Several things are curious about this optimism that a war of attrition favors NATO. It seems dependent upon historical nostalgia for World War II in which the images of Western allied competence may be discrepant from reality. Max Hastings's account of the Normandy invasion and its aftermath makes sober reading for optimists about U.S. and Western allied capabilities, then and now, to fight protracted conventional war.[55] His conclusion is worth quoting:

One lesson from the fighting in Normandy seems important for any future battle that the armies of democracy might be called upon to fight. If a Soviet invasion force swept across Europe from the east, it would be unhelpful if contemporary British or American soldiers were trained and conditioned to believe that the level of endurance and sacrifice displayed by the Allies in Normandy would suffice to defeat the invaders.[56]

Hastings goes on to suggest that the appropriate reference standard for competence of ground forces is the *Wehrmacht.* How current U.S. and NATO conventional forces would compare with the *Wehrmacht* in combat power or actual fighting efficiency we cannot know. Some historians have contrasted U.S./allied and German fighting power during World War II, however. Among these, Trevor N. Dupuy and Martin van Creveld reach similar conclusions. U.S. and Western allied forces were vastly inferior in fighting power to those of the *Wehrmacht,* and so, apparently were Soviet forces.[57]

The good news is that NATO flexible response strategy is not predicated on the assumption of turning a conventional war in Europe into a lengthy war of attrition. Although the prospect of a war of attrition might deter the Soviets from starting a war, it is not the assumption of flexible response that the United States and its NATO allies will attempt to replay the invasion of *Festung* (Fortress) Europe. This assumption is apparently wise. In addition to the capabilities of allied ground forces in protracted war that can be projected from historical experience, there is a further difficulty. For the USSR to believe in the prospect of a lengthy war of attrition in Europe, it would have somehow to take account of the role of nuclear weapons in NATO flexible response strategy. That is, it would have, either physically and militarily, to render those weapons useless by capturing them or destroying them preemptively, or find some other way to push them toward the back end, instead of the front end, of NATO strategy for the defense of Europe.

Unfortunately for the USSR, it cannot assume that this deemphasis upon the role of nuclear weapons will occur by choice among NATO political and military leaders, since among the European members of NATO in particular that choice would be controversial. Therefore, the USSR must count on preemptively destroying NATO's weapons, which can be done only by achieving a large measure of political and military surprise in an attack on the Central Front. However, such operational-tactical surprise could turn into strategic defeat. A sudden elimination of NATO's short-, medium-, and intermediate-range nuclear forces could succeed to the point of panic in NATO capitals, resulting in the launching of nuclear strikes by French, British, or U.S. national nuclear forces or by U.S. and British forces committed to NATO (the British case is ambiguous).

Given no feasible alternative, it might seem that NATO's dependence upon nuclear escalation is unavoidable. Colin S. Gray had argued assertively that it is not. According to Gray, nuclear weapons are no longer the trump card for NATO because the concept of extended nuclear deterrence has reached political obsolescence.[58] A nuclear deemphasis is called for that can be obtained, in Gray's judgment, only through assertive use of U.S. maritime power. The United States has essentially three generic choices of emphasis in future national military strategy: strategic forces; land/tactical air forces; and sea power. According to Gray, the choice favors sea power, which would allow the United States to confront the USSR with the prospect of extended or protracted war, even if nuclear weapons were not used. However, he does acknowledge that, for this extended deterrent based on U.S. sea power to be viable, several attendant conditions must be satisfied. First, the United States must maintain a very competent strategic nuclear counterdeterrent. Second, it must preserve overall maritime superiority compared with its opponents, although not necessarily superiority at every hotspot on the globe. Third, NATO ground and tactical air forces must be adequate to prevent a rapid Soviet victory in Western Europe so that U.S. maritime control over the Atlantic sea lines of communication (SLOCs) is mean-ingful.[59]

A third generic difficulty for advocates and critics of the Maritime Strategy is that neither group explains how the United States can expect to prevail in an extended conventional war against the Soviet Union. Although the preferability of an extended conventional war compared with a nuclear war is undoubted, preparedness cannot avoid the prospect of either, or both. A conventional war in Europe would be fought under the shadow of imminent potential nuclear escalation, however long that conventional war became. The losing side in a conventional war, however it might define losing, would be tempted to escalate unless it were phys-ically prevented from doing so or were willing to accept war termination on unfavorable terms. The winning side would always fear nuclear es-calation on the part of the loser, and might take precautionary measures to protect the survivability of its weapons as an incentive for preemption. There is another twist to the conventional-nuclear distinction in the context of global war, and this is the possible Soviet expectation that the war could be nuclear first and then conventional in its global, protracted phase. What deters Soviet leaders might not be the initial exchange of nuclear weapons as much as the possibility that, even if they prevail in that exchange, the West would not surrender, but carry on the war into subsequent, "broken back" struggles.

Thus U.S. and NATO forces unprepared for protracted theater and/ or strategic nuclear and conventional conflict would be unable to pose to their Soviet opponents a credible and deliberate threat to escalate to theater-strategic or strategic nuclear war. They could still threaten to blunder into nuclear war by the "threat that leaves something to chance" and by involving the Soviet Union in a process of escalation not fully controllable by both. But this threat of deliberate or inadvertent/acci-dental escalation is overrated by Maritime Strategy critics and advocates alike. The Soviet command structure for global war against the West is likely to be very well informed about U.S. and allied capabilities. U.S. deterrence strategists have failed to distinguish among the following: prewar deterrence of any Soviet aggression against vital interests; intra-war deterrence of Soviet escalation by U.S. escalation dominance; and crisis management by the manipulation of the risk of war, a risk that is not fully controllable by either side. Certainly this leaves room for mis-estimates of U.S. intentions, as Khrushchev discovered to his dismay in 1962. The fact remains that the USSR in all probability either will choose not to begin World War III or will enter it in the full knowledge of its potentially catastrophic character, with appropriate political and military preparedness. Under those conditions, nuclear escalation will not come as a surprise to them strategically, however it happens tactically.

U.S. policymakers who expect to prevail in a protracted conventional war against the Soviet Union and Warsaw Pact have failed to notice that should the Kremlin choose nuclear rather than conventional extended war, U.S. forces and C3I are ill-equipped for the task. Studies of the U.S. strategic C3I system by Desmond Ball, Bruce G. Blair, and Paul Bracken have documented the difficulties facing U.S. planners who have called for forces and commanders that can survive the early stages of superpower nuclear conflict and endure through the first exchanges of nuclear weapons.[60] As Blair noted with some emphasis, U.S. strategic C3 as of the early 1980s was barely adequate to fulfill the requirements of the assured destruction mission.[61] Other difficulties include the plausible unavailability of damage assessments beyond the earliest stages of war; the difficulties in making commanders survivable and authenticating who is in charge; the provision of postattack reconstitution and recovery for strategic forces; and the establishment of communications between surviving U.S. and Soviet leaderships in order to terminate the war before countersocietal destruction escapes control.[62]

It might be supposed that the USSR is no better off with regard to the survivability and endurance of its strategic C3, and there is some evidence to support equally pessimistic assessments of Soviet postattack C3 survivability.[63] However, this is not good news for Western commentators. If the Soviet command structure is more vulnerable as a result of explicitly designed U.S. targeting policies than it otherwise would be, then those same operational plans cannot be depended upon as the mechanisms that will bring about war termination. If that is the case, then it is even less plausible for the West to suppose that the gradual erosion of the strategic nuclear component of the correlation of forces will pay dividends (as Maritime Strategy proponents claim). Only if the USSR is prepared to participate in the graduated expansion of nuclear war, as opposed to the blunderbuss approach that might be expected on the basis of its history and traditions, does the counterforce attrition of Soviet SSBN fit the script for war termination. Western planners must recognize that deterring the Soviet Union *in* war is a very different matter from deterring the Soviet Union *from* war.

One might also question the validity of the strategic net assessment that counts on gradual attrition of the Soviet SSBN force to bring about war termination. Absent strategic defense for the U.S. and/or European homelands, and absent modernization of the U.S. ICBM force, attrition of the Soviet SSBN fleet amounts to the progressive deterioration of a capability in which the Soviets, relative to the West, are already deficient. The conquest of Western Europe might well be worth the loss of half the Soviet strategic submarine fleet, provided the USSR did not fear preemptive attack on its land-based strategic forces (which the United States does not have the wherewithal to attempt).

It might be supposed that the deployment of Trident II submarine-launched ballistic missiles by the United States, beginning in 1989, would provide sea-based prompt counterforce that could threaten imminent destruction of Soviet ICBMs. However, anticipating that U.S. development, the Soviets have begun deploying mobile ICBMs, modernizing their SSBN fleet, and developing newer bombers with cruise missiles in a move toward diversified survivability. Thus, threatening imminent destruction of the Soviet "Triad" of the 1990s will not be a convincing story for NATO even after significant attrition of the Soviet SSBN fleet has taken place. Note that this skepticism about the efficacy of counter-SSBN attacks differs from the reassurance that they do not matter because both sides preserve assured destruction capabilities even after much attrition of their sea-based strategic forces has taken place. Whether assured destruction capabilities prove to be useful in terminating a war, instead of escalating it, depends upon their utility for assured coercion of the opponent whose force structure, as well as cities, must be put at risk during war, although at different stages.

Maritime Strategy critics, on the other hand, posit no more plausible termination. Mearsheimer, for example, suggests that NATO has a reasonable chance to halt a Warsaw Pact blitzkrieg and turn the war into a stalemate. Perhaps so, but the unanswered question is "What do we do then?" The USSR is presumably squatting on half or more of West Germany and/or the Low Countries and part of Scandinavia. What combination of carrots and sticks will remove it? The Maritime Strategy recommendations for attacking the Soviet homeland with conventional forces could easily escalate into global nuclear war. A conventional retaliatory offensive of the kind proposed by Samuel Huntington, as a way of ending a stalemate and turning the tables in NATO's favor, lacks plausibility without greatly increased Western forces.[64] Air attacks against targets deep in the rear echelons of the Warsaw Pact (essentially deep into Poland and the Soviet Union), as called for in follow-on force attack concepts, could delay arrival of the Warsaw Pact second strategic echelon into the battle but will not remove Soviet tank and motorized rifle divisions from the Federal Republic.

There is, according to some, the possibility of raising a rumpus in the back yard of the Soviet Union by encouraging Chinese irredentism to regain lost territories or for other plausible motives. While Soviet expectations might preclude removing large numbers of divisions from the Eastern Front for use against NATO, the likelihood of Chinese belligerency against the USSR *before* the issue is decided in Western Europe is small. The same dilemma faces Tokyo as Beijing: premature belligerency would be costly, although failure to come in for the spoils amounts to a missed opportunity. But the spoils are likely to be negligible in the Far East unless the Soviet empire itself is cracking apart, in which case war termination becomes even more difficult for the superpowers to negotiate. The wariness of Soviet and Japanese leaderships during World War II about engaging in direct conflict illustrates the complexity of predicting decisions within the Russo-Sino-Japanese triangle.

A fourth issue that requires some additional sorting out is that of proximate versus systemic causes of crisis instability. Proximate causes are those embedded in the decision-making processes and military doctrines of the various state and other actors who decide between war and peace. Systemic causes are those inherent in the structure of the international system and in the collision courses between the basic political objectives of the major powers. This distinction can be confused, to the detriment of a clearer understanding of crisis stability under present conditions.

For example, it has been suggested that the conditions under which the major powers went to war in 1914 are similar to those that might prevail if the superpowers stumbled into nuclear war in the near future. The apparent similarities lie in the possibility of overly optimistic offensive military doctrines and in the crisis slide that might result from shared misperceptions of aggressive intent.[65] Doctrines and misperceptions are important indicators of possibly flawed decision-making processes, but by themselves they and other proximate or internal causes of decisions are insufficient.

The international context within which those decisions are made is equally important. In 1914, the major powers "stumbled" into war only if one ignores long-term factors and focuses exclusively upon short-term decisions and personalities. Undoubtedly, complex mobilization timetables were perceived to restrict alternatives in ways that fostered what we now call preemption. However, it is also the case that the major European powers had been skirmishing with one another outside Europe for some time, that they perceived one another as enemies that would sooner or later have it out militarily, and that several were committed to the extended deterrence of attacks against allies that required assertive mobilization planning and commitments inevitably perceived as hostile by potential opponents.[66] In addition, if the membership of the Triple Alliance and the Triple Entente is not a signal that systemic factors were pushing toward war sometime in that decade, then the reasons for those alliances were not the ones provided by those who made the commitments.

Analogies between 1914 and the present are misleading in another way. Present-day superpower leaders facing the prospect of nuclear war will not be under any illusions about the possible consequences, or at least of illusions that the consequences will be trivial. They will have a "crystal ball" that results from what we know already about the effects of even small numbers of nuclear explosions, let alone the prospect of uninhibited strategic exchanges.[67] Rapid mobilization analogous to that of 1914 in a superpower nuclear crisis (an alert followed by preemption or preventive attack) would not diminish the consequences of retaliation against the society of the opponent, although it might limit retaliation against military and other hard targets. This "crystal ball" available to national leaders today is the critical difference between 1914 and the present dilemma, and it explains why any crisis involving the possible use of nuclear weapons will be watched very closely by national command authorities on both sides (and perhaps more closely by Soviet than by U.S. leaders). This does not mean that escalation not intended by political leaders can never happen, but the prospect of nuclear war by inadvertent escalation can be overstated. Superpowers, even after the first nuclear weapons have been detonated, will have significant incentives to terminate the war.

## CONCLUSION: THE MARITIME STRATEGY AND WAR TERMINATION

Avoiding inadvertent escalation is not equivalent to bringing about war termination, especially under conditions favorable to the NATO alliance. It might happen that NATO could get the worst of a war that remains below the nuclear threshold. How, then, can maritime forces contribute to a NATO war termination strategy that leads to the attainment of positive war aims, in addition to the avoidance of negative ones?

The options in theory, whether they are available in practice or not, are these, based on the historical evidence: economic strangulation of the Soviet Union and its allies through some version of a blockade; gradual attrition of the Soviet surface and submarine fleets, until the West has virtual blue water preeminence that coerces the Warsaw Pact into returning to the status quo ante; offensive use of maritime forces against vital shore-based targets of the opponent, including naval installations, air bases, and military command centers in a manner to which the Soviet Union could not respond with proportionate reprisals; or a defensively cast operational maritime strategy that preserves the sealanes between the United States and allies needing reinforcements until the Soviet offensive on land reaches its "culminating point" in the face of NATO resistance on the Central Front.[68]

The first of these options, economic strangulation of the USSR, is unlikely to be accomplished by U.S. or NATO maritime forces, or by any other means. The USSR is not sufficiently dependent on an influx of wartime supplies and reinforcements to be vulnerable to being coerced in this fashion. In a war of several years' duration in which the United States somehow kept Japan and most of Western Europe out of Soviet hands, the Soviet dependence on outside sources of vital economic inputs might change. But a conventional war of that length without either side giving way to nuclear escalation is almost inconceivable. As we have seen from the historical evidence, overly optimistic assumptions about the effects of economic strangulation have helped to defeat some countries in this century (such as Germany World War I) and to expand the cost of obtaining victory for others (such as British area bombing in World War II). The Soviet Union has shown in its history that it has remarkable recuperative powers even when an invading army, such as Hitler's or Napoleon's, is well within its national border. That it could be bled into economic starvation by virtue of exclusion from the zones of Western commercial trade seems unlikely. Nor is the USSR, on the evidence, dependent upon scarce materials from the Third World without which it could not run its war machine.

The second option, of gradual attrition of the Soviet fleet, would be meaningful in an extended war if the Soviet ground and tactical air forces had somehow been prevented from obtaining their objectives in Central and Northern Europe. Even so, U.S. and allied NATO attrition of the Soviet Navy (VMF) will follow a gradient that correlates with the distance of dispersal of VMF components from the Soviet homeland. As the United States closes toward Soviet home waters, and especially the protected bastions for Soviet SSBNs, the rate of U.S. attrition, compared with the Soviet, may be unacceptable. The United States may win the war of attrition in the North Atlantic and so establish enduring control over the sea-lanes vital for European reinforcement. On the evidence NATO will also attempt to project its power forward into the Barents Sea and to contest Soviet submarine preeminence under the Arctic ice. In these relatively more unfavorable conditions, an offensive sea control strategy may encounter decisive obstacles.[69]

The third option, using maritime forces for countermilitary strikes against the Soviet coast, seems more promising for contingencies in the Western Pacific/Northeast Asia than it does as a coercive mechanism in Europe. The important Soviet coastal targets will be hard for U.S. carrier battle groups to reach. Battleships, cruisers, and destroyers, as well as submarines, armed with cruise missiles might have more success than carrier-based air power against shore targets. But even here, they will have to move within striking range of the Soviet coast in northern waters that may be controlled by Soviet land-based naval air power, surface ships, and submarines. Undoubtedly, if the war continues long enough, the United States and its allies will be able to strike at other coastal targets, using forces in the North, Norwegian, and Barents seas. There is also the battle of the Mediterranean, from which NATO, having emerged victorious, can expand its maritime salient into the Black Sea. NATO will also contest Soviet control over Baltic approaches and, if successful, be in a position to threaten inland targets of Soviet allies. So there is no question that, provided the war continues for several weeks without nuclear escalation, U.S. and allied maritime forces can begin to use their assumed maritime supremacy in outer and inner waters against vulnerable Soviet coastal and inland targets.

Such pressures are not war stoppers, however, because the USSR can absorb a substantial amount of punishment at all but a few coastal redoubts and still continue fighting. Murmansk and Petropavlovsk-Kamchatky are critical to the successful prosecution of an extended global conventional war or a nuclear one. But a short war on the Central Front will not be won or lost there. Moreover, the risk of escalation, once attacks against Soviet coastal or inland targets have begun, is considerable. In an earlier chapter we noted that coercive diplomacy requires for its successful execution that certain favorable environmental or background conditions be established. These conditions include having mechanisms that can induce cooperation as well as those that can inflict punishment. Presumably the cooperation in this case is the threat not to attack other Soviet homeland targets from the sea. However, once these attacks have begun, and the price has been paid to accomplish them, it is difficult to see how the USSR will accept them as tacit proposals for negotiation. Maritime attacks on the Soviet periphery have the drawback of raising the ante of escalation without the compensation of inducing Soviet cooperation.

A fourth alternative is the use of U.S. and allied maritime forces for defensive sea control. The tasking would be to establish control over the "Atlantic bridge" that carries U.S. reinforcements and supplies to Europe. In this view, aggressive forward operations of U.S. submarines and carrier task forces into Soviet home waters would not be necessary. The United States and NATO could preserve a maritime sanctuary south of the line connecting Greenland, Iceland, and Norway in order to protect convoys from marauding Soviet attack submarines and to keep transatlantic shipping out of the range of Soviet land-based air.[70]

The difficulty with this alternative is that it is not an alternative at all, but a minimum condition for NATO remaining in the war. Loss of defensive sea control means that Europe is on its own. Further, the line between defensive sea control and offensive sea control is somewhat ambiguous. It depends in part upon what the Soviets choose to do. If they surge their attack submarines into the Atlantic very early in war, or even before war begins, they will have established a preemptive threat to NATO shipping that will force a defensive sea control strategy onto the West.[71] Assuming this worst case for NATO does not materialize, the surface and subsurface battles surrounding the Norwegian Sea will still blur the line between defensive and offensive sea control. If the USSR is able to occupy northern Norway and to use Norwegian airfields to launch attacks on NATO maritime forces, controlling the Greenland-Iceland-Norway line will be a substantial task for NATO commanders.

The USSR could add to the predicament of NATO in this regard if it were to invade and occupy Iceland at the very outset of war, something that is not beyond the realm of possibility.

None of these alternatives appears to be decisive as a goad to war termination in and of itself, although in an actual conflict they might well be mixed with one another and with alternatives not summarized here. This does not change the essence of NATO's predicament. It must first stalemate the war on the Central Front with its ground and tactical air forces, allowing its maritime forces time to prolong the war, cause the Soviets to anticipate high attrition in their maritime forces as the war continues, and demonstrate the eventual vulnerability of Soviet homeland targets to war from the sea if the fighting continues. These things are all worth doing if it comes to that, but they best contribute to war termination and, under some conditions, are counterproductive.


**NOTES**

1. Adm. James D. Watkins, USN, "The Martime Strategy," *Proceedings of the U.S. Naval Institute,* January 1986, pp. 2–17. There is a substantial literature on U.S. maritime strategy and on the "Maritime Strategy" itself. An important bibliography compiled by Capt. Peter M. Swartz, USN, appeared in excerpted form in *Proceedings of the U.S. Naval Institute,* January 1986, pp. 41–47. I am grateful to John Allen Williams for his "Selected Bibliography of Sources on the Maritime Strategy."

2. John F. Lehman, Jr., "The 600-Ship Navy," *Proceedings of the U.S. Naval Institute,* January 1986, pp. 30–40.

3. Capt. Linton F. Brooks, USN, "Conflict Termination Through Maritime Leverage," ch. 10 in Stephen J. Cimbala and Keith A. Dunn, eds., *Conflict Termination and Military Strategy* (Boulder, Colo.: Westview Press, 1987), pp. 161–174, provides a succinct statement of the Navy's case.

4. Watkins, "The Maritime Strategy."

5. Edward N. Luttwak, *The Pentagon and the Art of War* (New York: Simon and Schuster, 1984), p. 51.

6. Even resource allocations are not primarily responsive to strategic needs. See Samuel P. Huntington, "Organization and Strategy," in Robert J. Art, Vincent Davis, and Samuel P. Huntington, eds., *Reorganizing America's Defense* (New York: Pergamon-Brassey's, 1985), pp. 230–254.

7. Vincent Davis, "The Evolution of Central U.S. Defense Management," in Art et al., eds., *Reorganizing America's Defense,* pp. 149–167.

8. Norman Friedman, "U.S. Maritime Strategy," *International Defense Review* 18, no. 7 (1985): 1071–1075, esp. p. 1074.

9. See Sen. Sam Nunn, "Improving NATO's Conventional Defense," *USA Today,* May 1985, pp. 21–25. Soviet attack on Western Europe is arguably improbable but represents the maximum standard upon which force planning must be predicated. A sensible assessment is that of Gen. Sir Hugh Beach, who acknowledges that force ratios of two or three to one (in ground and tactical air

forces) favoring the Warsaw Pact do not assure success. On the other hand, "The military view has always been that, given a fairly substantial Warsaw Pact incursion, properly orchestrated and in accordance with Soviet doctrine (though without the use of nuclear weapons by either side), Western defenses would become incoherent within a matter of days rather than weeks, and Western reserves exhausted well before the Warsaw Pact ran out of 'steam.'" See Beach, "On Improving NATO Strategy," in Andrew J. Pierre, ed., *The Conventional Defense of Europe* (New York: Council on Foreign Relations, 1986), pp. 152–185 (quotation from p. 155). Beach was deputy commander in chief of U.K. land forces from 1976 to 1977.

10. John J. Mearsheimer, *Conventional Deterrence* (Ithaca, N.Y.: Cornell University Press, 1983), pp. 165–188.

11. C. J. Dick, "Catching NATO Unawares: Soviet Army Surprise and Deception Techniques," *International Security Review* 19, no. 1 (1986): 21–26.

12. William W. Kaufmann, "Nonnuclear Deterrence," ch. 4 in John D. Steinbruner and Leon V. Sigal, eds., *Alliance Security and the No First Use Question* (Washington, D.C.: Brookings Institution, 1983), pp. 43–90.

13. Jeffrey Record, "Defending Europe Conventionally: An American Perspective on Needed Reforms,"*Air University Review* 36, no. 6 (September–October 1985): 55–64, esp. 61.

14. Paul Bracken, *The Command and Control of Nuclear Forces* (New Haven: Yale University Press, 1983), pp. 129–178.

15. Soviet capabilities allow for constrained salvos in theater war, but their doctrinal expressions of pessimism about controlled superpower exchanges are frequent. See Paul K. Davis and Peter J. E. Stan, *Concepts and Models of Escalation,* (Santa Monica, Calif.: Rand Corporation, 1984); and William T. Lee and Richard F. Staar, *Soviet Military Policy Since World War II* (Stanford, Calif.: Hoover Institution Press, 1986), p. 39 and passim.

16. Bracken notes, in this regard, that what seems anomalous to U.S. observers is considered quite sensible and realistic by Europeans: "What some observers see as a disorderly and thoughtless development of highly differentiated nuclear forces is in fact precisely the kind of force structure needed for a deterrence strategy whose implementation would be suicidal" (Bracken, *The Command and Control of Nuclear Forces*, p. 164). Compare the rationalist (from the U.S. perspective) argument of Henry Kissinger: "And therefore I would say, which I might not say in office, the European allies should not keep asking us to multiply strategy assurances that we cannot possibly mean, or if we do mean, we should not want to execute because if we execute, we risk the destruction of civilization" (Kissinger, "NATO: The Next Thirty Years," in Christoph Bertram, ed., *Strategic Deterrence in a Changing Environment* [Montclair, N.J.: Allenheld, Osmun, 1981], p. 109).

17. Benjamin S. Lambeth, "On Thresholds in Soviet Military Thought," in William J. Taylor, Jr., et al., eds., *Strategic Responses to Conflict in the 1980s* (Washington, D.C.: Center for Strategy and International Studies/Los Alamos National Laboratory, 1983) pp. 347–365.

18. See Stephen M. Meyer, "Soviet Perspectives on the Paths to Nuclear War," in Graham T. Allison et al, eds., *Hawks, Doves and Owls: An Agenda for Avoiding Nuclear War* (New York: W. W. Norton, 1985), pp.167–205.

19. A succinct discussion is provided in David N. Schwartz, *NATO's Nuclear Dilemmas* (Washington, D.C.: Brookings Institution, 1983).

20. For assessments, compare Mearsheimer, *Conventional Deterrence*, pp. 186–187; and Steven Canby, *The Alliance and Europe: Part IV—Military Doctrine and Technology*, Adelphi Papers no. 109 (London: International Institute for Strategic Studies, Winter 1974/1975), pp. 10–11.

21. The point is emphasized in Canby, *The Alliance and Europe*, p. 5.

22. See Christopher N. Donnelly, "Soviet Operational Concepts in the 1980s," in *Strengthening Conventional Deterrence in Europe: Proposals for the 1980s*, report of the European Security Study (New York: St. Martin's Press, 1983), pp. 105–136.

23. John G. Hines and Phillip A. Petersen, "The Warsaw Pact Strategic Offensive: The OMG in Context," *International Defense Review*, October 1983), pp. 1391–1395.

24. Charles J. Dick, "Soviet Operational Concepts: Part I," *Military Review* 65, no. 9 (September 1985): 29–45.

25. Gen. Bernard W. Rogers, "Follow-on Forces Attack (FOFA): Myths and Realities," *NATO Review* 32, no. 6 (December 1984): 1–9.

26. Phillip A. Petersen and Maj. John R. Clark, "Soviet Air and Antiair Operations," *Air University Review* 36, no. 3 (March–April 1985): 36–54.

27. Harriet Fast Scott and William F. Scott, *The Soviet Control Structure: Capabilities for Wartime Survival* (New York: Crane, Russak/National Strategy Information Center, 1983).

28. Samuel P. Huntington, "The Renewal of Strategy," Ch. 1 in Samuel P. Huntington, ed., *The Strategic Imperative: New Policies for National Security* (Cambridge, Mass.: Ballinger, 1982), pp. 1–52.

29. Ibid., pp. 21–32.

30. According to Admiral Watkins, "As the battle groups move forward, we will wage an aggressive campaign against all Soviet submarines. including ballistic missile submarines" (Watkins, "The Maritime Strategy," p. 11; italics added).

31. Benjamin S. Lambeth, "Uncertainties for the Soviet War Planner," *International Security* 7, no. 3 (Winter 1982/1983): 139–166. On Soviet maritime missions, see John Allen Williams, "The U.S. and Soviet Navies: Missions and Forces," *Armed Forces and Society* 10, no. 4 (Summer 1984): 507–528 and James John Tritten, *Soviet Naval Forces and Nuclear Warfare* (Boulder, Colo.: Westview, 1986).

32. Barry R. Posen, "Inadvertent Nuclear War? Escalation and NATO's Northern Flank," *International Security* 7, no. 2 (Fall 1982), repr. in Steven E. Miller, ed., *Strategy and Nuclear Deterrence* (Princeton: Princeton University Press, 1984), pp. 85–111.

33. Desmond Ball, "Nuclear War at Sea," reference paper no. 131, Strategic and Defense Studies Centre, Research School of Pacific Studies, Australian National University, Canberra, July 1985, suggests, quite correctly, that U.S. Tomahawk sea-launched cruise missiles pose problems for stability because they blur the distinctions between tactical and strategic warfare, and between conventional and nuclear war. Moreover, the nuclear-armed land attack version of

the Tomahawk is to comprise an important part of the strategic reserve force in a post-SIOP environment. One could well imagine that Soviet conventional attrition of U.S. SSNs armed with these missiles will have effects comparable with those of U.S. conventional attrition of Soviet SSBNs (if, under these circumstances, the distinction between conventional and nuclear use can be unambiguously preserved in any case). On the versatility of Tomahawk, see Com. S. J. Froggett, USN, "Tomahawk's Role," *Proceedings of the U.S. Naval Institute*, February 1987, pp. 51–54.

34. Bracken notes that NATO's nuclear deterrent "is politically and militarily credible because the governing command structure is so unstable and accident-prone that national leaders would exercise little practical control over it in wartime" *(The Command and Control of Nuclear Forces, p. 164)*. See also Stephen J. Cimbala, "Flexible Targeting, Escalation Control and War in Europe," *Armed Forces and Society* 12, no.3 (Spring 1986): 383–400.

35. Headquarters, Department of the Army, FM 100–5, *Operations* (Washington, D.C.: Headquarters, Department of the Army, August 1982) p. 2–1 and *passim*; FM 100–5, *Operations,* (Washington, D.C.: Headquarters, Department of the Army, May 1986), Chapter 2, pp. 9–26.

36. Both quotations are from ibid., August 1982, p. 2–1.

37. Ibid., p. 1–2.

38. Soviet military doctrine acknowledges the possibility of theater nuclear warfare that does not automatically escalate into U.S.-Soviet strategic exchanges against the opponent's homeland. See Meyer, "Soviet Perspectives on the Paths to Nuclear War," p. 185.

39. Joshua Epstein, "Horizontal Escalation: Sour Notes of a Recurrent Theme," *International Security* 8, no. 3 (Winter 1983–1984): 19–31.

40. Robert Komer, *Maritime Strategy or Coalition Defense?* (Cambridge, Mass.: Abt, 1984), esp. pp. 70–73, on the implications of horizontal escalation.

41. The correlation of forces is an impacted concept in Soviet writing that involves the comparison of socialist and capitalist coalitions along the dimensions of political, military, economic, and moral-ideological strength. See, for example, Col. S. Tyushkevich, "The Methodology for the Correlation of Forces in War," in *Selected Readings from MILITARY THOUGHT, 1963–1973*, selected and compiled by Joseph D. Douglass, Jr., and Amoretta M. Hoeber, vol. 5, part. II (Washington: D.C.: U.S. Government Printing Office, n.d.), pp. 57–71.

42. John J. Mearsheimer, "A Strategic Misstep: The Maritime Strategy and Deterrence in Europe," *International Security* 11, no. 2 (Fall 1986): 3–57.

43. Capt. Linton Brooks, "Naval Power and National Security: The Case for the Maritime Strategy," *International Security* 11, no. 2 (Fall 1986): 58–88.

44. Mearsheimer, *Conventional Deterrence*, pp. 165–171 and *passim*.

45. Ibid., p. 171.

46. On the relationship between planning and flexibility in Soviet doctrine and practice, see Nathan Leites, "The Soviet Style of War," in Derek Leebaert, ed., *Soviet Military Thinking* (London: Allen and Unwin, 1981), pp. 200–204.

47. Barry R. Posen, *The Sources of Military Doctrine: Britain, France and Germany between the World Wars* (Ithaca, N.Y.: Cornell University Press, 1984), pp. 205–215.

48. For an explication of blitzkrieg in historical context, see Larry H. Addington, *The Blitzkrieg Era and the German General Staff, 1865–1941* (New Brunswick, N.J.: Rutgers University Press, 1971).

49. The Soviets appear to be very much aware of the unpredictability of tactical engagements, although they stress constancy in following through on operational plans. According to one authoritative Soviet source:

The maneuver of personnel and equipment and the shifting of nuclear strikes and fire contribute to success in modern combat. Units and subunits must carry out maneuvers of personnel and equipment boldly, decisively and in good time. Skillful application of this principle makes it possible to seize and retain the initiative, to disrupt enemy plans, to conduct combat successfully in a situation which has changed, to achieve the objectives of an engagement in shorter periods of time and with fewer losses, and to defeat superior enemy forces in detail. (Lt. Gen. V. G. Reznichenko, ed., *Tactics* [Soviet Affairs Publications Division, Directorate of Soviet Affairs, Air Force Intelligence Service, May 1985], p. 51).

50. Posen, *The Sources of Military Doctrine,* p. 213.

51. See Hines and Petersen, "The Warsaw Pact Strategic Offensive"; and Petersen and Clark, "Soviet Air and Antiair Operations."

52. This is one of the reasons for Soviet emphasis upon speed and decisiveness, in order to disrupt the opponent's command and control and to preserve the essence of Soviet plans with minimum perturbation. See Leites, "The Soviet Style of War," pp. 198–199.

53. Charles J. Dick, "Soviet Operational Concepts: Part I."

54. See Donnelly, "Soviet Operational Concepts in the 1980s," p. 132.

55. Max Hastings, *Overlord: D-Day and the Battle for Normandy* (New York: Simon and Schuster, 1984).

56. Ibid., p. 319.

57. Martin van Creveld, *Fighting Power: German and U.S. Army Performance, 1939–45* (Westport, Conn.: Greenwood Press, 1982); Trevor N. Dupuy, *A Genius for War* (Englewood Cliffs, N.J.: Prentice-Hall, 1977), esp. pp. 253–254.

58. Colin S. Gray, *Maritime Strategy, Geopolitics and the Defense of the West* (New York: National Strategy Information Center, 1986).

59. Ibid., pp. 64–65 and *passim.* On the relationship between conventional maritime operations and nuclear deterrence, see Com. James John Tritten, USN, "(Non) Nuclear Warfare," *Proceedings of the U.S. Naval Institute,* February 1987, pp. 64–70.

60. Desmond Ball, *Can Nuclear War Be Controlled?* Adelphi Papers no. 169 (London: International Institute for Strategic Studies, Autumn 1981); Bracken, *The Command and Control of Nuclear Forces;* Bruce G. Blair, *Strategic Command and Control: Redefining the Nuclear Threat* (Washington, D.C.: Brookings Institution, 1985).

61. Blair, *Strategic Command and Control,* passim.

62. According to William R. van Cleave, "The standard of survivability against a well-executed surprise attack appears to have quietly given way to the assumption of effective strategic warning, generated alert, poorly executed attacks, and launch on warning." See Van Cleave, "U.S. Defense Strategy: A Debate," in George E. Hudson and Joseph J. Kruzel, eds., *American Defense Annual 1985–86* (Lexington, Mass. : D. C. Heath, 1985), p. 21.

63. Soviet political and military leaders apparently have more protection than their U.S. counterparts, including numerous command bunkers around Moscow and elsewhere. The Soviet civil defense program has been touted as important in declaratory policy, although there are disputes about its efficacy. See Desmond Ball, *The Soviet Strategic Command, Control, Communications and Intelligence (C3I system)* (Canberra: Strategic and Defense Studies Centre, Australian National University, 1985).

64. Samuel P. Huntington, "The Renewal of Strategy"; critiques of this proposal are presented in Keith A. Dunn and William O. Staudenmaier, eds., *Military Strategy in Transition: Defense and Deterrence in the 1990s* (Boulder, Colo.: Westview Press, 1984).

65. For interesting arguments and insights, see Posen, *The Sources of Military Doctrine;* and the discussion of the "owlish" perspective in Allison et al., eds., pp. 210–212. The authors summarize that the "owls" emphasize causes of war that are rooted in "organizational routines, malfunctions of machines or of minds, misperceptions, misunderstandings, and mistakes" (p. 210).

66. See Scott D. Sagan, "1914 Revisited: Allies, Offense and Instability," *International Security* 11, no. 2 (Fall 1986): 151–175.

67. Harvard Nuclear Study Group, *Living with Nuclear Weapons* (New York: Bantam Books, 1983), p. 44.

68. The notion of a culminating point is discussed in Edward N. Luttwak, *Strategy: the Logic of War and Peace* (Cambridge, Mass.: Belknap Press, 1987), ch. 3, esp. p. 43.

69. Mearsheimer, "A Strategic Misstep," pp. 35–45, discusses the problems with offensive sea control operations against the Soviet north.

70. Ibid., pp. 44–45.

71. There is some disagreement among academic strategists, about the importance of interdicting shipping, but an apparent consensus among naval commanders.

# 8

# Superpower Strategic Defenses, Deterrence, and War Termination

Interest in ballistic missile and air defenses is a long-standing component of the U.S., and the Soviet, military research and development communities. President Ronald Reagan's now famous speech of March 23, 1983, has taken on a character of gloss and novelty to which it was not really entitled.[1] The Soviets have, according to the restrictions of the ABM Treaty of 1972, actually deployed one ballistic missile defense (BMD) site around Moscow and are now upgrading it with new interceptors and improved radars.[2] The United States had a very heavily endowed air defense (defense against air-breathing weapons) system in the 1950s, and the Soviet Union deploys an extensive system today for the same purpose. Although both sides, by their signatures to arms control agreements, have avowed their acknowledgment of mutual deterrence based on offensive retaliation, neither has renounced the right to conduct research into technologies that might prove fruitful for future air or ballistic defenses.

Moreover, amid the clamor over the Reagan Strategic Defense Initiative (SDI), there was an apparent lack of recognition by U.S. observers of the difference between a strategic mission and a strategic technology. The mission of damage limitation is now assigned, in U.S. nuclear strategy, to strategic offensive forces. This is one rationale given for deploying weapons like the MX/Peacekeeper even in vulnerable fixed silos. It provides some very accurate counterforce that can be used promptly against the forces of the opponent. This has been judged significant by the last four U.S. administrations at least, although there is room for dispute. Having accepted the judgment that damage limitation is a necessary component of any war-fighting capability to support deterrence, policymakers have assigned that mission to offenses.

Offenses that are tasked for damage limitation have an ambiguous appearance to the opponent. They could also be optimal in first strikes because of their promptness and accuracy. Thus critics of MX/Peacekeeper point correctly to the probability that the Soviets will notice its compatibility with first-strike scenarios as well as second-strike counterforce. They will notice this even more if the missile is not deployed in a survivable basing mode. Nonetheless, U.S. policymakers and think tanks have endorsed the idea of damage limitation through prompt offensive retaliation and deployment of the forces with which to do it, notwithstanding their ambiguous status as quasi-first-strike forces.

Active defenses are another way to accomplish damage limitation, and they arguably can contribute to stable deterrence under some conditions. But missile defenses have been far more controversial in the U.S. policy debate than have prompt counterforce offenses. Perhaps this is because it is infrequently perceived that they would perform similar missions. Or perhaps defenses raise the hackles of those who imagine that U.S. strategic nuclear forces are actually targeted according to a countercity or assured destruction doctrine, which defenses are thought to undermine. Some defense analysts would recommend doing away with counterforce offenses *and* defenses on both sides of the East-West divide, and some of that recommendation is based on a national model of assured destruction that is textbook oriented, if not grounded in U.S. and Soviet war plans.

Confusion also is apparent when observers fail to distinguish between offensive and defensive strategies, on the one hand, and offensive or defensive technologies, on the other. It is sometimes said that we are in transition from an "offense dominant" to a "defense dominant" strategic environment; the Reagan administration has expressed the hope that this is so. However, this is a technological hope, not a strategic one. At present, defensive strategies dominate offensive strategies, not the reverse, because neither superpower can write a recipe for successful preemption. Superior offensive technology, relative to the capabilities of defenses, makes a defensive strategy—retaliation rather than preemption—pay. Conversely, the availability of defensive technology may make offensive strategies feasible when they previously were not. If either side could attack preemptively and then absorb a retaliatory strike with its defenses, the attacking side might yield to crisis temptations to do so. That the superpowers' currently dominant offensive technologies make defensive (retaliatory) strategies possible is not always appreciated in the public debate.

For this reason, too, command and control issues relative to SDI or any BMD program that may supplant it should be agenda items now.

If, for example, the command/control for defenses is to operate as it now does for offenses, then it cannot be taken for granted that stability is inherent in the force balances themselves. The ratio of Soviet warheads to U.S. aim points, and vice versa, is not a number that supersedes in importance any nuances in the U.S. or Soviet command/control system, provided those systems are survivable for purposes of immediate and gross Single Integrated Operational Plan (SIOP) execution. However, with defenses and offenses deployed on both sides, and the defenses perhaps deployed in space, the relative importance of counterforce fire-power ratios may go down, and that of postattack command fidelity, go up. Command systems of the future may be hard pressed to perform crisis and postattack assessment if those assessments involve conglom-erates of ballistic and air-breathing offenses, combined with space- and ground-based defenses. But this last observation is somewhat ahead of our story, which begins with a review of where we have been strategically in superpower relations, and then considers issues pertinent to SDI/C3 in sequence, with special emphasis on stability in a defense-competent environment.

## ORTHODOX AND HETERODOX THEORIES

Orthodox strategic thinking in the United States for several decades rested upon the premise of mutual vulnerability as the basis of U.S.-Soviet strategic nuclear deterrence. Mutual vulnerability held that both superpowers should deploy strategic offensive forces that were surviv-able against any conceivable surprise attack, and not attempt to protect their cities from enemy retaliation. Survivable forces and unprotected cities were the keys to deterrence. Cities would not necessarily be the first targets attacked in retaliation; more likely, the opponent's nuclear and other forces would be struck first. Nonetheless, countercity attacks were the ultimate deterrent, however far into war those strikes might be withheld.

During the 1970s dissatisfaction with orthodox deterrence strategy resulted in a reconsideration of some of its fundamental premises. As a result a neo-orthodox position developed in U.S. declaratory policy, and it was to some extent also represented in employment policy, or war plans.[3] The departures from orthodox mutual vulnerability (or mutual assured destruction) were basically two. First, there was an interest in providing capabilities for flexible targeting of retaliatory forces as a more credible deterrent to provocations less serious than all-out attack. Second, Nixon-Ford and Carter policymakers were interested in preserving es-calation control even after deterrence failed, in the hope that war could be terminated before it fully escaped control.[4] Escalation control de-pended partly, but not totally, on Soviet reciprocal targeting restraint.

It did not depend at all on a Soviet notion of intrawar deterrence comparable with the U.S. one. Nevertheless, the issue of intrawar deterrence is not a settled one in U.S. strategic thinking, and the advent of defenses probably will not eliminate the controversy.

The neo-orthodox position was variously labeled but its focus might be termed flexible nuclear response. Flexible nuclear response required that policymakers be more sensitized to the character of the forces over which they exercised control. This in turn required more confidence on their part in the strategic command, control, and communications (C3; C3I if "intelligence" is added). Several administrations, including the Reagan administration, have called for improvements in hardware and planning in order to address C3 weaknesses. It became clearer to U.S. planners as they reviewed the components of SIOP in the Carter and Reagan administrations that improved forces would not suffice for flexible nuclear response. The viability of the command system under unprecedented conditions of stress would be the key to the success or failure of selective options in early or later stages of war.

Although it did not actually repudiate the Carter version of flexible nuclear response, called countervailing strategy, the Reagan administration apparently concluded that by themselves improved offenses could lead to a dead end. Without defenses, offenses could improve the amount of destruction that the United States could inflict on Soviet targets in retaliation, but offenses could not protect the American people or military forces from the destruction caused by Soviet weapons. The Reagan "strategic concept" explained by Ambassador Paul H. Nitze called for a gradual strategic transition through three principal phases, from dependence upon offensive retaliation (punishment) to emphasis upon defensive protection (denial).[5] Since the new defenses would be based on nonnuclear kill mechanisms and the comparatively weak offenses would be based on nuclear weapons, the transition from offensively based to defensively oriented deterrence would remove the threat of U.S. and Soviet societal destruction if deterrence failed.

There was some suspicion on the part of Reagan critics that the administration sought to mirror the Soviet strategy, based on an incorrect appreciation of that strategy. Thus, according to those skeptical of Reagan programs, whatever the U.S. declaratory policy, the administration's force acquisitions and war plans were designed to provide improved offenses *and* competent defenses, in order to prevail in nuclear war should deterrence fail. President Reagan maintained, however, that a nuclear war "cannot be won and should not be fought," and arms control proposals called for large reductions in U.S. and Soviet strategic offensive forces and eventual substitution of mainly nonnuclear active defenses for superpower strategic nuclear offenses. The United States is attempting to modernize its offenses at the same time it is offering to reduce their numbers drastically, claiming that the modernized offensive forces are necessary as bargaining chips to induce Soviet willingness to negotiate. The Soviets, for their part, seem more interested in U.S. adherence to the ABM Treaty and U.S. plans for SDI while they, too, modernize their strategic offensive forces. The vision of a world without superpower strategic nuclear offenses seems more visionary than pragmatic at the present time.

To accomplish this vision, it would be necessary to do more than develop and deploy space- or ground-based defenses that could deter and defeat Soviet ballistic missile attacks. The United States would also have to work out a system for integrating the operations of offenses and defenses under probable wartime conditions. As noted below, the C3 required to make possible the efficient operation of defenses alone would be a vast improvement over present capabilities. When the complexity of defenses combined with offenses, even drastically reduced offenses, is considered, the problem grows exponentially.

This heterodox "defense emphasis" strategic concept had a neoheterodox variant that called for defenses not for the replacement of deterrence based on offensive retaliation, but for the improvement of deterrence based on offenses. In this amended version of the heterodox position, defenses would be deployed in order to protect U.S. retaliatory forces and command centers from Soviet preemption. They would thus contribute to the survivability of offensive forces, commanders, and the strategic communications that allow commanders to control their forces. In so doing, defenses would be compatible with an evolutionary shift away from mutual vulnerability rather than a sudden lurch into the unknown. For neoheterodox advocates, defenses deployed in the near term would improve deterrence by raising the uncertainties attendant to preemption against retaliatory forces.[6]

It may be possible to design BMD systems that provide some protection for military forces and some for populations. Actual technologies do not always require an "either-or" choice demanded by theorists. Although technology may not be constrained, budgets will be. Thus policymakers and defense planners will have to establish some priorities about near- and long-term missions for BMD. One can imagine, for example, that antitactical ballistic missile defenses and point defenses for silos could be building blocks for larger and more effective systems. One of the principal design issues in BMD is whether to design for single-mission efficiency or multimission flexibility. A single-mission point defense system, taking advantage of semipreferential defense techniques, could be very cost effective: it would raise the attack price against fixed or mobile ICBMs for a modest cost relative to the cost of offsetting it once it is in place. However, such a defense would have limited leverage against very large attacks, and none for the protection of cities or other area targets.

A more modular system including both space- and ground-based components might not be as efficient, but it could have the flexibility to adapt to an opponent's countermeasures and to perform more than one mission simultaneously. These kinds of choices—between very overdetermined programs with efficient cost parameters but limited shelf life, and underformulated programs that evolve gradually and adapt to their environment—will have important implications for the C3 networks of the systems.

If this admittedly oversimplified review of the central tendencies of strategic debates is fair, it admits of much legitimate disagreement about the roles of defenses in U.S. strategy. For the moment the technology tail is wagging the strategic dog; little is known about the potential of future defense technologies relative to the offenses that would oppose them, since those offenses would also be improved, relative to current offenses.[7] In addition to the unknown with regard to weapons and strategies, other uncertainties relative to the future requirements and vulnerabilities of U.S. strategic C3 would be important. Some of those requirements and vulnerabilities receive further consideration now.

## BATTLE MANAGEMENT/COMMAND-CONTROL: TECHNOLOGIES AND MISSIONS

A strategic command and control system is expected to do many things. In lay language, we might define these as seeing, thinking, acting, and adapting or reacting to the results of seeing, thinking and acting in the real world. The terms "seeing," "thinking," "acting," and "adapting" would have been used as metaphors in the past, in order to describe how organizations and machines might attempt to copy human behavior. In actuality, however, large bureaucratic organizations did not observe or think or act with the flexibility and conceptual skills of individual human beings. Instead, they acted according to standard operating procedures and organizational routines that were programmed (in the traditional sense of rehearsed activities) into the organization's repertoire.[8] These procedures and routines, together with the intraorganizational bargaining process that goes on in any large bureaucracy, were thought to predict most organizational behavior under all but exceptional conditions.[9] Organizational "knowledge" consisted of the trials and errors conducive to stable and predictable relationships between the organization and its environment; organizational adaptation to environmental change was assumed to occur within small tolerances of variation on a few key indicators of normal or perturbing conditions.[10]

The above description of traditional bureaucratic organizations can be applied to those in national security and defense. The advantages provided by organizations as described above are considerable when the organizations are assigned traditional missions within relatively stable environments. Under those conditions organizations slowly adjust the operating thermostat of their policymaking process to changes in the environment. Each individual adjustment may be adequate, although the cumulative pattern of adjustments may be maladaptive. For example, Leslie Gelb and Richard K. Betts have shown in their study of U.S. decision making during the Vietnam war that each administration struggled to cope with the problem long enough to pass it along to its successor.[11] Similarly, Robert W. Komer noted that no one was really in charge of the overall war effort in Vietnam. Authority and responsibility were fragmented and diffuse in Washington and in Southeast Asia for many reasons, among them the assumption of "business as usual" instead of real wartime or crisis discontinuity.[12]

At first it might seem that nuclear command and control organizations are different from those described above. Presidential control over nuclear release is thought to be tight, and nuclear alerts would obviously be employed during crises. These impressions are misleading. True, U.S. organizations for strategic C3 were developed differently from other military organizations to take account of the unique characteristics of nuclear forces. For example, the functions of warning/attack assessment and retaliation were separated: NORAD was assigned the former and SAC the latter, instead of assigning both to SAC.[13] Permissive action links or electronic locks prevent accidental or unauthorized launch of most U.S nuclear weapons, and other weapons (such as sea-based ballistic and cruise missiles) require that numerous procedural checks and balances be satisfied before release is authorized. Although it is a longstanding fear of fiction writers, experts assess the probability of a Dr. Strangelove scenario for U.S. strategic forces as slight to nonexistent.[14]

However, reducing the probability of accidental war does not necessarily preclude inadvertent loss of control during crises. The distinction between accidental and inadvertent escalation can be seen in the crises of July and August 1914 that resulted in World War I. No one mobilized by mistake in the sense that power was usurped by unauthorized military or political elites who then ordered mobilization. A series of action-reaction mobilizations that had been prepared in advance was set in motion without any preconception of how top policy officials might want to stop the chain reaction if they chose, at the last minute, to do so.[15] The implication of this for SDI is that Congress may be worried about the wrong problem to the extent that it is concerned about computers usurping the national command authority and firing space-based defenses without presidential authorization. The problem is much more subtle. Networks of sensors, weapons, and communications will have to be linked in real time so that the most efficient allocation of resources to perform the appropriate missions can be realized. The appropriate missions are seeing, thinking, acting, and adapting.

What these missions amount to in Strategic Defense Initiative Office (SDIO) terminology is surveillance, acquisition, tracking, and kill assessment.[16] The battle management/command and control system must provide for decentralized coordination in real time, that is, within the time cycle making possible effective response. In the case of attempted intercepts of ballistic missiles in their boost phases (the first few minutes of powered flight), this means that several things must be done very quickly. Attacking missile trajectories must be established; weapons must be allocated to those missiles on the basis of their location relative to the anticipated trajectories; firing must be authorized before or during actual launch; assessment of destroyed and surviving offensive missiles relative to defending platforms (satellites if based in space) must be made quickly; reallocation of interceptors relative to attackers must then take place until the defense is handed over to the next phase.[17]

Other phases involve similar distinctions and decisions plus some others. In midcourse, warheads and decoys move through space for approximately 20 minutes. Warheads must be distinguished or discriminated from clouds of objects that include aerosols, chaff, and other material designed to fool the defense sensors and interceptors. Both passive (observing the differences in heat radiated against the cold background of space) and active (tapping the warhead or decoy with directed energy and observing how it reacts) discrimination techniques have been studied by the U.S. defense community, and progress in active discrimination now appears to be fundamental to the successful deployment of any midcourse layer of defense. The post-boost phase, which precedes the midcourse phase and follows the boost phase, involves an effort to intercept reentry vehicles as they are being dispensed from the "bus" that carries multiple warheads aimed at separate targets. In the terminal phase, ground-based interceptors and radars aided by airborne optical adjuncts or object detection probes will provide the final layer of defense to absorb whatever warheads leak through the remainder of the defense.[18]

There is some distortion from a command/control standpoint in thinking of these layers of defense as separate entities. In one sense they are, and in another they are not. A certain amount of coordination is required to avoid unnecessary duplication of firing from the various defense constellations, and to permit one layer of the defense to pass along information about destroyed and surviving warheads to another. On the other hand, it is not necessary for a centralized brain to control every intercept that each of the various constellations of BMD satellites might have to make. Thus the various layers of the defense are both independent and interdependent. Failures in one layer have obvious implications for the difficulty facing subsequent layers of the defense: the more warheads that leak through earlier layers, the larger the task of interception for later layers. Yet it is not necessarily efficient for the coordination of interceptions to be overly dependent upon a central mechanism. The most efficient allocation of interceptors across all the defense satellite constellations might not optimize the use of interceptors relative to the problem as a whole. For example, a 10 percent redundancy rate in attacking threat objects with interceptors might be inefficient compared with no redundancy at all, but the cost of no redundancy might be loss of the entire system when the central coordinating mechanism mal-functions.

For this reason, SDIO has evolved in its thinking from earlier suggestions favoring high centralization to later suggestions, such as those proposed in the Eastport study, for more decentralized battle management/command-control BM/C3.[19] A decentralized approach would allow modular evolution of battle management to accompany the design of the overall defense system architecture. Instead of designing a system of weapons and sensors, and then attempting to configure an appropriate system of corresponding C3, the Eastport approach would allow evolutionary development of hardware and software along with the rest of the system design. This approach has much to recommend it in principle. If successfully implemented, it would allow for fault-tolerant execution of command decisions when one part of the system was not working or was producing anomalies. In a system with the probable interdependencies of an SDI BM/C3 system, the problem of anomalies is potentially more troublesome than the conceptually simpler complete failure of hardware or software components. When anomalies occur, an apparently correct system is producing misleading results that are not discovered until the erroneous messages are processed sequentially—if it is discovered at all. Anomalies can confound the system in undetermined ways while the central decision makers either think the system is functioning properly or cannot determine why it is not. A fault-tolerant decentralized system, if it can be implemented, offers the prospect of self-sealing punctures by transferring some communications and assessments first assigned to one part of the system to others if necessary. The U.S. common carrier telephone system prior to divestiture is an example of a distributed self-healing network of this type.

The successful approximation of a decentralized C3 system might circumvent some of the limits of software innovation that have been alleged to be so daunting as to preclude SDI. David Parnas, who formerly served the Department of Defense as an expert consultant on information sciences and battle management for SDI, later wrote that the software required for any comprehensive defense system would be impossible to design.[20] However, Parnas and others who forecast a requirement for some 10 million lines of computer code required for SDI apparently presumed a centralized system that is apparently no longer the preferred approach of SDIO. Additional research will be needed to confirm the validity of the decentralized approach to BM/C3, however.

SDIO has begun a knowledge-based software assistant project that will use artificial intelligence techniques to create a new capability for software development. If this approach were to be fruitful, complex software could be produced by automation, thus reducing the time required to change software systems in order to accommodate new design architectures.[21] There is no reason in principle why software cannot be designed in a modular fashion to accompany the growth and development of diverse architectures, provided too much is not expected of the computer programs at early stages. They will obviously have to undergo modification as simulation and other test results reveal weaknesses.

It has been stated by some experts that the SDI system, including its command/control components, could not be fully tested unless deterrence fails—when it is too late. This is true, but misleading insofar as it implies that a perfect system must be built or none at all. Any system will be far short of perfection, and probably error prone in ways that designers did not anticipate, but this unavoidable condition in research and development does not mean total catastrophe for the U.S. deterrent. It *would* mean something close to catastrophe if the United States were to disarm entirely its strategic offensive forces in the future and attempt to fulfill literally the vision of a world without nuclear weapons. Then the failure of defenses would be catastrophic because the entire deterrent would be based on them, and the modular approach to battle management would have to give way to something heroic. This is one among many reasons why the gradual evolution of defenses that is more likely in the real world than a sudden leap into defense dominance should not be accompanied by cavalier efforts to jettison the offensive retaliatory forces on which deterrence will be based for the foreseeable future.[22]

## CRISIS STABILITY AND COUNTERCOMMAND ATTACKS

We have discussed the implications of defenses for stability, and the technology and mission challenges pertinent to SDI BM/C3. Bearing in mind these discussions, we now consider some of the more important command and control difficulties that must be addressed when and if defenses are deployed. These more important C3 problems fall into four general categories that are not mutually exclusive.

First, the problem of countercommand attacks is important in its own right, including attacks that might defeat or tempt either side. Countercommand attacks are primarily designed to decapitate the leadership and selected communications of the opponent, or include command structure attacks as major components of other attacks.[23] Authoritative studies have noted that the USSR might, by using a small fraction of its strategic arsenal, destroy all the fixed-location command and control facilities in the continental United States, including the Pentagon's National Military Command Center, the Alternate National Military Command Center, Strategic Air Command headquarters, North American Aerospace Defense Command headquarters, and other principal components of the command system.[24] Communications among sensors based in space, command centers, and the retaliatory forces could be severed by well-structured attacks even if command centers themselves survive. Even the mobile command posts for principal military and political leadership, including the president, cannot provide for postattack survival beyond the first hours or days of combat.[25]

Defenses could create additional incentives for countercommand attacks beyond those already existing. Either U.S. or Soviet planners facing an opponent's offenses *and* defenses will be more uncertain about the likelihood of attaining a counterforce preemption. Indeed, this is partly the rationale for advocates of defense who argue for a modified version of SDI that would protect retaliatory forces instead of cities. The more uncertain that defenses make counterforce attacks once war has begun to seem imminent, however, the more the alternative, of attacking leadership and command centers, seems appealing. A small number of warheads, say several hundred, leaking through a defense might not destroy most of the opponent's silos in a first strike, but that number might be sufficient to disrupt its communications and postattack control, at least temporarily. In theory, it might be supposed that the Soviets could simply expend several thousand warheads to ensure the leakage of several hundred adequate to destroy or disrupt U.S. C3. In practice, however, this response is not without cost to them unless they have numerous warheads beyond their requirements for counterforce preemption *and* strategic reserve. BMD could be configured to defend command and control targets with selective emphasis, but until now this course has been preferred by Moscow, not the United States.

If defenses do not create additional incentives for countercommand attacks against the U.S. national command authorities and their Soviet counterparts, their communications, or the force commanders (in the U.S. case, the unified and specified commanders whose forces would include nuclear weapons), they might encourage decapitation of another kind. One could attack the defense itself. There are two ways to do this: attrition or suppression of its launchers and kill vehicles or mechanisms, in the case of direct-energy weapons, or by disrupting its central nervous system and brain.

Several alternatives might suggest themselves to Soviet planners. Instead of trying to exhaust the space-based interceptors with fake boosters, fast-burn boosters, and other near-term countermeasures, they might destroy or disrupt the communications links on which U.S. satellites and their sensors depend. This is one of the principal concerns about defenses developed in space even before they are capable BMD weapons; they might be very credible antisatellite weapons that could disrupt satellite communications and memory. It is not inconceivable that false messages and disinformation could be introduced into the U.S. communications chain, along with the traditional techniques of jamming and spoofing satellite communications.[26]

Whether defenses invite attack against themselves is a distinct issue from the issue of command system sensitivity to preemption with or without defenses. Under present conditions, there has been a tendency on the part of some U.S. analysts to exaggerate the vulnerability of the U.S. nuclear command system to disruption. A Soviet "bolt from the blue" attack against the command system could certainly disrupt a coherent retaliation against a comprehensive military target set.[27] But it could not preclude an immensely destructive U.S. retaliation against Soviet cities. Nor, under present conditions, could the USSR execute a "surgical" attack against the U.S. nuclear command system. To be certain that the U.S. system was disrupted or destroyed comprehensively, the Soviets would have to launch a massive attack involving significant collateral damage.[28] Moreover, although the U.S. strategic nuclear command system might be expected to survive extremely heavy attacks in order to provide for some massive retaliatory response, or to provide for flexible targeting and selective options in a protracted but less than total conflict, it need not be tasked or expected to do both.[29]

Adding defenses to the present condition of command sensitivity complicates the issue. It is usually supposed that defenses that are vulnerable must not be deployed. But the problem of vulnerability is not a simple one. It is the compound vulnerability of U.S. and/or Soviet defenses *and* defense suppression forces that is central to stability. If both sides have vulnerable defense suppression forces as well as vulnerable defenses, then the situation is extremely unstable.[30] It is not so clear what happens if either has vulnerable defenses and survivable defense suppression forces, or vice versa, especially if defenses and defense suppression forces are both based in space. We might represent the problem as the U.S. having four possible combinations for its forces, and the USSR four possible combinations, yielding a matrix shown in Chart 1. Movement from the upper left to the lower right of this matrix obviously results in more stability, but the intermediate cases are not so clear. If we imagine a command vulnerability matrix superimposed upon the table above, a three dimensional cube would be needed to represent even crudely the

**Chart 1**
**Possible Combinations of U.S.-Soviet Defense and Defense-Suppression Vulnerabilities**

|  | SOVIET FORCES | | | |
|---|---|---|---|---|
|  | Defenses (V) Suppression (V) | Defenses (V) Suppression (S) | Defenses (S) Suppression (V) | Defenses (S) Suppression (S) |
| **U.S. FORCES** | | | | |
| Defenses (V) Suppression (V) | less stable | | | |
| Defenses (V) Suppression (S) | | | | |
| Defenses (S) Suppression (V) | | | | |
| Defenses (S) Suppression (S) | | | | more stable |

Note: S = survivable;  V = vulnerable.

simple relationships among the various components. Even then, the problem would be grossly oversimplified.

We have suggested that defenses might increase the temptation for decapitation attacks, or their marginal utility whatever the temptation. The second general concern about C3 related to defense deployments is the problem of synergistic complexity. Synergistic complexity means that in addition to the usual problems of component failure, a more complicated system may develop problems because of unforeseen relationships between components. The consequences of component failure can be serious: In 1979 and 1980, the NORAD command center in Cheyenne Mountain, Colorado, was perturbed by a number of false alerts that later resulted in congressional investigation. System failures are different, and result from the unexpected interaction of problems that were previously thought to be independent. In system rather than component failures, it might happen that warning systems provided false alerts that were observed by the opponent. Having observed the United States moving to higher levels of alert, the Soviet Union might begin to generate its forces and otherwise prepare itself against the perceived possibility of a U.S. first strike, which the United States would perceive and react to, and so forth. Thus the warning and assessment systems of the two superpowers are coupled to each other in a perverse and ironic way; each reacts to what the other does, and in a crisis each might be triggered into unlocking those standard operating procedures and restrictions against nuclear devolution that under normal circumstances prevent launching of strategic forces.

The argument here is that system failures, as opposed to component failures, are more important when defenses are deployed along with offenses. An illustration of the problem of increased complexity is provided by the issue of attack assessment. With offenses alone, attack assessment requires a gross, undifferentiated estimate that the nation is under attack and that the attack is generally targeted against forces, cities, or whatever. Future systems may be more refined technically, but there are limits to the dividends paid by refined attack assessments when the expectations of policy are based totally on offensive retaliation. Having deployed defenses, however, the United States will want interactive discrimination in real time among warheads, decoys, and penetration aids, and will want to reassess the status of the battle after each phase and integrate those reassessments progressively from one state to another. Although some notional BMD systems have described how enemy re-entry vehicles (RVs) should be winnowed out or filtered from one stage to another, few have noted that the sequentially phased, but functionally integrated, attack assessments must accompany the process of destroying warheads, and the former process is more demanding upon software than the latter.

A third way in which defenses might increase incentives for command attacks is that defense could be used offensively. The possibility that space-based defenses could be used against the opponent's warning and communications satellites has already been discussed in the open literature. Some extrapolations of this prospect are divorced from reality, but others are quite realistic. Of course, with present nuclear arsenals, the superpowers could attack each other's forces and cities much more efficiently than by deploying space-based lasers for either job. Under defense-competent and reduced-offensive regimes, however, the offensive use of space-based defensive weapons will occur to each side as something to be feared if the opponent chooses to attempt it. Among those fears would be countercommand attacks against launch facilities, BMD and air defense radars, satellite control stations, and other targets that are important parts of the C3 infrastructure.

Fourth, the United States in all likelihood will not be fighting by itself if deterrence fails. U.S. expectations are that deterrence and defense are matters for coalition management. Therefore, the role of defenses within the compass of acceptable deterrence doctrines will be a matter of NATO concern. The command and control problem is complicated enough in the U.S.-Soviet bilateral case. During crises, and after deterrence fails, it would become more complicated, even without defenses. NATO European allies will want to know the effects of defenses on crisis stability and to have some say in how defenses are deployed, and in what doctrines govern their employment or withholding. Some U.S. allies might want to build their own defenses. Others could demand a "finger on the trigger" of the U.S. system and improved offenses of their own to compensate for improved Soviet defenses, which might threaten to negate the retaliatory power of the British and French national deterrents.[31]

These illustrations are not exhaustive, but they provide examples of the command and control difficulties that may accompany the deployment of competent, although less than perfect, defenses in a world that remains dominated by offenses. This picture might seen one-sidedly gloomy. Equally against conventional wisdom, however, we contend that defenses could contribute to improved strategic stability. But they cannot do so without some adjustment of prevailing strategic thinking.

Defenses in an offense-dominant world could contribute to stability if they helped to protect the survivability of U.S. strategic command and assets that otherwise invited attack on themselves. This means, inter alia, that the major command centers, communications links, and warning sensors must be protected from cheap shots that would otherwise be insufficient to prevent retaliation. Deployment of weapons in space is unnecessary to accomplish this objective.

As a study by the U.S. Office of Technology Assessment makes clear, the United States has within the grasp of near-term technology the capability to deploy ground-based defenses that would protect key command and control targets against inexpensive attacks.[32] Slightly more expanded defenses would have exoatmospheric (outside the atmosphere) and endoatmospheric (inside the atmosphere) interceptors with the appropriate sensors and radars for battle management. They would be unambiguously designed not to threaten the deterrent of the other side, but to provide "hard site" defense for some military targets, and both point and area defenses that would help to protect attractive command targets.[33]

The pertinent question is: Since the United States has the capability, or soon will, to provide for limited but effective defenses of important countercommand targets, why does it not do so? There are several answers. First, the U.S. defense establishment almost never prefers to apply acceptable technology to solving manageable problems. The customary preference is to define problems that challenge the state of the art in technology and then postpone "what for" decisions for resolution later, if at all.

The second reason is that SDI means many different things to the diverse constituencies that are its supporters. To President Reagan it provides an affirmation that Americans would rather defend lives than avenge them. For SDIO, it is necessary to tack with the wind of changing congressional interests and budgetary appropriations. For the Congress, the reactions of constituents are balanced against the views of party, the White House, and the press about the entire Reagan economic program, not just the defense program.

The third reason is that the U.S. defense community has been preoccupied with the technological aspects of strategy to the exclusion of the strategic ones.[34] It is of no small interest that the Soviet counterparts to Pentagon planners have insisted on deploying their own, and imperfect, missile defense system around Moscow. [35] They have not argued about whether it is perfect; they care only that it might be good enough to contribute to the survival of important Soviet leaders. However fatalistic their Western counterparts have become about the effect of nuclear war, Soviet planners assume that war might be forced upon them under less than favorable conditions. War survival and postattack recovery in the traditional sense would be impossible, but destruction of Soviet political and military leadership is to be precluded if at all possible.[36]

A fourth and final reason is that the U.S. defense community thinks very little about the problem of war termination as it applies to nuclear war between the superpowers. The problem of ending wars on terms acceptable to both sides short of Armageddon cannot be approached without some semblance of authenticated and survivable leadership on both sides after the first exchanges of weapons. U.S. national complacency about this problem of survivable commanders for war termination has been jolted by well-crafted proposals for nuclear risk reduction centers by a group cochaired by senators Sam Nunn and John Warner.[37]

## COMMAND RECIPROCITY

The ironies of deterrence based on offensive retaliation are considerable. Not the least of them is that both sides hold their societies vulnerable to destruction in order to preserve deterrence, although it has been noted that the Soviet Union acquiesces to this state of mutual vulnerability as a condition, not as a preference.[38] Unless U.S. or Soviet strategic defenses can remove their societies from hostage status, deterrence based on retaliation will remain the guarantor of their security. Thus some of the command and control dilemmas of the offensive retaliation syndrome will carry over when offenses are combined with defenses of whatever kind, unless the defenses are perfect.

One of the dilemmas that will carry over from the mutual vulnerability condition is that of preserving command and control of nuclear forces during war as well as before war. Although much thought was given to prevention of nuclear accidents by the government of the two superpowers, this was seen for the most part as a unilateral activity not subject to negotiation and discussion. An exception to this propensity toward unilateralism in strategic command and control was the "hot line" agreement that codified procedures for contact between heads of state during crises. Another exception was the Accidents Measures Agreement, which provided for prenotification of missile tests with launch trajectories outside the homeland of either superpower and in the direction of the other.[39] The Reagan administration also has explored with Soviet principals the possibility of establishing crisis command centers for civilian and/or military personnel.

Both U.S. and Soviet leaders have an interest in the prevention of accidental nuclear war in the correct sense of that term. Stated differently, neither can gain if it loses control over its own forces during a crisis and war begins despite policy preferences to avoid it.[40] However, the prevention of accidental war is one of those rare illustrations of a positive-sum game in which the payoffs to all players can only be favorable. The more subtle and demanding problem is inadvertent escalation from a crisis or limited war, when escalation takes place despite policymakers' efforts to avoid it. World War I is often used as a classical illustration of a process of competitive alerts and mobilizations that captured the political leaders in its momentum.[41] Provided the case is not overstated, it is important to note the ways in which alerts and crises that can get out of control might trigger nuclear war. Robert S. McNamara, secretary of defense under presidents Kennedy and Johnson, provides reminders of the fragile structure of crisis management in his book on nuclear strategy.[42] According to McNamara, several crises involving the United States and the Soviet Union could easily have escalated to the use of nuclear weapons against forces or cities. During each of those crises, U.S. leaders thought it important to send clear signals to the Soviet Union of their intention to resolve the crisis without war.

The problem with crisis management or the manipulation of nuclear risk is that it depends upon adversaries with great sensitivity to the decision problems of their opponents. During the Cuban missile crisis of 1962, President John F. Kennedy insisted that his advisers keep in mind the predicament of Khrushchev, seen from his perspective.[43] The Soviet leader had to be given a face-saving exit that allowed him to back down gracefully; otherwise, he might impulsively order attacks against the United States or, more likely, against U.S. allies such as West Germany. Kennedy found that his grasp was not as sure as his reach during the Cuban crisis. Several U–2 reconnaissance aircraft were involved in unpredictable mishaps that could have triggered war, and U.S. naval operations in the Atlantic forced Soviet submarines to surface under conditions the USSR might well have considered provocative.[44]

It is worth noting in this regard that U.S. and Soviet strategic nuclear forces have never gone simultaneously on full alert. Once alerted, both sides' forces might be difficult to control. The pressure to "use them or lose them" if the opponents appeared to be preparing a preemptive strike could be difficult to resist. To some extent, then, hair-trigger responses can be mitigated by strategic defenses that protect retaliatory forces and command centers. Each side's C3I is an invitation to destruction and a warning against taking the invitation too seriously. Decapitated opponents are not necessarily weaker. Without the U.S. president or a clearly designated political successor at the helm, it is not clear that the Soviets would be better off. As Paul Bracken has noted, authority *or* retaliatory capacity could be delegated before a crisis reached its boiling point, or even under normal peacetime conditions.[45] The Soviets cannot know exactly how and to whom this delegation has taken place. A reasonable supposition by them is that U.S. unified and specified military commanders can retaliate, if they are not forbidden to do so by higher authorities, under the mandate to protect their forces from preemptive destruction.

Given that both sides have undoubtedly provided for at least a trans-SIOP response of some kind, and that this response would in each case destroy much of the society of the other, then both sides have a shared reciprocal interest in preserving the opponent's command structures even after deterrence fails. It has been argued, in contrast with our case for command preservation, that Soviet military doctrine calls for the prompt destruction of the enemy's command and communications.[46] Suppressing the command decision apparatus of your opponent makes sense, provided you have the capabilities for comprehensive disarming first strike against the combined elements of its retaliatory forces. In the instance of an overwhelming first-strike capability for one side compared with the other, however, there would be little likelihood of war because the weaker side would have to capitulate during crises. Under conditions such that forces are more symmetrical in their prelaunch survivability and in their ability to penetrate any defenses, command destruction does not appeal to them.

It might seem from the standpoint of classical strategy that destroying the opponent's commanders and their organizations would provide a force multiplier for the side that did it first. But, again, this presupposes that there is the possibility of one side's delivering a rapid knockout blow against the forces of the other, so as to preclude any significant retaliation. If retaliation cannot be prevented beyond levels that are unacceptable to the attacker, then once deterrence fails, the door must be left open for negotiation and war termination.[47] Victory cannot be imposed by one party on another, and both will have to use up their arsenals in mutual fury or come to some terms of nonendearment. It seems improbable that this can happen in the aftermath of a U.S.-Soviet nuclear exchange, but it is not any more improbable than some of the processes by which wars have been terminated in the past.

One of the cases made for U.S. strategic defense might be that it would help to preserve postattack command survivability so that whatever negotiations were possible could still be conducted by a surviving national command authority. However, this use for strategic defenses will not justify large and comprehensive deployments of the kind that would protect society as a whole. C3 protection is at best only part of the rationale for a limited BMD system, and no partial system would guarantee the survival of all commanders and their respective commands. A disaggregated U.S. command structure is sure to follow from even the early exchanges of weapons during superpower nuclear conflict. The difference between disaggregated and disintegrated, however, might mean the difference between zero probability of war termination and some low, but still significant, probability. But there is another side to the argument that defenses should be deployed to protect command and control. As defenses mature, some of that C3 will have to be deployed in space, where it may be more vulnerable to preemptive attack than the command and control infrastructure based on land. The more automated a space-based defense system becomes, the more complicated will be the checks and balances to assure that it does not fire accidentally or inadvertently.

## SOVIET RESPONSES

Obviously U.S. planners will have to take into account the possibility of Soviet countermeasures to any U.S. SDI deployment. These counter measures might take any of several paths. First, the Soviets might attack the system itself and attempt to destroy its sensor or weapons platforms. This is defense suppression. Second, they might overwhelm the system with so many offensive launchers and reentry vehicles that the defense interceptors would be exhausted, or the sensors confused, before they could inflict meaningful losses against the offense. A third approach to countermeasures is to outsmart the defense by means of electronic or electro-optical deception or disruption. This third approach merits more discussion that it has previously received.

U. S. sensors and weapons platforms will depend upon sensitive components to monitor the flight of Soviet missiles and reentry vehicles, to track their trajectories, to determine whether they have been intercepted or missed, and to transmit information to national command authorities, who must make political decisions in a very short time. The attacker has every incentive to make these tasks for an SDI system difficult instead of easy. Several techniques might be available to a determined attacker.

Two well-known techniques are jamming and spoofing. Jamming is the transmission of noise or competing signals on the same frequencies as true signals, with the intent of distorting or preventing reception of the true signals. Spoofing is more sophisticated, at least in concept. The target satellite is given false signals that cause it to perform its mission in a faulty or misleading way, or not at all. If Soviet jammers and spoofers know the relevant frequencies, they will attempt to jam the uplinks from ground controllers to satellites or the downlinks in the other direction.

In addition, future satellite systems will make more use of crosslinks from one satellite to another; these, too, might be disrupted by space-to-space or earth-to-space interference. Finally, there are the through-links or ground-to-ground links through a satellite. Modern satellites rely on uplinks as command channels; disruption of those channels would result in physical (drifting out of orbit) or electronic failures.[48]

Sometimes the opponent may simply want to collect information from U.S. signals without revealing that the information has been obtained. This collection may be difficult to detect. Encryption of signals is one defense against hostile collection. In addition to preventing collection of some signals, the United States might want other signals to be completely unknown to potential opponents. In those cases low-probability-of-intercept (LPI) approaches are employed, including burst transmissions and spread-spectrum techniques.[49] Protection against spoofing requires encryption plus authentication protocols or digital signals that can require the authentication of the sender or the message. Counter-countermeasures to jamming could include increases in the power of the indented signal relative to incidental and antagonistic noise, or LPI techniques such as frequency hopping and pseudo noise.[50]

Soviet military and political leaders have shown increasing awareness of the importance of space-based assets for communications, early warn-ing, and reconnaissance. They depend upon their satellite early warning systems and their over-the-horizon backscatter ground-based radars for early detection of any U.S. ICBM launch.[51] Satellites are important to Soviet planners and commanders for missions such as signals intelli-gence, ocean surveillance, and space surveillance. Their fifth-generation photographic reconnaissance satellites transmit digital electronic signals in real time to geosynchronous relay satellites, which retransmit them to ground stations.[52] Soviet intelligence organizations, including the KGB and GRU (military intelligence), collect a great deal of signals intelli-gence, including the interception of U.S. and other military communi-cations.

Since 1970 the Soviet Union has had a constellation of electronic in-telligence (ELINT) satellites that, among other assignments, can monitor the emissions of U.S. warning and space-tracking radars.[53] Soviet space reconnaissance and ELINT assets are coordinated with ground-based platforms for intercepting U.S. and allied communications. The com-munications intelligence facility at Lourdes, Cuba, the largest non-U.S. operation of its kind in the Western Hemisphere, intercepts civilian and military communications, including communications to and from Cape Canaveral related to U.S. military space missions.[54] Two types of ocean surveillance and reconnaissance satellites are operated by the USSR: radar ocean reconnaissance satellites (RORSATs) and ELINT ocean re-connaissance satellites (EORSATs). EORSATs and RORSATs provide real-time detection and tracking data to Soviet surface ships, submarines, and ground stations. They could be used in conjunction if EORSATs established the presence and signal pattern of a U.S. ship and RORSATs provided more detailed information for targeting of antiship weapons launched from Soviet naval vessels or Backfire bombers.[55]

A study by the U.S. Office of Technology Assessment reported in 1985 that the Soviet Union's co-orbital antisatellite (ASAT) weapon could attack U.S. satellites in low earth orbit.[56] For the time being, the Soviet ASAT poses no apparent threat to U.S. launch detection and communications satellites in higher orbits, although the USSR might increase the capacity of its boosters in order to reach satellites in higher orbits. Soviet research and development efforts have apparently included kinetic and directed-energy weapons that might be employed in an ASAT mode. According to the U.S. Department of Defense, the USSR already has ground-based lasers that have a limited capability to attack U.S. satellites, and they could have a prototype space-based ASAT laser weapon by the end of the 1980s.[57] The USSR, according to the Pentagon, has conducted research on radio frequency signals that could interfere with the electronic components of satellites.[58] If necessary, the Soviets' already deployed Galosh ABM system might be used in a limited ASAT role, although its nuclear warhead, if detonated, could create unintended disturbances in the functioning of Soviet as well as U.S. space assets.

The relationship between the Soviets' military doctrine and their possible response to a U.S. SDI technology program or deployment is admittedly unclear. In terms of the present discussion, Soviet military doctrine would suggest an unwillingness to depend upon tactical warning of attack against their early warning or communications satellites. Soviet planners apparently assume that a U.S.-Soviet nuclear war might begin in one of several ways: a deliberate U.S. attack "out of the blue," escalation from a superpower crisis (as in Cuba), or expansion from a conventional war into nuclear exchanges.[59] A "bolt from the blue" now seems improbable to them relative to the possibilities of escalation or expansion from conventional war, in which cases they would presumably have strategic warning from a variety of political and military indicators. Under those conditions, the USSR might choose to preempt an anticipated Western attack on its satellites or other warning and communications media. Although the Soviet Union is not now as dependent as is the United States upon satellites for day-to-day military communications, it should not be assumed that destruction of its satellites would be unimportant to it. Depending upon the other indicators they were watching, Soviet leaders might conclude during a crisis that destruction of their warning and communications satellites (or maneuvering of U.S. space- or ground-based ASATs into position to destroy those Soviet satellites) was a sign of imminent U.S. preemptive attack.

One example of how this fear of ASAT preemption might lead to the deterioration of crisis stability is provided by the importance of Soviet RORSATS and EORSAT in targeting U.S. fleets. U.S. naval planners have indicated that they desire the U.S. ASAT (miniature homing vehicle) primarily for its potential to threaten or destroy Soviet RORSATs and EORSATs that would provide targeting information against the U.S. fleet in time of war. Soviet observers of U.S. ASAT launch preparation might consider this part of a broader preparedness for preemptive attack against an entire constellation of Soviet space assets. Thus, U.S. or Soviet ASATs present two kinds of threats to crisis stability: they might be used for preemptive attack against the warning and communications satellites of the other superpower, and their vulnerability to disruption or destruction might invite attack. We have been emphasizing the opportunities for disruption more than those for destruction, although in some instances ASAT technologies make the distinction academic.

## ARTIFICIAL INTELLIGENCE AND SDI

The preceding discussion raises the possibility that the performance of active defense systems and their battle management/command functions could be improved significantly by applications of artificial intelligence. It must be acknowledged that many potential applications are, at this writing, speculative. Artificial intelligence also suffers from its nomenclature, which sounds pretentious and hubristic. Even its practitioners are sometimes cultish about advertising their expertise, and some premature applications were accompanied by embarrassing failures.

The first and most important contribution, in general, will be the developments in decision support systems. This implies both hardware and software systems. Future systems, compared with present systems, will be cheaper, more versatile, and smarter. They will be included in networks of increased diversity and sophistication. Future decision support systems will be more portable than their predecessors. They will also have simultaneous voice and video capabilities. Some of their memories will be prodigious. Management functions that are now performed repeatedly in military and other organizations will be performed a single time, and then learned into the memory of the artificially intelligent decision support system.[60]

These projections for the decision supports of the 1990s, if valid, turn out to have interesting implications for SDI. For example, at the present time, command centers for the control of nuclear forces are few in number, and therefore potentially vulnerable to a small number of nearby detonations.[61] In the future, it may be possible to proliferate command centers with the aid of decision support systems. The command centers could also be made more mobile because they could handle the same information functions with a smaller gross size. Instead of SAC, NORAD, National Military Command Center, Alternate NMCC, and the various command posts for the commanders in chief who are assigned nuclear forces, one can imagine literally hundreds, if not thousands, of mobile command posts that could not possibly be destroyed in toto. With the appropriate software, the information environment of the postattack period might be reconstructed, not only in the central command posts in the Pentagon and Cheyenne Mountain but also at various points throughout the United States, virtually everywhere there is a military installation or a local police station. Such a distributed network of postattack command stations could be programmed to accept input from persons who in time of peace were not necessarily authenticated to send messages, and it could be shrewd enough to maintain a file on whose authentications should receive priority. This last function becomes extremely important should the president and the secretary of defense (together with their successors, the national command authority) be killed in early attacks or the main bases for NORAD and SAC be attacked. Someone will have to establish a pecking order for transmission and receipt of important messages.

The proliferation of command stations reassures against fears of a nuclear decapitation, but it raises other issues. True, no one wants the U.S. retaliatory arsenal to lie paralyzed if the Soviet first strike on North America is attempted. On the other hand, no one wants Colonel Jones to start a war without National Command Authority authorization, or even to issue improper orders that might confuse the chain of command. There is a real dilemma here, between allowing appropriate initiative to subordinates, as a reward for good past performance and as an incentive to future excellence, and restriction, to protect against the possible combination of powerful technology and exuberant commanders. At the moment, the problem of preventing accidental or unauthorized launch of U.S. nuclear forces is thought to be very much in hand.[62] And there is certainly an upper limit beyond which it would not make much sense for the controls over the U.S. use of force to go. The temptation for presidents to play sergeant by exploiting real-time communications with faraway subordinates may disrupt the plans of commanders, who count on a certain distance or autonomy from the top. While modern communications and a small number of key command centers now make this presidential control relatively easy, in the future proliferated command centers may make it more difficult, especially if the numerous commanders in the field and their subordinates have access to better information that their superiors.

The second major application made possible by artificial intelligence technology, relative to the C3 requirements of SDI, has already been alluded to: distributed data processing and dispersed assessment. We have already seen that strategic defense systems can be designed to work from a centralized or decentralized basic architecture. The same is true for the BM/C3 components of defenses.[63] Centralized and decentralized models are ideal types; any system actually deployed will have features of both. Nevertheless, the matter of relative emphasis is still important.

A distributed base of data files for assessment and warning will allow spaceborne commanders to plug into national C3 networks for nearly instantaneous feedback about the status of targets following strikes and counterstrikes. Included in these status reports will be information deemed vital to efforts to attain war termination on some mutually acceptable terms. An expert system (artificial intelligence analogue to a human expert in a particular domain) could make preliminary attack assessments and select from a menu of postattack options which were optimal from the standpoint of effective targeting. The advantage of doing this in space is that it could be done with direct satellite-to-space-station crosslinks without the requirement for downlinks to terrestrial fusion centers, which may have been destroyed. Of course, more sophisticated C3 based in space has all the vulnerabilities that anything based in space has. Vulnerability of enemy BMD or ASAT weapons is the most immediate concern. On the other hand, a distributed data base with spaceborne expert systems can make decisions in real time for the survivability of space reconnaissance and other satellite-based capabilities, including the giving of instructions for the satellites to change orbit, speed, and photographic or electronic coverage of relevant targets.

Third, in order for a layered defense system to work synergistically, so that the whole is greater than the sum of its parts, the system must optimize rather than suboptimize across a variety of possible intercept priorities. If, for example, the midcourse phase of the defense system can be given discrimination capabilities in real time to distinguish enemy warheads from decoys, it will, to accomplish that mission, have to avoid being deceived by simulation and antisimulation tactics of the offense.[64] Simulation makes decoys look like real warheads; antisimulation is the opposite of simulation. The computer programs that will have to provide instructions for sensors and weapons in the midcourse phase may be the most complicated ever written; literally hundreds of thousands of warheads and decoys may be coming at the defender at once. Discrimination and response that are of high fidelity relative to the offense's countermeasures will allow the defense to get by with a more manageable terminal defense. Conversely, if the midcourse problem is not managed successfully, then it is likely that a large number of warheads surviving the midcourse phase will leak through to the terminal defense, and overwhelm it.

The assessment functions that must be performed in the midcourse phase are extremely challenging. The boost phase of the defense is the most difficult to weaponize, according to some scientists, but it does not present information overload problems comparable with those of midcourse discrimination. In the boost phase, the problem will be to intercept "mere" hundreds of launch vehicles, like ICBMs, before they disperse their multiple warheads in the postboost phase. If this can be done, then the amount of stress on the remaining layers of the defense is reduced. It matters a great deal whether the midcourse defense is dealing with hundreds of thousands, or hundreds, of warheads and decoys. Artificial intelligence systems of the 1990s and beyond may provide the only possible way to implement such a demanding mission requirement, through the use of expert systems and other extensions of the man-machine interface in command systems.

Fourth, and finally, artificial intelligence may make possible the "proactive" reaction of the defense to what looks like a first strike by the offense. This concern—that SDI might falsely anticipate an attack and so provoke one—has been voiced by politicians and scientists. On the other hand, U.S. planners will be hard pressed to justify a system that is so slow-reacting that it can be nullified by simple countermeasures, such as faster-burning boosters or ablative coating for missile casing.[65] The ability of artificial-intelligence-based systems to discriminate between false alarms and real attacks will depend upon the kinds of software written to provide this capability, and also upon the tightness or looseness of the decision rules by which they operate. These decision rules will be the rules that political and military leaders desire to be programmed into the system. Leaders will have to make known to programmers their priorities in peacetime, during crises, and in wartime.

Peacetime criteria, for the Reagan administration, have included survivability and cost effectiveness at the margin for any deployable SDI system.[66] Both criteria will demand larger information bases, and smarter ways of understanding them, than now exist. There is no hope of coping with the sophistication of attacks that might happen if deterrence failed, during the 1990s or beyond, without some significant exploitation of artificial intelligence for sensors, information processing, and command/control. At the same time, artificial intelligence technologists should not promise to attain results in SDI/C3 that are beyond the state of the art. Politicians will still make the decisions that provide the strategic and financial boundaries for U.S. retaliatory forces, including the BM/C3 that supports them. In the past, command systems have not received the fiscal or strategic emphasis that weapons delivery platforms have, and interest in C3 improvements have been dispersed, and thus fragmented, throughout the defense bureaucracy. The creation of the position of assistant secretary of defense for C3I in the Reagan administration shows timely recognition of the importance of command systems and their subordinate functions to the future of defense, including spaceborne and terrestrial missile defenses. Those defenses, should they be deployed, could help to protect U.S. C3 system that are now vulnerable to disruption or destruction.

It is also the case that U.S. strategic intelligence during crisis and war may be the intended victim of deception.[67] The potential of artificial intelligence for assisting decision makers who want to avoid being deceived has barely been tapped. Already some important uses can be foreseen. Enemy attempts to jam electronic signals or spoof the behavior of U.S. satellites and their control systems must be prevented if the reliable command and control of forces is not to be lost. If the USSR is the opponent in wartime, it will attempt to mask its own behavior by providing deceptive signals about its intentions and capabilities. The difference by the 1990s will be that the Soviets may be able to do this real time, and the U.S. response may be too delayed to be useful. Or penetration of U.S. artificial intelligence systems by hostile agents may allow a foreign power to introduce, in advance of the outbreak of war, deceptive instructions that will cause the system to fail or to perform its mission in unexpected ways. Expert systems and other decision supports may be the "moles" of the next century whose bona fides will be scrutinized more carefully than those of their human users. Thus the role of artificial intelligence in counterintelligence will increase as the plausibility of threats to intelligent systems increases.

As important as it is to recognize the potential of artificial intelligence for SDI, it is equally important not to overpromote it in this context. Some of the problems attendant to SDI cannot be resolved by artificial intelligence or any foreseeable information technology. The weaponization of space platforms requires the provision of power supplies and a more efficient way of getting those supplies into orbit, compared with present approaches. The U.S. civilian and military use of space will also depend upon a clear sense of priorities about what missions must be accomplished there. Department of Defense software and hardware development will have to consider how space-based sensors, communications, and weapons will contribute to the termination of war on earth. These issues are foreseeable only in a very general way at present. Moving into another medium for military operations obviously requires additional logistics, technology, and strategy. Whether these three elements can be combined into a coherent whole by U.S. planners will depend partly, but only so, on how innovative software and instrumentation can be. Artificial intelligence expert systems and other decision aids can provide force multipliers for policymakers and commanders who already know where they want to go. If they do not know, then no improvement in their tools will substitute for lack of goal consensus.

It would also be misguided to assume that, with or without the enhancements of artificial intelligence, the essential decision-making problems attendant to crisis and war can be bypassed by the deployment of defenses. The most disconcerting thing about the proposed deployment of SDI is not the interest in new hardware and software, but the tendency to treat personal and group decision-making processes as unwelcome perturbation of an otherwise attainable steady state. The psychological factors pertinent to crisis and wartime decisions will become more, instead of less, important if policymakers attempt to draw upon artificial intelligence methodologies as analogues of actual crisis or wartime behavior.[68] Models have the advantage of parsimony, which allows us to focus on the few important relationships among many interactions that occur at the same time. Models also have disadvantages, including the tendency for analysts to ontologize them, to attribute to models the behavioral attributes of individuals, in order to make possible a more concise presentation of hypotheses and inferences. However, if we are to put policymakers into a black box in this fashion, we will have to allow the box to have permeable boundaries and, on occasion, a chameleonlike ability to change colors.[69]

## SDI AND WAR TERMINATION

What impact would SDI or its Soviet counterpart have on the possibility of terminating a nuclear war, regional or global, after it had begun? Answering this question involves venturing into the unknown, but it must be posed now. We have seen that the command and control issues attendant to SDI must be confronted in its early stages. So, too, must the question of war termination. And the possibility of U.S. or Soviet ground- or space-based missile defenses cuts more than one way with regard to ending nuclear conflict after it has begun. Let us consider the impact of SDI in terms of the three generic components of war termination outlined in Chapter 1: an agreed battle, escalation control, and coercive diplomacy.

The notion of an agreed battle would be compatible with a war fought only in space and then stopped for fear of spreading it to earth. One side might be tempted, for example, to strike selectively at the space-based surveillance or weapons-carrying satellites of the opponent, hoping to escape with impunity. When it became clear that the other side had correctly detected this move, then its opposite number might desist. Or both sides could destroy some but not all of the warning and communications satellites of the other, stopping at that point for fear of provoking terrestrial war. It seems that tacit limitations might be built around the space-versus-terrestrial threshold, with "terrestrial" defined to include atmospheric defenses and offenses.

An agreed battle in space might follow a crisis. Exchanges of ASAT salvos against the satellites of the opponent might follow immediately upon the collapse of crisis management. However, this would still leave room, although precious little, for prevention of nuclear war on earth. The brinkmanship-minded leadership that risked strikes against space-based sensors or weapons might be emboldened by the thought that, even if detected, the collateral damage attendant to the attack (in terms of human lives) would be in the range of limited to nonexistent. Risks could appear to be asymmetrical when they were not. The defender might conclude that the attacker had launched the first salvos of World War III, instead of interpreting the strikes as coercive measures (see below).

The concept of an agreed battle already exists, in the form of a tacit recognition by Soviet and U.S. leaders since the ABM Treaty of 1972 that neither will attempt to deploy a credible first-strike capability against the other. This does not preclude research on defenses, or even limited deployments. It does preclude comprehensive city and territorial defenses, which would negate retaliatory strikes. There is also another side to this agreed battle based on mutual deterrence, in addition to its arms control implications. This other side is the shared recognition that countercity retaliation is the ultimate deterrent, but not necessarily the first move or the militarily most important move. Each would target its early strikes primarily against the remaining military forces of the opponent, holding cities in reserve to be threatened with later destruction. Here the first stages of nuclear war might resemble an agreed battle with a large element of coercive diplomacy based on cities held hostage. However, there is a cost to maintaining this notion of an agreed battle. To the extent that both sides forego counterforce capabilities and enduring command systems, they are working with an attenuated ladder of escalation that has essentially two rungs: very limited theater nuclear strikes and total disaster.

The second component of the war termination concept is escalation control. Defenses could assist in the control of escalation after nuclear war had broken out under certain very specific conditions. They would have to be defenses that could help to protect assured destruction forces and command centers, but not defenses that threatened to eliminate the opponent's capacity for retaliation. Maintaining defenses within this zone of not too weak and not too strong would be difficult even if only one side deployed them. If both did, then some arms control agreement would have to be devised to pace their deployments at equally competitive rates. Otherwise, the slower to deploy would begin to fear that the other side was about to obtain a first-strike capability.

In the current U.S.-Soviet condition of stability based on offensive retaliation with limited defenses on one side and none on the other, defenses could improve stability by protecting command centers and other C3 elements. Earlier chapters noted that an attack against the entire strategic nuclear command system of either superpower would probably be counterproductive and might fail. A selective attack is another matter, and the temptation to preempt against the more vulnerable components of the Soviet or U.S. command system will grow as a crisis deepens and war appears to be inevitable. It may also be that following an initial attack, the defender will judge its best option to be a counter-command attack against those fixed command centers and other nodes that support the remaining forces of the attacker.[70] Although limited defenses for C3 protection would be theoretical options for both super-powers, in practice the U.S. alternatives are politically constrained. A U.S. version of the Galosh system deployed around Washington, D.C., would invite charges of provocative preparation for nuclear war against any administration that proposed it. Thus U.S. C3 defenses would have to be dedicated initially to some other mission, probably force protection, and benefits for the command system would be residuals.

Defenses would contribute to escalation control not only by helping to protect the command system against a limited attack but also by increasing policymakers' confidence that they could absorb an accidental or catalytic strike from an "Nth" country arsenal. Some U.S. advocates of SDI have pressed this argument far beyond its justification. Terrorists have other and more manageable ways to wreak nuclear havoc, as do Third World states not constrained by the Nonproliferation Treaty. Even limited BMD seems an expensive safeguard against terrorist strikes that would not be confused with a superpower attack in any event, since the latter would be of a completely different size and character. Defenses might have the psychological effect of convincing commanders that they had more time and sanctuary to make decisions than they did without defenses. This could contribute to prevention of hair-trigger response after an accidental or unauthorized launch.

On the other hand, defenses deployed in space could contribute to crisis instability, for reasons already noted, if they invite defense suppression. And after war began on earth, space-based military assets could be impediments instead of complements to a war termination desired by both sides. Space surveillance would improve the accuracy of nuclear and conventional weapons targeting. Ocean reconnaissance and ELINT satellites would provide timely information for attacks against maritime forces. Weather satellites could make available timely forecasts of cloud cover and other conditions that would facilitate attack planning and coordination.[71] For these reasons even conventional war between U.S. and Soviet forces or their allies in Europe would create strong pressures for the use of ASATs if they were available. There is no question that the United States has become dependent upon satellite reconnaissance, surveillance, communication, and navigation for the conduct of conventional war worldwide. Thus the onset of war, or even its likelihood, could tempt Soviet planners to remove these eyes and ears in order to restrict U.S. wartime options and to improve their own.

Command assets, too, will increasingly be based in space, perhaps on space stations as well as satellites. Transponders for one C3 mission can be carried on satellites designed primarily for other jobs. Thus, for example, NAVSTAR-GPS navigation satellites and DSP warning satellites both carry nuclear explosion detectors. The NAVSTAR-GPS version, NDS (for nuclear detection system, formerly IONDS), will provide information about the yield and height of burst within minutes.[72] From a war termination perspective, this is a mixed blessing. Nuclear explosion detection provides information for restrikes in an extended war. It also provides information that would be needed to verify that detonations had ceased in order to bring the war to an end. Conversely, loss of this information in wartime would make extended counterforce war harder to fight, and it would also make agreement on an armistice or truce more difficult to obtain.

This is not an academic point in the pejorative sense. The military uses of space, including space-based defenses, are not, for the most part, unambiguously supportive of, or destructive of, strategic stability as we now know it. And even if simple labels could be attached, the entire meaning of stability changes if either or both sides deploy defenses of sufficient competence to protect cities. Then physical protection or denial of countercity attacks will replace forbearance as the mechanism by which populations are protected. Unless the physical protection is nearly perfect, the partially effective defenses may be more useful in the mission of protecting each side's deterrent from preemptive strike. Stability would remain as a condition based on offensive retaliation, and defenses would reinforce deterrence instead of undermining it. And if deterrence failed, defenses would provide some limited protection for force that leaders might otherwise launch hastily for fear of losing them altogether.

Another long-run possibility, although a much-disputed one as to the actual odds, is the prospect for space-based reconnaissance and communications systems that would change the nature of undersea warfare. If, for example, ballistic missile submarines no longer had to come near the surface to receive rapid-rate communications, U.S. and Soviet leaders could employ them more flexibly in limited and prompt attack roles. This would add to fears of counterforce vulnerability against the prompt launch of sea-based ballistic force. Another potential development is the deployment of satellite-based technology for detection of submarines at normal operating depths. This would threaten prelaunch survivability of U.S. and Soviet ballistic missile submarines, and possibly contribute to more hair-trigger deterrent forces, or deployments of additional submarines to foil antisubmarine assets based in space.

These space-based systems might add complexity to an already apparent threat from the sea to existing defenses, that of cruise missiles with nuclear and conventional warheads. Soviet air defenses would need to be improved to cope with futuristic U.S. versions of these sea-based weapons. U.S. air defenses would be terribly stressed by Soviet equivalents of the U.S. Tomahawk deployed on submarines and surface craft. In regional war that has not yet expanded into global superpower conflict, sea-launched cruise missiles could play havoc with both sides' conventional and nuclear forces based in Europe. European air defenses are also vulnerable to rapid interdiction by Soviet air offensives and conventional ballistic missile salvos. Conventional sea-launched cruise missiles and theater ballistic missiles, if deployed in Europe without arms control restraints, could chase Soviet and NATO war planners back to their drawing boards in planning ground and tactical air campaigns. In turn, improved space-based reconnaissance of U.S. and Soviet submarines could make cruise-missile-launching attack and ballistic-missile submarines more vulnerable, and mobile land-based ballistic missiles suddenly more attractive.

The third component of war termination, coercive diplomacy, has already appeared in discussion of the agreed battle and escalation control. Defenses could protect either side against counterforce coercion by an opponent willing to engage in limited nuclear options but unwilling to go further. One of the disturbing possibilities inherent in Soviet BMD deployments is that they might rob the United States of limited nuclear options (LNOs) and thus of the compellence attendant to limited nuclear options in Europe.[73] Related to that, Soviet defenses might also deny French and British deterrents their assured retaliation while the U.S. force retained it. Therefore limited defenses make sub-SIOP employment options less credible. This might be good or bad, depending on the scenario. It could inhibit the foolish initiation of small nuclear attacks in the mistaken optimism that further escalation would be easy to control. And limited defenses could also increase a false sense of security about the costs of limited nuclear war. U.S. maritime strategy, which depends at least in part on the coercive use of conventional war at sea against Soviet nuclear reserve forces, would be less credible if the USSR were not so fearful of losing its SSBNs to gradual attrition. And it might not be less credible if highly competent BMD deployments that protected much of Eastern Europe and the western USSR reassured Soviet leaders that they could afford to wait out the results of the U.S. antisubmarine campaign.

Finally, in terms of coercive diplomacy, BMD could have two possibly offsetting effects on policymakers' crisis and wartime bargaining strategies. If they had high confidence in their defenses, they might be bolder in resisting coercion of the adversary. But if they lacked confidence in their defenses—as they well might, given the absence of tests under realistic conditions—defenses could be albatrosses around their necks. Vulnerable defenses in future crises could be very similar to U.S. Jupiter missiles deployed in Turkey in 1962. The U.S. missiles were liabilities instead of assets, and targets instead of deterrents. That this was so perceived by President Kennedy and his "ExComm" advisers is evident from transcripts of their deliberations on October 27. The president continued to entertain notions of trading missiles in Turkey for missiles in Cuba, although some of his advisers, on grounds of NATO solidarity and future credibility, were dead set against it.[74] The effects of weapons systems on crisis management and intrawar deterrence, to say nothing of war termination, will be specific to the vagaries of the scenario as it unfolds. Nothing would be more misleading than to assert categorical imperatives, with regard to the implications of strategic defenses for war termination, independently of the nuances of national leaders' objectives and fears.

## NOTES

1. President Reagan's speech is reprinted in the *New York Times* of March 24, 1983; pertinent excerpts appear in Arms Control Association, *Star Wars Quotes* (Washington, D.C.: Arms Control Association, 1986), pp. 118–119.

2. U.S. Department of Defense, *Soviet Military Power: 1987* (Washington, D.C.: U.S. Government Printing Office, March 1987), pp. 46–47.

3. Desmond Ball, "Counterforce Targeting: How New? How Viable?" *Arms Control Today* 11, no. 2 (February 1981), repr. with revisions in John F. Reichart and Steven R. Sturm, eds., *American Defense Policy* (Baltimore: Johns Hopkins University Press, 1982), pp. 227–234.

4. Desmond Ball, "The Development of the SIOP, 1960–1983," ch. 3 in Desmond Ball and Jeffrey Richelson, eds., *Strategic Nuclear Targeting* (Ithaca, N.Y.: Cornell University Press, 1986), pp. 57–83.

5. Paul H. Nitze, "On the Road to a More Stable Peace," February 20, 1985, U.S. Department of State, repr. in Keck Center for International Strategic Studies, *The Strategic Defense Initiative* (Claremont, Cal.: Claremont McKenna College, 1985) pp. 33–38.

6. Ashton B. Carter, "BMD Applications: Performance and Limitations," in Ashton B. Carter and David N. Schwartz, eds., *Ballistic Missile Defense* (Washington, D.C.: Brookings Institution, 1984), pp. 98–181.

7. U.S. Office of Technology Assessment, *Ballistic Missile Defense Technologies*, OTA-ISC–254 (Washington, D.C.: U.S. Government Printing Office, (September 1985), p. 11.

8. Bruce G. Blair, *Strategic Command and Control: Redefining the Nuclear Threat* (Washington, D.C.: Brookings Institution, 1985).

9. Graham T. Allison, *Essence of Decision: Explaining the Cuban Missile Crisis* (Boston: Little, Brown, 1971).

10. John D. Steinbruner, *The Cybernetic Theory of Decision* (Princeton: Princeton University Press, 1974), esp. pp. 57–61.

11. Leslie H. Gelb with Richard K. Betts, *The Irony of Vietnam: The System Worked* (Washington, D.C.: Brookings Institution, 1979), esp. pp. 323–343.

12. Robert W. Komer, *Bureaucracy at War: U.S. Performance in the Vietnam Conflict* (Boulder, Colo.: Westview Press, 1986), pp. 81–110.

13. Paul Bracken, *The Command and Control of Nuclear Forces* (New Haven: Yale University Press, 1983).

14. Albert Carnesale et al., *Living with Nuclear Weapons* (New York: Bantam Books, 1983), pp. 59–60.

15. See Scott D. Sagan, "1914 Revisited: Allies, Offense and Instability," *International Security* 11, no. 2 (Fall 1986): 151–175. A standard historical reference is Barbara W. Tuchman, *The Guns of August* (New York: Macmillan, 1962).

16. See Office of Technology Assessment, *Ballistic Missile Defense Technologies*, ch. 7.

17. Ibid., pp. 197–218.

18. See John R. Southern, Carl G. Davis, and Melvin P. Edwards, "Army BM/C³ in the SDI Program," in Stephen J. Andriole, ed., *High Technology Initiatives in C³I* (Washington, D.C.: AFCEA International Press, 1986), pp. 358–369.

19. Eastport Study Group, *A Report to the Director, Strategic Defense Initiative Organization: Summer Study 1985* (Washington, D.C.: Department of Defense, December 1985).

20. David Lorge Parnas, "Software Aspects of Strategic Defense Systems," *American Scientist* 73 (September–October 1985): 432–439.

21. Director, SDIO, *SDI: A Technical Progress Report* (Washington, D.C.: SDIO, June 1985), p. 10.

22. See James R. Schlesinger, "Rhetoric and Realities in the Star Wars Debate," *International Security* 10, no. 1 (Summer 1985): 3–24; and Harold Brown, "Is SDI Technically Feasible?" *Foreign Affairs* 64, no. 3 (1986): 435–454.

23. John Steinbruner, "Nuclear Decapitation," *Foreign Policy* no. 45 (Winter 1981–1982): 16–28.

24. Blair, *Strategic Command and Control*, p. 187.

25. Desmond Ball, *Can Nuclear War Be Controlled?* Adelphi Papers, no. 169 (London: International Institute for Strategic Studies, Autumn 1981); comments by Lt. Gen. Brent Scowcroft, *Strategic Nuclear Weapons, Policies and the C3 Connection* (Bedford, Mass.: Electronic Systems Division, USAF, and MITRE Corp., October 1981).

26. Colin S. Gray, *American Military Space Policy* (Cambridge, Mass.: Abt Books, 1982), pp. 69–70.

27. Peter Pringle and William Arkin, *SIOP: The Secret U.S. Plan for Nuclear War* (New York: W. W. Norton, 1983), p. 34.

28. Ashton B. Carter, "Assessing Command System Vulnerability," ch. 17 in Ashton B. Carter, John D. Steinbruner, and Charles A. Zraket, eds., *Managing Nuclear Operations* (Washington, D.C.: Brookings Institution, 1987), pp. 555–610.

29. See Albert Wohlstetter and Richard Brody, "Continuing Control as a Requirement for Deterring," ch. 5 in Carter, Steinbruner, and Zraket, eds., *Managing Nuclear Operations*, pp. 142–196.

30. Dean Wilkening, Kenneth Watman, Michael Kennedy, and Richard Darilek, "Strategic Defenses and First Strike Stability," *Survival* 29, no. 2 (March/April 1987): 137–165.

31. "Allies Uncertain About 'Star Wars,'" *Long Island Newsday,* October 24, 1985, p. 19, repr. in *Current News,* spec. ed. *Strategic Defensive Initiative,* November 19, 1985, p. 50.

32. Office of Technology Assessment, *Ballistic Missile Defense Technologies,* p. 200.

33. Ibid., pp. 202–203.

34. Michael Howard, *The Causes of Wars,* 2nd. ed. (Cambridge, Mass.: Harvard University Press, 1984), pp. 104–105 and passim, for clarification of this distinction.

35. U.S. Department of Defense, *Soviet Military Power: 1986* (Washington, D.C.: U.S. Government Printing Office, March 1986), p. 42.

36. See Harriet Fast Scott and William F. Scott, *The Soviet Control Structure: Capabilities for Wartime Survival* (New York: Crane, Russak/National Strategy Information Center, 1983), pp. 9–12, 121, 129–138, and passim.

37. Barry M. Blechman and Michael Krepon, *Nuclear Risk Reduction Centers* (Washington, D.C.: Center for Strategic and International Studies, Georgetown University, 1986).

38. See Raymond L. Garthoff, "Mutual Deterrence, Parity and Strategic Arms Limitation in Soviet Policy," in Derek Leebaert, ed., *Soviet Military Thinking* (London: Allen and Unwin, 1981), pp. 92–124.

39. See Albert Carnesale, *Learning from Experience with Arms Control: a Final Report* (Cambridge, Mass.: John F. Kennedy School of Government, Harvard University, September 1986), ch. 3.

40. The distinction between accidental and inadvertent nuclear war is discussed by Paul Bracken, "Accidental Nuclear War," ch. 2 in Graham T. Allison, Albert Carnesale, and Joseph S. Nye, Jr., eds., *Hawks, Doves and Owls: An Agenda for Avoiding Nuclear War* (New York: W. W. Norton, 1985), pp. 25–53.

41. Tuchman, *The Guns of August,* provides important historical background. See esp. pp. 71–83.

42. Robert S. McNamara, *Blundering into Disaster* (New York: Pantheon Books, 1986).

43. Allison, *Essence of Decision.*

44. Elie Abel, *The Missile Crisis* (Philadelphia: J. B. Lippincott, 1966), discusses these and other near-miss incidents during the crisis.

45. Bracken, *The Command and Control of Nuclear Forces,* pp. 224–232. The impact of unexpected stresses upon disaggregated command systems is best appreciated by insightful review of case studies of other complex organizations, especially Charles Perrow, *Normal Accidents: Living with High Risk Technologies* (New York: Basic Books, 1984), esp. chs. 3 and 8.

46. Fritz W. Ermarth, "Contrasts in American and Soviet Strategic Thought," in Leebaert, ed., *Soviet Military Thinking,* p. 66.

47. For examples, see Fred Charles Ikle, *Every War Must End* (New York: Columbia University Press, 1971). See also George H. Quester, "The Difficult Logic of Terminating a Nuclear War," ch. 3 in Stephen J. Cimbala, ed., *Strategic War Termination* (New York: Praeger, 1986), pp. 53–74. On countercommand attacks, see Jeffrey Richelson, "The Dilemmas of Counterpower Targeting," ch. 7 in Ball and Richelson, eds., *Strategic Nuclear Targeting,* pp. 159–170; and

Stephen J. Cimbala, "Countercommand Attacks and War Termination," in Cimbala, ed., *Strategic War Termination,* pp. 134–156.

48. George F. Jelen, "Space System Vulnerabilities and Countermeasures," ch. 4 in William J. Durch, ed., *National Interests and the Military Use of Space* (Cambridge, Mass.: Ballinger, 1984), p. 98.

49. Ibid., p. 104.

50. Ibid., pp. 105–107.

51. Stephen M. Meyer, "Soviet Nuclear Operations," *Signal,* December 1986, pp. 41–56, esp. pp. 42–43, on Soviet warning systems.

52. Jeffrey Richelson, *Sword and Shield: The Soviet Intelligence and Security Apparatus* (Cambridge, Mass.: Ballinger, 1986), p. 92.

53. Ibid., p. 97.

54. Ibid., p. 100.

55. Ibid., p. 104.

56. U.S. Office of Technology Assessment, *Anti-Satellite Weapons, Countermeasures, and Arms Control* (Washington, D.C.: U.S. Government Printing Office, 1985), p. 6, quotes Richard Perle, assistant secretary of defense, who states: "[that] this Soviet anti-satellite capability is effective against critical U.S. satellites in relatively low orbit, that in wartime we would have to face the possibility, indeed the likelihood, that critical assets of the United States would be destroyed by Soviet anti-satellite systems...."

57. U.S. Department of Defense, *Soviet Military Power: 1986,* p. 47.

58. Ibid.

59. Stephen M. Meyer, "Soviet Perspectives on the Paths to Nuclear War," in Allison, Carnesale, and Nye, eds., *Hawks, Doves and Owls,* pp. 167–205.

60. Stephen J. Andriole, "Next Generation Decision Support Systems Technology," in Andriole, ed., *High Technology Initiatives in C3I.* See Also Stephen J. Cimbala, "Artificial Intelligence and SDI: Corollaries or Compatriots?" ch. 11 in Cimbala, ed., *Artificial Intelligence and National Security* (Lexington, Mass.: Lexington Books, 1987), pp. 203–214.

61. For background on the subject of nuclear command centers see Albert E. Babbitt, "Command Centers," ch. 9 in Carter, Steinbruner, and Zraket, eds., *Managing Nuclear Operations,* pp. 322–351.

62. Paul Bracken, "Accidental Nuclear War," ch. 2 in Allison, Carnesale, and Nye, eds., *Hawks, Doves and Owls,* pp. 25–53.

63. See Theodore Jarvis, "Nuclear Operations and Strategic Defense," ch. 20 in Carter, Steinbruner, and Zraket, eds., *Managing Nuclear Operations,* pp. 661–678.

64. Office of Technology Assessment, *Ballistic Missile Defense Technologies,* pp. 162–164, 170–172. For a discussion of the battle management problems attendant to SDI and previous attempts to solve them, see John R. Southern, Carl G. Davis, and Melvin P. Edwards, "Army BM/C3 in the SDI Program," in Andriole, ed., *High Technology Initiatives in SDI,* pp. 358–369. On the issue of NCA control over space-based C3 and weapons, see James Offutt and J. Bryan Danese, "Communications for SDI," in ibid, pp. 370–383. Offutt and Danese offer the following assessment, pertinent to many concerns of participants in the SDI debate: "The role of human control (man in the loop) is connected closely to the type of weapon and tier. This is currently under study, particularly

for the boost phase intercept (BPI) system. It is clear that man will be in the loop and will have the power to activate or intervene and deactivate the system at any time" (p. 374).

65. A nontechnical explanation of possible countermeasures to SDI appears in Office of Technology Assessment, *Ballistic Missile Defense Technologies*, pp. 170–177.

66. Paul H. Nitze, "On the Road to a More Stable Peace," U.S. Department of State, *Current Policy* no. 657 (February 20, 1985), pp. 1–3.

67. An important anthology on this topic is Brian D. Dailey and Patrick J. Parker, eds., *Soviet Strategic Deception* (Lexington, Mass.: D. C. Heath/Lexington Books, 1987).

68. Among studies pertinent to the issue of crisis decision making, those with obvious applications here include Richard Ned Lebow, *Between Peace and War* (Baltimore: Johns Hopkins University Press, 1981), *Nuclear Crisis Management* (Ithaca, N.Y.: Cornell University Press, 1986), "Windows of Opportunity: Do States Jump Through Them?" *International Security* 9, no. 1 (Summer 1984):147–186, and "The Cuban Missile Crisis: Reading the Lessons Correctly," *Political Science Quarterly*, 98, no. 3.(Fall 1983):431–458; Robert Jervis, *Perception and Misperception in International Politics* (Princeton: Princeton University Press, 1976); Irving L. Janis, *Groupthink*, 2nd ed. (Boston: Houghton Mifflin, 1982); and Patrick M. Morgan, *Deterrence: A Conceptual Analysis*, 2nd. ed. (Beverly Hills, Calif.: Sage, 1983), chs. 3, 4 and 5.

69. The most substantial effort to apply artificial intelligence to national command decision problems is directed by Paul K. Davis at Rand Corporation. See Paul K. Davis, Steven C. Bankes, and James P. Kahan, *A New Methodology for Modeling National Command Level Decisionmaking in War Games and Simulations* (Santa Monica, Calif.: Rand Strategy Assessment Center, July 1986).

70. Bracken, *The Command and Control of Nuclear Forces*, p. 97.

71. The value of military satellites in superpower conventional ground, air, and naval operations is discussed in Paul B. Stares, *Space and National Security* (Washington, D.C.: Brookings Institution, 1987), pp. 53–66.

72. Blair, *Strategic Command and Control*, pp. 261–262. IONDS/NDS packages on NAVSTAR-GPS will provide, according to Blair, "real-time measurements of nuclear explosions anywhere in the world" and damage assessments to the U.S. national command authority, which may have been transferred to airborne command posts. It will complement the planned MILSTAR satellite system, which will provide, inter alia, for jam-resistant extremely high frequency voice communications among the National Emergency Airborne Command Post and the commanders in chief of U.S. forces in Europe, the Pacific, the Atlantic and the Strategic Air Command.

73. Gary L. Guertner, "Nuclear War in a Defense Dominant World," ch. 1 in Stephen J. Cimbala, ed., *The Technology, Strategy and Politics of SDI* (Boulder, Colo.: Westview Press, 1987), pp. 13–24.

74. See McGeorge Bundy, transcriber, and James G. Blight, editor, "October, 27, 1962: Transcripts of the Meetings of the ExComm," *International Security* 12, no. 3 (Winter 1987/1988):30–92, esp. 85.

# 9

## Assessments and Prospects: U.S. Nuclear Strategy and Conflict Termination

This chapter summarizes our conclusions about the problem of war termination as it applies to superpower nuclear conflict. This conflict could be a direct U.S.-Soviet confrontation motivated by issues having nothing to do with Europe. Or it could begin as a conventional war in Europe and then escalate. Or it could begin outside of Europe—for example, in the Persian Gulf—and then spread to Europe. There are many paths by which the United States and the Soviet Union might end up on the edge of nuclear war, but these three seem to be among the possibilities most frequently studied by Western analysts.[1]

The probability that any of these wars, once begun, could be terminated in a rational way is unknown. As Gregory Treverton has noted, a "classic" literature on this subject appeared during the 1960s and suggests some general propositions that might apply to war termination in Europe:

1. termination planning must be in place before war begins;
2. communications with the opponent must be continued during the fighting (although communication need not be direct);
3. thresholds, pauses and prominent features can be exploited in order to increase the probability of successful termination;
4. some forces (perhaps substantial forces) should be held as intra-war deterrents and not used immediately;
5. the fog of war makes agreements difficult to verify; thus cooperative measures, including unilateral gestures, might be necessary while fighting continues.[2]

The same requirements might apply to a U.S.-Soviet direct nuclear exchange, whether it grew out of regional war or not. These requirements are process oriented. They impose obligations on U.S. and Soviet, or NATO and Warsaw Pact, decision-making processes that may be as important as force structure requirements or nuclear war-fighting strategies. Simply put, deliberate war termination requires that U. S. and Soviet adversaries, and their alliance partners, be able to make the most difficult kinds of decisions under unprecedented stresses. Further, national or bloc leaders must be able to enforce these decisions down the chain of command to far-flung military forces with fractured communications and uncertain organizational cohesion. Even if we assume that once war begins, the bloc partners will follow their Soviet and U.S. leaders, which is a large assumption, important obstacles remain to prevent war termination under conditions acceptable to both sides.

If nuclear war termination under conditions that are acceptable to both superpowers is unattainable, three basic alternatives remain. First, the Soviet Union attains its objectives and the United States or NATO no longer resists. Second, the reverse outcome occurs, with Soviet leaders yielding to the objectives of the United States and the West. Third, both sides lose so much, by virtue of damage to their societies, that neither attains any meaningful political objectives. Once nuclear detonations on the U.S. or Soviet homeland would exceed several tens of weapons, the likelihood of this third outcome is very strong. This makes the case for avoiding nuclear war as imperative as any political imperative can be.

Nevertheless, NATO declaratory policy and U.S. vital interests make it apparent that there are conditions under which the United States would be willing to engage in nuclear war against the Soviet Union. And it is not determined how such a conflict would turn out. It could *conceivably* be terminated well short of a mutually destructive exhaustion of superpower nuclear arsenals. However, the fact that outcomes short of holocaust are conceivable does not make them probable. Nor should conceivable outcomes be treated as equally desirable in policy planning. The apparent opposite is also true: that intermediate outcomes are difficult to conceive of does not make them inconceivable.

## LIMITATION POSSIBILITIES

Despite the foregoing observations, there are reasons why a conventional war in Europe might be limited below the nuclear threshold. And there are other reasons why a limited nuclear war in Europe would not necessarily expand into a general nuclear war. These reasons are worth reviewing.

Most important, the use of military forces has something to do with the policy objectives for which a nation is fighting. Surely this will be recalled in Moscow, where there are many devotees of Clausewitz. Given the potential destructive power of U.S. and Soviet strategic nuclear arsenals, there is no point—if there ever was—to unconditional surrender or other absolutist statements of policy objectives. In a nuclear war, unconditional surrender is a formula for mutual suicide of nations and their inhabitants. Policy objectives must therefore be formulated with sharper ends and these should be thought through before any war begins.

For example, if Soviet forces cross the inter-German border and proceed to move against Frankfurt, what is NATO's political objective, from which its military objective is presumably derived? Is it to annihilate the Soviet forces in West Germany, or to push them back across the border? And in either case, what is the political objective that corresponds to this military objective? The temptation among U.S. officials might be to punish the Warsaw Pact for having committed aggression against the defenders; U.S. history is replete with such morality-of-revenge tales. However, revenge is poor policy objective, even near the next election. In this instance it risks escalation that cannot be controlled by NATO to its advantage. So NATO will somehow have to make clear that its political objectives are limited, and perhaps commensurate with Soviet ones, whereas its staying power and military potential are superior.

The last statement implies that NATO must not lose its identity as a defensive political alliance even in wartime, when it might have to undertake operational and tactical military offensives. The same applies to the United States in a two-way confrontation with the Soviet Union, for example, in Cuba in 1962. President Kennedy chose the blockade or quarantine because it was a military operation that suggested very specific political objectives and was tied to the possibility of very intimidating escalation if Khrushchev did not comply. What the United States wanted was the removal of the Soviet missiles from Cuba. There was no demand for Castro to resign or to be deposed. Nor was there an effort by the United States to impose horizontal escalation on the Kremlin by attacking at some other point on the globe where Soviet vital interests might be threatened. The Kennedy administration kept the political issue to the specific point: withdrawal of the missiles from Cuba.

Kennedy's advisors (the ExComm, or Executive Committee of the National Security Council) also avoided being sucked into a closure of deescalatory alternatives in face of escalatory ones. This almost happened as a result of the two very different messages received by Kennedy from the Soviet Union on October 26 and 27, and following several incidents on October 27 that seemed to point toward deterrence failure in the near term.[3] One of these incidents was an off-course U.S. U–2 spy plane that strayed into Soviet territory, and the other was the shooting down of a similar reconnaissance aircraft over Cuba.[4] The second incident was especially ominous because it was clear to U.S. intelligence that the U.S. plane had been shot down by Soviet surface-to-air missiles (SAMs). Some U.S. authorities suspected the Cubans had control of SAM launches. Had the United States stuck to its original plan, formulated the preceding Tuesday, it would have responded to the downing of the U–2 by taking out the offending SAM site with conventional air strikes, risking the killing of Soviet personnel. However, President Kennedy demurred at the brink, preferring to resist the temptation to even the score, so to speak, at the tactical or operational level, in order to preserve the hope of attaining the U.S. strategic objective which to was to remove the Soviet missiles from Cuba without war.

The blockade was an exercise in coercive diplomacy of the kind that we have been discussing throughout. But the success of the crisis for the United States was in many ways a near miss. Some of Kennedy's intimate advisers were disappointed that the U–2 downing over Cuba did not provide the pretext for an air strike or even an invasion; an opportunity to get rid of Castro and to demonstrate U.S. resolve to the Soviets had been missed, in their views.[5] On the other hand, President Kennedy was apparently more impressed with Khrushchev's determination, or reck-lessness, than his advisers were. Or Kennedy may have felt more vul-nerable to the same fates that drove the major powers over the brink in World War I. Here the issue was not preemptive mobilization followed by a conflict spiral, as in World War I, but preventive conventional war that might escalate into nuclear war.[6]

Kennedy resisted a temptation to which others had fallen prey. The opportunity for an operationally advantageous campaign is so attractive that the costs of continued fighting, if the campaign fails to end the war, are not fully considered. This mistaken inference, or omitted reasoning, was characteristic of German and Japanese planning in World War II. Hitler could not resist the opportunity to attack the Soviet Union in 1941, although his strategic objectives would have been better served by continuing the nonaggression pact and fighting on one front, against England. And after Japan attacked Pearl Harbor on December 7, 1941, Hitler gratuitously declared war on the United States. Admittedly he would have done this anyway, but Hitler accelerated the date on which England acquired a guarantee against eventual defeat, since there was not the faintest hope that Germany could defeat the United States in an extended war. The Japanese attack against Pearl Harbor, as is well known, was a brilliant tactical and operational coup. Its military planning was impeccable. However, the Japanese refused to confront the full implications of a protracted war against the United States. Their military objectives absorbed their political ones. Roberta Wohlstetter's classic study of Pearl Harbor, on the topic of Japanese long-range military estimation, makes the following observation:

The Japanese did have the material for making some relevant long-range predictions. The intelligence estimates released by USSBS (United States Strategic Bombing Survey), for example, show that their assessment of our war potential in aircraft manufacture, shipbuilding, and rate of training of the necessary crews was much more accurate than our own for 1941, 1942, and 1943. The relation between this material and the decision to take on the United States as an opponent is simply not explicable in rational terms.[7]

If the USSR has studied the history of World War II as carefully as one would think, Soviet leaders have drawn several lessons from the experience of their German and Japanese adversaries. First, under the right conditions, lightning campaigns like that in Manchuria in 1945 can pay large dividends. Second, one should not get entangled in an extended war against a foe superior in economic and military potential. Third, the command and control of military operations must be adapted to the unique circumstances of the theater of war, the capabilities and objectives of the opponent, and one's own objectives and capabilities.

In the case of the Manchurian campaign, the Soviet Union can be said to have applied all of these lessons correctly. The Japanese Kwantung army was overwhelmed by a three-front combined arms offensive along a 5,000-kilometer front line in six days.[8] Although the Japanese forces had serious technological weakness and numerical inferiority, Soviet analyses of this campaign have attributed the Soviets' victory to the surprise, speed, depth, and strength of their offensive. Soviet studies of the Manchurian campaign have also noted the Kremlin was concerned about being trapped into a protracted war, and devised solutions to avoid this potential problem.[9] Although the basic concept of operations proved to be sound, this did not eliminate difficulties in the execution, including deficient tactical intelligence, lack of basic supplies, and a fragile troop control network.[10]

The third lesson, that command and control of operations had to be adapted to local circumstances, was evident in the Soviet command organization for the Manchurian campaign. Forces in the Far East and trans-Baikal regions were grouped into a unified command under Marshal A. M. Vasilevsky. The shuttle arrangements used earlier in the war, in which coordinators from Moscow would be sent to control multifront operations on behalf of Headquarters, Supreme High Command (STAVKA), were discarded. The geographical size and diversity of the theater of war dictated the creation of a new Far East Command with overall responsibility for land, sea, and air operations in the Far East and trans-Baikal regions.[11] This unprecedented arrangement was not without its apparent frictions, but Soviet military historians have judged that it was appropriate to the commanders' and policymakers' requirements.

The Manchurian campaign provided a textbook case of the effectiveness of strategic surprise against a less-well-equipped foe. Soviet marshals would be loath to assume that this illustration could be transposed into a strategic (or theater-strategic, in Soviet terminology) offensive against Western Europe. The Kwantung army in Manchuria was doomed in the long run. The USSR had concluded its war against Germany in the west. It was a matter of time until the superior Soviet war potential crushed the nearly defeated Japanese, who were being battered by the United States and its European allies. However, although not transferable to the Europe of today in literal terms, the Manchurian campaign suggests to Soviet planners the limitations of any proposed initiative in Europe— that such an offensive, with the objective of conquering West Germany and/or the Low Countries, is not in the cards unless some very favorable conditions come together unexpectedly:

1. The societies of Western Europe begin to come apart as a result of domestic instabilities and contradictions.
2. Elements within those societies appeal to the Soviet Union for "fraternal" socialist assistance to parties or forces that are obviously prepared to seize power, and seem to have credible means to do so.
3. The United States, for reasons of being deterred or for other causes, is likely to stay out of the war beyond absorbing the casualties to its divisions already stationed in the Federal Republic of Germany
4. If 3 is unlikely, the U.S. intervention will be limited to conventional war and not cross the nuclear threshold, and the rest of NATO Europe will so forbear, including France.

The coming together of these contingencies is highly improbable, if not impossible. But many wars have started from seemingly improbable or impossible causes. What we have been saying above is that for the Manchurian campaign to provide a model for what the USSR might want to accomplish in present-day Europe, the appropriate operational methods (operational art in Soviet terms) have to be mated to the appropriate policy objectives. The appropriate objectives, for the Soviet Union with regard to Europe, would have to include the Sovietization of the parliamentary-democratic regimes located there. Skirmishing with NATO ground and tactical air forces, however invigorating as an exercise, is not an end in itself.

The last sentence is stated somewhat facetiously, out of exasperation. For years U.S. and NATO war games, as well as academic and think tank analyses, have concocted detailed scenarios for war in Europe. These scenarios rarely take into account the reasons why the war is supposedly being fought, or the Marxian character of Soviet foreign policy objectives. The Soviets of today are not (merely) interested in winning battles over pieces of territory; they are not modern-day replacements for Frederick the Great. Soviet foreign policy objectives, and therefore Soviet politico-military strategy, pass through filter whose components include the distilled thinking of Marx, Lenin, and their philosophical offspring. As we have seen, this filtration process separates those who think of war as an end in itself, as something self-sufficiently glorious and nationally enriching, from those who understand that war has specific, and limited, utility.

## REVOLUTION AND WAR

For Soviet Marxians, this utility is that war is part of the midwifery of revolution. Societies ripe for revolution because of basically indigenous failures can be given a helpful push at a timely moment. Lenin's deviation from Marx even allowed that this timely push could come about in a society not theoretically prepared for it. "Theoretically" here has two meanings, one objective and one subjective. Objectively, precapitalist societies should be early laboratories for a proletarian revolution, regardless of the state of political consciousness of their peoples. Subjectively, the peoples themselves may not be prepared with proper revolutionary ardor and education. More than once Marx and Lenin admitted that revolutionary intellectuals would have to lead the proleteriat, even when the objective social conditions were congenial, into the promised land.

For Marxian Soviet members of the Politburo, as they all are, to contemplate these objective and subjective requirements for extending the proletarian revolution to Western Europe, they must conclude that the proper conditions are far from having been fulfilled. Western Europe is not ripe for revolution, at least not by revolutionary working-class movements. There is a widespread alienation that is felt by the well-educated middle class, but this phenomenon is not restricted to Europe, or to Western Europe. Nor does it present to the USSR the material that can be exploited in order to turn the societies of Western Europe into socialized paradises. On the contrary, the Soviets must see that the trends are going against any hopes they may have of a nineteenth-century-style working-class rising.

To be sure, the Soviet Union can exploit divisions within Western democratic polities, but these divisions are not necessarily signs of weakness that would contribute to a Soviet victory in war. There is a great deal of difference in the cohesion of democracies between their peacetime and wartime experience, assuming something as momentous as a war in Europe would be. In peacetime, parliamentary-democratic regimes are divided houses, and disputation rules the day. In wartime they are apt to become mobilized monsters, unforgiving and ultrademanding of punishment against any presumed aggressor. One can imagine that the Dutch and the Belgians might demur in a crisis of very ambiguous origin, and there is some risk that an ambiguous crisis could spill over into war in Europe. But if the crisis truly arose from misunderstanding and did not result from an attempted conquest of NATO European territory, the USSR would have as many incentives to terminate the fighting as NATO would. On the other hand, the USSR could not turn a presumed crisis growing out of misperception or inadvertence into a full-scale war without making its intentions clear very soon. At the point it became clear that full-scale war was on, the Dutch, Belgians, and everybody else in NATO would be getting on board, for they would have no other realistic option.

Soviet planners, then, would have to assume that the conditions are not ripe for the plucking of Western Europe, meaning that the class struggle is not in the proper phase and the peoples are not properly indoctrinated with the secular religion of Marxian deliverance. If war broke out, the USSR could expect resistance instead of willing subjection. Given these unfavorable portents in West European domestic politics, Soviet leaders would have to expect that any conflict not terminated quickly would become a protracted conventional war, to their ultimate disadvantage, or escalate into a nuclear war, even more disadvantageous. So there is some strong incentive on the Soviet side to get the fighting stopped in the short term, whatever the putative causes that started it. As we have just been saying there is one exception to this, and that is the unlikely circumstance that the class struggle in Europe is so advanced (from the Soviet standpoint) that the policy objective of conquering and occupying one or more West European countries is now appealing. Actually, the class struggle in Marxian terms is more advanced in Eastern than in Western Europe, if the Polish group Solidarity is any indication. One has to wonder how the Kremlin would deal with the occupation of Western Europe on a permanent basis without also subduing the United States, where the class struggle is hopelessly retrograde.

Another incentive for the USSR to terminate any war in Europe shortly after it begins, and prior to nuclear escalation, also relates to the class struggle. In this case it is the international class struggle, of which the Kremlin claims undisputed leadership. However, Beijing lays claim to the same roles, and would undoubtedly see a war between the Warsaw Pact and NATO as an opportunity from which it would benefit even by inaction. The first problem for the Soviets here is that they would be forced to fight a two-front war if the Chinese decided to intervene. But even if the PRC stayed out, Beijing would benefit at Soviet expense. Of course, the USSR might win a conventional war in Europe, provided the United States did not intervene. But, regardless, Moscow would still have the problem of facing the Americans eventually. And the Americans, seeing Europe imperiled, would open their war chests and embark on a sustained military buildup of the kind that Moscow could never hope to match. The USSR would be hard pressed to run a protracted war machine-building contest with the United States after the latter had opened the spigot of war production. Such a postwar (in Europe) production race would, at long last, demonstrate the superior economic competence of capitalism. Meanwhile, the USSR would have fewer resources to devote to containment of its potential PRC adversaries. A war in Europe, if stalemated or lost, could turn the Soviet Union into the world's second most important Marxian power. For some Soviet leaders past and present, and certainly for Mr. Brezhnev, playing second fiddle to the PRC would have been the worst outcome of all.

So, contrary to the supposition of pessimists, there is some hopeful indication that, should war in Europe start, it might be important for the USSR to terminate it quickly. Granted that a Soviet attack is unlikely in the first place, but we are assuming here that this unlikely event, however improbable, has begun. And we are further assuming that the Soviets' interest in deliberate and purposeful war termination thereafter is not precluded by their ideology or prewar plans (admittedly this assumption is open to challenge). This means that if NATO, too, sought to bring about a purposeful end to the fighting, there might be a meeting of the minds at some salient threshold, either before nuclear weapons were used or before very many were used against certain kinds of targets. A number of these salient points have been suggested by theorists. One dividing line is between no use of nuclear weapons and first use by either side. Another is between selective, constrained uses of battlefield nuclear weapons once authority for their use has been delegated, and continuous and sustained employment with the objective of destroying the opponent's capacity for theater nuclear war.[12] Still another is the line between attacks on Soviet and U.S. homelands with nuclear weapons, and regional uses of nuclear weapons by the superpowers outside of Europe, but with potential spillover to Europe.[13]

Albert Wohlstetter and Richard Brody suggest an interesting variation of the theater versus strategic threshold, illustrating the complexity of observing distinctions under fire. The Soviet Union might strike at a restricted number of military bases in the United States during a conventional war in Europe, in order to prevent U.S. reinforcements from crossing the Atlantic.[14] This would be limited war on the U.S. strategic homeland, perhaps comparable with the scenarios in which the United States fires limited strategic strikes against Soviet oil refineries or conventional forces north of Iran.

However, to say that policy objectives of the Soviet Union and NATO during conventional or theater nuclear war in Europe would permit war termination is not to prove that the mechanisms for it would be in place when and where needed. The mechanisms have to do with the doctrines, organizations, and equipment of the two sides' forces as they pitch forward into battle. The fog of war would be immense even in the first few hours of contact between Warsaw Pact and NATO forces in West Germany. Intelligence systems would be dumping large amounts of data into fusion centers that might not be able to collate the material, even if they survived deliberate attacks. Both sides might be tempted to attack space-based as well as ground-based photographic and electronic reconnaissance assets, including satellite-based ones. Lacking a clear picture of the battlefield, corps commanders would have to proceed by "dead reckoning," according to rehearsed standard operating procedures that had become irrelevant.

## SOVIET STYLE OF WAR

This last point, about the vulnerability of command systems to information overload or direct attack, is obviously going to be exploited by the Soviet Union, with consequences for efforts to terminate war. This brings us to the topic of Soviet operational art writ large, and requires that we say something about the Soviet style of war and its implications for war termination in Europe.

The first implication we have already seen: that the vulnerability of NATO theater command systems will be a temptation to Soviet attackers. But where does exploitation of that NATO vulnerability fit into Soviet strategy, and, what, if any, are the Soviet command and control vulnerabilities? The larger issue of Soviet operational art for war in Europe has been studied by Western experts, including C. N. Donnelly of the United Kingdom and John Hines and Phillip A. Petersen of the U.S. Department of Defense.[15] The Soviets have also written a great deal about their own military operations and theories of war, and much of this literature is readily available in Western libraries. [16] Some notion of how the USSR would attack Western Europe, in the event that this option somehow presented itself as an attractive one (but see above), can be learned from these and other sources.

In general, the Soviet approach to military operations in a continental theater such as Western Europe would emphasize the accomplishment of five basic missions or functions: penetration; exploitation and encirclement; disruption; deceptions; and pursuit. Penetration is the piercing of the front-line defenses that NATO has deployed forward in West Germany in eight corps sectors. Soviet advance detachments and combined-arms armies in the first echelon would attempt to penetrate in depth during the first day or days of fighting. However, this penetration is temporary unless it is exploited, and the exploitation is to be accomplished by operational maneuver groups (OMGs) when the moment is ripe. OMGs are tank heavy, specially tasked units at army or front level that exploit the most promising initial penetrations of the opponent's forward defenses. These and adjunct raiding forces will move rapidly into the opponent's operational depth in order to frustrate its effort to reinforce its forward defenses, maintain communications, and preserve organizational cohesion in its fighting units.[17]

At the same time these operational raiding forces are exploiting deep penetrations into the defender's rear, rapid encirclement of the defender's forces is taking place. This encirclement is really a three-dimensional envelopment of the defender's ground and tactical air forces, brought about by combined-arms air and ground offensives. The air offensive includes the early use by the USSR of ground-to-ground short-range ballistic missiles to destroy NATO air defenses, runways, and other important targets, and thereby pave the way for follow-up destruction by Soviet frontal aviation against other NATO fixed and mobile targets. Among those targets will be NATO command systems, nuclear weapons storage sites, and nuclear-capable delivery vehicles.

Disruption of the opponent's command systems and his organizational cohesion have already been noted. Deception or *maskirovka* (the Soviet generic term) adds another dimension, and it involves both tactical and operational deception on small and large scale. The STAVKA Plan Uranus, by which the Soviets eventually prevailed at Stalingrad during World War II, illustrates the successful use of operational-level deception.[18] Repetition of such a feat of concealment might be thought impossible under conditions of modern reconnaissance, but the Soviet interest in deception is considerable, and the U.S. capacity for observation is not invulnerable to destruction. For approximately one year following the U.S. *Challenger* space shuttle disaster, the United States had a single modern reconnaissance satellite (KH–11) in orbit.[19] The United States does not depend upon low-orbiting satellites for tactical warning of Soviet missile launches, but it does depend on close-look satellites like KH–11 (and its near-term successor, KH–12) for detailed evidence of Soviet noncompliance with arms control agreements and other authentication of intelligence information. As Paul B. Stares has shown, the U.S. antisatellite weapon that was undergoing testing during the Reagan administration, and the Soviet antisatellite weaponry that was already operational, would both threaten some significant number of the other's satellites; more satellites performed vital peacetime and wartime functions.[20] The U.S. Navy is particularly interested in negating the Soviet radar ocean reconnaissance (RORSAT) and ELINT (electronic intelligence) satellites early in a global or regional conventional war, in order to prevent the prompt Soviet detection and destruction of carrier battle groups.

Moreover, the Soviet view of deception is not that it is an aggregate of measures in themselves. It is a way of thinking about the conduct of war itself. Active and passive deception is something that competent commanders and planners "naturally" do. Tactical deception is something that Western planners are familiar with, such as the deployment of individual dummy tanks or formations. But Soviet *maskirovka* includes an entire menu of approaches to anticipating the intelligence and decision-making cycles of the opponent. The latter is then allowed to believe that it has discerned the applicable Soviet plans when it has not, or is thrown off balance by an attack along more than one axis of advance.[21] The illustrations of *maskirovka* are seemingly endless, and the point is not to multiply illustrations. It is to advance the notion that the Soviet conduct of war has embedded in it the concept of deception in its active and passive forms.[22] Thus a Soviet attack on NATO might be preceded by a large military exercise that continued into a different, and more sinister, phase. The USSR might, if it feared an outbreak of war for which its military leaders judged it unprepared, go through a demonstrative "mobilization" in Eastern Europe and the western Soviet Union that was designed to intimidate U.S. and West European officials and their publics.

In this regard, the Soviet civil defense program has been cited as providing an active defense asset that the United States, by comparison, lacks in comparable scope and effectiveness. Others have said the Soviet program would not actually provide very much protection in the event of nuclear war, but that it adds to the Soviet prewar deterrent. Few have noticed the possibility that the Soviet civil defense program may have a deception component, not unlike the impressive bomber aircraft that overflew the reviewing stands in Moscow during parades in the 1950s (impressions of a larger-than-actual force were created by repeatedly overflying the stand with the same few planes). Americans have difficulty understanding the Soviet civil defense program because of their assumption that the purpose of civil defense is population protection. Instead, the primary purpose of the Soviet civil defense system may be to protect the political and military leadership from all attacks except those dedicated specifically against them.

Pursuit, as a component of Soviet operational methods, is the following up of a defender on the run. Defensive forces moving backward from their initial positions and attempting to regroup would be hard pressed to reconstitute a movable fire base, to reestablish survivable command

and control, or to take the offensive against the flanks of advancing Soviet armored divisions. Assuming at least a standoff in the air battle over Western Europe, these Soviet armored divisions would be provided with some substantial close air support and mobile artillery that would be very destructive to forces undergoing regroupment. In this regard NATO has set itself for additional difficulties by lacking the echelons-above-corps grasp of the fog of war that the USSR will have, in all likelihood, as a result of its intermediate commands between front and Supreme Headquarters.[23]

Nor should it be forgotten that a critical component of the pursuit, deception, and disruption missions will be the probable use of Soviet *spetsnaz* (forces of special designation, including but not limited to "special operations" as used in U.S. nomenclature.[24] They will certainly conduct commando raids against NATO political and military targets, and perhaps even preemptive strikes if the Soviets decide that war is unavoidable. But they will also be a moving finger that can be used to pinpoint vulnerable civilian and military command centers, warning systems, and communications networks. As NATO corps sectors move to reestablish their command and control systems under the duress of Soviet operational maneuvers by conventional ground and air armies, special designation forces will be eating away from within at the NATO command and communications infrastructure.

What all of this amounts to is summarized very concisely by the U.S. Army Combined Arms Center, Soviet Army Studies Office, at Ft. Leavenworth, Kansas:

Forces within the theater of war (TV) will seek to achieve rapid victory by conducting successive *front* operations without pause in the theater's TVDs (TSMAs). A first strategic echelon will consist of combat-ready forces (fronts) within the TVD (TSMA) (primarily forward) backed by a second strategic echelon and a strategic reserve comprising *fronts* (and in some cases individual armies) mobilized within the Soviet Union on the basis of the strength and status of each military district. Stronger peacetime military districts will provide second strategic echelon forces and weaker districts will provide reserves. The strategic offensive will probably rely for success on the use of first strategic echelon forces to preserve strategic surprise by avoiding more than essential pre-hostility mobilization and reinforcement.[25]

This says a great deal about the likely Soviet style of war, and one of the things it says is that turning this kind of offensive off, after having turned it on the confined spaces of Western Europe, will be no small challenge for NATO. However, we have presented the Soviets' operational design from the standpoint of their most optimistic expectations. What about their own vulnerabilities, especially their ability to command and control an operation of unprecedented ferocity, complexity, and potential destructiveness?

Soviet planners contemplating a conventional war in Europe would not be as sanguine as Western analysts who attribute to the USSR the capability for rapid and decisive victory against NATO. This is more than professional pessimism. Apart from the Soviet policymakers' skepticism that the class struggle in Europe has taken a turn in their favor, there is the military professional's awareness of shortcomings in the training and competence of Soviet ground forces. These are primarily in the ranks of enlisted personnel rather than officers, who can be expected to have undergone at least a rigorous professional education, if not the Soviets' best academic one. However, Soviet conscripts, who must bear the brunt of the fighting, are not of the same quality as their officers, and no one can be more aware of this deficiency than those very officers, especially the Soviet division and brigade commanders, who will have to succeed or fail on the basis of these soldiers' performances. It would be mistaken to describe either Soviet officers or rank and file as automatons, but it does concern Soviet planners that many of their rank and file do not feel that their officers are competent, or that they care about the welfare of their men as opposed to their own career advancement.[26]

In the ground forces of any modern army, this expectation by the "grunts" that their officers are "careerist" to the extent that they are negligent of the troops' welfare is the kiss of death for combat effectiveness. In Vietnam, U.S. Army officers learned this only too well. If research seems to show that cohesion is the sine qua non for the effectiveness of armed forces in combat, and especially for the successful performance of their missions by small units, then the Soviet commanders who must motivate their troops under fire certainly have a long way to go before they are satisfied. Nor can Kremlin planners have forgotten those who left the front in World War I and became a reserve army of the revolutionary unemployed, eventually the coercive arm of rising that ousted the czar. Would Soviet soldiers take the opportunity of their arrival in Western Europe to defect? Probably not, if the war were short and favorable to Moscow. But in an extended war, the temptation of defection might be harder to resist, especially if maltreatment in the peacetime Soviet armed forces were as widespread as some defectors have suggested it has been in the recent past.

A more serious issue for Soviet war planners, compared with dissatisfied "grunts" and defectors, is the question of whether the Soviet propensity for "top down" command systems is compatible with the kinds of fluid meeting engagements and encounter battles their armed forces may have to fight in Europe. The short answer is "no," and the potential incompatibility is recognized in Soviet writings and exercises.[27] A centralized command system is not necessarily inferior to one that is decentralized and relies on a great deal of tactical initiative. Much depends on the national culture and training of the soldiers in question. Thus

*Wehrmacht* officers in World War II were able to draw upon a tradition of excellence and training going as far back as the origins of the German General Staff. The expectation of fighting according to *auftragstaktik*, orders that assign a general mission while allowing a great deal of flexibility and initiative in the way it is accomplished, was thus part of the German military psyche.[28]

The Israelis apparently are infected with this virus as well. A virus is a good analogy, because the indeterminacy of such a system plays havoc with the desire of topmost political and military leaders for management of the details of operations, on which larger outcomes sometimes depend. So, for example, in the Cuban missile crisis, former U.S. Secretary of Defense Robert McNamara visited the U.S. Navy command center in the Pentagon and wanted to know about the detailed procedures for intercepting Soviet ships if they ran the blockade. An argument ensued between McNamara and Admiral Anderson, chief of naval operations, with the latter quite properly reflecting military service skepticism about the interference of civilians in the details of operational planning.[29] In this instance McNamara was asserting the important point that the president sought to control the situation, even if this meant toleration for some extraordinary operational procedures.

However, top-level micro-management can lead to military disaster. During the ill-fated Desert One rescue mission in Iran in 1980, the U.S. command system was so top-heavy that it encumbered the proper formulation and execution of the operation. And after events went awry, the unfortunate commander on the scene was forced to decide whether to continue the operation or abort it, while higher military and civilian commanders (including the president) copped a plea.[30] The U.S. war effort in Vietnam was similarly blessed with a cornucopia of irrelevant command levels, in Washington and in Saigon, and experts have testified to the operational malfeasance that resulted from this self-sustaining bureaucratic excess.[31] Military bureaucracies, given their druthers, are as bureautropic as any other large formal organization. However, the armed forces have a different mission, which depends on limiting the bureautropic syndrome to manageable proportions. In this regard the Soviets seem to be well on the way to imitating their Western counterparts, if not exceeding them, and there is an all too dangerous tendency for the USSR to compensate for bureaucratic inefficiency with numbers, mass, and artificial exercises.

The related issue, suggested by the topic of administrative overdrive, is the question of accountability. This might seem on the surface to be a Soviet strong point and a Western, and especially American, weak one. Witness the U.S. investigation of the bombing of the Marine barracks in Beirut in October 1983, for which no high-ranking military officer was seriously disciplined or demoted. President Reagan took the blame for this unfortunate episode, which was correct in the larger political sense for his having decided to commit U.S. combat forces to the ambiguous peacekeeping mission there. It was also correct in a second sense, in that his minions in the White House and Pentagon enshackled U.S. Marine forces in rules of engagement that made them vulnerable to terrorism and surprise. That having been said, the U.S. military chain of command was a Frankenstein monster of incompetence for what ought to have been a small-time operation (after all, these are the armed forces that are supposed to be ready to face the Soviet Union if need be).[32]

In the U.S. case in Lebanon and elsewhere, it certainly appears that the phrase "chain of command" is apropos, extending all the way up to the level of the joint chiefs of staff. There is the additional tidbit that at one time U.S. Defense Secretary Caspar Weinberger had some 40 persons reporting to him directly, which is quite a span of control even for a cabinet officer of Weinberger's budgetary reach and responsibility. One might argue that this is a strictly managerial issue not pertinent to operations as such. However, the U.S. experience in Lebanon and elsewhere argues against the separation of management control methodology from operational results. Compare the U.S. chain of irresponsibility for the situation in Lebanon with the Soviets' response to the penetration of their air space by an intrepid West German youth who landed in Red Square in 1987. Mikhail Gorbachev did not offer to take the blame for this incident; instead, he sacked leading members of the armed forces high command, including the defense minister.

The U.S., Soviet, and German (World War II and earlier) examples suggest, then, that there is no one right or wrong way to organize a command system, for war in Europe or anywhere else. And so there is no one right or wrong way to prepare that system for the conduct of war termination. There are two problems here: one is negotiating war termination at some senior level. The other is enforcing it through both national chains of command. One commonality that does seem to cross cultures is that both sides must still have some capacity to fight (else why negotiate?) and some means of communicating a preference to stop fighting now, as opposed to continuing to fight. Neither the Soviet command system with its apparent rigidity nor the U.S. system with its pluralist confusion appears to have maximized the opportunity for wartime interaction directed toward the objective of war termination. Instead, each might be taxed to maintain effective troop control, as the Soviets call it, without being able to task commanders with any more subtle or ambitious objectives until the fighting had almost stalemated at some clear line of demarcation.

So if Soviet forces invading West Germany were to be bottled up at the Weser and fighting were to stabilize there, the USSR might be responsive to tacit and explicit overtures for war termination instead of preferring nuclear escalation. This would seem even more appealing to them if NATO had not yet struck into Soviet territory but maintained residual capabilities to do so. As discussed in an earlier chapter, this makes the coordination of naval and land warfare a difficult matter. Nuclear weapons could be introduced into one of those environments before it seemed sensible to do so in the other, and in so doing one side might throw cold water on a process of conflict termination that was just getting under way.

## NUCLEAR ESCALATION AND CONTROL

Suppose, now, that the line between conventional and nuclear war has been crossed, in regional theaters of action adjacent to the Soviet Union, on Soviet and U.S. soil directly, or both. U.S. officials and nuclear pundits have sometimes suggested with wry humor that Europeans would prefer to see the United States and the Soviet Union fight a nuclear war "over their heads" while they were exempted from collateral damage. This scenario is unlikely, but it does reflect the possibility of war beginning as a direct superpower nuclear conflict, and then spilling into Europe. This has been one of Western Europe's major fears for many years: being dragged inadvertently into a U.S.-Soviet crisis and ensuing war. The opposite fear, of being abandoned in time of need, plagues other Europeans, although this fear has more to do with their expectations about U.S. help during conventional war in Europe. In the first instance, fear of involvement in nuclear war, West Europeans fear too much immersion in U.S.-Soviet disputes that are essentially bilateral. In the second case, they fear too little U.S. immersion in their defense planning and deterrence signals.

Are there salient thresholds at which nuclear war between superpowers, even war that has escalated to U.S. and Soviet homelands, can be stopped, even temporarily? Let us take the harder case, of nuclear strikes against U.S. or Soviet homelands, since we have previously discussed the problem of limiting war in Europe. Let us set a hypothetical experiment, in which the Soviet Union has carried out an attack against some portion of the U.S. strategic retaliatory force but mostly spared U.S. cities, economic infrastructure, and war-supporting industry. The USSR indicates that if the United States will avoid retaliation against the Soviet homeland, and not resist Soviet occupation of Europe with conventional forces, the Soviet Union will not make additional attacks against U.S. forces or society.

This is what Herman Kahn would have called a "constrained force reduction salvo," in which one side attempts to destroy a small but significant portion of the opponent's retaliatory force in a single strike, as a basis for further bargaining on advantageous terms.[33] (Kahn's "ladder of escalation" has this one rung *above* "slow motion counterforce war," although he admits that the two thresholds might be reversed).[34] This scenario has become part of the standard lexicon of surrogate warfare among policy analysts, as a result of Paul Nitze's application of it to the problem of U.S. deterrent, and especially ICBM, vulnerability.[35] U.S. rationales for limited strategic options in the 1970s called for counterforce weapons that would allow the tables to be turned against the USSR, as in selective U.S. strategic strikes against Soviet military or economic assets in response to Soviet conventional war in Europe or Southwest Asia.[36]

The first thing to be said about this scenario is how improbable it is. The second thing to be said is that, however improbable it is, it is more probable than an unrestrained exhaustion of U.S. and Soviet arsenals against each other's territories. Whether the United States could or would respond to a limited nuclear attack in a limited fashion is another matter. The requirements for doing so would be severe. The U.S. president would somehow have to know the size of the Soviet attack, the targets struck, the approximate collateral damage, and the forces and options remaining for retaliation. Most important, the president would have to have some sense of what the United States wanted to accomplish in the trans-attack period (encompassing the earliest exchanges of weapons), and in the postwar world.

There are two kinds of nonanswers to these questions. The first is to deny that the line between limited war and total war is meaningful. The second is to assert that the effort to distinguish between limited and total wars implies tolerance for, even interest in, the costs of nuclear war without sufficient concern for the consequences in ethical terms. This discussion has nothing to commend it to either school, although the frame of reference is deserving of some understanding. The impulse to prevent nuclear war along with defending equally important political and moral values is not disputed. The moral high ground on this issue of war prevention and limitation, properly understood, is one that requires sensitivity to value trade-offs as well as value absolutes.[37]

## DISMAL ALTERNATIVES

We will assume for purposes of discussion that the point of the last sentence is at least provisionally accepted by readers. The U.S. president wants to respond in some fashion, and it is not obviously in the U.S. interest to respond with everything remaining in its strategic nuclear arsenal. One can question, however, whether the United States would be able to deliver constrained counterforce attacks against a precisely defined Soviet target set in the aftermath of even limited Soviet attacks on the U.S. homeland.

The first issue is whether U.S. strategic command, control, and communications (C3) can pull itself together in order to deliver a constrained but effective retaliation against a plausible Soviet military target set. This set would probably, although not exclusively, emphasize Soviet prompt counterforce systems capable of further attacks against surviving U.S. forces. The United States would have to have a very reliable attack assessment of its own surviving forces, communicate this assessment to national command authorities, and ensure the reception of the proper launch orders by the retaliatory forces. These forces would then have to respond according to largely preprogrammed strike plans, for there would be little or no time to improvise.[38] None of these command system prerequisites for launching discriminate and controlled attacks can be guaranteed. Attack assessments might be muddled or inaccurate. National command authorities might not receive a timely assessment even if it were accurate, or if they did, it might be misinterpreted. And the reprogramming of forces after the survivors have been polled, in order to optimize strikes against surviving Soviet targets, would be done under conditions that would fall short of the standard implicit in peacetime models.[39] A growing problem is that more of the future Soviet force than the present one may be mobile, and thus difficult to target.

A complication for the command system is that it must support the various components of the U.S. strategic nuclear "triad" (ICBMs, SLBMs, and bombers equipped with various weapons) in their operational settings, which are not identical. ICBMs deployed in fixed silos must be launched on warning or under attack in order to perform their missions, or run the risk of being rendered impotent by early Soviet attacks against their silos and command centers. Bomber operations are extremely complicated from the standpoint of demands made upon the command system. Bombers must take off to holding positions from which they will receive further, confirmatory orders that authorize them to proceed to target. Only about 30 percent of the U.S. strategic bomber force is maintained on strip alert; the rest are, at least theoretically, at risk from Soviet SLBMs launched from normal submarine patrol areas off the U.S. Atlantic and Pacific coasts.[40] Missiles on board submarines are less vulnerable to preemptive attack, but submarine communications are doubtfully dependable for any tasking other than serving to attack preplanned, fixed targets, most of which are in urban areas.[41] Thus the most survivable weapons platforms under a condition of little or no warning are those with which the national command authority might have the most difficulty communicating in order to revise its previous plans. This does not raise too many complications as long as the ballistic missile submarines' mission is to survive the initial exchanges and complete World

War III. But if policymakers expect more of them, as they might following the introduction of Trident II into the fleet in 1989, then the fidelity of SSBN communications, under a greater diversity of combat conditions, will become an important agenda item.

The second issue is whether the United States wants to retaliate promptly, and if it does, what it wants to accomplish. The canonical scenarios posit an immediate and large U.S. retaliation against a comprehensive Soviet military target set, including C3 assets related to Soviet countermilitary potential. This is made quite clear in authoritative U.S. government policy documents, such as the report of the Scowcroft Commission during the first term of the Reagan administration. The commission recommended that the United States deploy MX/Peacekeeper ICBMs immediately and Midgetman small, mobile, and singe-warhead ICBMs in the 1990s. The rationale for the MX/Peacekeeper was that it would threaten the Soviets with the destruction of their missile silos and supporting command and control, and so pose to them the same threat that Soviet capabilities now pose to U.S. ICBMs.[42] The implied theory of war termination seems to be that squeezing the Soviet countermilitary potential, by rapidly evening up U.S. losses with theirs, would quickly disabuse the Kremlin of any interest in continuing the war. In fairness, the Scowcroft Commission (officially the President's Commission on U.S. Strategic Forces) was tasked to focus mainly on deterrence and placed less emphasis on how a war might actually be fought.

This assessment can be disputed. It would be equally logical to argue that the Soviet Union will have used the most effective proportion of its land-based strategic missile force in its opening attack. What remains in silos will be a large number of warheads of lesser lethality, although still a substantial force. A U.S. prompt launch against remaining Soviet ICBMs might simply cause the Soviets to launch their remaining land-based missiles on tactical warning, causing more immediate damage to the United States and no additional net damage to Soviet missile silos. It is also suggested in some analyses that the Soviet military and political command centers, regional and national, would be targets for prompt counterforce. Such destruction could either kill party, government, and military leaders in their bunkers or disconnect those bunkers from the military forces and other command nodes with which they need to communicate. In some models these countercommand attacks spare national command centers but destroy regional political and military ones. In other models the national command centers themselves are attacked.[43]

## COMMAND PRESERVATION

Such attacks, even if they could wreak havoc on Soviet postattack command and control, might not be advisable. U.S. war plans apparently provide for withholding of attacks against national command centers while striking at regional ones. If top Soviet officials felt that they faced nearly certain personal destruction, they would have few incentives to withhold the most comprehensive retaliatory strikes possible. Presumably U.S. plans provide that national command centers could be attacked only as last resorts, in order to influence the behavior of Soviet leaders instead of destroying them.[44] If the initial Soviet attack greatly degraded U.S. counterforce potential, the temptation to retaliate immediately against Soviet political and military command centers of all kinds would undoubtedly occur. Retaliatory attacks against an opponent's command system might seem to provide a more economical way of striking back with comparatively fewer forces than a counterforce duel in which the second striker would be disadvantaged. This economy of force could be a policy disaster, if it left the opponent with no motivation except that of a dying sting.

Even if U.S. policymakers determine that large retaliatory strikes against Soviet forces and command nodes are advisable, there is no overwhelming case for launching them as rapidly as possible. Soviet ICBMs will be launched on warning or under attack before American ICBMs can destroy them in their silos. The command centers are not going to move, so there is no hurry about attacking them unless they are mobile. And if they are mobile, they are going to be hard to find and to hit. U.S. sources report that the Soviet Union has dug hundreds of command bunkers around Moscow and that other survivable command posts for the political and military leadership have been dispersed throughout the country.[45] An attack against the Soviet command system is a very much larger and more complicated enterprise than an attack against a target list of fixed command centers. The Soviet command system in the largest sense includes the organizations, technologies, and war plans that integrate the various parts into a composite whole. Even the Soviet nuclear command system, if such a thing can be isolated, is, taken in its entirety, going to present U.S. target planners with a formidable list. As the results of the U.S. strategic bombing survey after World War II showed quite clearly, the destruction of targets is not the same thing as the immobilization of an organization or an entire national defense system. Both Great Britain and Germany in World War II overestimated the effects of strategic air bombardment on the morale of the opponent's civilian population.[46]

If the United States is going to aspire to a war of attrition against Soviet forces and the Soviet military command system, it would be preferable to spread that attrition out in time, in order to draw a measure of coercive influence from the use of force. Doing the destruction as rapidly as possible simply encourages lack of restraint. Slowing it down and allowing the opponent additional time to consider whether the continuing costs of war are worth the potential gains, if any, makes more sense if one wants to conduct a war subordinated to policy.[47] Slowing down the pace of strategic nuclear war, or any war, probably makes sense if one objective of campaign planning is to allow time and opportunity for war termination. Such a planning initiative would run against the grain of military common sense, which has always believed in "getting there fustest with the mostest." The other side of the argument, which should be acknowledged, is that a response that is too drawn out may leave you nothing to respond with, while the other side retains competent forces.

This suggestion that war plans might attempt to slow the pace of nuclear war also has implications for the kind of force structure that U.S. planners favor. Survivable weapons with high counterforce accuracies could be delivered by slow as well as prompt launchers. Air-ground- and sea-launched cruise missiles can be given accuracies that make their conventional, as well as nuclear, warheads lethal to military targets in the USSR or its East European allies. Submarine-launched ballistic missiles, beginning with Trident II, will have accuracies comparable with the most lethal U.S. strategic land-based missiles. Future generations of cruise and ballistic missiles with conventional warheads could destroy over great distances targets that now require a nuclear warhead within several hundred meters to assure a high probability of kill.[48] The prospects for strategic nonnuclear war may be far off as long as both sides fear the use of nuclear strategic missiles on the heels of conventionally armed ones, and they will as long as both sides retain large inventories of the nuclear-armed missiles. No conventional weapons could completely capture the terror effect of nuclear warheads for the purpose of intimidation or to establish national prestige. A superpower shift toward retaliatory forces that are mainly conventionally armed, with only token numbers of nuclear weapons, is an arms controller's hope more than it is a realistic near-term possibility.

## POSSIBLE COMPONENTS

But it is *not* unrealistic to suppose that the combination of improved accuracies, increasingly sophisticated communication and control systems, and at least partly effective nonnuclear defenses against strategic nuclear weapons can make some difference in future U.S. and Soviet war plans.[49] Albert Wohlstetter has noted that these trends, separately and in combination, raise the possibility that limited and controlled war might become more realistic to contemplate, and so find its way into actual war plans.[50] One should not give the impression that this would be altogether new, and even advocates of assured-destruction declaratory doctrines sought to include in operational plans the possibility of selective and limited nuclear strikes.[51]

Until the "Schlesinger doctrine" of 1974, these "selective" options were still very large. And the Carter administration sought to refine the Schlesinger doctrine still further. The Nixon-Ford emphasis on the destruction of a certain proportion of the Soviet economy-for-recovery was deemed less important and less feasible than the ability to damage Soviet war-supporting industry. Soviet nuclear and conventional forces were subject to large strikes, but under the Carter policy PD–59 national command authorities and population centers were presumably spared from initial retaliatory strikes.[52] The Reagan administration's nuclear war plans have apparently continued the trends, begun under Nixon, Ford, and Carter, toward increasing the number of targeting options in the Single Integrated Operational Plan (SIOP) and providing policymakers with options to attack or withhold from attack political, military, and economic target sets (or building blocks).

Carter and Reagan war plans may have anticipated the possibility of slowing down the pace of nuclear war in another way. The Carter plans purportedly called for an increased emphasis upon capabilities to fight an extended or protracted nuclear war over many weeks or months. The Reagan administration's national guidance for military force planning apparently took this notion one step further in attempting to turn the Carter emphasis into actual programs for force structure and command system improvement.[53] There is reason to be skeptical about how far this process of continuing control into the extended phases of a nuclear war can go. Brookings Institution analyst Bruce G. Blair has offered a summary of the reasons for skepticism about the capabilities of the U.S. nuclear command system to support a policy of extended nuclear war fighting.[54] The policy expectations imposed by a doctrine of extended nuclear war, according to Blair, exceed the capabilities of the current U.S. command system. And this situation is likely to continue into the foreseeable future. Moreover, the U.S. nuclear command system of the present may, under some conditions, not be able to fulfill the requirements of assured destruction. More ambitious objectives imposed upon the system could simply confuse it precisely when it was most needed. As Colin S. Gray has noted, with regard to the introduction of additional subtlety in U.S. strategic nuclear war plans:

If the Soviet Union should choose to counterescalate to, and within, central war in only a very measured way (which is far from certain)—responding to U.S. countermilitary attack options and, eventually, to selective countereconomic recovery options, in kind and with roughly the same weight of attack—the United States soon would find its employment options paralyzed through the functioning of self-deterrence.[55]

It may seem that the desire to introduce selectivity into nuclear options below the full SIOP response is an objective different in kind from the goal of fighting extended nuclear war. On the contrary, selective options are more related than unrelated to the idea of extended nuclear war fighting. If the superpowers respond to any nuclear provocation by unleashing a full SIOP or its Soviet equivalent in the first hour of war, what will have happened is something other than a war, that is, something that occurs outside the province of conflict subordinated to policy. The inhumanity of such an undertaking will be as obvious as its absurdity. The idea of extended nuclear (and conventional) war implies that less than total or nearly total responses can be expected when conflict really begins. Otherwise, national command systems will be destroyed rapidly, and war turned into a mindless series of exchanges without political point.

Future U.S. and Soviet nuclear command modernization programs will attempt to overcome this problem by proliferating and hardening command posts for national leaders and military force commanders; by improving the survivability and redundancy of communications; by providing active and passive defenses for parts of the retaliatory force or command system, if technologies prove to be feasible and affordable; and by elaborating theories of controlled conflict that draw upon important contributions of the past. We have already noted the future conjunction of increasingly accurate offenses, partial defenses, and enhanced control and communications technologies relative to the possibility that conventional or nuclear wars, even between superpowers, might be limited. Of course, an equally plausible, and to my mind more convincing, argument can be made that the political parameters of the conflict, not the available technology, will determine whether it is limited. One needs to ask what the war is about.

## SOVIET INTEREST IN CONTROL

This last question leads to the third issue, which is the Soviet interest in, or capability for, limiting nuclear war. The question of Soviet doctrine has been touched on earlier, although some additional and summary comments are appropriate here. The first issue with regard to the Soviet Union and war limitation is whether there is any apparent interest in the basic concept of escalation control on their part. The second aspect of this issue is whether, interest notwithstanding, there is any apparent Soviet capability for limited nuclear war. A third aspect is whether the reciprocal interaction between U.S. and Soviet command systems can be structured so that the capabilities for, and interest in, war termination can be exploited in a timely way.

The first question, Soviet interest, has no definitive answer. The specific circumstances would determine much. One can quote Soviet writers on all sides of the issue, up to a point. This is the point at which nuclear weapons strike Soviet territory or at which the USSR decides that such an attack is inevitable. At this point, war limitation is not impossible, but extremely difficult, by all accounts, in Soviet doctrine. Any war that extends onto Soviet soil, even conventional war, is an implied threat to the survival of the regime and its domination of the peripheral Eurasian heartland. On the other hand, future technologies may make limitations possible if the Soviets wish to impose them. President Reagan raised European hackles when he told an interviewer that he could "conceive" of a nuclear war limited to relatively few weapons fired in Europe. However, U.S. strategists have been conceiving of the same thing for many years. And it is official NATO doctrine that the West, if it embarks on first use of nuclear weapons, will not fire them indiscriminately. They will be fired at very specific targets in packages tailored to the requirements of the situation. There are two reasons for this requirement of specific targets and packages for NATO nuclear first use, or any early use. The first is that larger uses will require a longer time to obtain political authorization. The second is that larger uses are less controllable, in that they are less distinguishable by the victim from attacks with specific and limited objectives.

Clearly, the Soviets have not precluded limited nuclear war in Europe, or elsewhere, if it is judged advantageous to them. The U.S.-Soviet treaty on the destruction of intermediate nuclear forces will make each nuclear weapon deployed in Eastern or Western Europe that much more important. Thus these weapons may be used sparingly, if at all, and their restricted ranges (less than 500 kilometers for the remaining ground-based missiles) will encourage attacks that are more discriminating and appropriate to the evolution of development near the forward line of troops. Some have raised the issue of whether these battlefield nuclear weapons should not be withdrawn from Europe as well as their longer-range cousins. NATO would then depend on conventional forces deployed in Europe, plus the U.S., British, and French strategic nuclear deterrents.[56] Authoritative studies have contended that affordable changes in NATO doctrine and technology would allow it to provide a credible conventional defense without resort to early nuclear first use.[57] Former U.S. Secretary of Defense Robert McNamara has been an outspoken advocate of limiting NATO nuclear weapons to the role of retaliatory deterrents, in response to nuclear aggression only.[58]

A smaller number of nuclear weapons deployed in Europe could have various effects on the problem of escalation control, depending on the remaining balance of conventional and strategic nuclear forces in the two blocs. Scenarios in which the USSR overwhelms NATO conventional forces with its conventional forces and then counts on its nuclear forces to deter NATO escalation attribute to Soviet leaders great willingness to run risks, in the face of a NATO declaratory strategy that promises early nuclear use. In the equations of model builders, NATO would not take those risks, because the use of its theater and strategic deterrents would only result in the destruction of European and U.S. cities. However, in the real world of high politics and high crisis-time temperatures on the part of national leaders, NATO may value credibility more than rationality, or revenge more than prudence.

On the other hand, if a drastic imbalance in superpower strategic nuclear capabilities were to evolve in the Soviets' favor, the situation might be less stable. The USSR could use its strategic deterrent to compel support of a process of escalation, much to the disadvantage of the West. In this situation, it would matter more whether the battlefield nuclear weapons on the two sides were of approximately equal capability, or unbalanced in favor of either side. They would be potential detonators of the larger deterrents that were themselves unstable as a result of imbalance. Of course, from the Soviet perspective, the same instability would result from a strategic nuclear imbalance drastically favoring the United States and NATO. It is sometimes argued that the United States had this one-sidedly favorable balance during the 1940s and 1950s and did not exploit it. Therefore the consequences would not be the same as they would for an imbalance favoring the USSR. However, the argument transposes the U.S.-Soviet relations of the past into the future, with uncertain parallelism. The Soviet perspective is unlikely to be so accommodating of anachronism in order to derive a benevolent model of U.S. intentions.

## SOVIET CAPABILITIES

A second aspect of the Soviet motivation for war limitation was whether the USSR would have the capabilities to limit a nuclear war even if its leaders were interested. Here the answer is more straightforward, for there is no question that the USSR, if it chose to do so, could limit its own use of nuclear weapons in Europe. It could even impose some restraints in its own targeting requirements for other continental and oceanic theaters of operation, depending on the objective of these strikes and the reactions of opponents.[59] However, it is problematic whether the Soviet leadership would be very interested in limiting any war that has escalated to selected strikes against Soviet homeland-based forces, economic resources, or cities. There is a substantial question whether the Soviet command and control system could, for example, distinguish reliably between a limited U.S. countersilo attack and a larger anticity or antirecovery strike. Nor is it obvious that the Soviets could, with partially destroyed strategic forces and command systems, conduct a selective and calibrated tit-for-tat exchange with the Americans while feeling confident that their relations with other possibly hostile powers, including China, were secure. So the issue of Soviet capability or willingness to fight a limited nuclear war in Europe must be brought down to scale. Prior to large numbers of detonations of NATO nuclear weapons on Soviet territory or near it, Soviet self-limitation of nuclear responses is at least conceivable. Once things have gone beyond that boundary, continued restraint on escalation is much less likely.

It is more realistic to believe that the USSR could limit a conventional war from going nuclear; and its declaratory policy against nuclear first use, which does not preclude preemption under some conditions, should be considered in this light. U.S. maritime strategy straddles this difficult juncture, involving strategic attacks other than those with nuclear weapons, meaning that conventional weapons are used to attack targets of strategic importance. These include Soviet SSBNs in their protected ports, naval air bases, and other war-related targets, some of which will be located on Soviet soil. How would the USSR react? The assumption made by the U.S. Navy in its declaratory strategy is that the Soviet Union will feel threatened, but that nuclear escalation is not a necessary response to that threat unless the USSR is desperate for other reasons.[60] Critics feel that this assumption of Soviet acquiescence in U.S. conventional attacks that threaten the survival of their strategic assets is overly optimistic. But it is no more optimistic than the belief that even if the U.S. Navy stayed home from war in Europe, NATO ground and tactical air forces could defeat their opponents without resorting to nuclear escalation. The U.S. maritime strategy runs the risk of not being sufficiently credible if the USSR wins too quickly in Central Europe, however, that is a deficiency not of naval strategy but of NATO strategy more generally.

The U.S. Navy's assumption that the USSR might observe a threshold of conventional theater-strategic, although nonnuclear, war remains controversial. So does another potential Soviet threshold, in which nuclear weapons are exploded in Eastern and Western Europe but not on the superpower homelands. Although a potential threshold, it is an imbalanced one. Eastern Europe is much more a part of the Soviet conventional defense perimeter than Western Europe is for the United States; geographical propinquity, as well as recent historical memory by the Soviets of Hitler's invasion, makes it so. NATO nuclear weapons launched into Eastern Europe may not provoke Soviet attacks on the United States, and if the NATO strikes are sufficiently irrelevant to the final war outcome, they may not be met by nuclear retaliation. NATO's dilemma here is acute: if small, demonstrative packages of tactical nuclear weapons are used, they may not be taken seriously (although not all small attacks would necessarily be demonstrative). If more comprehensive attacks are made, they may be taken too seriously. There is some evidence in Soviet writing and exercises that their leaders might recognize a threshold between regional and global nuclear use. Apparently Soviet representatives on at least one occasion approached their U.S. counterparts about the likely U.S. reaction to a preventive Soviet nuclear attack on the PRC.[61]

A third aspect of the Soviet motivation for limited strategic war or limited nuclear war is the interaction between the superpowers' respective command systems during nuclear crises and wars. We have had no nuclear wars from which to generalize, but nuclear crises have provided little in the way of solid information about the interaction of U.S. and Soviet warning and intelligence systems. We have not a single instance, of which Western analysts are aware, in which both sides have mobilized their strategic nuclear or other nuclear forces simultaneously. The fear of President Kennedy and his advisers during the Cuban missile crisis was more the anticipation of Soviet conventional pressure on Berlin, although this might have led, ultimately, to nuclear confrontation in Europe.

A more interesting illustration of the possible effects on the two sides' intelligence and response systems was the confrontation in the Middle East in 1973. In that crisis, the United States made at least oblique nuclear threats against the potential intervention by the Soviet Union with its conventional forces in the immediate theater of war.[62] However, the extent to which the United States was willing to use its nuclear, as opposed to general-purpose, forces in the Mediterranean, if the Soviets had actually intervened, is unclear. The fear in Washington was of Soviet airborne landings in Egypt to rescue the beleaguered Egyptian Third Army from destruction by Israel. This scenario lacked plausibility as a sufficient rationale for an alert of U.S. strategic nuclear forces. Soviet airborne landings in Egypt would have confronted Israeli forces with superior firepower at the time and place of contact. The USSR, to make this intervention meaningful, would have to follow it up with support from other forces, which would surely draw in additional U.S. forces.

This episode reminds us of the potential for modern day "Balkan" crises to involve the superpowers. The danger would be if one of these crises was compounded by another, simultaneous crisis at some other trouble spot where superpower allies called for assistance. Of course, in the case of the 1973 war, some U.S. accounts have papered over the dilatory U.S. diplomacy that allowed the regional conflict to expand into more direct Soviet-U.S. exchanges. The United States initially sought to restrain the Israelis, and some U.S. government officials felt that a stalemated military outcome would lead to a postwar political settlement. For this and other reasons, including overconfidence in Israel's military competence compared with the Arabs', U.S. officials delayed in responding to Israeli needs for replenishment of equipment losses. This ultimately dragged out the war and led to Soviet remonstrances about unilateral intervention and U.S. worldwide DefCon 3 alert. The United States would have been well advised to make clear its willingness to resupply Israel earlier and to do so in a more timely manner. There is the justification that a stalemated outcome restored Arab pride better than an Israeli victory would have, and that this contributed to a postwar peace settlement. Perhaps so, although if this was the design of U.S. policy, one could argue equally well that preventing war was better than allowing it to start and hoping for a military stalemate.

To a remarkable extent, the superpowers have kept their forces from direct confrontation, and they have avoided tweaking their respective command systems with provocative measures during crises. However, the danger always exists that, in a future crisis, the U.S. and Soviet warning and intelligence systems will reinforce worst case interpretations of each other's behavior, and so contribute to war. In similar fashion, the interactions between superpower command systems would be critical to terminating a war if both sides desired to do so. The problem is that peacetime procedures must be instituted within military and political organizations in order to provide any hope that, in the midst of nuclear war, authorities will feel confident about limiting it and ending it. When we say "procedures," we speak not only of the rules and regulations that are written down, but also of the expectations of persons who work in organizations. Do they really expect that nuclear war will come? And, if it does, what will they do if they think that they are losing but, are ordered by superior authorities to stop firing? Will U.S. submarine commanders, who may have contingent authority to fire their weapons under certain very specific conditions, be told that a cease-fire has been implemented? Can Soviet antisubmarine forces that are tracking them be interrupted in midcourse?

The two problems embedded here are political and provincial control.[63] Political control has to do with the larger issues of grand strategy and high politics; provincial control refers to the efficient application of military forces in their strategic and tactical missions. In the U.S. case, the provincial control of the military has generally been left to military professionals, while grand strategy has been the domain of political leadership. Most Western countries follow a similar path, although there is variation among them on the extent to which truly independent military voices are heard in the highest grand strategic councils. In the Soviet Union, the picture is somewhat different. The Western references to grand strategy and high politics, as distinct from military operations, imply a cleavage or separation that is not so neat in Soviet theory or practice. In Soviet military doctrine, as we have seen, what we are now calling "provincial" control is the domain of military professionals up to a point. The point is that beyond which there are no party-political controversies that remain unresolved.

For example, during the 1950s Khrushchev attempted to shift the balance of Soviet military investment from conventional to nuclear forces, resulting in great turbulence within the Soviet military establishment. This establishment focused on the problem of provincial control that it would have in executing less than nuclear missions, and so became discontented with Khrushchev's emphasis upon the decisiveness of nuclear weapons per se. The military's perceived problem of provincial control led to a problem of political control for Khrushchev and his allies in the Politburo, and ultimately contributed to their political demise.[64] Of course, the USSR has since its inception been concerned with the relationship of provincial and political control, and its military doctrine has emphasized the predominant role of the party in deciding upon which wars to fight, and to what ends. Moreover, the pervasive system of internal controls reassures Soviet leaders, at least in peacetime, that no one will rise to the top of the military professional ladder who has not been purged of "Bonapartist" tendencies or is lacking in sufficient *partinost* (party commitment and sensitivity to party policy nuances).

But peacetime conditions and wartime conditions are very different. Even an intense crisis could bring about changes in the relationship between provincial and political control for both superpowers, with results that made war termination more difficult. Once a serious crisis or war had begun, both sides' command systems and forces would be poised to retaliate, and the strict peacetime controls against accidental or unauthorized launch, somewhat relaxed. Both systems would shift gradually from negative to positive control; protections against accidental or inadvertent war would be less important than avoiding the loss of key forces or command systems.[65] As the Soviet and U.S. command systems shift from "safety on" to "safety off" positions, expectations of those on the receiving end of nuclear strikes will change. Warning indicators that might be interpreted in peacetime as innocuous will have a sinister meaning during crisis or after some weapons have actually been fired.

Expectations for the efficient management of force application (provincial control) will predominate at the sharp end of the military organizations that are in contact worldwide: armies, fleets, and air forces. These expectations will include assumptions about rules of engagement that, if authorities understood their implications, they might want to revoke. Under crisis or wartime conditions commanders will assume that they have authority not to take what appear to be unseemly risks from a purely tactical standpoint. But policymakers might want to accept these risks, in order to avoid escalation if war had started, or to prevent war as the time for crisis management ran short. As the run-in between the U.S. Navy and Defense Secretary Robert McNamara during the Cuban missile crisis suggests, the provincial control of military operations (efficient blockade) can conflict with the political control required to prevent escalation (avoiding nuclear war).

When both sides have alerted forces over which they are trying to reconcile political and provincial control, the problem is compounded. In addition, the implications of political and provincial control are different for nuclear and conventional forces.[66] NATO nuclear weapons deployed with alliance general-purpose forces will be in forward and potentially vulnerable positions. Battlefield or naval commanders may want contingent authorization to fire them before they are lost in a Soviet attack with conventional forces only. This presents NATO with an acute dilemma: losing on the battlefield in order to preserve political control at the expense of provincial control, or escalating, and thereby risking the loss of political control in order to restore provincial control. Nor is this less of a problem for the USSR, even during a crisis:

On alert, the Soviets' dispersal of nuclear weapons might proceed randomly, their electronic warfare might inadvertently jam their own military frequencies, civil defense evacuations might be spontaneous and uncontrolled, weapons depots might explode as munitions are outloaded, and go-code disseminations might begin accidentally as radio operators were overwhelmed and confused by events.[67]

## TRANSCENDING DETERRENCE

We have reviewed three aspects of the issue of whether a superpower nuclear conflict might be limited. There remains one other possibility, of a more speculative nature. Deterrence based entirely on offensive retaliation might give way to something else. Generally the alternative is thought to be deterrence by denial (to the opponent, of its objectives) as opposed to deterrence by punishment. This implies a combination of active and passive defenses, including ballistic missile defense, air defenses, and civil defense, although the last has rarely been a priority for U.S. planners. An earlier chapter looked at some of the command and control issues pertinent to strategic ballistic missile defense, so we will take a broader compass now, considering the overall mission of defenses and whether they can be substituted for offenses. If so, what, if anything, would it mean for war termination?

An understanding of first principles is essential here. Deterrence in the most inclusive sense works on the psychology of the opponent. This occurs at two levels. The opponent is presumably a rational actor who to some extent estimates the probable costs and benefits of alternative actions. This model is useful for academic and other analysts in simplifying reality, in order to explain it to students and other interested readers. However, in actuality few decisions are made entirely, or mainly, according to the rational model, at least in politics as opposed to economics. Instead an approximation of pseudorationality that is best described as intellectual groping is what the besieged policymaker does.[68] This pseudorationality is the kind of reasoning process characteristic of individual decision makers. On the second level of analysis, that of group dynamics and the larger governmental policymaking process in general, there is even less likelihood of approximating the rational model. Of course, deterrence does not depend on the rational model being realized, by either individuals or groups, in its entirety (or, one might say, its entire simplicity). But deterrence depends on a pseudo-rational approximation of rationality: the decision maker needs to have some intuitive notion of the larger potential losses, and gains, attendant to war.

There are ways in politics and in economics for the policymaking process to compensate for the pseudorationality of high-level decision making. If the Federal Reserve Board flubs the setting of interest rates, the market will soon signal that this has happened and a course correction will be offered. And in politics, individual voters may not be rational, but the aggregate of the U.S. electorate contains so many conflicting and contrasting elements that, in the long run at least, extreme and improbable nostrums are filtered out. But one must not confuse the compensatory mechanisms available to large national aggregates, either consumers or voters, with the compensations available to small decision-making groups, such as the Politburo and the National Security Council.

If these principles are properly understood, then the deployment of defenses, in order to make deterrence by offensive retaliation obsolete, is not going to happen in our lifetime. Real policy makers, as opposed to notional ones who turn up in models of economic and political rationality, are not going to bet the fate of their societies on defensive technologies that have never been tested in war. What we are likely to see in actuality on the part of the Americans and the Soviets is the deployment of partially effective defenses along with continued modernization of offenses. The key question is how they will interact.

Defenses can have one of three kinds of effects on the present balance of terror (discussed in an earlier chapter.). They can leave it essentially the way it is, by providing some flexibility for fighting and terminating limited nuclear wars below the threshold of assured destruction. This was claimed as one of the virtues of near-term BMD deployment by the Future Security Strategy Study (Hoffman Report) commissioned by the Reagan administration.[69] Second, they can introduce uncertainty into the attacker's and defender's calculations about the results of first and second strikes. Third, they can, in the vision of the Reagan administration's "strategic concept," eventually replace offensive dominance with defensive dominance, insofar as the relative potency of technologies is concerned.[70]

In the first case, defenses might simply perform the roles of Marxist parties, midwifing history in a direction in which it is already moving. Defenses would be part of a package of evolutionary technologies and emerging policy guidance for the conduct of less-than-total nuclear wars, or wars of comparable destructiveness with conventional weapons.[71] Such wars would conceivably be more amenable to termination than total wars would be. There will be various judgments within the academic and policy communities as to whether this is in fact an evolutionary trend, or one that is dependent on the whims of any particular administration. Advocates of assured destruction abhor any thought of making nuclear wars fightable, controllable, and winnable. Therefore, they will insist that technologies that make any of these things possible, including defensive technologies, be put back into the proverbial bottle. It should be noted here that these emerging technologies that are gnawing at the foundation of assured destruction are not all related to missile or air defenses. Antisubmarine warfare is an illustration of something that has nothing to do with BMD and strategic air defenses in a technological sense, but it is intimately related to them in a strategic sense. An antisubmarine warfare "breakthrough" by either superpower against the other's ballistic missile submarine force would have serious consequences for the stability of the balance of terror, although by the 1990s the deployment of mobile land-based strategic missiles should help to offset this potential vulnerability.[72]

In the second case, defenses increase the uncertainty attendant to offensive attacks, thereby purportedly improving crisis stability and making preemption less attractive. However, if both sides deploy defenses, this alleged benefit from increasing the attacker's uncertainty is likely to be cancelled out. Now the defender's retaliatory strike can no longer penetrate the attacker's already alerted defenses with certainty.[73] In a worst case, both sides deploy limited defenses of uncertain effectiveness. Each thinks that the other has a defense that is sufficient to absorb its retaliatory strike, although insufficient to defeat any first strike. Therefore the incentive for preemption is increased. Mutually deployed U.S. and Soviet defenses need not approximate this worst case. A defense capable of absorbing the other side's retaliation against current offenses, or anything even comparable in size and diversity, is very far from being realized technologically.

Thus the uncertainties introduced by defenses will be less drastic. Defenses may be deployed to provide limited protection for ICBM silos, command centers, and other targets that might be destroyed in preemptive attack, and so protect against smaller, as opposed to total, attacks.

For this mission it remains to be demonstrated that defenses are the most efficient and effective way of accomplishing it, compared with arms control limitations, ICBM mobility and hardening, and other responses. Although conceptually these approaches are not antithetical and may in some circumstances be complementary, the problem of finite resources means that there will be difficult marginal trade-offs among funds invested in development and deployment of the various approaches.

In the third situation, the Reagan administration found itself in the peculiar position of arguing for a transition to defense dominance while contending that this was a particular strong point of Soviet doctrine and strategy. Perhaps the assumption was that the United States with its superior technology, would catch up to and overtake Soviet BMD deployments, with the corollary strain created on the Soviet economy and technology base. And even former U.S. defense officials claimed that SDI, whether deployed or not, served as a useful "bargaining chip" to get the USSR to agree to offensive force reductions.[74] The assumption that the USSR assumes it will lose a technology race with the United States in the long run might not be warranted. Short of war, there will be no definitive test of either side's space- or ground-based defense systems. The Soviets have successfully deployed an antisatellite and a BMD system, although of limited effectiveness in each case.[75] The Soviet space program is not noticeably inferior to the U.S. one.[76]

The suspicion was that the rationale for U.S. BMD was technology with a patina of strategy added as an afterthought. The best case was that the technologies would work eventually, and meanwhile the USSR would be intimidated from adventurism that it would otherwise contemplate. But this seemed a very "iffy" rationale for such an expensive system, estimated by some experts at a trillion dollars or more.[77] In addition, if SDI were not carefully managed in its implementation, it could divide the Western alliance on issues of arms control and military strategy. Europeans were not uniform in their reaction, although generally they were less suspicious of a mini-SDI for Western Europe if technology were to make it available.[78] The problem with a mini-SDI for Europe was that it might engender a Soviet mini-BMD for Eastern Europe, and so negate several options for the West, including the conventional deep attack strategies that were becoming more attractive to NATO military planners.

One might ask how this is related to the problem of war termination. The answer is that without active defenses war termination becomes difficult to impossible to arrange once more than a few nuclear weapons have been exploded in Western or Eastern Europe. Defenses may raise the probability that damage can be limited, and command systems preserved as functioning entities, after small nuclear wars have been conducted. On the other hand, one does not want to deploy defenses in order to have small nuclear wars, and from the European standpoint, small nuclear wars are large ones if those weapons are exploding on European territory. So theater defenses based in Europe or strategic defenses that include Europe but are based in North America will, unless comprehensive, raise dilemmas of policy and strategy. They will multiply options for flexible targeting, escalation control, and war termination after deterrence fails, but they may also erode the core superpower relationship of mutual deterrence based on offensive retaliation and societal vulnerability. In short, defenses may improve the bath water but throw out the baby.

The third scenario of defense dominance was to unfold through a transition stage, and this became the most difficult to conceptualize unambiguously.[79] Observers of the debate could easily imagine a continuation of the present condition, or its polar opposite, with offenses reduced to near token levels and very competent defenses. It was the strategy for getting from one to the other that was controversial. Some advocates of BMD within the Reagan administration favored near-term deployment of viable technologies for late midcourse and terminal intercept. Others favored waiting for research and development breakthroughs that would allow for the development of boost-phase defenses, based on space-based kinetic-kill vehicles or directed-energy weapons.[80] Critics also were divided in their arguments against SDI/BMD research and development, or deployment, or both. Some opposed BMD because they considered it to be futile; the Soviet Union, in their judgment, would always be able to offset any defense with cheaper countermeasures. Others opposed BMD for fear that it might work, and therefore upset deterrence stability based on offensive retaliation.[81]

Of the three possibilities, the one most imminently related to nuclear war termination was the possible deployment of partially effective defenses. These might protect retaliatory forces and command system components, with residual protection for some countervalue targets. Assuming preferential defense schemes in which some retaliatory forces and other assets are deliberately defended more heavily than others (via a preference ordering presumably unknown to the attacker), the attack price for a prospective first striker could be raised significantly.[82] This could also be accomplished by other means that appeared to be less expensive, especially for U.S. strategic retaliatory forces that might take advantage of additional mobility, hardening, and concealment. There was also the question of how far to push the attack price down the throat of any putative attack planners. Would the need to rely on five warheads as opposed to two or three to destroy hardened ICBMs deter an attacker who was desperate enough to contemplate nuclear war in the first place? The arithmetic of the arms debate became an ontology of its own for proponents and opponents of SDI.

Beyond deterrence, and before escalation totally escaped control, defenses might help U.S. and Soviet policymakers to improve their prospects for war termination if (1) neither defense thréatened the other's second-strike capability; (2) neither defense could be used to suppress the other's defense preemptively, and so to promote crisis instability; (3) U.S. allies in Europe were persuaded that defenses would increase U.S. willingness to initiate nuclear war on their behalf, instead of causing decoupling of U.S. strategic nuclear forces from European-based nuclear and conventional forces. This last point was argued on both sides by expert analysts.[83] Defenses might also serve to protect national command authorities and their communications to retaliatory forces from disruption by small attacks; attacks designed to destroy the U.S. or Soviet command infrastructure would probably succeed unless defenses were sufficiently competent to protect entire societies. But, as we suggested earlier, attacks designed to destroy the opponent's command system signal something else, with or without defenses. They signal that the entire notion of an agreed battle, a war with some restraint, is now history; and at that point the capabilities of surviving defenses will matter less than whether national leaders, or their alternates, can reestablish some political boundaries around violence.

## SUMMING UP

The unknowns with regard to nuclear war termination outnumber the knowns by a considerable margin. This has proved discouraging to analysts and policymakers, and even more so to military planners. Why, then, pursue the subject? The argument here is that the pursuit is worth the price, for at least three reasons:

1. War termination is a very much neglected subject. The more events are studied from this perspective, the more spillover to other conceptual issues in strategy and deterrence can be expected.

2. War termination cannot be guaranteed, even if policy planners and military commanders work hard at it.

3. If the United States does not work at the problem of nuclear war termination, and nuclear war occurs, it is likely to end badly for Americans and for much of mankind.

These summations might not be bankable assets compared with the benefits of war avoidance, but that avoidance is not unconditional. War avoidance is not the sole objective of policy, and sometimes not the most important. The case for nuclear war avoidance seems self-evident, under conditions that we have lived through in the nuclear age. Yet conditions change. If national leaders in Washington or Moscow ever decide that the conditions are propitious for nuclear attack, it will be important whether the subsequent control of violence and destruction can be managed effectively. It has been the judgment of the academic and policy communities for the most part, at least until now, that the problem of postattack control is an irrelevant and dangerous subject matter. Consideration of the problem at length might make nuclear war seem more fightable, controllable, and winnable. The obverse seems more likely. By avoiding war termination as a topic and planning component the United States has deliberately staked its society on the premise that there is no gradation between deterrence failure and Armageddon. And not only U.S. society, if studies of the possible effects of nuclear winter can be credited. If this is not the ultimate in the revenge of the guilty against the innocents, it fairly competes for the honor.

## NOTES

1. For representative topical essays, see Graham T. Allison, Albert Carnesale, and Joseph S. Nye, Jr., eds., *Hawks, Doves and Owls: An Agenda for Avoiding Nuclear War* (New York: W. W. Norton, 1985).

2. Gregory F. Treverton, "Ending Major Coalition Wars," ch. 6 in Stephen J. Cimbala and Keith A. Dunn, eds., *Conflict Termination and Military Strategy: Coercion, Persuasion and War* (Boulder, Colo.: Westview Press, 1987), p. 93. See also Thomas C. Schelling, *Arms and Influence* (New Haven: Yale University Press, 1966).

3. McGeorge Bundy, transcriber, and James G. Blight, editor, "October 27, 1962: Transcripts of the Meetings of the ExComm," *International Security* 12, no. 3 (Winter 1987/1988):30–92.

4. Graham T. Allison, *Essence of Decision: Explaining the Cuban Missile Crisis* (Boston: Little, Brown, 1971), pp. 140–141; Elie Abel, *The Missile Crisis* (New York: Bantam Books/J. B. Lippincott, 1966), pp. 167–172.

5. According to Elie Abel, ExComm deliberations reviewed six options or tracks. Track E called for a surprise air strike against the offensive missile installations while minimizing collateral damage. Track F was an invasion of Cuba. Abel, *The Missile Crisis*, p. 50.

6. For discussion of the conflict spiral model, see Robert Jervis, *Perception and Misperception in International Politics* (Princeton University Press, 1976). ch. 3.

7. Roberta Wohlstetter, *Pearl Harbor: Warning and Decision* (Stanford, Calif.: Stanford University Press, 1962), p. 352.

8. For an analysis of the Manchurian campaign, see Lilita I. Dzirkals, *Lighting War in Manchuria: Soviet Military Analysis of the 1945 Far East Campaign* (Santa Monica, Calif.: Rand Corp., January 1976).

9. Ibid., p. 9.

10. Ibid., p. 11.

11. Lt. Col. David M. Glantz, *August Storm:The Soviet 1945 Strategic Offensive in Manchuria* (Ft. Leavenworth, Kan.: Combat Studies Institute, U.S. Army Command and General Staff College, February 1983), p. 39.

12. On this point see Treverton, "Ending Major Coalition Wars," passim.

13. See Francis Fukuyama, "Escalation in the Middle East and the Persian Gulf," ch. 5 in Allison, Carnesale, and Nye, eds., *Hawks, Doves and Owls*, pp. 115–147.

14. Albert Wohlstetter and Richard Brody, "Continuing Control as a Requirement for Deterring," ch. 5 in Ashton B. Carter, John D. Steinbruner, and Charles A. Zraket, eds., *Managing Nuclear Operations* (Washington, D.C.: Brookings Institution, 1987), pp. 142–196.

15. John G. Hines and Phillip A. Petersen, "The Warsaw Pact Strategic Offensive: The OMG in Context," *International Defense Review*, October 1983, pp. 1391–1395; C. N. Donnelly, "The Soviet Operational Maneuver Group: A New Challenge for NATO," *International Defense Review* (1982): 177–1186.

16. See V. Ye. Savkin, *The Basic Principles of Operation Art and Tactics* (Moscow: 1972). Translated and published under the auspices of the U.S. Air Force.

17. An authoritative study is Soviet Army Studies Office, U.S. Army Combined Arms Center, *The Soviet Conduct of War* (Ft. Leavenworth, Kan.: Soviet Army Studies Office, March 1987).

18. See Earl F. Ziemke, "Stalingrad and Belorussia: Soviet Deception in World War II," ch. 11 in Donald C. Daniel and Katherine L. Herbig, eds., *Strategic Military Deception* (New York: Pergamon Press, 1981), pp. 243–276.

19. Jeffrey Richelson, *American Intelligence and the Soviet Espionage Target* (New York: William Morrow, 1987), p. 243.

20. For a discussion of satellite missions during peacetime and wartime, see Paul B. Stares, *Space and National Security* (Washington, D.C.: Brookings Institution, 1987), ch. 3.

21. In addition to previously cited sources on this campaign, see Peter H. Vigor, *Soviet Blitzkrieg Theory* (New York: St. Martin's Press, 1983), ch. 9.

22. See John J. Dziak, "Soviet Deception: The Organizational and Operational Tradition," ch. 1 in Brian D. Dailey and Patrick J. Parker, eds., *Soviet Strategic Deception* (Lexington, Mass.: D.C. Heath/Lexington Books, 1987), pp. 3–20.

23. John G. Hines and Phillip A. Petersen, "The Changing Soviet System of Control for Theater War," in Stephen J. Cimbala, ed., *Soviet C3* (Washington, D.C.: AFCEA International Press, 1987), pp. 191–219.

24. Comparison of U.S. and Soviet approaches is provided by John M. Collins, *U.S. and Soviet Special Operations* (Washington, D.C.: Congressional Research Service, Library of Congress, 1986).

25. Soviet Army Studies Office, *The Soviet Conduct of War*, pp. 26–27.

26. See Andrew Cockburn, *The Threat: Inside the Soviet Military Machine* (New York: Random House, 1983).

27. John Hemsley, *Soviet Troop Control: The Role of Command Technology in the Soviet Military System* (New York: Brassey's Publishers Ltd., 1982), pp. 159ff.

28. Martin Van Creveld, *Command in War* (Cambridge, Mass.: Harvard University Press, 1985), p. 270.

29. Allison, *Essence of Decision*, p. 131.

30. On problems attendant to the Iran rescue operation (Desert One), see Richard A. Gabriel, *Military Incompetence: Why the American Military Doesn't Win* (New York: Hill and Wang, 1985), ch. 4, pp. 85–116.

31. An account of this is provided in Van Creveld, *Command in War*, pp. 232–260.

32. Edward N. Luttwak, *The Pentagon and the Art of War* (New York: Simon and Schuster, 1984), p. 52.

33. Herman Kahn, *On Escalation: Metaphors and Scenarios* (New York: Frederick A. Praeger, 1965), p. 173.

34. Ibid.

35. Paul Nitze, "Assuring Strategic Stability in an Era of Detente," *Foreign Affairs* 54 (1976): 207–233.

36. Joshua M. Epstein, *Strategy and Force Planning: The Case of the Persian Gulf* (Washington, D.C.: Brookings Institution, 1987), ch. 2, pp. 11–29, discusses U.S. plans for nuclear escalation in case of war with the Soviet Union over Iran.

37. Moral judgments involving the use of nuclear weapons are at least three-dimensional: they concern motives, means, and consequences. See Joseph S. Nye, Jr., *Nuclear Ethics* (New York: The Free Press, 1986), pp. 20–26.

38. A good discussion of this appears in Bruce G. Blair, *Strategic Command and Control* (Washington, D.C.: Brookings Institution, 1985), ch. 3, pp. 50–78.

39. See Theodore A. Postol, "Targeting," ch. 11 in Carter, Steinbruner, and Zraket, eds., *Managing Nuclear Operations*, pp. 373–406.

40. According to Blair, *Strategic Command and Control*, p. 189, half of the 400 primary and secondary U.S. strategic C3I targets "could be attacked by Soviet missile submarines on routine patrol." Many of these include the U.S. strategic bomber force and components of the airborne command network for postattack control.

41. U.S. ballistic missile submarine communications are evaluated in terms of SSBN missions in Ashton B. Carter, "Assessing Command System Vulnerability," ch. 17 in Carter, Steinbruner, and Zraket, eds., *Managing Nuclear Operations*, pp. 574–578.

42. President's Commission on U.S. Strategic Forces (Scowcroft Commission), *Report* (Washington, D.C., April 1983).

43. See Jeffrey Richelson, "The Dilemmas of Counterpower Targeting," ch. 7 in Desmond Ball and Jeffrey Richelson, eds., *Strategic Nuclear Targeting* (Ithaca, N.Y.: Cornell University Press, 1986), pp. 159–170; Stephen J. Cimbala, "Countercommand Attacks and War Termination," ch. 7 in Cimbala, ed., *Strategic War Termination* (New York: Praeger, 1986), pp. 134–156.

44. Desmond Ball, "The Development of the SIOP, 1960–1983," ch. 3 in Ball and Richelson, eds., *Strategic Nuclear Targeting*, p. 82.

45. U.S. Department of Defense, *Soviet Military Power:1987* (Washington, D.C.: U.S. Government Printing Office, 1987), p. 15; Desmond Ball, *The Soviet Strategic Command, Control, Communications and Intelligence (C3I) System* (Canberra: Strategic and Defense Studies Centre, Australian National University, May 1985).

46. This is not to say that air power was unimportant in the combined ground-air-maritime war against Germany, for it certainly was. See Thomas A. Fabyanic, "Air Power and Conflict Termination," in Cimbala and Dunn, eds., *Conflict Termination and Military Strategy*, pp. 145–148.

47. Stephen J. Cimbala, "How Shall We Retaliate? Slow Down and Live," in Cimbala, ed., *Challenges to Deterrence: Resources, Technology and Policy* (New York: Praeger, 1987), pp. 268–288.

48. See Carl H. Builder, "The Impact of New Weapons Technologies," ch. 8 in Cimbala, ed., *Strategic War Termination*, pp. 157–173.

49. Albert Wohlstetter, "Swords Without Shields," *The National Interest*, Summer 1987, pp. 31–57.

50. Albert Wohlstetter, "Between an Unfree World and None," *Foreign Affairs* 63, no. 5 (Summer 1985): 962–994.

51. See Desmond Ball, "Counterforce Targeting: How New? How Viable?" *Arms Control Today* 11, no. 2 (February 1981), repr. with revisions in John F. Reichart and Steven R. Sturm, eds., *American Defense Policy* (Baltimore: Johns Hopkins University Press, 1982), pp. 227–234.

52. Ball, "The Development of the SIOP, 1960–1983"; Ball, "Counterforce Targeting"; and Leon Sloss and Marc Dean Millot, "U.S. Nuclear Strategy in Evolution," *Strategic Review*, Winter 1984, pp. 19–28.

53. Richard Halloran, *To Arm a Nation: Rebuilding America's Endangered Defenses* (New York: Macmillan, 1986), ch. 9, pp. 268–298.

54. Blair, *Strategic Command and Control*, pp. 287–288.

55. Colin S. Gray, "Targeting Problems for Central War," ch. 8 in Ball and Richelson, eds., *Strategic Nuclear Targeting*, pp. 175–176. See also ch. 14 of the same volume, George H. Quester, "War Termination and Nuclear Targeting Strategy."

56. See Dennis M. Gormley, " 'Triple Zero' and Soviet Strategy," in *Arms Control Today*, January/February 1988, pp. 17–20.

57. European Security Study, *Strengthening Conventional Deterrence in Europe: Proposals for the 1980s* (New York: St. Martin's Press, 1983).

58. Robert S. McNamara, *Blundering into Disaster* (New York: Simon and Schuster, 1986).

59. According to William T. Lee and Richard F. Staar, Soviet nuclear targeting strategy "appears to be insensitive to three basic Soviet scenarios for nuclear war. Whether the USSR succeeds in preempting, launches on tactical warning under attack, or is forced into a second strike situation after absorbing an enemy attack, its targeting priorities remain the same." See Lee and Staar, *Soviet Military Policy Since World War II* (Stanford, Calif.: Hoover Institution Press, 1986), p. 139.

60. Lt. Comm. Michael N. Pocalyko, USN, "25 Years After the Blink," *Proceedings of the U.S. Naval Institute*, September 1987, pp. 41–47.

61. Stephen M. Meyer, "Soviet Perspectives on the Paths to Nuclear War," ch. 7 in Allison, Carnesale, and Nye, eds., *Hawks, Doves and Owls*, p. 193, notes possible Soviet probing of U.S. reactions to a preemptive strike on Chinese nuclear facilities in 1969.

62. Barry M. Blechman and Douglas H. Hart, "The Political Utility of Nuclear Weapons: The 1973 Middle East Crisis," in Steven E. Miller, ed., *Strategy and Nuclear Deterrence* (Princeton: Princeton University Press, 1984), pp. 273–297.

63. Paul Bracken, "Delegation of Nuclear Command Authority," ch. 10 in Carter, Steinbruner, and Zraket, eds., *Managing and Nuclear Operations*, p. 355.

64. Oleg Penkovskiy, *The Penkovskiy Papers* (Garden City, N.Y.: Doubleday, 1965), pp. 223–260.

65. This usage is consistent with that of Blair, *Strategic Command and Control*, and John D. Steinbruner, "Choices and Trade-offs," ch. 16 in Carter, Steinbruner, and Zraket, eds., *Managing Nuclear Operations*, pp. 535–554. This can be

misleading to nonspecialists. "Positive control launch" refers to launch of the bomber force to a fail-safe point, after which they must return unless additional, confirmatory orders to attack are received. In this sense positive control launch is an *operation* that performs a negative control function, that of preventing unauthorized attacks while still improving bomber survivability.

66. Paul Bracken, "Delegation of Nuclear Command Authority," p. 355.

67. Paul Bracken, "War Termination," in Carter, Steinbruner, and Zracket, eds., *Managing Nuclear Operations*, pp. 199–216. See P. 211.

68. On rationality and deterrence, see Patrick M. Morgan, *Deterrence: A Conceptual Analysis* (Beverly Hills, Calif.: Sage, 1983), chs. 4 and 5; and Robert Jervis, "Perceiving and Coping with Threat," ch. 2 in Robert Jervis, Richard Ned Lebow, and Janice Gross Stein, *Psychology and Deterrence* (Baltimore: Johns Hopkins University Press, 1985), pp. 13–33.

69. See Fred S. Hoffman, study director, *Ballistic Missile Defenses and U.S. National Security*, summary report, prepared for the Future Security Strategy Study, repr. in Steven E. Miller and Stephen Van Evera, eds., *The Star Wars Controversy* (Princeton: Princeton University Press, 1986).

70. Paul H. Nitze, "On the Road to a More Stable Peace," U.S. Department of State, *Current Policy* no. 657 (February 20, 1985): 1–3.

71. This is discussed in Builder, "The Impact of New Weapons Technologies."

72. See Donald C. Daniel, *Anti-Submarine Warfare and Superpower Strategic Stability* (Urbana: University of Illinois Press, 1986).

73. Charles L. Glaser, "Do We Want the Missile Defenses We Can Build?" in Miller and Van Evera, eds., *The Star Wars Controversy*, pp. 108–110, notes the difficulties inherent in the assumption that defenses necessarily create more uncertainty for attackers than for defenders. The impact of uncertainty also depends on whether decision makers are risk averse or optimistically dismissive of risks. On the latter point, see Richard Ned Lebow, "The Deterrence Deadlock: Is There a Way out?" ch. 8 in Jervis, Lebow, and Stein, *Psychology and Deterrence*, pp. 180–202.

74. James R. Schlesinger, "Rhetoric and Realities in the Star Wars Debate," *International Security* 10, no. 1 (Summer 1985), repr. in Miller and Van Evera, eds., *The Star Wars Controversy*, pp. 15–24.

75. On the effectiveness of the Soviet antisatellite weaponry, see Paul B. Stares, *Space and National Security*, pp. 85–95.

76. See Gen. Robert T. Herres, USAF, "Soviet Military Use of Space," *Signal* 41, no. 4 (December 1986): 61–70.

77. Schlesinger, "Rhetoric and Realities in the Star Wars Debate," p. 16, provides a "rough and ready" estimate of $1 trillion for the "complete" SDI.

78. Lawrence Freedman, "The Star Wars Debate: The Western Alliance and Strategic Defence: Part II," in Robert O'Neill, ed., *New Technology and Western Security Policy* (Hamden, Conn.: Archon Books, 1985), pp. 149–165.

79. Keith B. Payne and Colin S. Gray, "Nuclear Policy and the Defensive Transition," *Foreign Affairs* 62, no. 4 (Spring 1984): 820–842.

80. Office of Technology Assessment, *Ballistic Missile Defense Technologies* (Washington, D.C.: U.S. Government Printing Office, September 1985). There is a companion report, *Anti-Satellite Weapons, Countermeasures and Arms Control* (Washington, D.C.: U.S. Government Printing Office, September 1985).

81. See, for example, John Tirman, ed., *Empty Promise: The Growing Case Against Star Wars* (Boston: Beacon Press, 1986).

82. On the concept of an attack price, see Ashton B. Carter, "BMD Applications: Performance and Limitations," in Ashton B. Carter and David N. Schwartz, eds., *Ballistic Missile Defense* (Washington, D.C.: Brookings Institution, 1984), pp. 110–126.

83. On the implications of SDI for Europe, see Keith B. Payne, *Strategic Defense: Star Wars in Perspective* (Lanham, Md.: Hamilton Press, 1986), ch. 10.

# Selected Bibliography

Allison, Graham T., *Essence of Decision: Explaining The Cuban Missile Crisis.* Boston: Little, Brown, 1971.

Allison, Graham T., Albert Carnesale, and Joseph S. Nye, Jr., eds. *Hawks, Doves and Owls: An Agenda for Avoiding Nuclear War.* New York: W. W. Norton, 1985.

Ball, Desmond. *Can Nuclear War Be Controlled?* Adelphi Papers no. 169. London: International Institute for Strategic Studies, 1981.

———. "The Development of the SIOP, 1960–1983." Ch. 3 in Desmond Ball and Richelson, eds., *Strategic Nuclear Targeting,* pp. 57–83. Ithaca, N.Y.: Cornell University Press, 1986.

———. *The Soviet Strategic Command, Control and Communications and Intelligence (C3I) System.* Canberra: Strategic and Defense Studies Centre, Australian National University, 1985.

Ball, Desmond, and Jeffrey Richelson, eds. *Strategic Nuclear Targeting.* Ithaca, N.Y.: Cornell University Press, 1986.

Beres, Louis R. *Mimicking Sisyphus: America's Countervailing Nuclear Strategy.* Lexington, Mass.: D. C. Heath/Lexington Books, 1983.

Berman, Robert P., and John C. Baker. *Soviet Strategic Forces: Requirements and Responses.* Washington, D.C.: Brookings Institution, 1982.

Betts, Richard K. *Surprise Attack: Lessons for Defense Planning.* Washington, D.C.: Brookings Institution, 1982.

———. *Nuclear Blackmail and Nuclear Balance.* Washington, D.C.: Brookings Institution, 1987.

Bialer, Seweryn. *Stalin's Successors: Leadership, Stability and Change in the Soviet Union.* Cambridge: Cambridge University Press, 1980.

Blair, Bruce G. *Strategic Command and Control: Redefining the Nuclear Threat.* Washington, D.C.: Brookings Institution, 1985.

Bracken, Paul. *The Command and Control of Nuclear Forces.* New Haven: Yale University Press, 1983.

Byely, B., et al. *Marxism-Leninism on War and Army.* Moscow: 1972. Progress Publishers, translated and published under the auspices of the U.S. Air Force.

Carter, Ashton B., John D. Steinbruner, and Charles A. Zraket, eds. *Managing Nuclear Operations.* Washington, D.C.: Brookings Institution, 1987.

Cimbala, Stephen J. "How Should We Retaliate? Slow Down and Live." In Stephen J. Cimbala, ed., *Challenges to Deterrence: Resources, Technology and Policy* pp. 268–288. New York: Praeger, 1987.

———. ed., *Strategic War Termination.* New York: Praeger, 1986.

Cimbala, Stephen J., and Keith A. Dunn, eds. *Conflict Termination and Military Strategy.* Boulder, Colo.: Westview Press, 1987.

Daniel, Donald C., and Katherine L. Herbig, eds. *Strategic Military Deception.* New York: Pergamon Press, 1981.

Davis, Paul K., and Peter J. E. Stan. *Concepts and Models of Escalation.* Santa Monica, Calif.: Rand Corporation, 1984.

Douglass, Joseph D., Jr., and Amoretta M. Hoeber. *Soviet Strategy for Nuclear War.* Stanford, Calif.: Hoover Institution Press, 1979.

Erickson, John. *The Soviet High Command.* New York: St. Martin's Press, 1962.

Ermarth, Fritz W. "Contrasts in American and Soviet Strategic Thought." Ch. 3 in Derek Leebaert, ed., *Soviet Military Thinking.* London: Allen and Unwin, 1981.

Garthoff, Raymond L. *Detente and Confrontation: American-Soviet Relations from Nixon to Reagan.* Washington, D.C.: Brookings Institution, 1985.

———. "Conflict Termination in Soviet Military Thought and Strategy." Ch. 3 in Stephen J. Cimbala and Keith A. Dunn, eds., *Conflict Termination and Military Strategy,* pp. 33–58. Boulder, Colo.: Westview Press, 1987.

George, Alexander L., David K. Hall, and William R. Simons, *The Limits of Coercive Diplomacy: Laos, Cuba, Vietnam.* Boston: Little, Brown, 1971.

Gray, Colin S. *American Military Space Policy.* Cambridge, Mass.: Abt Books, 1983.

Huntington, Samuel P., ed. *The Strategic Imperative.* Cambridge, Mass.: Ballinger, 1982.

Ikle, Fred Charles. *Every War Must End.* New York: Columbia University Press, 1971.

Jervis, Robert. *The Illogic of American Nuclear Strategy.* Ithaca, N.Y.: Cornell University Press, 1984.

Kahn, Herman. *On Escalation: Metaphors and Scenarios.* New York: Frederick A. Praeger, 1965.

Knorr, Klaus, and Patrick Morgan, eds. *Strategic Military Surprise: Incentives and Opportunities.* New Brunswick, N.J.: Transaction Books, 1983.

Lambeth, Benjamin S. "On Thresholds in Soviet Military Thought." In William J. Taylor, Jr., Steven A. Maaranen, and Gerrit W. Gong, eds., *Strategic Responses to Conflict in the 1980s,* Washington, D.C.: pp. 347–365. Center for Strategic and International Studies/Los Alamos National Laboratory, 1983.

Lebow, Richard Ned. *Nuclear Crisis Management.* Ithaca, N.Y.: Cornell University Press, 1987.

Martel, William C., and Paul L. Savage. *Strategic Nuclear War: What the Superpowers Target and Why.* Westport, Conn.: Greenwood Press, 1986.

MccGwire, Michael. *Military Objectives in Soviet Foreign Policy.* Washington, D.C.: Brookings Institution, 1987.

McNamara, Robert S. *Blundering into Disaster: Surviving the First Century of the Nuclear Age.* New York: Pantheon Books, 1986.

Mearsheimer, John J. *Conventional Deterrence.* Ithaca, N.Y.: Cornell University Press, 1983.

Meyer, Stephen M. "Soviet Nuclear Operations." Ch. 15 in Ashton B. Carter, John D. Steinbruner, and Charles A. Zraket, eds., *Managing Nuclear Operations,* pp. 470–543. Washington, D.C.: Brookings Institution, 1987.

Nitze, Paul H. "Assuring Strategic Stability in an Era of Detente." *Foreign Affairs* 54 (1976):207–233.

Ogarkov, Marshal N.V. *Always in Readiness to Defend the Homeland.* Foreign Broadcast Information Service, JPRS L/10412, March 25, 1982.

Perrow, Charles. *Normal Accidents: Living with High Risk Technologies.* New York: Basic Books, 1984.

Pipes, Richard. "Why the Soviet Union Thinks It Could Fight and Win a Nuclear War." *Commentary,* July 1977, pp. 21–34.

President's Commission on U.S. Strategic Forces (Scowcroft Commission). *Report.* Washington, D.C., April 1983.

Pringle, Peter, and William Arkin, *SIOP: The Secret U.S. Plan for Nuclear War.* New York: W. W. Norton, 1983.

Sarkesian, Sam C. *Beyond the Battlefield: The New Military Professionalism.* New York: Pergamon Press, 1981.

Schelling, Thomas C. *Arms and Influence.* New Haven: Yale University Press, 1966.

Scott, Harriet Fast, and William F. Scott. *The Soviet Control Structure: Capabilities for Wartime Survival.* New York: Crane, Russak/National Strategy Information Center, 1983.

Sigal, Leon V. *Nuclear Forces in Europe: Enduring Dilemmas, Present Prospects.* Washington, D.C.: Brookings Institution, 1984.

Skirdo, Col. M. P. *The People, the Army, the Commander.* Moscow: 1970. Translated by the DGIS Multilingual Section, Secretary of State Department, Ottawa. Published by the U.S. Air Force.

Smoke, Richard. *War: Controlling Escalation.* Cambridge, Mass.: Harvard University Press, 1977.

Steinbruner, John D. "Nuclear Decapitation." *Foreign Policy* no. 45 (Winter 1981–1982):16–28.

Talbott, Strobe, ed. *Khrushchev Remembers.* Boston: Little, Brown, 1971.

U.S. Department of Defense. *Soviet Military Power.* Washington, D.C.: U.S. Government Printing Office, various years.

Van Creveld, Martin. *Command in War.* Cambridge, Mass.: Harvard University Press, 1985.

Vigor, Peter. *Soviet Blitzkrieg Theory.* New York: St. Martin's Press, 1983.

William, Phil. *Crisis Management: Confrontation and Diplomacy in the Nuclear Age.* New York: John Wiley and Sons, 1976.

Wohlstetter, Albert. "The Delicate Balance of Terror." *Foreign Affairs* 37, no. 2 (January 1959):209–234.

Zemskov, Maj. Gen. V. "Characteristic Features of Modern Wars and Possible Methods of Conducting Them." In *Selected Readings from MILITARY THOUGHT, 1963–1973*, selected and compiled by Joseph D. Douglass, Jr., and Amoretta M. Hoeber, pp. 48–56. Washington, D.C.: U.S. Government Printing Office, 1971.

# Index

**ABOUT THE AUTHOR**

STEPHEN J. CIMBALA is professor of political science at Pennsylvania State University and teaches at its Delaware County Campus, Media. He has contributed to the field of national security studies for many years and is the author of *Rethinking Nuclear Strategy* and *Nuclear Strategy: Unfinished Business*.